BARRON'S
FOREIGN LANGUAGE GUIDES

ITALIAN
Vocabulary

THIRD EDITION

Marcel Danesi, Ph.D.
University of Toronto

BARRON'S

All inquiries should be addressed to:
Barron's Educational Series, Inc.
250 Wireless Boulevard
Hauppauge, New York 11788
www.barronseduc.com

ISBN: 978-0-7641-4769-2

Library of Congress Control Number: 2012931840

PRINTED IN CHINA
9 8 7 6 5 4

CONTENTS

CONTENTS

CONTENTS

CONTENTS

PREFACE TO THE THIRD EDITION

This third edition of *Italian Vocabulary* has been modified and expanded in various ways. First and foremost, the list of entries has been updated to reflect the changes that have occurred in Italy (and the world) since the first edition came out in 1990—to mention just one example, Italy has replaced its *lira* currency with the *euro*. Specifically, in this third edition you will find that:

- more "call-outs" explaining points of form and meaning, or providing further vocabulary information (such as idiomatic expressions), have been added;
- a number of sections have been renamed or reorganized to provide more clarity and information on their content;
- new sections have been added (e.g., Internet vocabulary, telecommunications vocabulary, etc.) reflecting the many changes in the world that have come to pass since 2003.

All in all, the number of vocabulary items has almost doubled since the first edition, making this book a contemporary and comprehensive study guide to the learning of Italian vocabulary.

Marcel Danesi
University of Toronto, 2012

HOW TO USE THIS BOOK

THIS IS NOT JUST ANOTHER DICTIONARY!

When you learn another language, there comes a time when you will feel the need to fill in the vocabulary gaps left by the learning process, so that you can truly speak about any topic in your new language. But an ordinary dictionary, which simply lists words in alphabetical order, is of no use to you in helping you fill in the gaps in a systematic fashion.

This book will help you do exactly *that* in Italian. It is not a dictionary, although it can be used as one. It is a comprehensive and structured study guide to over 10,000 Italian words, all of which you will need to be able to speak about virtually anything, from the weather to controversial issues such as the environment and drugs. The book guides you systematically through the ways in which the Italian language organizes its vocabulary into categories of thought and communication. These form the knowledge base upon which you will be able to acquire a comprehensive control of the kind of vocabulary you will need to carry out everyday communicative tasks.

OVERALL DESIGN

This book consists of a pronunciation guide, nine main thematic sections (*Basic Information, People,* etc.), an appendix of the irregular verbs that are found in it, and an English-Italian *Wordfinder*. The pronunciation guide gives you the essential details of how to pronounce Italian words, phrases, and sentences.

Each thematic section is divided into subcategories (44 in all). For example, the section dealing with *People* sets up the study of this topic in terms of three subcategories: *Family and Friends, Describing People,* and *The Body*. Each of these is then subdivided into more specific themes (e.g., *Family Members, Age Concepts,* etc.). This section is thus designed to provide you with a structured access to the kind of vocabulary you will invariably need when talking about people in Italian.

USING THIS BOOK FOR DIFFERENT LEARNING GOALS

If you are attempting to learn Italian from scratch, you will find that this book provides you with an effective framework for acquiring the basic vocabulary tools of the Italian language. If you already have some knowledge of the language, you will find the way in which it has organized vocabulary items to be extremely useful for helping you increase or reinforce your control of vocabulary. If you are a student of Italian, enrolled in some program of study, you will find this book to be an effective aid in helping you prepare for oral classroom tasks and for written assignments on specific topics.

FEATURES

The English concept is given to you on the left-hand side of the page; the Italian equivalent or equivalents appear in the middle of the page; and a pronunciation guide appears on the right-hand side. Complete phonetic transcriptions are given mainly for difficult items. Frequently occurring items, easily pronounceable words, and many one-syllable items (such as prepositions) are not transcribed.

ENGLISH CONCEPT	ITALIAN EQUIVALENT	PRONUNCIATION
↓	↓	↓
five	cinque	*'čin-kwe*

The English concepts are arranged in alphabetical order, unless the nature of the category requires some other logical system of organization (e.g., numbers). Related items, concepts, or specific uses are indented under the main item.

ENGLISH CONCEPT	ITALIAN EQUIVALENT	PRONUNCIATION
birth	nascita	*'na-ši-ta*
• **birth certificate**	certificato di nascita	*čer-ti-fi-'ka-to*
• **birth pains**	doglie	*'do-lye*
• **birth rate**	tasso di natalità	*'tas-so*
• **(to) give birth**	partorire	*par-to-'ri-re*
• **premature birth**	parto prematuro	*'par-to pre-ma-'tu-ro*

Each noun is given in its singular form, unless it does not occur in this form within a specific category.

Regular Italian Nouns

• A masculine noun ends in *-o* (*ragazzo* "boy") or in *-e* (*padre* "father")
• A feminine noun ends in *-a* (*ragazza* "girl") or in *-e* (*madre* "mother")

The gender of nouns ending in –e will thus be marked throughout the book as either masculine (m) or feminine (f)

Nouns that have a different masculine and feminine form will be indicated accordingly. For example, the concept "nurse" is rendered as *infermiere* in reference to male nurses and as *infermiera* in reference to female ones. This will be shown in the following way:

infermiere (-a)

Adjectives will be given in their masculine singular form (*alto* "tall", *grande* "big"). Invariable adjectives (i.e., those having only one form, singular and plural) are identified with (inv).

Verbs will be listed in their infinitive form as follows:

(to) eat   mangiare   *man-'ja-re*

If a verb has an irregular conjugation, it will be marked with an asterisk (*). All such verbs are found in the *Irregular Verbs* section at the back. Verbs conjugated with *essere* in compound tenses are indicated with (ess). And third conjugation verbs that are conjugated with *–isc* in present tenses (e.g., *finisco* "I finish") are also identified for your convenience with (isc).

ABBREVIATIONS

FOR NOUNS

m   =   masculine

f   =   feminine

s   =   singular

pl   =   plural

fam   =   familiar

inv   =   invariable

pol   =   polite

FOR VERBS

*   =   irregular

ess   =   conjugated with *essere* in compound tenses (since *essere* itself is
conjugated with *essere*, this will not be indicated in its own case)

isc   =   a third-conjugation verb conjugated with *–isc* in present tenses

IN GENERAL

subj   =   subject

obj   =   object

inv   =   invariable

pol   =   polite form

fam   =   familiar form

CONSONANTS: II

The following letters are pronounced in different ways, as indicated in the chart:

Alphabet Letters	English Equivalents	Examples	Symbols Used
c	<u>c</u>at	Used in front of *a, o, u,* and any consonant.	*k*
		cane / dog *come* / how *cuore* / heart *classe* / class *cravatta* / tie	
ch	<u>ch</u>emistry	Used in front of *e* and *i*.	*k*
		che / what *chi* / who *chiesa* / church	
c	<u>ch</u>in	Used in front of *e* and *i*.	*č*
		cena / dinner *cinema* / movies	
ci	<u>ch</u>at	Used in front of *a, o, u*.	*č*
		ciao / hi, bye *cioccolata* / chocolate	
g	<u>g</u>ood	Used in front of *a, o, u,* and any consonant.	*g*
		gatto / cat *gola* / throat *guanto* / glove *gloria* / glory *grande* / big, large	
gh	<u>g</u>et	Used in front of *e* and *i*.	*g*
		spaghetti / spaghetti *ghiaccio* / ice	

Alphabet Letters	English Equivalents	Examples	Symbols Used
g	just	Used in front of *e* and *i*.	*j*
		gente / people	
		giro / turn, tour	
gi	Belgian	Used in front of *a, o, u*.	*j*
		giacca / jacket	
		giorno / day	
		giugno / June	
sc	<u>sc</u>ale	Used in front of *a, o, u*, or any consonant.	*sk*
		scala / staircase	
		scopa / broom	
		scuola / school	
		scrivere / to write	
sch	<u>sch</u>ool	Used in front of *e* and *i*.	*sk*
		scherzo / prank	
		schifo / disgust	
sc	<u>sh</u>ine	Used in front of *e* and *i*.	*š*
		scena / scene	
		sciocco / unsalted, flavorless	
sci	<u>sh</u>uffle	Used in front of *a, o, u*.	*š*
		sciopero / labor strike	
		sciupare / to waste	
s	<u>s</u>oul	*sapone* / soap	*s*
		specchio / mirror	
s	pre<u>s</u>ent	Used in front of *b, d, g, l, m, n, r, v*; and between vowels.	*z*
		sbaglio / mistake	
		casa / house	

Alphabet Letters	English Equivalents	Examples	Symbols Used
gn	ca*ny*on	*sogno* / dream *giugno* / June	*ny*
gli	mi*lli*on	*figlio* / son *luglio* / July	*ly*
z	ca*ts* do*gs*	*zio* / uncle *zucchero* / sugar	*ts* *dz*

CONSONANTS: III

Most of the above consonants can have a corresponding double articulation. The pronunciation of double consonants lasts twice as long as that of the corresponding single consonant. In this book, double consonants will be indicated with double symbols, belonging to separate syllables:

fato ("fate") = *'fa-to*   *fatto* ("fact") = *'fat-to*
caro ("dear") = *'ca-ro*   *carro* ("cart") = *'kar-ro*

SYLLABICATION

Syllables will be separated by hyphens, and the stressed syllable will be indicated with a preceding mark.

amico ("friend") = *a-'mi-ko*

BASIC INFORMATION

1. MATHEMATICS

A. CARDINAL NUMBERS

zero	zero	*'dze-ro*
one	uno	*'u-no*
two	due	*'du-e*
three	tre	*tre*
four	quattro	*'kwat-tro*
five	cinque	*'čin-kwe*
six	sei	*'se-i*
seven	sette	*'set-te*
eight	otto	*'ot-to*
nine	nove	*'no-ve*
ten	dieci	*'dye-či*
eleven	undici	*'un-di-či*
twelve	dodici	*'do-di-či*
thirteen	tredici	*'tre-di-či*
fourteen	quattordici	*'kwat-'tor-di-či*
fifteen	quindici	*'kwin-di-či*
sixteen	sedici	*'se-di-či*
seventeen	diciassette	*di-čas-'set-te*
eighteen	diciotto	*di-čot-to*
nineteen	diciannove	*di-čan-'no-ve*
twenty	venti	*'ven-ti*
twenty-one	ventuno	*ven-'tu-no*
twenty-two	ventidue	*ven-ti-'du-e*
twenty-three	ventitré	*ven-ti-'tre*
twenty-four	ventiquattro	*ven-ti-'kwat-tro*
twenty-five	venticinque	*ven-ti-čin-kwe*
twenty-six	ventisei	*ven-ti-'se-i*
twenty-seven	ventisette	*ven-ti-'set-te*
twenty-eight	ventotto	*ven-'tot-to*
twenty-nine	ventinove	*ven-ti-'no-ve*
thirty	trenta	*'tren-ta*
thirty-one	trentuno	*tren-'tu-no*
thirty-two	trentadue	*tren-ta-'du-e*
thirty-three	trentatré	*tren-ta-'tre*
...		

forty	quaranta	*kwa-'ran-ta*
forty-one	quarantuno	*kwa-ran-'tu-no*
forty-two	quarantadue	*kwa-ran-ta-'du-e*
forty-three	quarantatré	*kwa-ran-ta-'tre*
...		
fifty	cinquanta	*čin-'kwan-ta*
fifty-one	cinquantuno	*čin-kwan-'tu-no*
fifty-two	cinquantadue	*čin-kwan-ta-'du-e*
fifty-three	cinquantatré	*čin-kwan-ta-'tre*
...		
sixty	sessanta	*ses-'san-ta*
...		
seventy	settanta	*set-'tan-ta*
...		
eighty	ottanta	*ot-'tan-ta*
...		
ninety	novanta	*no-'van-ta*
...		
one hundred	cento	*'čen-to*
one hundred and one	centouno, centuno	*čen-'to-u-no, čen-'tu-no*
one hundred and two	centodue	*čen-to-'du-e*
...		
two hundred	duecento	*du-e-'čen-to*
two hundred and one	duecentouno, duecentuno	*du-e-čen-'to-u-no*
...		
three hundred	trecento	*tre-'čen-to*
...		
one thousand	mille	*'mil-le*
one thousand and one	milleuno	*mil-le'u-no*
...		
two thousand	duemila	*du-e-'mi-la*
two thousand and one	duemilauno	*du-e-mi-la'u-no*
...		
three thousand	tremila	*tre-'mi-la*
...		
four thousand	quattromila	*kwat-tro-'mi-la*
...		
five thousand	cinquemila	*čin-kwe-'mi-la*
...		
one hundred thousand	centomila	*čen-to-'mi-la*
...		
two hundred thousand	duecentomila	*du-e-čen-to-'mi-la*
...		
one million	un milione	*un mi-'lyo-ne*
...		
two million	due milioni	*'du-e mi-'lyo-ni*
...		

3

ORDINAL NUMBERS 1b

three million	tre milioni	'tre mi-'lyo-ni
...		
one hundred million	cento milioni	'čen-to mi-'lyo-ni
...		
one billion	un miliardo	un mi-'lyar-do
...		
two billion	due miliardi	du-e mi-'lyar-di

Formation Rule

In front of *uno* and *otto* (the two numbers that start with a vowel), drop the final vowel of the tens number:

| 21 | *venti* | → | *vent-* + *uno* | → | *ventuno* |
| 38 | *trenta* | → | *trent-* + *otto* | → | *trentotto* |

When *tre* is added on, it must be written with an accent (to show that the stress is on the final vowel):

| 23 | *venti* + *tre* | → | *ventitré* |
| 33 | *trenta* + *tre* | → | *trentatré* |

B. ORDINAL NUMBERS

first	primo	'pri-mo
second	secondo	se-'kon-do
third	terzo	'ter-tso
fourth	quarto	'kwar-to
fifth	quinto	'kwin-to
sixth	sesto	'ses-to
seventh	settimo	'set-ti-mo
eighth	ottavo	ot-'ta-vo
ninth	nono	'no-no
tenth	decimo	'de-či-mo
eleventh	undicesimo	un-di-'če-zi-mo
twelfth	dodicesimo	do-di-'če-zi-mo
thirteenth	tredicesimo	tre-di-'če-zi-mo
...		
twenty-third	ventitreesimo	ven-ti-tre-'e-zi-mo
thirty-third	trentatreesimo	tren-ta-tre-'e-zi-mo
forty-third	quarantatreesimo	kwa-ran-ta-tre-'e-zi-mo
...		
hundredth	centesimo	čen-'te-zi-mo
...		

thousandth	millesimo	*mil-'le-zi-mo*
...		
millionth	milionesimo	*mi-lyo-'ne-zi-mo*
...		
billionth	miliardesimo	*mi-lyar-'de-zi-mo*

Formation Rule

> The ordinals greater than *decimo* are formed by adding
> the suffix *-esimo* to the corresponding cardinal number.
> The final vowel of the cardinal is dropped in the process:
>
> e.g., *undici* + *-esimo* = *undicesimo* (= eleventh).
>
> *Exception:* the *-e* in cardinal numbers ending in *-tré* is
> retained without the accent mark: *ventitrè* + *-esimo* =
> *ventitreesimo* (= twenty-third)

Useful Expressions

double	=	il doppio
two by two	=	a due a due
three by three	=	a tre a tre
...		
a dozen	=	una dozzina
about twenty	=	una ventina
about thirty	=	una trentina
...		
about a hundred	=	un centinaio
about two hundred	=	due centinaia
about three hundred	=	tre centinaia
...		
about one thousand	=	un migliaio
about two thousand	=	due migliaia
about three thousand	=	tre migliaia
...		

C. FRACTIONS

General Rule

2	→	due (= cardinal number)
3	→	terzi (= ordinal number)
two thirds = due terzi		

one-half	metà (f)	*me-'ta*
	mezzo	*'met-tso*
one-third	un terzo	*un 'ter-tso*
one-quarter	un quarto	*un 'kwar-to*
...		
two-thirds	due terzi	*du-e 'ter-tsi*
two-fifths	due quinti	*du-e 'kwin-ti*
...		
three-elevenths	tre undicesimi	*tre un-di-če-zi-mi*
three-twenty-fifths	tre venticinquesimi	*tre ven-ti-čin-'kwe-zi-mi*

D. TYPES OF NUMBERS

Arabic	arabo	*'a-ra-bo*
cardinal	cardinale	*car-di-'na-le*
complex	complesso	*com-'ples-so*
decimal	decimale	*de-či-'ma-le*
digit	cifra	*'či-fra*
even	pari (inv)	*'pa-ri*
fraction	frazione (f)	*fra-'tsyo-ne*
• **fractional**	frazionario	*fra-tsyo-'na-ri-o*
imaginary	immaginario	*im-ma-ji-'na-ri-o*
integer	intero	*in-'te-ro*
irrational	irrazionale	*ir-ra-tsyo-'na-le*
negative	negativo	*ne-ga-'ti-vo*
number	numero	*'nu-me-ro*
• **(to) number**	numerare	*nu-me-'ra-re*
• **numeral**	numerale (m)	*nu-me-'ra-le*
• **numerical**	numerico	*nu-'me-ri-ko*
odd	dispari (inv)	*'dis-pa-ri*
ordinal	ordinale	*or-di-'na-le*
positive	positivo	*po-zi-'ti-vo*
prime	primo	*'pri-mo*
rational	razionale	*ra-tsyo-'na-le*
real	reale	*re-'a-le*
reciprocal	reciproco	*re-'či-pro-ko*
Roman	romano	*ro-'ma-no*
square	quadrato	*kwa-'dra-to*

E. BASIC OPERATIONS

arithmetical operations	operazioni aritmetiche	o-per-a-'tsyo-ni a-rit-'me-ti-ke
(to) add	addizionare	ad-di-tsyo-'na-re
• **(to) add on**	aggiungere*	aj-'jun-je-re
• **addition**	addizione (f)	ad-di-'tsyo-ne
• **plus**	più	pyu
• **two plus two equals four**	due più due è uguale a quattro	—
(to) subtract	sottrarre*	sot-'trar-re
• **subtraction**	sottrazione (f)	sot-tra-'tsyo-ne
• **minus**	meno	—
• **three minus two equals one**	tre meno due è uguale a uno	—
(to) multiply	moltiplicare	mol-ti-pli-'ka-re
• **multiplication**	moltiplicazione (f)	mol-ti-pli-ka-'tsyo-ne
• **multiplication table**	tavola pitagorica	'ta-vo-la pi-ta-'go-ri-ka
• **multiplied by**	moltiplicato per	mol-ti-pli-'ka-to per
• **three times two equals six**	tre per due è uguale a sei	—
(to) divide	dividere*	di-'vi-de-re
• **division**	divisione (f)	di-vi-'zyo-ne
• **divided by**	diviso (per)	di-'vi-zo
• **six divided by three equals two**	sei diviso (per) tre è uguale a due	—
(to) raise to a power	elevare alla potenza di	e-le-'va-re 'al-la po-'ten-dza di
• **power**	potenza	po-'ten-dza
• **squared**	al quadrato	al kwa-'dra-to
• **cubed**	al cubo	—
• **to the fourth power**	alla quarta potenza	al-la 'kwar-ta po-'ten-dza
• **to the nth power**	all'ennesima potenza	al-len-'ne-zi-ma po-'ten-dza
• **two squared equals four**	due al quadrato è uguale a quattro	—
(to) extract the root	estrarre* la radice	es-'trar-re la ra-'di-če
• **root**	radice (f)	ra-'di-če
• **square root**	radice quadrata	ra-'di-če kwa-'dra-ta
• **cube root**	radice cubica	ra-'di-če 'ku-bi-ka
• **nth root**	ennesima radice	en-'ne-zi-ma ra-'di-če
• **the square root of nine equals three**	la radice quadrata di nove è uguale a tre	—
ratio, proportion	proporzione (f)	pro-por-'tsyo-ne
• **twelve is to four as nine is to three**	dodici sta a quattro come nove sta a tre	—

Summary of Arithmetical Operations

Addition
2 + 3 = 5   →   due più tre è uguale a cinque
or
due più tre fa cinque

Subtraction
9 − 3 = 6   →   nove meno tre è uguale a sei
or
nove meno tre fa sei

Multiplication
4 × 2 = 8   →   quattro per due è uguale a otto
or
quattro per due fa otto
or
quattro moltiplicato due è uguale a otto
or
quattro moltiplicato due fa otto

Division
10 ÷ 2 = 5   →   dieci diviso (per) due è uguale a cinque
or
dieci diviso (per) due fa cinque

Raising to a power
$3^2 = 9$ →   tre al quadrato è uguale a nove
$2^3 = 8$ →   due al cubo è uguale a otto
$5^4 = 625$ →   cinque alla quarta potenza è uguale a
                 seicentoventicinque

Extraction of a root
$\sqrt[2]{4} = 2$ →   la radice quadrata di quattro è uguale a due
$\sqrt[3]{27} = 3$ →   la radice cubica di ventisette è uguale a tre

Ratio
12:4 = 6:2   →   dodici sta a quattro come sei sta a due

F. GENERAL MATHEMATICAL CONCEPTS

algebra	algebra	*'al-je-bra*
• **algebraic**	algebrico	*al-'je-bri-ko*
algorithm	algoritmo	*al-go-'rit-mo*
arithmetic	aritmetica	*a-rit-'me-ti-ka*
• **arithmetical**	aritmetico	*a-rit-'me-ti-ko*

average	media	'me-di-a
(to) calculate	calcolare	kal-ko-'la-re
• calculation	calcolo	kal-'ko-lo
constant	costante (f)	kos-'tan-te
(to) count	contare	kon-'ta-re
decimal	decimale (m)	de-či-'ma-le
difference	differenza	dif-fe-'ren-tsa
equality	uguaglianza	u-gwa-'lyan-tsa
equation	equazione (f)	e-kwa-'tsyo-ne
• (to) be equal to	essere* uguale a	'es-se-re u-'gwa-le a
• (to) be equivalent to	essere* equivalente a	e-kwi-va-'len-te
• (to) be greater than	essere* maggiore di	maj-'jo-re
• (to) be less than	essere* minore di	mi-'no-re
• (to) be similar to	essere* simile a	'si-mi-le
• equation in one unknown	equazione (f) a una incognita	in-'ko-nyi-ta
• equation in two unknowns	equazione (f) a due incognite	in-'ko-nyi-te
exponent	esponente (m)	es-po-'nen-te
factor	fattore (m)	fat-'to-re
• (to) factor	fattorizzare	fat-to-ri-'dza-re
• factorization	fattorizzazione (f)	fat-to-ri-dza-'tsyo-ne
function	funzione (f)	fun-'tsyo-ne
logarithm	logaritmo	lo-ga-'rit-mo
• logarithmic	logaritmico	lo-ga-'rit-mi-ko
mathematician	matematico (-a)	ma-te-'ma-ti-ko
minus	meno	—
multiple	multiplo	'mul-ti-plo
percent	percento	per 'čen-to
• percentage	percentuale (f)	per-čen-tu-'a-le
plus	più	pyu
problem	problema (m) (problemi, pl)	pro-'ble-ma
• problem to solve	problema (f) da risolvere	ri-'zol-ve-re
product	prodotto	pro-'dot-to
proposition	proposizione (f)	pro-po-zi-'tsyo-ne
quotient	quoziente (m)	kwo-'styen-te
set	insieme	in-'sye-me
solution	soluzione (f)	so-lu-'tsyo-ne
• (to) solve	risolvere*	ri-'zol-ve-re
statistical	statistico	sta-'tis-ti-ko
sum	somma	'som-ma
• (to) sum up	sommare	som-'ma-re
symbol	simbolo	'sim-bo-lo
theorem	teorema (m) (teoremi, pl)	te-o-'re-ma
unknown	incognita	in-'ko-nyi-ta
variable	variabile (f)	va-'rya-bi-le

G. BRANCHES OF MATHEMATICS

accounting, bookkeeping	contabilità (f, inv)	*kon-ta-bi-li-'ta*
	ragioneria	*ra-jo-ne-'ri-a*
algebra	algebra	*'al-je-bra*
• **set algebra**	algebra di insiemi	*in-'sye-mi*
• **linear algebra**	algebra lineare	*li-ne-'a-re*
arithmetic	aritmetica	*a-rit-'me-ti-ka*
calculus	calcolo	*'kal-ko-lo*
• **differential calculus**	calcolo differenziale	*dif-fe-ren-'tsya-le*
• **integral calculus**	calcolo integrale	*in-te-'gra-le*
geometry	geometria	*je-o-me-'tri-a*
• **analytical geometry**	geometria analitica	*a-na-'li-ti-ka*
• **descriptive geometry**	geometria descrittiva	*des-krit-'ti-va*
• **Euclidean geometry**	geometria euclidea	*eu-kli-'de-a*
• **non-Euclidean geometry**	geometria non euclidea	—
• **projective geometry**	geometria proiettiva	*pro-yet-'ti-va*
• **solid geometry**	geometria solida	*'so-li-da*
mathematics	matematica	*ma-te-'ma-ti-ka*
statistics	statistica	*sta-'tis-ti-ka*
topology	topologia	*to-po-lo-'ji-a*
trigonometry	trigonometria	*tri-go-no-me-'tri-a*

2. GEOMETRY

A. FIGURES

circle	cerchio	*'čer-kyo*
• **arc**	arco	*'ar-ko*
• **center**	centro	*'čen-tro*
• **circumference**	circonferenza	*čir-kon-fe-'ren-tsa*
• **diameter**	diametro	*di-'a-me-tro*
• **radius**	raggio	*'raj-jo*
• **tangent**	tangente (f)	*tan-'jen-te*
cone	cono	—
cube	cubo	—
cylinder	cilindro	*či-'lin-dro*
decagon	decagono	*de-'ka-go-no*
dodecahedron	dodecaedro	*do-de-ka-'e-dro*
figure	figura	*fi-'gu-ra*
• **plane figure**	figura piana	*'pya-na*
• **four-sided figure**	figura a quattro lati	—
• **solid figure**	figura solida	*'so-li-da*
heptagon	ettagono	*et-'ta-go-no*
hexagon	esagono	*e-'za-go-no*
icosahedron	icosaedro	*i-ko-za-'e-dro*
octagon	ottagono	*ot-'ta-go-no*

octahedron	ottaedro	*ot-ta-'e-dro*
parabola	parabola	*pa-'ra-bo-la*
parallelepiped	parallelepipedo	*pa-ral-le-le-'pi-pe-do*
parallelogram	parallelogramma (m) (parallelogrammi, pl)	*pa-ral-le-lo-'gram-ma*
pentagon	pentagono	*pen-'ta-go-no*
polygon	poligono	*po-'li-go-no*
polyhedron	poliedro	*po-li-'e-dro*
prism	prisma (m) (prismi, pl)	*'priz-ma*
• right prism	prisma retto	—
pyramid	piramide (f)	*pi-'ra-mi-de*
quadrilateral	quadrilatero	*kwa-dri-'la-te-ro*
rectangle	rettangolo	*ret-'tan-go-lo*
rhombus	rombo	*'rom-bo*
solid	solido	*'so-li-do*
sphere	sfera	*'sfe-ra*
square	quadrato	*kwa-'dra-to*
tetrahedron	tetraedro	*te-tra-'e-dro*
trapezium	trapezio	*tra-'pe-zi-o*
triangle	triangolo	*tri-'an-go-lo*
• acute-angled	acutangolo	*a-ku-'tan-go-lo*
• equilateral	equilatero	*e-kwi-'la-te-ro*
• isosceles	isoscele	*i-'zo-še-le*
• obtuse-angled	ottusangolo	*ot-tu-'zan-go-lo*
• right-angled	rettangolo	*ret-'tan-go-lo*
• scalene	scaleno	*ska-'le-no*

B. CONCEPTS

angle	angolo	*'an-go-lo*
• acute	acuto	*a-'ku-to*
• adjacent	adiacente	*a-dya-'čen-te*
• bisector	bisettrice (f)	*bi-set-'tri-če*
• complementary	complementare	*kom-ple-men-'ta-re*
• concave	concavo	*kon-'ka-vo*
• consecutive	consecutivo	*kon-se-ku-'ti-vo*
• convex	convesso	*kon-'ves-so*
• obtuse	ottuso	*ot-'tu-zo*
• opposite	opposto	*op-'pos-to*
• right	retto	—
• side	lato	—
• straight	piatto	*'pyat-to*
• supplementary	supplementare	*sup-ple-men-'ta-re*
• vertex	vertice (m)	*'ver-ti-če*
axis	asse (m)	*'as-se*
coordinate	coordinata	*ko-or-di-'na-ta*
• abscissa	ascissa	*a-'šis-sa*
• ordinate	ordinata	*or-di-'na-ta*

Plane Figures

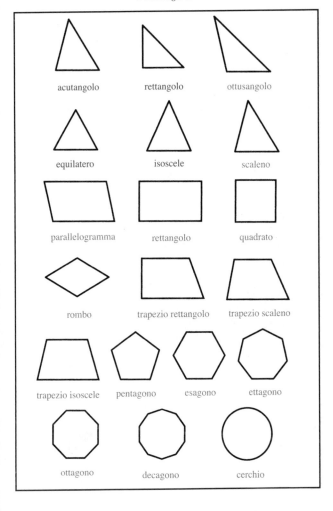

acutangolo	rettangolo	ottusangolo
equilatero	isoscele	scaleno
parallelogramma	rettangolo	quadrato
rombo	trapezio rettangolo	trapezio scaleno
trapezio isoscele	pentagono	esagono	ettagono
ottagono	decagono	cerchio

Solid Figures

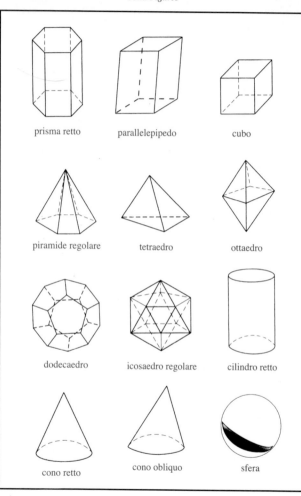

prisma retto

parallelepipedo

cubo

piramide regolare

tetraedro

ottaedro

dodecaedro

icosaedro regolare

cilindro retto

cono retto

cono obliquo

sfera

degree	grado	—
diagonal	diagonale	*di-a-go-'na-le*
drawing instruments	strumenti del disegno	*stru-'men-ti di-'ze-nyo*
• **compass**	compasso	*kom-'pas-so*
• **(to) draw**	disegnare	*di-ze-'nya-re*
• **eraser**	gomma	*'gom-ma*
• **pen**	penna	*'pen-na*
• **pencil**	matita	*ma-'ti-ta*
• **protractor**	goniometro	*go-ni-'o-me-tro*
• **ruler**	riga	—
• **template**	sagoma	*'sa-go-ma*
geometry	geometria	*je-o-me-'tri-a*
• **geometrical**	geometrico	*je-o-'me-tri-ko*
hypotenuse	ipotenusa	*i-po-te-'nu-za*
line	linea	*'li-ne-a*
• **broken**	spezzata	*spe-'tsa-ta*
• **curved**	curva	*'kur-va*
• **horizontal**	orizzontale	*o-ri-dzon-'ta-le*
• **parallel**	parallela	*pa-ral-'le-la*
• **perpendicular**	perpendicolare	*per-pen-di-ko-'la-re*
• **straight**	retta	*'ret-ta*
• **vertical**	verticale	*ver-ti-'ka-le*
perimeter	perimetro	*pe-'ri-me-tro*
point	punto	—

Lines

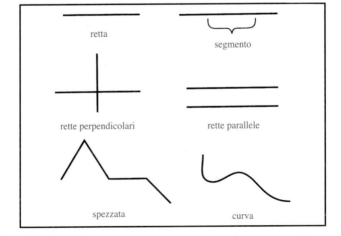

Angles

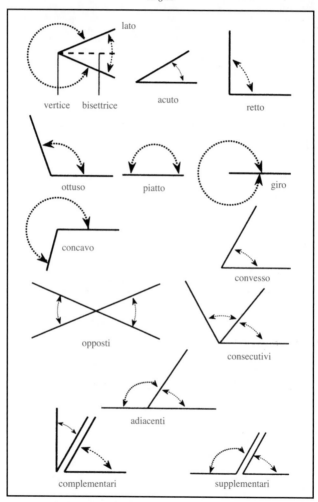

Pythagorean theorem	teorema di Pitagora	*te-o-'re-ma pi-'ta-go-ra*
segment	segmento	*seg-'men-to*
space	spazio	*'spa-tsyo*
trigonometry	trigonometria	*tri-go-no-me-'tri-a*
• cosecant	cosecante (f)	*ko-se-'can-te*
• cosine	coseno	*ko-'se-no*
• cotangent	cotangente (f)	*ko-tan-'jen-te*
• secant	secante (f)	*se-'kan-te*
• sine	seno	—
• tangent	tangente (f)	*tan-'jen-te*
• trigonometric	trigonometrico	*tri-go-no-'me-tri-ko*
vector	vettore (m)	*vet-'to-re*

3. QUANTITY, SPACE, SHAPE, AND MOVEMENT

A. WEIGHTS AND MEASURES

area	area	*'a-re-a*
	superficie (f)	*su-per-'fi-če*
• hectare	ettaro	*'et-ta-ro*
• square centimeter	centimetro quadrato	*čen-'ti-me-tro kwa-'dra-to*
• square kilometer	chilometro quadrato	*ki-'lo-me-tro*
• square meter	metro quadrato	*'me-tro*
• square millimeter	millimetro quadrato	*mil-'li-me-tro kwa-'dra-to*
height	altezza	*al-'te-tsa*
• centimeter	centimetro	*čen-'ti-me-tro*
• foot	piede (m)	*'pye-de*
• inch	pollice (m)	*'pol-li-če*
• meter	metro	—
length	lunghezza	*lun-'ge-tsa*
• centimeter	centimetro	*čen-'ti-me-tro*
• kilometer	chilometro	*ki-'lo-me-tro*
• meter	metro	—
• millimeter	millimetro	*mil-'li-me-tro*
speed, velocity	velocità (f)	*ve-lo-či-'ta*
• per hour	all'ora	—
• per minute	al minuto	—
• per second	al secondo	—
volume	volume (m)	*vo-'lu-me*
• cubic centimeter	centimetro cubico	*čen-'ti-me-tro 'ku-bi-ko*
• cubic kilometer	chilometro cubico	*ki-'lo-me-tro*
• cubic meter	metro cubico	—
• cubic millimeter	millimetro cubico	*mil-'li-'me-tro*
• liter	litro	—
• quart	quarto	*'kwar-to*

weight	peso	'*pe-zo*
• **gram**	grammo	'*gram-mo*
• **hectogram**	ettogrammo	
	etto	*et-to-'gram-mo*
• **kilogram**	chilogrammo	*ki-lo-'gram-mo*
	chilo	
• **pound**	libbra	
width	larghezza	*lar-'ge-tsa*
• **centimeter**	centimetro	*čen-'ti-me-tro*
• **kilometer**	chilometro	*ki-'lo-me-tro*
• **meter**	metro	—
• **millimeter**	millimetro	*mil-'li-me-tro*

B. BASIC CONCEPTS OF QUANTITY, SIZE, AND MEASUREMENT

a lot, much	molto	—
	tanto	
all, everything	tutto	'*tut-to*
• **everyone**	tutti	'*tut-ti*
	ciascuno	*čas-'ku-no*
	ognuno	*o-'nyu-no*
almost, nearly	circa	'*čir-ka*
	quasi	'*kwa-zi*
approximately	approssimativamente	*ap-pros-si-ma-ti-va-* '*men-te*
as much as	tanto…quanto	—
balance/scale	bilancia	*bi-'lan-ča*
big	grande	—
• **(to) become big**	ingrandire (isc, ess)	*in-gran-'di-re*
• **(to) make bigger**	aggrandire (isc)	*ag-gran-'di-re*
both	ambedue	*am-be-'du-e*
	tutti e due	—
capacity	capienza	*ka-'pyen-tsa*
	capacità (f, inv)	*ka-pa-či-'ta*
compact	compatto	*kom-'pat-to*
decrease	diminuzione (f), calo	*di-mi-nu-'tsyo-ne, 'ka-lo*
• **(to) decrease, diminish**	diminuire (isc)	*di-mi-nu-'i-re*
• **(to) reduce**	ridurre*	*ri-'dur-re*
dense	denso	'*den-so*
• **density**	densità (f, inv)	*den-si-'ta*
dimension	dimensione (f)	*di-men-'syo-ne*
double	doppio	'*dop-pyo*
• **(to) double**	raddoppiare	*rad-dop-'pya-re*
each, every	ogni	'*o-nyi*
empty	vuoto	'*vwo-to*
enough	abbastanza	*ab-bas-'tan-dza*
• **(to) be enough**	bastare (ess)	*bas-'ta-re*
	essere* abbastanza	'*es-se-re ab-bas-* '*tan'dza*

entire	intero	*in-'te-ro*
expansion	espansione (f)	*es-pan-'syo-ne*
• (to) expand	espandere* (ess)	*es-'pan-de-re*
extension	estensione (f)	*es-ten-'syo-ne*
full	pieno	*'pye-no*
• (to) fill	riempire	*ri-em-'pi-re*
• fullness	ampiezza, pienezza	*am-'pye-tsa, pye-'ne-tsa*
growth	crescita	*'kre-ši-ta*
• (to) grow	crescere* (ess)	*'kre-še-re*
half	metà (f, inv)	*me-'ta*
	mezzo	*'me-dzo*
handful	manciata, manata	*man-'ča-ta, ma-'na-ta*
heavy	pesante	*pe-'zan-te*
high, tall	alto	—
how much	quanto	*'kwan-to*
increase	aumento	*au-'men-to*
	incremento	*in-kre-'men-to*
• (to) increase	aumentare	*au-men-'ta-re*
	incrementare	*in-kre-men-'ta-re*
large	grande	*'gran-de*
	grosso	*'gros-so*
less	meno	*'me-no*
level	livello	*li-'vel-lo*
light	leggero	*lej-'je-ro*
little, small	piccolo	*'pik-ko-lo*
• a little	un po'	*un po*
long	lungo	*'lun-go*
mass	massa	*'mas-sa*
massive	massivo	*mas-'si-vo*
maximum	massimo	*'mas-si-mo*
measure, size	misura	*mi-'zu-ra*
• (to) measure	misurare	*mi-zu-'ra-re*
• measuring tape	metro	*'me-tro*
medium	medio	*'me-dyo*
minimum	minimo	*'mi-ni-mo*
more	più	*pyu*
	di più	*di pyu*
narrow	stretto	*'stret-to*
no one	nessuno	*nes-'su-no*
nothing	nulla	*'nul-la*
	niente	*'nyen-te*
pair	paio (paia, f, pl)	*'pa-yo ('pa-ya)*
part	parte (f)	—
partial	parziale	*par-'tsya-le*
piece	pezzo	*'pet-tso*
pile	mucchio	*'muk-kyo*

	catasta	*ka-'tas-ta*
portion	porzione (f)	*por-'tsyo-ne*
quantity	quantità (f, inv)	*kwan-ti-'ta*
reduction	riduzione (f)	*ri-du-'tsyo-ne*
several	parecchio	*pa-'rek-kyo*
short	corto	—
• **(to) shorten**	accorciare	*ak-kor-'ča-re*
size	misura	*mi-'zu-ra*
small	piccolo	*'pik-ko-lo*
• **(to) become small**	impiccolire (isc)	*im-pik-ko-'li-re*
	rimpiccolire (isc)	*rim-pik-ko-'li-re*
some	alcuni (m)	*al-'ku-ni*
	alcune (f)	*al-'ku-ne*
	qualche	*'kwal-ke*
• **some of it**	ne	—
• **I want some**	ne voglio	*'vo-lyo*
sufficient	sufficiente	*suf-fi-čen-te*
• **(to) be sufficient**	essere* sufficiente	—
supplement	supplemento	*sup-ple-'men-to*
thickness	spessore (m)	*spes-'so-re*
• **thick**	spesso	*'spes-so*
	fitto	*'fit-to*
• **thin, fine**	fino	*'fi-no*
ton	tonnellata	*ton-nel-'la-ta*
too much	troppo	*'trop-po*
total	totale (m)	*to-'ta-le*
triple	triplo	*'tri-plo*
weight	peso	*'pe-zo*
• **(to) weigh**	pesare	*pe-'za-re*
wide	largo	*'lar-go*

C. BASIC CONCEPTS OF LOCATION, SPACE, AND DISTANCE

above	sopra	*'so-pra*
across	attraverso	*at-tra-'ver-so*
ahead, forward	avanti	*a-'van-ti*
among, between	fra	
	tra	—
away	via	*'vi-a*
back	dietro	*'dye-tro*
• **backward**	indietro	*in-'dye-tro*
behind	dietro	*'dye-tro*
beside, next to	accanto a	*ak-'kan-to*
beyond	oltre	*'ol-tre*
bottom	fondo	*'fon-do*
• **at the bottom**	in fondo	—
compass	bussola	*'bus-so-la*
depth	profondità (f, inv)	*pro-fon-di-'ta*
• **deep**	profondo	*pro-fon-do*

diffusion, spread	diffusione (f)	*dif-fu-'zyo-ne*
• (to) spread	diffondere*	*dif-'fon-de-re*
• (to) spread out	spargere*	*'spar-je-re*
dimension	dimensione (f)	*di-men-'syo-ne*
direction	direzione (f)	*di-re-'tsyo-ne*
distance	distanza	*dis-'tan-dza*
down	giù	*ju*
east	est	—
• eastern	orientale	*o-ryen-'ta-le*
• north-east	nord-est	—
• south-east	sud-est	—
• to the east	ad est	—
edge	orlo	*'or-lo*
	margine (m)	*'mar-ji-ne*
extension	estensione (f)	*es-ten-'syo-ne*
far	lontano	*lon-'ta-no*
from	da	—
front	fronte (f)	*'fron-te*
	facciata	*fač-'ča-ta*
• in front	di fronte	—
	davanti	—
here	qui	—
horizontal	orizzontale	*o-ri-dzon-'ta-le*
in	in	—
inside	dentro	*'den-tro*
left	sinistra	*si-'nis-tra*
• to the left	a sinistra	—
length	lunghezza	*lun-'ge-tsa*
• (to) lengthen	allungare	*al-lun-'ga-re*
level	livello	*li-'vel-lo*
mile	miglio (miglia, f, pl)	*'mi-lyo*
middle	mezzo	*'me-dzo*
• in the middle	in mezzo (nel mezzo)	—
narrow	stretto	*'stret-to*
near	vicino	*vi-'či-no*
	presso	*'pres-so*
nearly	quasi	*'kwa-zi*
north	nord	—
• northern	settentrionale	*set-ten-tryo-'na-le*
• to the north	a nord	—
nowhere	da nessuna parte	—
on	su	—
outside	fuori	*'fwo-ri*
place	posto	*'pos-to*
	luogo	*'lwo-go*
position	posizione (f)	*po-zi-'tsyo-ne*
right	destra	*'des-tra*
• to the right	a destra	—
section	sezione (f)	*se-'tsyo-ne*

somewhere	da qualche parte	*'kwal-ke*
south	sud	—
• **southern**	meridionale	*me-ri-dyo-'na-le*
• **to the south**	a sud	—
space	spazio	*'spa-tsyo*
• **spacious**	spazioso	*spa-'tsyo-zo*
surface	superficie (f)	*su-per-'fi-če*
there	là	
	lì	—
through	per	—
	attraverso	*at-tra-'ver-so*
to, at	a	—
• **to someone's place**	da	—
• **to Sarah's place**	da Sara	—
top	cima	*'či-ma*
• **on top**	in cima	—
toward	verso	*'ver-so*
under	sotto	*'sot-to*
up	su	—
vertical	verticale	*ver-ti-'ka-le*
west	ovest	—
• **western**	occidentale	*oč-či-den-'ta-le*
• **north-west**	nord-ovest	—
• **south-west**	sud-ovest	—
• **to the west**	ad ovest	—
where	dove	—
wide, broad	largo	*'lar-go*
zone	zona	*'dzo-ona*

D. SHAPES AND PATTERNS

boundary	confine (m)	*kon-'fi-ne*
check	quadretto	*kwa-'dret-to*
• **checkered**	a quadretti	—

Compass Points

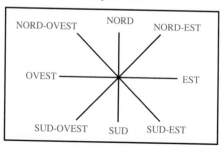

circuit	circuito	*čir-ku-'i-to*
circular, round	circolare	*čir-ko-'la-re*
	rotondo	*ro-'ton-do*
column	colonna	*ko-'lon-na*
conical	conico	*'ko-ni-ko*
cross	croce (f)	*'kro-če*
curve	curva	*'kur-va*
cylindrical	cilindrico	*či-'lin-dri-ko*
design	disegno	*di-'ze-nyo*
disk	disco	*'dis-ko*
dot	punto	*'pun-to*
emblem	emblema (m)	*em-'ble-ma*
	(emblemi, pl)	
enclosed, surrounded	circoscritto	*čir-ko-'skrit-to*
	racchiuso	*rak-'kyu-zo*
enclosure	recinto	*re-čin-to*
even	uguale	*u-'gwa-le*
form	forma	*'for-ma*
frame	cornice (f)	*kor-'ni-če*
furrow	solco	*'sol-ko*
graph	grafico	*'gra-fi-co*
irregular	irregolare	*ir-re-go-'la-re*
labyrinth, maze	labirinto	*la-bi-'rin-to*
layout	stesura	*ste-'zu-ra*
lined	a righe	*'ri-ge*
marbled	marmorizzato	*mar-mo-ri-'dza-to*
margin	margine (m)	*'mar-ji-ne*
orbit	orbita	*'or-bi-ta*
outline, profile	profilo	*pro-'fi-lo*
	contorno	*kon-'tor-no*
pattern	modello	*mo-'del-lo*
• **(to) pattern**	modellare	*mo-del-'la-re*
• **patterned**	modellato	*mo-del-'la-to*
periphery, outskirts	periferia	*pe-ri-fe-'ri-a*
pyramidal	piramidale	*pi-ra-mi-'da-le*
rectangular	rettangolare	*ret-tan-go-'la-re*
relief	rilievo	*ri-'lye-vo*
ring	anello	*a-'nel-lo*
row	fila	*'fi-la*
schema	schema (m)	
	(schemi, pl)	
		'ske-ma
silhouette	sagoma	*'sa-go-ma*
slice	fetta	*'fet-ta*
sphere	sfera	*'sfe-ra*
spherical	sferico	*'sfe-ri-ko*
spiral	spirale (f)	*spi-'ra-le*
spotted	macchiato	*mak-'kya-to*
	chiazzato	*kya-'tsa-to*

square	quadrato	*kwa-'dra-to*
star	stella	*'stel-la*
streaked	vergato	*ver'ga-to*
stripe, streak	striscia	*'stri-ša*
• **striped**	a strisce	*a stri-'še*
stroke	tratto	*'trat-to*
surveying	topografia	*to-po-gra-'fi-a*
tortuous	tortuoso	*tor-'two-zo*
triangular	triangolare	*tri-an-go-'la-re*
twisting, winding	avvolgente, serpeggiante	*av-vol-'jen-te —*
uneven	disuguale	*diz-u-'gwa-le*
veined, grainy	venato	*ve-'na-to*
wavy, undulating	ondulato	*on-du-'la-to*
zigzag	zigzag (inv)	*dzig-'dzag*

E. CONTAINERS

bag, sack	sacco	*'sak-ko*
barrel	botte (f)	*'bot-te*
basket	canestro, cesto	*ka-'nes-tro, 'čes-to*
	cestino	*'čes-'ti-no*
• **flower basket**	canestro di fiori	*'fyo-ri*
• **fruit basket**	canestro di frutta	—
box	scatola	*'ska-to-la*
• **cardboard box**	scatola di cartone	*kar-'to-ne*
• **round box**	scatola rotonda	*ro-'ton-da*
• **square box**	scatola quadrata	*kwa-dra-ta*
• **tin box**	scatola di latta	*'lat-ta*
• **wood box**	scatola di legno	*'le-nyo*
bucket	secchio	*'sek-kyo*
case	cassa	*'kas-sa*
cask	barile (m)	*ba-'ri-le*
container	contenitore (m)	*kon-te-ni-'to-re*
• **(to) contain**	contenere*	*kon-te-'ne-re*
• **contents**	contenuto	*kon-te-'nu-to*
handbag	borsa	*bor-sa*
jar, tin	barattolo	*ba-'rat-to-lo*
packing crate	cassa d'imballaggio	*'kas-sa dim-bal-'laj-jo*
receptacle	recipiente (m)	*re-či-'pyen-te*
reservoir	cisterna	*čis-'ter-na*
safe, strongbox	cassaforte (f)	*kas-sa-'for-te*
tank	serbatoio	*ser-ba-'to-yo*
toolbox	cassetta degli arnesi	*kas-'set-ta 'de-lyi ar-'ne-zi*
toy box	scatola dei balocchi	*'ska-to-la dei ba-'lok-ki*
trunk	baule (m)	*ba-'u-le*
tub	vasca	*'vas-ka*
water tank	cisterna dell' acqua	*čis-'ter-na*

F. MOVEMENT

English	Italian	Pronunciation
(to) accelerate	accelerare	ač-če-le-'ra-re
(to) approach	avvicinarsi a	av-vi-či-'nar-si
ascent	salita	sa-'li-ta
	ascesa	a-'še-za
(to) arrive	arrivare (ess)	ar-ri-'va-re
(to) avoid	evitare	e-vi-'ta-re
back and forth	avanti e indietro	a-'van-ti e in-'dye-tro
(to) begin	cominciare	ko-min-'ča-re
(to) bend	piegare	pye-'ga-re
(to) blink	battere le palpebre	'bat-te-re le 'pal-pe-bre
bow	inchino	in-'ki-no
• (to) bow	inchinarsi	in-ki-'nar-si
(to) brush against	sfiorare	sfyo-'ra-re
(to) bump into	imbattersi in	im-'bat-ter-si
(to) bustle about	darsi* da fare	'dar-si da 'fa-re
(to) catch	afferrare	af-fer-'ra-re
(to) chase	inseguire	in-se-'gwi-re
circulation	circolazione (f)	čir-ko-la-'tsyo-ne
• (to) circulate	circolare	čir-ko-'la-re
(to) clap	applaudire (isc)	ap-plau-'di-re
(to) climb, (to) go up	salire* (ess)	sa-'li-re
(to) cling on	appiccicarsi	ap-pi-či-'kar-si
	stringersi*	'strin-jer-si
(to) collapse	crollare	krol-'la-re
(to) come	venire* (ess)	ve-'ni-re
(to) crash	fracassare	fra-kas-'sa-re
(to) crawl	strisciare carponi	stri-'ša-re kar-'po-ni
descent	discesa	di-'še-za
• (to) descend	scendere* (ess)	'šen-de-re
(to) dodge	schivare	ski-'va-re
(to) drive	guidare	gwi-'da-re
(to) embrace, hug	abbracciare	ab-brač-'ča-re
(to) end	finire, terminare	fi-'ni-re
(to) enter	entrare (ess)	en-'tra-re
fall	caduta	ka-'du-ta
• (to) fall	cadere* (ess)	ka-'de-re
• (to) fall down	cadere* per terra	—
fast	veloce	ve-'lo-če
(to) fling	lanciare	lan-'ča-re
(to) follow	seguire	se-'gwi-re
gesture	gesto	'jes-to
(to) get going	cominciare	kom-in-'ča-re
(to) get up, rise	alzarsi	al-'tsar-si
(to) go	andare* (ess)	an-'da-re
• (to) go across	attraversare	at-tra-ver-'sa-re
• (to) go around	andare* (ess) in giro	an-'da-re in 'ji-ro

• (to) go away	andare* (ess) via	—
	andarsene*	an-'dar-se-ne
• (to) go backwards	andare* (ess) indietro	in-'dye-tro
• (to) go forward	andare* (ess) avanti	—
• (to) go on foot	andare* (ess) a piedi	—
• (to) go out, exit	uscire* (ess)	u-'ši-re
• (to) go toward	andare* (ess) verso	—
(to) grab	afferrare	af-fer-'ra-re
(to) greet	salutare	sa-lu-'ta-re
(to) handle	maneggiare	ma-nej-'ja-re
(to) hit	colpire (isc)	kol-'pi-re
	picchiare	pik-'kya-re
(to) hold hands	tenersi* per mano	te-'ner-si
(to) hurry	affrettarsi	af-fret-'tar-si
	sbrigarsi	sbri-'gar-si
(to) jump	saltare	sal-'ta-re
(to) kick	dare* un calcio	'da-re un 'kal-čo
	prendere* a calci	'pren-de-re a 'kal-či
(to) kneel	inginocchiarsi	in-ji-nok-'kya-rsi
(to) knock	bussare	bus-'sa-re
(to) lean against	appoggiarsi a	ap-poj-'jar-si
(to) leap	balzare	bal-'tsa-re
(to) leave, (to) depart	partire (ess)	par-'ti-re
(to) lie down	sdraiarsi	zdra-'yar-si
(to) lift	alzare	al-'za-re
(to) march	marciare	mar-'ča-re
movement	movimento	mo-vi-'men-to
• (to) move	muovere*	'mwo-ve-re
	muoversi*	'mwo-ver-si
(to) nod	fare* un cenno	'fa-re un 'čen-no
(to) pass by	passare davanti	pas-'sa-re da-'van-ti
(to) pass near	passare vicino	pas-'sa-re vi-'či-no
(to) pinch	pizzicare	pi-tsi-'ka-re
(to) precede	precedere	pre-'če-de-re
(to) proceed	procedere	pro-'če-de-re
(to) pull	tirare	ti-'ra-re
(to) push	spingere*	'spin-je-re
(to) put	mettere*	'met-te-re
• (to) put down	posare	po-'za-re
quickly	velocemente	ve-lo-če-'men-te
(to) raise	sollevare	sol-le-'va-re
(to) reach	raggiungere*	raj-'jun-jere
(to) return	tornare (ess)	tor-'na-re
(to) rub	strofinare	stro-fi-'na-re
(to) run	correre*	'kor-re-re
• (to) run away	scappare (ess)	skap-'pa-re
(to) send	inviare, mandare	in-vi-'a-re, man-'da-re
(to) shake	agitare	a-ji-'ta-re
(to) shake hands	dare* la mano	—

(to) shake one's head	scuotere* la testa	*'skwo-te-re*
(to) sit down	sedersi*	*se-'der-si*
(to) slide, slip	scivolare	*ši-vo-'la-re*
slow	lento	*'len-to*
• **(to) slow down**	rallentare	*ral-len-'tar-e*
• **slowly**	lentamente	*len-ta-'men-te*
(to) squat	rannicchiarsi	*ran-nik-'kyar-si*
(to) stand up, get up	alzarsi	*al-'tsar-si*
(to) step forward	fare* un passo avanti	—
(to) stop	fermare	*fer-'ma-re*
(to) stretch	stirare	*sti-'ra-re*
(to) stroke	lisciare	*li-'ša-re*
(to) stroll	passeggiare	*pas-sej-'ja-re*
	fare* una passeggiata	*pas-sej-'ja-ta*
(to) stumble	inciampare	*in-čam-'pa-re*
(to) throw	gettare	*jet-'ta-re*
(to) tiptoe	camminare in punta	*kam-mi-'na-re*
	di piedi	
(to) touch	toccare	*tok-'ka-re*
(to) turn	girare	*ji-'ra-re*
• **(to) turn around**	girarsi	*ji-'rar-si*
• **(to) turn left**	girare, voltare a sinistra	—
• **(to) turn right**	girare, voltare a destra	—
(to) twist	torcere*	*'tor-če-re*
walk	camminata	*kam-mi-'na-ta*
• **(to) walk**	camminare	*kam-mi-'na-re*
(to) wander	girovagare	*ji-ro-va-'ga-re*

4. TIME

A. TELLING TIME

What time is it?	Che ora è?	*ke 'o-ra e*
	Che ore sono?	*ke 'ore so-no*
• **It's 1:00.**	È l'una.	—
• **It's 2:00.**	Sono le due.	—
• **It's 3:00.**	Sono le tre.	—
• **It's 3:00 on the dot.**	Sono le tre in punto.	—
• **It's 1:10.**	È l'una e dieci.	*'dye-či*
• **It's 4:25.**	Sono le quattro e	
	venticinque.	*ven-ti-'čin-kwe*
• **It's 3:15.**	Sono le tre e quindici.	*'kwin-di-či*
	Sono le tre e un quarto.	
• **It's 3:30.**	Sono le tre e trenta.	
	Sono le tre e mezzo	
	(mezza).	*'me-dzo*
• **It's 2:45.**	Sono le due e	
	quarantacinque.	*kwa-ran-ta-'čin-kwe*
	Sono le due e tre quarti.	

The 24-Hour Clock

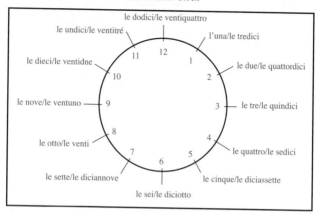

	Sono le tre meno un quarto.	
• It's 5:50.	Sono le cinque e cinquanta.	*cin-'kwan-ta*
	Sono le sei meno dieci.	*'dye-či*
• It's 5:00 A.M.	Sono le cinque.	*'čin-kwe*
• It's 5:00 P.M.	Sono le diciassette.	*di-čas-'set-te*
• It's 10:00 A.M.	Sono le dieci.	*'dye-či*
• It's 10:00 P.M.	Sono le ventidue.	*ven-ti-'du-e*
At what time?	A che ora?	*a ke 'o-ra*
• At 1:00.	All'una.	—
• At 2:00.	Alle due.	—
• At 3:00.	Alle tre.	—

B. CLASSIFYING AND MEASURING TIME

afternoon	pomeriggio	*po-me-'rij-jo*
• in the afternoon	nel pomeriggio	—
	di pomeriggio, del pomeriggio	
• this afternoon	questo pomeriggio	—
	oggi pomeriggio	*'oj-ji*
• tomorrow afternoon	domani pomeriggio	—
century	secolo	*'se-ko-lo*
dawn, sunrise	alba	*'al-ba*

Alternatives

As the next hour approaches, an alternative way of express-
ing the minutes is (as shown above), the next hour minus
(*meno*) the number of minutes left to go.

 8:58 = *le otto e cinquantotto* or *le nove meno due*
10:50 = *le dieci e cinquanta* or *le undici meno dieci*

The expressions *un quarto* (a quarter), and *mezzo (mezza)*
(half) can be used for the quarter and the half hour.

3:15 = *le tre e quindici* or *le tre e un quarto*
4:30 = *le quattro e trenta* or *le quattro e mezzo (mezza)*
5:45 = *le cinque e quarantacinque* or *le sei meno un
         quarto* or *le cinque e tre quarti* (three quarters)

day	giorno	*'jor-no*
• **all day**	tutta la giornata	*jor-'na-ta*
• **daily**	quotidianamente	*kwo-ti-dya-na-'men-te*
decade	decennio	*de-'čen-nyo*
evening	sera	*'se-ra*
• **in the evening**	di sera	—
• **last evening**	ieri sera	*ye-ri 'se-ra*
• **this evening**	questa sera, stasera	—
• **tomorrow evening**	domani sera	—
hour	ora	—
instant	istante (m)	*is-'tan-te*
midnight	mezzanotte (f)	*me-dza-'not-te*
• **at midnight**	a mezzanotte	—
millennium	millennio	*mil-'len-ni-o*
minute	minuto	*mi-'nu-to*
moment	momento	*mo-'men-to*
month	mese (m)	*'me-ze*
• **monthly**	mensile	*men-'si-le*
morning	mattina	*mat-'ti-na*
	mattino	
• **in the morning**	di mattina, della mattina	—
• **this morning**	questa mattina, stamani	—
• **tomorrow morning**	domani mattina	—
night	notte (f)	*'not-te*
• **at night**	di notte, della notte	—
• **last night**	ieri notte	*'ye-ri*
• **this night**	questa notte, stanotte	—
• **tomorrow night**	domani notte	—

noon	mezzogiorno	*me-dzo-'jor-no*
• at noon	a mezzogiorno	—
second	secondo	*se-'kon-do*
sunrise	alba	*'al-ba*
sunset, twilight	tramonto	*tra-'mon'to*
time (in general)	tempo	*'tem-po*
• time (hour)	ora	—
• time (occurrence)	volta	—
today	oggi	*'oj-ji*
tomorrow	domani	*do-'ma-ni*
• day after tomorrow	dopodomani	*do-po-do-'ma-ni*
tonight	stasera (*evening*)	*sta-'se-ra*
	stanotte (*night*)	*sta-'not-te*
week	settimana	*set-ti-'ma-na*
• weekly	settimanalmente	*set-ti-ma-nal-'men-te*
year	anno	*'an-no*
• yearly	annuo	*'an-nu-o*
	annuale	*an-'nwa-le*
yesterday	ieri	*'ye-ri*
• day before yesterday	l'altro ieri	*lal-tro 'ye-ri*
• yesterday morning, afternoon, etc.	ieri mattina	*mat-'ti-na*
	ieri pomeriggio	*po-me-'rij-jo*
	ecc.	

C. GENERAL TIME CONCEPTS AND EXPRESSIONS

after	dopo	*'do-po*
again	ancora (una volta)	*an-'ko-ra*
	di nuovo	*di 'nwo-vo*
ago	fa	—
• two years ago	due anni fa	—
almost always	quasi sempre	*kwa-zi 'sem-pre*
almost never	quasi mai	*kwa-zi 'ma-i*
already	già	*ja*
always	sempre	*'sem-pre*
anterior, before	anteriore	*an-te-'ryo-re*
as soon as	appena	*ap-'pe-na*
at the same time	allo stesso tempo	*'stes-so*
(to) be about to	stare* (ess) per	*'sta-re*
(to) be on the point, verge of	essere* sul punto di	*'es-se-re*
(to) be on time	essere* in orario	*o-'ra-ryo*
(to) be punctual	essere* puntuale	*pun-tu-'a-le*
before	prima	—
brief	breve	*'bre-ve*
• briefly	brevemente	*bre-ve-'men-te*

by now, already	ormai	or-'ma-i
duration	durata	du-'ra-ta
during	durante	du-'ran-te
early	presto	'pres-to
• **(to) be early**	essere* in anticipo	'es-se-re in an-'ti-ci-po
end	fine (f)	'fi-ne
• **(to) end, finish**	finire (isc)	fi-'ni-re
equinox	equinozio	e-kwi-'no-tsyo
every once in a while	di tanto in tanto	—
frequent	frequente	fre-'kwen-te
from now on	d'ora in poi	dora in 'po-i
future	futuro	fu-'tu-ro
(to) happen, occur	accadere* (ess)	ak-ka-'de-re
	avvenire* (ess)	av-ve-'ni-re
in an hour's time (in two hours time, etc.)	tra un'ora	—
	tra due ore	
	ecc.	
in the long run, term	a lungo andare	a lun-go an-'da-re
	a lungo termine	'ter-mi-ne
in the meanwhile	intanto	in-'tan-to
	nel frattempo	frat-'tem-po
in the short term	a breve termine	'ter-mi-ne
in time	in orario	o-'ra-ryo
jet lag	fuso orario	—
just, as soon as	appena	ap-'pe-na
last	scorso	'skor-so
• **last month**	il mese scorso	—
• **last year**	l'anno scorso	—
(to) last	durare (ess)	du-'ra-re
• **(to) last a long time**	durare (ess) a lungo	
• **(to) last a short time**	durare (ess) poco	'po-ko
late	tardi	'tar-di
• **(to) be late**	essere* in ritardo	'es-se-re in ri-'tar-do
long-term	a lunga scadenza	lun-ga ska-'den-tsa
(to) look forward to	non vedere* l'ora di	ve-'de-re
never	mai	'ma-i
now	ora	—
	adesso	a-'des-so
• **from now on**	d'ora in poi	—
• **nowadays**	oggigiorno	oj-ji-'jor-no
occasionally	di tanto in tanto	—
	ogni tanto	
often	spesso	'spes-so
once	una volta	—
• **once in a while**	ogni tanto	o-nyi 'tan-to
past	passato	pas-'sa-to
posterior	posteriore	pos-te-'ryo-re
present	presente (m)	pre-'zen-te
• **presently**	attualmente	at-twal-'men-te

rare	raro	—
• **rarely**	raramente	*ra-ra-'men-te*
recent	recente	*re-'čen-te*
• **recently**	recentemente	*re-čen-te-'men-te*
regular	regolare	*re-go-'la-re*
• **regularly**	regolarmente	*re-go-lar-'men-te*
right away	subito	*'su-bi-to*
short-term	a breve scadenza	*ska-'den-tsa*
simultaneous	simultaneo	*si-mul-'ta-ne-o*
• **simultaneously**	simultaneamente	*si-mul-ta-ne-a-'men-te*
since, for	da	—
• **since Monday**	da lunedì	*lu-ne-'di*
• **since yesterday**	da ieri	*'ye-ri*
• **for three days**	da tre giorni	*'jor-ni*
soon	tra poco, presto	*'po-ko, 'pres-to*
• **as soon as**	appena	*ap-'pe-na*
• **sooner or later**	prima o poi	*pri-ma o 'po-i*
(to) spend (time)	passare	*pas-'sa-re*
	trascorrere*	*tras-'kor-re-re*
sporadic	sporadico	*spo-'ra-di-ko*
• **sporadically**	sporadicamente	*spo-ra-di-ka-'men-te*
still	ancora	*an-'ko-ra*
(to) take place	avere* luogo	*a-'ve're 'lwo-go*
	svolgersi*	*'zvol-jer-si*
temporary	temporaneo	*tem-po-'ra-ne-o*
• **temporarily**	temporaneamente	*tem-po-ra-ne-a-'men-te*
then	allora	*al-'lo-ra*
	poi	*'po-i*
timetable, schedule	orario	*o-'ra-ryo*
to this day, till now	tutt'oggi, tuttora	*tut-'toj-ji, tut-'to-ra*
until	fino a	—
	finché (*conjunction*)	*fin-'ke*
usually	di solito	*di 'so-li-to*
(to) wait (for)	aspettare, attendere	*as-pet-'ta-re, at-'ten-de-re*
when	quando	*'kwan-do*
while	mentre	*'men-tre*

Idiomatic Expressions

Time is money!	=	Il tempo è denaro!
Time flies!	=	Il tempo vola!
Time is short!	=	Il tempo stringe!
Once upon a time	=	C'era una volta
It was high time!	=	Era ora!
Better late than never!	=	Meglio tardi che mai!

within	entro	*'en-tro*
• **within two days**	entro due giorni	*'jor-ni*
yet	ancora	*an-'ko-ra*

D. TIMEPIECES

alarm clock	sveglia	*'sve-lya*
cell phone	cellulare (m)	*če-lu-'la-re*
clock	orologio	*o-ro-'lo-jo*
dial	quadrante (m)	*kwa-'dran-te*
grandfather clock	orologio a pendolo	*o-ro-'lo-jo a 'pen-do-lo*
hand (of a clock, watch)	lancetta	*lan-'čet-ta*
watch	orologio	*o-ro-'lo-jo*
• **digital watch**	orologio digitale	*di-ji-'ta-le*
• **The watch is fast.**	L'orologio va avanti.	*a-'van-ti*
• **The watch is slow.**	L'orologio va indietro.	*in-'dye-tro*
• **wristwatch**	orologio da polso	*'pol-so*
(to) wind	caricare	*ka-ri-'ka-re*

5. DAYS, MONTHS, AND SEASONS

A. DAYS OF THE WEEK

day of the week	giorno della settimana	*'jor-no set-ti-'ma-na*
• **Monday**	lunedì (m, inv)	*lu-ne-'di*
• **Tuesday**	martedì (m, inv)	*mar-te-'di*
• **Wednesday**	mercoledì (m, inv)	*mer-ko-le-'di*
• **Thursday**	giovedì (m, inv)	*jo-ve-'di*
• **Friday**	venerdì (m, inv)	*ve-ner-'di*
• **Saturday**	sabato	*'sa-ba-to*
• **Sunday**	domenica	*do-'me-ni-ka*
holiday	giorno festivo	—
weekend	fine (m) settimana	*'fi-ne set-ti-'ma-na*
What day is it?	Che giorno è?	*ke 'jor-no*
workday	giorno lavorativo, feriale	*'jor-no la-vo-ra-'ti-vo, fe-'ria-le*

B. MONTHS OF THE YEAR

calendar	calendario	*ka-len-'da-ryo*
leap year	anno bisestile	*an-no bi-ses-'ti-le*
month	mese (m)	*'me-ze*
• **January**	gennaio	*jen-'na-yo*
• **February**	febbraio	*feb-'bra-yo*
• **March**	marzo	*'mar-tso*
• **April**	aprile	*a-'pri-le*
• **May**	maggio	*'maj-jo*
• **June**	giugno	*'ju-nyo*
• **July**	luglio	*'lu-lyo*

• **August**	agosto	*a-'gos-to*
• **September**	settembre	*set-'tem-bre*
• **October**	ottobre	*ot-'to-bre*
• **November**	novembre	*no-'vem-bre*
• **December**	dicembre	*di-'čem-bre*
monthly	mensile	*men-'si-le*
	mensilmente	*men-sil-'men-te*
school year	anno scolastico	*'an-no sko-'las-ti-ko*
What month is it?	Che mese è?	—

Jingle

> **Trenta giorni ha novembre,
> con aprile, giugno e settembre,
> di ventotto ce n'è uno,
> tutti gli altri ne han(no) trentuno**
>
> Thirty days has November,
> as does April, June, and September,
> there is only one with twenty-eight
> all the others have thirty-one

C. SEASONS

season	stagione (f)	*sta-'jo-ne*
• **autumn**	autunno	*au-'tun-no*
• **winter**	inverno	*in-'ver-no*

The Seasons

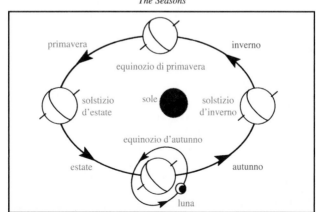

• spring	primavera	*pri-ma-'ve-ra*
• summer	estate (f)	*es-'ta-te*
Earth	Terra	*'ter-ra*
equinox	equinozio	*e-kwi-'no-tsyo*
moon	luna	*'lu-na*
planet	pianeta (m) (pianeti, pl)	*pya-'ne-ta*
solstice	solstizio	*sol-'sti-tsyo*
star	stella	*'stel-la*
sun	sole (m)	*'so-le*

D. THE ZODIAC

horoscope	oroscopo	*o-'ros-ko-po*
zodiac	zodiaco	*dzo-'di-a-ko*
• signs of the zodiac	segni dello zodiaco	*'se-nyi*
• **Aquarius**	Acquario (21 gennaio-18 febbraio)	*ak-'kwa-ryo*
• **Aries**	Ariete (m) (21 marzo-20 aprile)	*a-'rye-te*
• **Cancer**	Cancro (22 giugno-22 luglio)	*'kan-kro*
• **Capricorn**	Capricorno (22 dicembre-20 gennaio)	*ka-pri-'kor-no*
• **Gemini**	Gemelli (pl) (22 maggio-21 giugno)	*je-'mel-li*
• **Leo**	Leone (23 luglio-23 agosto)	*le-'o-ne*
• **Libra**	Bilancia (24 settembre-23 ottobre)	*bi-'lan-ča*
• **Pisces**	Pesci (pl) (19 febbraio-20 marzo)	*'pe-ši*
• **Sagittarius**	Sagittario (23 novembre-21 dicembre)	*sa-jit-'ta-ri-o*
• **Scorpio**	Scorpione (m) (24 ottobre-22 novembre)	*skor-'pyo-ne*
• **Taurus**	Toro (21 aprile-21 maggio)	*'to-ro*
• **Virgo**	Vergine (f) (24 agosto-23 settembre)	*'ver-ji-ne*

> For the planets, see §13a

E. EXPRESSING THE DATE

What's the date?	Che data è?	*ke 'da-ta 'e*
• **October first**	il primo ottobre	*ot-'to-bre*
• **September 15**	il quindici settembre	*'kwin-di-či set-'tem-bre*
• **June 23**	il ventitré giugno	*'ju-nyo*

What year is it?	Che anno è?	—
• **It's 2015.**	È il duemila quindici	—
When were you born?	Quando è nato (m, pol)?	—
	Quando sei nato (m, fam)?	
	Quando è nata (f, pol)?	
	Quando sei nata (f, fam)?	
• **I was born in 1994**	Sono nato (-a) nel	—
	mille novecento novantaquattro	

F. IMPORTANT DATES

Christmas	Natale	*na-ta-le*
• **Merry Christmas!**	Buon Natale!	*bwon na-'ta-le*
Easter	Pasqua	*'pas-kwa*
• **Happy Easter!**	Buona Pasqua!	*'bwo-na 'pas-kwa*
Feast of the Assumption	Ferragosto	*fer-ra-'gos-to*
holiday	giorno festivo	*'jor-no fes-'ti-vo*
holidays	ferie (f, pl)	*'fe-rye*
New Year	Anno Nuovo	*'an-no 'nwo-vo*
• **Happy New Year!**	Felice Anno Nuovo!	*fe-'li-če*
New Year's	Capodanno,	*ka-po-'dan-no,*
	Buon Anno!	*bwon 'an-no*
New Year's Eve	Vigilia di Capodanno	*vi-'ji-li-a*
vacation	vacanza	*va-'kan-dza*

Useful Expressions

prossimo	next
la settimana prossima	next week
il mese prossimo	next month
scorso	last
la settimana scorsa	last week
il mese scorso	last month
a domani, a giovedì, ecc.	till tomorrow, till Thursday, etc.
il giorno	the day
la giornata	the whole day (long)
la sera	the evening
la serata	the whole evening (long)
oggi	today
ieri	yesterday
domani	tomorrow
avantieri	the day before yesterday
dopodomani	the day after tomorrow

Distinctions and Patterns

Use the ordinal **primo** for the first of each month, and cardinal numbers
for the other days

il primo gennaio = January first
il due gennaio = January second

Use **Quanti ne abbiamo?** when the complete date is not required:

Quanti ne abbiamo?	What's the date?
Ne abbiamo quindici	It's the fifteenth
Ne abbiamo ventuno	It's the twenty-first

---

6. TALKING ABOUT THE WEATHER

A. GENERAL WEATHER VOCABULARY

air	aria	*'a-rya*
atmosphere	atmosfera	*at-mos-'fe-ra*
• **atmospheric conditions**	condizioni atmosferiche	*kon-di-'tsyo-ni at-mos-'fe-ri-ke*
(to) be bad (awful) weather	fare* brutto, cattivo tempo	*'fa-re 'brut-to kat-'ti-vo 'tem-po*
(to) be good (beautiful) weather	fare* bel tempo	—
(to) be windy, blow wind	tirare vento	*ti-'ra-re 'ven-to*
clear	sereno	*se-'re-no*
• **The sky is clear.**	Il cielo è sereno.	*'če-lo*
climate	clima (m)	*'kli-ma*
• **continental**	continentale	*kon-ti-nen-'ta-le*
• **dry**	asciutto	*a-'šut-to*
• **humid**	umido	*'u-mi-do*
• **Mediterranean**	mediterraneo	*me-di-ter-'ra-ne-o*
• **tropical**	tropicale	*tro-pi-'ka-le*
cloud	nuvola	*'nu-vo-la*
• **cloudy**	nuvoloso	*nu-vo-'lo-zo*
• **cloudburst**	nubifragio	*nu-bi-'fra-jo*
cold	freddo	*'fred-do*
• **(to) be cold**	fare* freddo	—
cool	fresco	*'fres-ko*
• **(to) be cool**	fare* fresco	—
dark	buio	*'bu-yo*
• **It's dark today.**	Oggi è buio.	*'oj-ji e 'bu-yo*
dew	rugiada	*ru-'ja-da*
drizzle	pioggerellina, pioggerella, pioviggine	*pyoj-je-rel-'li-na pyoj-je-'rel-la pyo-vij-ji-ne*
• **drizzly**	piovigginoso	*pyo-vij-ji-'no-zo*

drop	goccia	'goč-ča
dry	asciutto	a-'šut-to
	secco	'sek-ko
flash of lightning	lampo	'lam-po
• **(to) flash**	lampeggiare,	lam-pej-'ja-re,
	fulmine (m)	'ful-mi-ne
fog	nebbia	'neb-'bya
• **foggy**	nebbioso	neb-'byo-zo
foul weather	tempaccio	tem-'pač-čo
frost	gelo	'je-lo
• **(to) freeze**	gelare	je-'la-re
• **frozen**	gelato	je-'la-to
	ghiacciato	gyač-'ča-to
hail	grandine (f)	'gran-di-ne
• **(to) hail**	grandinare	gran-di-'na-re
• **hailstorm**	tempesta di grandine	tem-'pes-ta
hoarfrost	brina	'bri-na
hot	caldo	'kal-do
• **(to) be hot**	fare* caldo	—
humidity	umidità (f, inv)	u-'mi-di-'ta
• **humid, damp**	umido	'u-mido
hurricane	uragano	u-ra-'ga-no
ice	ghiaccio	'gyač-čo
light	luce (f)	'lu-če
lightning (bolt of)	lampo	'lam-po
	fulmine (m)	'ful-mi-ne
• **There's lightning**	Sta lampeggiando.	lam-pej-'jan-do
mild	mite	'mi-te
• **(to) be mild**	essere* mite	—
mist, haze	foschia	fos-'ki-a
moon	luna	'lu-na
• **moonbeam**	raggio della luna	'raj-jo
mugginess	afa	'a-fa
• **muggy**	afoso	a-'fo-zo
rain	pioggia	'pyoj-ja
• **(to) rain**	piovere	'pyo-ve-re
• **(to) rain heavily**	piovere a dirotto	di-'rot-to
• **rainy**	piovoso	'pyo-vo-zo
• **pouring rain**	pioggia torrenziale	'pyoj-ja tor-ren-'tsya-le
sea	mare (m)	'ma-re
shadow, shade	ombra	'om-bra
shower	acquazzone (m)	a-kwa-'tso-ne
sky	cielo	'če-lo
sleet	nevischio	ne-'vis-kyo
slippery	scivoloso	ši-vo-'lo-zo
snow	neve (f)	'ne-ve
• **(to) snow**	nevicare	ne-vi-'ka-re
• **snowball**	palla di neve	'pal-la

Idiomatic Expressions

(to) have one's head in the clouds	=	avere la testa fra le nuvole
The weather is foul.	=	Fa un tempo da cani.
It's raining cats and dogs.	=	Piove a catinelle.
		Piove a dirotto.

• **snow-capped**	coperto di neve	*ko-'per-to*
• **snowflake**	fiocco di neve	*'fyok-ko*
• **snowman**	pupazzo di neve	*pu-'pa-tso*
• **snowstorm**	bufera di neve	*bu-'fe-ra*
star	stella	*'stel-la*
storm	tempesta	*tem-'pes-ta*
sun	sole	*'so-le*
• **(to) sunbathe**	prendere* sole	*'pren-de-re*
• **sunbeam**	raggio di sole	*'raj-jo*
• **sunglasses**	occhiali da sole	*ok-'kya-li*
• **sunny**	pieno di sole	*'pye-no*
thaw	disgelo	*diz-'je-lo*
• **(to) thaw**	sgelare	*zje-'la-re*
thunder	tuono	*'two-no*
• **(to) thunder**	tuonare	*two-'na-re*
• **thunderstorm**	temporale (m)	*tem-po-'ra-le*
tornado	tornado	—
typhoon	tifone (m)	*ti-'fo-ne*
weather	tempo	*'tem-po*
wind	vento	*'ven-to*
• **(to) be windy**	tirare vento	*ti-'ra-re*
• **wind gust**	raffica di vento	*'raf-fi-ka*
• **windstorm, snowstorm**	bufera	*bu-'fe-ra*

B. REACTING TO THE WEATHER

(to) be cold	avere* freddo	*a-'ve-re 'fred-do*
(to) be hot	avere* caldo	*a-'ve-re 'kal-do*
(to) bear	sopportare	*sop-por-'ta-re*
• **I can't stand the cold.**	Non sopporto il freddo.	*sop-'porto*
• **I can't stand the heat.**	Non sopporto il caldo.	—
(to) have chills	avere* i brividi	*a-'ve-re i 'bri-vi-di*
How's the weather?	Che tempo fa?	—
	Com'è il tempo?	—
• **It's bad (weather).**	Fa brutto (tempo).	—
• **It's cloudy**	È nuvoloso.	*nu-vo-'lo-zo*
• **It's cold.**	Fa freddo.	*'fred-do*
• **It's very cold.**	Fa molto freddo.	*'fred-do*
• **It's cool.**	Fa fresco.	*'fres-ko*

• It's hot, warm.	Fa caldo.	'kal-do
• It's very hot.	Fa molto caldo.	—
• It's a bit hot.	Fa un po' caldo.	—
• It's humid.	È umido.	'u-mi-do
• It's mild.	È mite.	'mi-te
• It's muggy.	È afoso.	a-'fo-zo
• It's nice (weather).	Fa bello.	—
	Fa bel tempo.	—
• It's pleasant.	È piacevole.	pya-če-vo-le
	È bello.	—
• It's raining	Piove.	'pyo-ve
• It's snowing	Nevica.	'ne-vi-ka
• It's sunny.	C'è il sole.	ce il 'so-le
• It's thundering.	Tuona.	'two-na
• It's windy.	Tira vento.	'ti-ra 'ven-to
• There's lightning.	Lampeggia.	lam-'pej-ja
(to) perspire	sudare	su-'da-re
(to) warm up	riscaldarsi	ris-kal-'dar-si

C. WEATHER-MEASURING INSTRUMENTS AND CONCEPTS

barometer	barometro	ba-'ro-me-tro
• barometric pressure	pressione barometrica	pres-'syo-ne bar-o-'me-tri-ka
boiling point	temperatura dell'acqua bollente	tem-pe-ra-'tu-ra del-'lak-kwa bol-'len-te
Celsius	Celsius (m, inv)	'čel-si-us
Centigrade	centigrado	čen-'ti-gra-do
degree	grado	'gra-do
Fahrenheit	Fahrenheit (m, inv)	—
maximum	massimo	'mas-si-mo
• maximum temperature	temperatura massima	tem-pe-ra-'tu-ra
(to) melt	sciogliere*	'šo-lye-re
• melting point	temperatura del ghiaccio fondente	'gyač-čo fon-'den-te
mercury	mercurio	mer-'ku-ri-o
minimum	minimo	'mi-ni-mo
• minimum temperature	temperatura minima	—
minus	meno	—
plus	più	pyu
temperature	temperatura	tem-pe-ra-'tu-ra
thermometer	termometro	ter-'mo-me-tro
thermostat	termostato	ter-'mos-ta-to
weather bulletin	bollettino meteorologico	bol-let-'ti-no me-te-o-ro-'lo-ji-ko
weather conditions	condizioni meteorologiche	kon-di-'tsyo-ni me-te-o-ro-'lo-ji-ke

weather forecast	previsioni, (f, pl)	*pre-vi-'zyo-ni*
	del tempo	
zero	zero	*'dze-ro*
• above zero	sopra zero	—
• below zero	sotto zero	—

7. COLORS

A. BASIC COLORS

What color is it?	Di che colore è?	*di ke co-l'o-re 'e*
black	nero	*'ne-ro*
• pitch black	nero come la pece	*'pe-če*
blue	azzurro	*a-'dzur-ro*
• dark blue	blu (inv)	—
• light blue, sky blue	celeste	*če-'les-te*
brown	marrone (inv)	*mar-'ro-ne*
gold	oro (inv)	—
gray	grigio	*'gri-jo*
• pearl gray	grigio perla (inv)	*'per-la*
green	verde	*'ver-de*
• military green	verde militare (inv)	*mi-li-'ta-re*
ivory	avorio	*a-'vo-ryo*
lemon	limone (inv)	*li-'mo-ne*
mauve	malva (inv)	*'mal-va*
orange	arancione (inv)	*a-ran-'čo-ne*
pink	rosa (inv)	*'ro-za*
plum	prugna (inv)	*'pru-nya*
pure	puro	*'pu-ro*
purple, violet	viola (inv)	*'vyo-la*
red	rosso	*'ros-so*
silver	argento (inv)	*ar'jen-to*
turquoise	turchino	*tur-'ki-no*
white	bianco	*'byan-ko*
yellow	giallo	*'jal-lo*

B. DESCRIBING COLORS AND COLORING ACTIVITIES

bright	acceso	*ač-če-zo*
	brillante	*bril-'lan-te*
color	colore (m)	*ko-'lo-re*
• (to) color	colorare, colorire (isc)	*ko-lo-'ra-re, ko-lo-'ri-re*
• colored	a colori	—
chocolate	cioccolato	*cok-ko-'la-to*
dark	scuro	*'sku-ro*
dull	cupo	*'ku-po*
	spento	*'spen-to*
light	chiaro	*'kya-ro*
lively	vivace	*vi-'va-če*

Color Idioms

(financially) broke	al verde
1-800 number	numero verde
carte blanche	carta bianca
dark mood	umore nero
dull life	vita grigia
extremely angry	giallo dalla rabbia
help line	telefono azzurro
information radio	onda verde
mystery story	giallo
national Italian team	squadra azzurra
rare thing	mosca bianca
red light	luci rosse
sleepless night	notte bianca
Snow White	Bianca Neve
terrified	verde di paura
(to) be extremely angry	essere verde dalla rabbia
(to) become embarrassed	diventare rosso
yellow pages	le pagine gialle

opaque	opaco	*o-'pa-ko*
painting	pittura	*pit-'tu-ra*
	dipinto	*di-'pin-to*
	quadro	*'kwa-dro*
• **(to) paint**	pitturare	*pit-tu-'ra-re*
	dipingere*	*di-'pin-je-re*
• **painter**	pittore (-trice)	*pit-'to-re*
pen	penna	*'pen-na*
• **felt pen**	pennarello	*pen-na-'rel-lo*
• **pencil**	matita	*ma-'ti-ta*
• **brush**	pennello	*pen-'nel-lo*
tint	tinta	*'tin-ta*
• **(to) tint**	tingere*	*'tin-je-re*
transparent	trasparente	*tras-pa-'ren-te*

8. BASIC GRAMMAR

A. GRAMMATICAL TERMS

adjective	aggettivo	*aj-jet-'ti-vo*
• **demonstrative**	dimostrativo	*di-mos-tra-'ti-vo*
• **descriptive**	qualificativo	*kwa-li-fi-ka-'ti-vo*
• **indefinite**	indefinito	*in-de-fi-'ni-to*
• **interrogative**	interrogativo	*in-ter-ro-ga-'ti-vo*
• **possessive**	possessivo	*pos-ses-'si-vo*

adverb	avverbio	*av-'ver-byo*
alphabet	alfabeto	*al-fa-'be-to*
• **accent**	accento	*ač-'čen-to*
• **consonant**	consonante (f)	*kon-so-'nan-te*
• **letter**	lettera	*'let-te-ra*
• **phonetics**	fonetica	*fo-'ne-ti-ka*
• **pronunciation**	pronuncia	*pro-'nun-ča*
• **vowel**	vocale (f)	*vo-'ka-le*
article	articolo	*ar-'ti-ko-lo*
• **definite**	determinativo	*de-ter-mi-na-'ti-vo*
• **indefinite**	indeterminativo	*in-de-ter-mi-na-'ti-vo*
clause	proposizione (f)	*pro-po-si-'tsyo-ne*
• **main**	principale	*prin-či-'pa-le*
• **relative**	relativa	*re-la-'ti-va*
• **subordinate**	subordinata	*su-bor-di-'na-ta*
conjunction	congiunzione (f)	*kon-jun-'tsyo-ne*
discourse	discorso	*dis-'kor-so*
• **direct**	diretto	*di-'ret-to*
• **indirect**	indiretto	*in-di-'ret-to*
gender	genere (m)	*'je-ne-re*
• **feminine**	femminile	*fem-mi-'ni-le*
• **masculine**	maschile	*mas-'ki-le*
grammar	grammatica	*gram-'ma-ti-ka*
interrogative	interrogativo	*in-ter-ro-ga-'ti-vo*
mood	modo	—
• **conditional**	condizionale	*kon-di-tsyo-'na-le*
• **imperative**	imperativo	*im-pe-ra-'ti-vo*
• **indefinite**	indefinito	*in-de-fi-'ni-to*
• **indicative**	indicativo	*in-di-ka-'ti-vo*
• **subjunctive**	congiuntivo	*kon-jun-'ti-vo*
noun	nome (m)	*'no-me*
• **substantive**	sostantivo	*sos-tan-'ti-vo*
number	numero	*'nu-me-ro*
• **singular**	singolare	*sin-go-'la-re*
• **plural**	plurale	*plu-'ra-le*
object	complemento, oggetto	*kom-ple-'men-to, oj-'jet-to*
• **direct**	diretto	*di-'ret-to*
• **indirect**	indiretto	*in-di-'ret-to*
participle	participio	*par-ti-'či-pi-o*
• **past**	passato	*pas-'sa-to*
• **present**	presente	*pre-'zen-te*
partitive	partitivo	*par-ti-'ti-vo*
person	persona	*per-'so-na*
• **first**	prima	*'pri-ma*
• **second**	seconda	*se-'kon-da*
• **third**	terza	*'ter-tsa*
predicate	predicato	*pre-di-'ka-to*

preposition	preposizione (f)	*pre-po-zi-'tsyo-ne*
• **prepositional contraction**	preposizione articolata	*ar-ti-ko-'la-ta*
pronoun	pronome (m)	*pro-'no-me*
• **demonstrative**	dimostrativo	*di-mos-tra-'ti-vo*
• **interrogative**	interrogativo	*in-ter-ro-ga-'ti-vo*
• **object**	di complemento, oggetto	*kom-ple-'men-to, oj-'jet-to*
• **personal**	personale	*per-so-'na-le*
• **possessive**	possessivo	*pos-ses-'si-vo*
• **reflexive**	riflessivo	*ri-fles-'si-vo*
• **relative**	relativo	*re-la-'ti-vo*
• **subject**	soggetto	*soj-'jet-to*
sentence	frase (f), periodo	*'fra-ze, pe-'ri-o-do*
• **declarative**	dichiarativa	*di-kya-ra-'ti-va*
• **interrogative**	interrogativa	*in-ter-ro-ga-'ti-va*
• **exclamatory**	esclamativa	*es-kla-ma-'ti-va*
subject	soggetto	*soj-'jet-to*
tense	tempo	*'tem-po*
• **future**	futuro	*fu-'tu-ro*
• **imperfect**	imperfetto	*im-per-'fet-to*
• **past**	passato	*pas-'sa-to*
• **past absolute**	passato remoto	*re-'mo-to*
• **perfect**	perfetto	*per-'fet-to*
• **present perfect**	passato prossimo	*'pros-si-mo*
• **pluperfect**	trapassato	*tra-pas-'sa-to*
• **present**	presente	*pre-'zen-te*
verb	verbo	*'ver-bo*
• **active**	attivo	*at-'ti-vo*
• **conjugation**	coniugazione (f)	*kon-yu-ga-'tsyo-ne*
• **gerund**	gerundio	*je-'run-di-o*
• **infinitive**	infinito	*in-fi-'ni-to*
• **intransitive**	intransitivo	*in-tran-si-'ti-vo*
• **irregular**	irregolare	*ir-re-go-'la-re*
• **modal**	modale	*mo-'da-le*
• **passive**	passivo	*pas-'si-vo*
• **reflexive**	riflessivo	*ri-fles-'si-vo*
• **regular**	regolare	*re-go-'la-re*
• **transitive**	transitivo	*tran-si-'ti-vo*

B. ARTICLES

a, an

• **a boy**	un ragazzo	*ra-'ga-tso*
• **a girl**	una ragazza	*ra-'ga-tsa*
• **an uncle**	uno zio	*'dzi-o*
• **a friend**	un amico (m)	*a-'mi-ko*
• **a friend**	un'amica (f)	*a-'mi-ka*

the
• the boy	il ragazzo	ra-'ga-tso
• the boys	i ragazzi	ra-'ga-tsi
• the uncle	lo zio	'dzi-o
• the uncles	gli zii	'dzi-i
• the friend	l'amico (m)	a-'mi-ko
• the friends	gli amici (m)	lyi a-'mi-či
• the girl	la ragazza	ra-'ga-tsa
• the girls	le ragazze	ra-'ga-tse
• the friend	l'amica (f)	a-'mi-ka
• the friends	le amiche (f)	a-'mi-ke

C. PARTITIVES

some
• some boys	dei ragazzi	de-i ra-'ga-tsi
	alcuni ragazzi	al-'ku-ni ra-'ga-tsi
	qualche ragazzo	'kwal-ke ra-'ga-tso
• some friends	degli amici (m)	de-lyi a-'mi-či
	alcuni amici	al-'ku-ni a-'mi-či
	qualche amico	'kwal-ke a-'mi-ko
• some uncles	degli zii	de-lyi 'dzi-i
	alcuni zii	al-'ku-ni 'dzi-i
	qualche zio	'kwal-ke 'dzi-o
• some girls	delle ragazze	'del-le ra-'ga-tse
	alcune ragazze	al-'ku-ne ra-'ga-tse
	qualche ragazza	'kwal-ke ra-'ga-tsa
• some friends	delle amiche (f)	'del-le a-'mi-ke
	alcune amiche	al-'ku-ne a-'mi-ke
	qualche amica	'kwal-ke a-'mi-ka

a bit, little, some
• some, a bit of butter	del burro	del 'bur-ro
	un po' di burro	—
• some, a bit of sugar	dello zucchero	del-lo 'dzuk-ke-ro
	un po' di zucchero	—
• some, a bit of cake	della torta	del-la 'tor-ta
	un po' di torta	—
• some, a bit of water	dell'acqua	del-'lak-kwa
	un po' acqua	—

D. DEMONSTRATIVES

this, these
• this boy	questo ragazzo	'kwes-to ra-'ga-tso
• these boys	questi ragazzi	'kwes-ti ra-'ga-tsi
• this girl	questa ragazza	'kwes-ta ra-'ga-tsa
• these girls	queste ragazze	'kwes-te ra-'ga-tse

that, those
- **that boy**   quel ragazzo   *kwel ra-'ga-tso*
- **those boys**   quei ragazzi   *kwe-i ra-'ga-tsi*
- **that uncle**   quello zio   *kwel-lo 'dzi-o*
- **those uncles**   quegli zii   *kwe-lyi 'dzi-i*
- **that friend**   quell'amico (m)   *kwel-la-'mi-ko*
- **those friends**   quegli amici (m)   *kwel-lyi a-'mi-či*
- **that girl**   quella ragazza   *kwel-la ra-'ga-tsa*
- **those girls**   quelle ragazze   *kwel-le ra-'ga-tse*
- **that friend**   quell'amica (f)   *kwel-la-'mi-ka*
- **those friends**   quelle amiche (f)   *kwel-le a-'mi-ke*

E. POSSESSIVES

my
- **my book**   il mio libro   *'mi-o 'li-bro*
- **my books**   i miei libri   *'mye-i 'li-bri*
- **my pen**   la mia penna   *'mi-a 'pen-na*
- **my pens**   le mie penne   *'mi-e 'pen-ne*

your (s, fam)
- **your book**   il tuo libro   *'tu-o*
- **your books**   i tuoi libri   *'two-i*
- **your pen**   la tua penna   *'tu-a*
- **your pens**   le tue penne   *'tu-e*

his, her, its, your (s, pol)
- **his, her, your book**   il suo libro   *'su-o*
- **his, her, your books**   i suoi libri   *'swo-i*
- **his, her, your pen**   la sua penna   *'su-a*
- **his, her, your pens**   le sue penne   *'su-e*

our
- **our book**   il nostro libro   *'nos-tro*
- **our books**   i nostri libri   *'nos-tri*
- **our pen**   la nostra penna   *'nos-tra*
- **our pens**   le nostre penne   *'nos-tre*

your (pl, fam)
- **your book**   il vostro libro   *'vos-tro*
- **your books**   i vostri libri   *'vos-tri*
- **your pen**   la vostra penna   *'vos-tra*
- **your pens**   le vostre penne   *'vos-tre*

their, your (pl, pol)
- **their, your book**   il loro libro   *'lo-ro*
- **their, your books**   i loro libri   —
- **their, your pen**   la loro penna   —
- **their, your pens**   le loro penne   —

F. PREPOSITIONS

above	sopra	'so-pra
among	fra	—
	tra	—
at	a	—
	in	—
below	sotto	'sot-to
between	fra	—
	tra	—
by	da	—
for	per	—
from	da	—
in	in	—
of	di	—
on	su	—
over	sopra	'so-pra
	su	
through	per	—
to	a	—
with	con	—
without	senza	'sen-tsa

G. PERSONAL PRONOUNS

I	io	'i-o
• me	mi (*before verb*)	—
	me (*after verb*)	—
• to me	mi (*before verb*)	—
	a me	—
• myself	mi (*before verb*)	—
you (s, fam, subj)	tu	—
• you	ti (*before verb*)	—
	te (*after verb*)	—
• to you	ti (*before verb*)	—
	a te	—
• yourself	ti (*before verb*)	—

Prepositional Contractions

+	il	i	lo	l'	gli	la	le
a	al	ai	allo	all'	agli	alla	alle
da	dal	dai	dallo	dall'	dagli	dalla	dalle
di	del	dei	dello	dell'	degli	della	delle
in	nel	nei	nello	nell'	negli	nella	nelle
su	sul	sui	sullo	sull'	sugli	sulla	sulle

he	lui, egli	*'lu-i*
• **him**	lo *(before verb)*	—
	lui *(after verb)*	*'lu-i*
• **to him**	gli *(before verb)*	*lyi*
	a lui	*'lu-i*
• **himself**	si *(before verb)*	—
she	lei, ella	*'le-i*
• **her**	la *(before verb)*	—
	lei *(after verb)*	—
• **to her**	le *(before verb)*	—
	a lei	*'le-i*
• **herself**	si *(before verb)*	—
you (s, pol)	Lei	—
• **your**	Lo *(before verb)*	—
	Lei *(after verb)*	—
• **to you**	Le *(before verb)*	—
	a Lei	—
• **yourself**	si *(before verb)*	—
we	noi	*'no-i*
• **us**	ci *(before verb)*	*či*
	noi *(after verb)*	—
• **to us**	ci *(before verb)*	—
	a noi	—
• **ourselves**	ci *(before verb)*	*či*
you (pl, fam)	voi	*'vo-i*
• **you**	vi *(before verb)*	—
	voi *(after verb)*	—
• **to you**	vi *(before verb)*	—
	a voi	—
• **yourselves**	vi *(before verb)*	—
they, you (pl, pol)	loro, Loro	*'lo-ro*
• **them**	li (m) *(before verb)*	—
	le (f) *(before verb)*	—
• **to them**	gli *(before verb)*	*lyi*
	a loro *(after verb)*	—
• **themselves**	si *(before verb)*	—

H. OTHER PRONOUNS

everyone	tutti	*'tut-ti*
	ognuno	*o-nyu-no*
everything	tutto	*'tut-to*
many	molti (molte, f)	*'mol-ti*
	tanti (tante, f)	*'tan-ti*
one (in general)	si *(before verb)*	—
others	altri (altre, f)	*'al-tri*
some, of it, of them	ne *(before verb)*	—

some (people)	alcuni (alcune, f)	*'al-ku-ni*
someone	qualcuno	*kwal-'ku-no*
something	qualcosa	*kwal-'ko-za*

I. CONJUNCTIONS

also	anche	*'an-ke*
although	benché	*ben-'ke*
	sebbene	*seb-'be-ne*
and	e	—
as	come	*'ko-me*
as if	come se	—
as soon as	appena	*ap-'pe-na*
because	perché	*per-'ke*
but	ma	—
	però	*pe-'ro*
despite	malgrado	*mal-'gra-do*
	nonostante	*no-nos-'tan-te*
even though	anche se	*'an-ke*
however	comunque	*ko-'mun-kwe*
	tuttavia	*tut-ta-'vi-a*
if	se	—
in fact	infatti	*in-'fat-ti*
in the event that	nel caso che	*nel 'ka-zo ke*
on account of	a causa di	*a 'kau-za di*
provided that	purché	*pur-'ke*
since	poiché	*poy-'ke*
so that	affinché	*af-fin-'ke*
	perché	*per-'ke*
thanks to	grazie a	*'gra-tsye*
therefore	quindi	*'kwin-di*

J. COMMON ADVERBS

again	di nuovo	*'nwo-vo*
almost	quasi	*'kwa-zi*
already	già	*ja*
also, too	anche	*'an-ke*
as a matter of fact	anzi	*'an-tsi*
bad(ly)	male	*'ma-le*
	malamente	*ma-la-'men-te*
by chance	per caso	*per 'ka-zo*
by now	ormai	*or-'ma-i*
early	presto	*'pres-to*
enough	abbastanza	*ab-bas-'tan-dza*
far	lontano	*lon-'ta-no*
first	prima	*'pri-ma*

in a hurry	in fretta	*'fret-ta*
in a little while	fra (tra) poco	*'po-ko*
in the meanwhile	nel frattempo	*frat-'tem-po*
instead	invece	*in-'ve-če*
just, barely	appena	*ap-'pe-na*
late	tardi	*'tar-di*
near(by)	vicino	*vi-'či-no*
nowadays	oggigiorno	*oj-ji-'jor-no*
only	solo	*'so-lo*
rather	piuttosto	*pyut-'tos-to*
right away	subito	*'su-bi-to*
still, yet, again	ancora	*an-'ko-ra*
then	allora	*al-'lo-ra*
• **then, after**	poi	*'po-i*
there	lì	—
	là	—
this evening	stasera	*sta-'se-ra*
this morning	stamani	*sta-'ma-ni*
today	oggi	*'oj-ji*
together	insieme	*in-'sye-me*
tomorrow	domani	*do-'ma-ni*
unfortunately	purtroppo	*pur-'trop-po*
until now	finora	*fi-'no-ra*

K. NEGATIVES

neither...nor	non...né...né	—
never	non...mai	—
no more, no longer	non...più	*pyu*
no one	non...nessuno	*nes-'su-no*
not even	non...neanche	*ne-'an-ke*
	non...nemmeno	*nem-'me-no*
	non...neppure	*nep-'pu-re*
not really, not quite	non...mica	*'mi-ka*
nothing	non...niente	*'nyen-te*
	non...nulla	—

9. INFORMATION

A. REQUESTING INFORMATION

answer	risposta	*ris-'pos-ta*
• **(to) answer**	rispondere*	*ris-pon-de-re*
(to) ask (for)	chiedere*	*'kye-de-re*
• **(to) ask a question**	fare* una domanda	*'fa-re u-na do-'man-da*
Can you tell me...?	Mi sa dire... (pol)?	—
	Mi sai dire... (fam)?	—

How?	Come?	'ko-me
How come?	Come mai?	—
How much?	Quanto?	'kwan-to
I don't understand.	Non capisco.	ka-'pis-ko
So?	E allora?	al-'lo-ra
	E con ciò?	kon čo
What?	Che?	ke
	Cosa?	'ko-za
	Che cosa?	ke 'ko-za
What does it mean?	Che significa?	ke si-'nyi-fi-ka
	Che vuol dire?	ke vwol 'di-re
When?	Quando?	'kwan-do
Where?	Dove?	'do-ve
Which (one)?	Quale?	'kwa-le
Who?	Chi?	ki
Why?	Perché?	per-'ke

B. GENERAL CONCEPTS

communication	comunicazione (f)	ko-mu-ni-ka-'tsyo-neh
• **communication media**	mezzi (m, pl) di comunicazione	—
cyberspace	ciberspazio	—
information	informazione (f)	in-for-ma-'tsyo-ne
• **information booth**	sportello informazioni	—
• **information media**	mezzi (m, pl) d'informazione	—
• **information theory**	teoria dell'informazione	te-o-'ri-a
Internet	Internet (m, inv)	—
• **on the Internet**	su Internet	—
mass communications	comunicazione (f) di massa	—
news item	notizia	no-'ti-tsya
press	stampa	—
radio	radio (f)	—
television	televisione (f)	te-le-vi-'syo-ne
transmission	trasmissione (f)	tras-mi-'syo-ne
• **(to) transmit**	trasmettere*	tras-'met-te-re
unit of information	unità d'informazione	u-ni-'ta
website	sito web	—

PEOPLE

10. FAMILY AND FRIENDS

A. FAMILY MEMBERS

aunt	zia	*'dzi-a*
• **great-aunt**	prozia	*pro-'dzi-a*
brother	fratello	*fra-'tel-lo*
• **brother-in-law**	cognato	*ko-'nya-to*
• **half-brother**	fratellastro	*fra-tel-'las-tro*
cousin	cugino (m)	*ku-'ji-no*
	cugina (f)	—
child	bambino (-a)	*bam-'bi-no*
• **godchild**	figlioccio (-a)	*fi-'lyoč-čo*
dad	papà (m, inv), babbo	*pa-'pa, 'bab-bo*
daughter	figlia	*'fi-lya*
• **daughter-in-law**	nuora	*'nwo-ra*
• **stepdaughter**	figliastra	*fi-'lyas-tra*
family	famiglia	*fa-'mi-lya*
• **family relation**	parentela	*pa-ren-'te-la*
father	padre (m)	*'pa-dre*
• **father-in-law**	suocero	*'swo-če-ro*
• **godfather**	padrino	*pa-'dri-no*
• **stepfather**	patrigno	*pa-'tri-nyo*
fraternal	fraterno	*fra-'ter-no*
grandchild	nipote (m/f)	*ni-'po-te*
• **great grandchild**	pronipote (m/f)	*pro-ni-'po-te*
grandfather	nonno	—
• **great grandfather**	bisnonno	*biz-'non-no*
grandmother	nonna	—
• **great grandmother**	bisnonna	*biz-'non-na*
head of the family	capofamiglia	*ka-po-fa-'mi-lya*
household	casa	*'ka-za*
	domicilio	*do-mi-'či-lyo*
	focolare	*fo-ko-'la-re*
husband	marito	*ma-'ri-to*
maternal	materno	*ma-'ter-no*
mother	madre (f)	*'ma-dre*
• **godmother**	madrina	*ma-'dri-na*
• **mother-in-law**	suocera	*'swo-če-ra*
• **mom**	mamma	—
• **stepmother**	matrigna	*ma-'tri-nya*
nephew	nipote (m)	*ni-'po-te*

niece	nipote (f)	ni-'po-te
parent	genitore (-trice)	je-ni-'to-re
paternal	paterno	pa-'ter-no
relative	parente (m/f)	pa-'ren-te
sister	sorella	so-'rel-la
• half-sister	sorellastra	so-rel-'las-tra
• sister-in-law	cognata	ko-'nya-ta
son	figlio	fi-lyo
• son-in-law	genero	'je-ne-ro
• stepson	figliastro	fi-'lyas-tro
twin	gemello (-a)	je-'mel-lo
uncle	zio	'dzi-o
• great-uncle	prozio	pro-'dzi-o
wife	moglie (f)	'mo-lye

B. FRIENDS AND SIGNIFICANT OTHERS

acquaintance	conoscenza	ko-no-'šen-dza
boyfriend	amico	a-'mi-ko
	ragazzo (amorous)	ra-'ga-tso
chum	compagno (-a)	kom-'pa-nyo
colleague	collega (m/f)	kol-'le-ga
enemy	nemico (-a)	ne-'mi-ko
fiancé	fidanzato	fi-dan-'tsa-to
fiancée	fidanzata	fi-dan-'tsa-ta
friend	amico (-a)	a-'mi-ko
• (to) become friends	diventare (ess) amici	di-ven-'ta-re a-'mi-či
	fare* amicizia	'fa-re a-mi-'či-tsya
• (to) break off a friendship	rompere* un'amicizia	'rom-pe-re
• close friend	amico (-a) intimo (-a)	a-'mi-ko 'in-ti-mo
• dear friend	caro (-a) amico (-a)	—
• family friend	amico (-a) di famiglia	a-'mi-ko di fa-'mi-lya
• friendship	amicizia	a-mi-'či-tsya
girlfriend	amica	a-'mi-ka
	ragazza (amorous)	ra-'ga-tsa
lover	amante (m/f)	a-'man-te
• love affair	relazione (amorosa)	re-la-'tsyo-ne
people	gente (f)	'jen-te
person	persona	per-'so-na
relationship	relazione (f)	re-la-'tsyo-ne

11. DESCRIBING PEOPLE

A. GENDER AND PHYSICAL APPEARANCE

adorable	adorabile	a-do-'ra-bi-le
agile	agile	'a-ji-le

alert	sveglio	'zve-lyo
athletic	atletico	at-'le-ti-ko
attractive	attraente	at-tra-'en-te
average height	altezza media	al-'te-tsa 'me-dya
baldness	calvizie (f, inv)	kal-'vi-tsye
• bald	calvo	'kal-vo
(to) be slightly built	avere* un fisico debole	a-'ve-re un 'fi-zi-ko 'de-bo-le
(to) be strongly built	avere* un fisico forte	'for-te
beauty	bellezza	bel-'le-tsa
• beautiful, handsome	bello (-a)	—
(to) become fat	ingrassare	in-gras-'sa-re
(to) become thin	dimagrire (isc)	di-ma-'gri-re
big	grande	'gran-de
• big, huge	grosso	'gros-so
blond	biondo	'byon-do
• blonde	bionda	—
(to) blush	arrossire (isc)	ar-ros-'si-re
body	corpo	'kor-po
bow legs	gambe storte	'gam-be 'stor-te
boy	ragazzo	ra-'ga-tso
brawny	poderoso	po-de-'ro-zo
broad chin	mento largo	'men-to 'lar-go
broad forehead	fronte spaziosa	'fron-te spa-'tsyo-za
broad-shouldered	con le spalle larghe	'spal-le 'lar-ge
brown eyes	occhi castani	'ok-ki kas-'ta-ni
brown skin	pelle bruna	'pel-le 'bru-na
build	fisico	'fi-zi-ko
chapped hands	mani screpolate	skre-po-'la-te
chubby	grassottello	gras-sot-'tel-lo
clean	pulito	pu-'li-to
clear skin	pelle chiara	'pel-le 'kya-ra
(to) color one's hair	tingersi* i capelli	'tin-jer-si i ka-'pel-li
(to) comb oneself	pettinarsi	pet-ti-'nar-si
corpulent	corpulento	kor-pu-'len-to
curly	riccio	'rič-čo
cute	simpatico, carino (-a)	sim-'pa-ti-ko, ka-'ri-no
dark skin	pelle nera	'pel-le 'ne-ra
dark-haired	bruno	'bru-no
delicate, frail	delicato	de-li-'ka-to
dimple	fossetta (del mento)	fos-'set-ta
dirty	sporco	'spor-ko
double chin	doppio mento	'dop-pyo 'men-to
dry skin	pelle secca	'pel-le 'sek-ka
emaciated	emaciato	e-ma-'ča-to
energetic	energico	e-'ner-ji-ko
expression	espressione (f)	es-pres-'syo-ne
face, countenance	faccia	'fač-ča
	viso	'vi-zo
fascinating	affascinante	af-fa-ši-'nan-te

fat	grasso	'gras-so
female	femmina	'fem-mi-na
• **feminine**	femminile	fem-mi-'ni-le
fleshy	carnoso	kar-'no-zo
frail, slender	gracile	'gra-či-le
freckles	lentiggini (f)	len-'tij-ji-ni
• **freckled**	lentigginoso	len-tij-ji-'no-zo
frizzy, fuzzy hair	capelli crespi	ka-'pel-li 'kres-pi
gentleman	signore (m)	si-'nyo-re
giant	gigante	ji-'gan-te
good complexion	carnagione bella	kar-na-'jo-ne 'bel-la
good figure, shapely	bella figura	'bel-la fi-'gu-ra
gray hair	capelli grigi	ka-'pel-li 'gri-ji
haggard face	viso stravolto	'vi-zo stra-'vol-to
hairstyle	acconciatura	ak-kon-ča-'tu-ra
	(dei capelli)	
hairy	peloso	pe-'lo-zo
happy face	viso allegro	'vi-zo al-'le-gro
(to) have a slim waistline	avere* una vita snella	a-'ve-re u'na 'vi-ta 'znel-la
heavy	pesante	pe-'zan-te
hefty	robusto	ro-'bus-to
height	altezza	al-'te-tsa
• **short**	basso	'bas-so
• **tall**	alto	'al-to
high forehead	fronte alta	—
hunched	curvo	'kur-vo
husky, manly	aitante	ai-'tan-te
lady	signora	si-'nyo-ra
• **young lady**	signorina	si-nyo-'ri-na
lanky, long-legged	slanciato	zlan-'ča-to
large	grosso	'gros-so
lean	magro	'ma-gro
(to) lose one's hair	perdere* i capelli	'per-de-re i ka-'pel-li
(to) lose weight	perdere* peso	'per-de-re 'pe-zo
low forehead	fronte bassa	'fron-te 'bas-sa
male	maschio	'mas-kyo
man	uomo (uomini, pl)	'wo-mo ('wo-mi-ni)
• **masculine**	maschile	mas-'ki-le
midget	nano (-a)	—
muscular	muscoloso	mus-ko-'lo-zo
mustache	baffi (pl)	'baf-fi
obese	obeso	o-'be-zo
olive skin	pelle olivastra	'pel-le o-li-'vas-tra
pale cheeks	guance pallide	'gwan-če 'pal-li-de
parted hair	capelli con la scriminatura	skri-mi-na-'tu-ra
paunch	pancia	'pan-ča
pimple	foruncolo	fo-'run-ko-lo

pleasant, friendly face	viso simpatico	'vi-zo sim-'pa-ti-ko
plump	pasciuto	pa-'šu-to
pot-bellied	panciuto	pan-'ču-to
pretty	carino (-a)	ka-'ri-no
pudgy	tozzo	'to-tso
puny	smunto	'zmun-to
red hair	capelli rossi	ka-'pel-li 'ros-si
robust, strong	robusto	ro-'bus-to
rosy cheeks	guance rosee	'gwan-če 'ro-ze-e
rough skin	pelle ruvida	'pel-le 'ru-vi-da
round face	viso rotondo	'vi-zo ro-'ton-do
scrawny, skin and bones	scheletrico	ske-'le-tri-ko
seductive	seducente	se-du-'čen-te
sex	sesso	'ses-so
short	basso	'bas-so
skinny	magro	'ma-gro
slant eyes	occhi a mandorla	'ok-ki a 'man-dor-la
slim, lean	snello	'snel-lo
small, little	piccolo	'pik-ko-lo
smile	sorriso	'sor-'ri-zo
• **(to) smile**	sorridere*	sor-'ri-de-re
stocky	tarchiato	tar-'kya-to
straight hair	capelli lisci	ka-'pel-li 'li-ši
streaked hair	capelli striati	ka-'pel-li stri-'a-ti
strength	forza	'for-tsa
• **strong**	forte	'for-te
tall	alto	—
toothless	sdentato	zden-'ta-to
ugly	brutto	'brut-to
untidy, disheveled hair	capelli sfatti	ka-'pel-li 'sfat-ti
vigorous	vigoroso	vi-go-'ro-zo
virile	virile	vi-'ri-le
waistline	vita	—
wavy hair	capelli ondulati	ka-'pel-li on-du-'la-ti
weakness	debolezza	de-bo-'le-tsa
• **weak**	debole	'de-bo-le
weight	peso	'pe-zo
well-built	ben fatto	—
woman	donna	—
wrinkles	rughe (f, pl)	'ru-ge
youthful	giovanile	jo-va-'ni-le

B. AGE CONCEPTS

adolescence	adolescenza	a-do-le'-šen-tsa
• **adolescent, teenager**	adolescente (m/f)	a-do-le-'šen-te
adulthood, maturity	maturità (f, inv)	ma-tu-ri-'ta
• **adult**	adulto	a-'dul-to

age	età (f, inv)	e-'ta
• (to) be...years old	avere*...anni	—
• I am 55 years old.	Ho cinquantacinque anni.	čin-kwan-ta-'čin-kwe
baby, child	bambino (-a)	bam-'bi-no
• children	bambini	—
big (in the sense of old)	grande	'gran-de
boy	ragazzo	ra-'ga-tso
childhood	fanciullezza	fan-cul-'le-tsa
girl	ragazza	ra-'ga-tsa
(to) grow up	crescere* (ess)	'kre-še-re
infancy	infanzia	in-'fan-tsya
• infantile	infantile	in-fan-'ti-le
mature person	persona matura	per-'so-na ma-'tu-ra
middle age	mezza età	'me-dza e-'ta
newly-born	neonato (-a)	ne-o-'na-to
old	vecchio	'vek-kyo
• old age	vecchiaia	vek-'kya-ya
	terza età	'ter-tsa e-'ta
• older	maggiore	maj-'jo-re
	più vecchio	pyu 'vek-kyo
	più grande	pyu 'gran-de
• older brother	fratello più grande	—
	fratello maggiore	—
• older person	vecchio (-a)	—
• senior	anziano (-a)	an-'tsya-no
• (to) become old	invecchiarsi	in-vek-'kyar-si
puberty	pubertà (f, inv)	pu-ber-'ta
• senile	senile	se-'ni-le
youth	gioventù (f, inv)	jo-ven-'tu
	giovinezza	jo-vi-'ne-tsa
• young	giovane	'jo-va-ne
• younger	minore	mi-'no-re
	più piccolo	pyu 'pik-ko-lo
• younger sister	sorella più piccola	so-'rel-la
	sorella minore	mi-'no-re
• young lady	signorina	si-nyo-'ri-na
• young man	giovanotto	jo-va-'not-to
• young person	giovane (m/f)	'jo-va-ne

C. MARRIAGE AND THE HUMAN LIFE CYCLE

abortion	aborto	a-'bor-to
• (to) abort	abortire (isc)	a-bor-'ti-re
adoption	adozione (f)	a-do-'tsyo-ne
• (to) adopt	adottare	a-dot-'ta-re
adultery	adulterio	a-dul-'te-ryo
alimony	alimenti (m, pl)	a-li-'men-ti
ancestor	antenato (-a)	an-te-'na-to

anniversary	anniversario	*an-ni-ver-'sa-ryo*
• **diamond**	di diamante	*dya-'man-te*
• **golden**	d'oro	—
• **silver**	d'argento	*dar-'jen-to*
artificial insemination	fecondazione (f)	*fe-kon-da-'tsyo-ne*
	artificiale	*ar-ti-fi-'ča-le*
baby bottle	biberon (m, inv)	*bi-be-'ron*
bachelor	scapolo (-a)	*'ska-po-lo*
(to) be born	nascere* (ess)	*'na-še-re*
(to) be in mourning	essere* in lutto	*'es-se-re in 'lut-to*
(to) be pregnant	essere* incinta	*'es-se-re in'čin-ta*
best man	testimone (dello sposo)	*tes-ti-'mo-ne 'del-lo*
		'spo-zo
birth	nascita	*'na-ši-ta*
• **birth certificate**	certificato di nascita	*čer-ti-fi-'ka-to*
• **(to) give birth**	partorire (isc)	*par-to-'ri-re*
• **premature birth**	parto prematuro	*'par-to pre-ma-'tu-ro*
birthday	compleanno	*kom-ple-'an-no*
• **Happy Birthday!**	Buon compleanno!	—
(to) breast-feed	allattare	*al-lat-'ta-re*
bride	sposa	*'spo-za*
bridesmaid	damigella	*da-mi-'jel-la*
burial	sepoltura	*se-pol-'tu-ra*
• **(to) bury**	seppellire (isc)	*sep-pel-'li-re*
cadaver	cadavere (m)	*ka-'da-ve-re*
(to) care for	volere bene a	*vo-'le-re 'be-ne 'a*
childbirth	parto	—
coffin	bara	—
(to) cohabit, live together	convivere*	*kon-'vi-ve-re*
cohabitation	convivenza	*kon-vi-'ven-tsa*
cremation	cremazione (f)	*kre-ma-'tsyo-ne*
death	morte (f)	*'mor-te*
• **death certificate**	certificato di morte	*čer-ti-fi-'ka-to*
• **deceased, late**	defunto	*de-'fun-to*
• **(to) die**	morire* (ess)	*mo-'ri-re*
dependent	persona a carico	*per-'so-na a 'ka-ri-ko*
divorce	divorzio	*di-'vor-tsyo*
• **(to) divorce**	divorziare	*di-vor-'tsya-re*
• **divorced**	divorziato (-a)	*di-vor-'tsya-to*
dowry	dote	*'do-te*
engagement	fidanzamento	*fi-dan-tsa-'men-to*
• **(to) get engaged**	fidanzarsi	*fi-dan-'tsar-si*
estate	successione (f)	*suc-ces-'syo-ne*
expectant mother	futura mamma	*fu-'tu-ra 'mam-ma*
family tree	albero genealogico	*'al-be-ro*
		je-ne-a-'lo- ji-ko
first-born	primogenito	*pri-mo-'je-ni-to*
funeral	funerale (m)	*fu-ne-'ra-le*
groom	sposo	*'spo-zo*

heredity	eredità (f, inv)	e-re-di-'ta
honeymoon	luna di miele	'lu-na di 'mye-le
husband	marito	ma-'ri-to
(to) inherit	ereditare	e-re-di-'ta-re
• inheritor	erede (m/f)	e-'re-de
kiss	bacio	'ba-čo
• (to) kiss	baciare	ba-'ča-re
late	fu	—
life	vita	—
• (to) live	vivere*	'vi-ve-re
love	amore (m)	a-'mo-re
• (to) love	amare, volere bene a	a-'ma-re
• (to) fall in love	innamorarsi	in-na-mo-'rar-si
• in love	innamorato	in-na-mo-'ra-to
maid-of-honor	damigella d'onore	da-mi-'jel-la do-'no-re
marital status	stato civile	'sta-to či-'vi-le
marriage, matrimony	matrimonio	ma-tri-'mo-ni-o
• marriage vow	promessa di matrimonio	pro-'mes-sa
• (to) marry	sposare	spo-'za-re
• matrimonial	matrimoniale	ma-tri-mo-'nya-le
• (to) get married	sposarsi	spo-'zar-si
• married	sposato (-a)	spo-'za-to
• unmarried	celibe (m)	'če-li-be
	nubile (f)	'nu-bi-le
miscarriage	aborto spontaneo	a-'bor-to spon-'ta-ne-o
newborn	neonato (-a)	ne-o-'na-to
newlyweds	novelli sposi	no-'vel-li 'spo-zi
offspring	discendenza	di-šen-'den-tsa
orphan	orfano (-a)	'or-fa-no
• orphanage	orfanotrofio	or-fa-no-'tro-fi-o
pregnancy	gravidanza	gra-vi-'dan-dza
• pregnant	incinta	in-'čin-ta
(to) remarry	risposarsi	ri-spo-'zar-si
separation	separazione (f)	se-pa-ra-'tsyo-ne
• separated	separato (-a)	se-pa-'ra-to
single	single (inv)	—
spouse	coniuge (m/f)	'kon-yu-je
	consorte (m/f)	kon-'sor-te
test-tube baby	figlio in provetta	'fi-lyo in pro-'vet-ta
tomb	tomba	—
• tombstone	lapide (f)	'la-pi-de
veil	velo	—
wedding	nozze (f, pl),	'no-tse, ma-tri-'mo-nio,
	matrimonio, sposalizio	spo-za-'lit-tsio
• wedding invitation	partecipazione (f)	par-te-ci-pa-'tsyo-ne
• wedding ring	fede (f)	'fe-de
widow	vedova	've-do-va
• widower	vedovo	—
wife	moglie	'mo-lye

will	testamento	tes-ta-'men-to
witness	testimone (m/f)	tes-ti-'mo-ne
wreath	ghirlanda	gir-'lan-da

D. RELIGION

abstinence	astinenza	a-sti-'nen-dza
agnostic	agnostico	a-'nyos-ti-ko
• altar	altare (m)	al-'ta-re
• altar-boy	chierichetto	kye-ri-'ket-to
• high altar	altare maggiore	maj-'jo-re
angel	angelo	'an-je-lo
archbishop	arcivescovo	ar-či-'ves-ko-vo
Ash Wednesday	Ceneri (f, pl)	'če-'ne-ri
atheism	ateismo	a-te-'iz-mo
• atheist	ateo	'a-te-o
(to) atone for one's sins	scontare i propri peccati	skon-'ta-re i 'pro-pri pek-'ka-ti
baptism	battesimo	bat-'te-zi-mo
• baptismal font	fonte battesimale	'fon-te bat-te-zi-'ma-le
baptistery	battistero	bat-tis-'te-ro
belief	credenza	kre-'den-dza
• (to) believe	credere	'kre-de-re
• believer	credente (m/f)	kre-'den-te
bell-tower	campanile (m)	kam-pa-'ni-le
Benedictine	benedettino	be-ne-det-'ti-no
Bible	Bibbia	'bib-bya
bishop	vescovo	'ves-ko-vo
blasphemy	blasfemia	blas-'fe-mya
blessing	benedizione (f)	be-ne-di-'tsyo-ne
• (to) bless	benedire* (isc)	be-ne-'di-re
Buddhism	buddismo	bud-'diz-mo
• Buddhist	buddista (m/f)	bud-'dis-ta
cardinal	cardinale (m)	kar-di-'na-le
catechism	catechismo	ka-te-'kiz-mo
cathedral	cattedrale (f)	kat-te-'dra-le
Catholicism	cattolicesimo	kat-to-li-'če-zi-mo
• Catholic	cattolico (-a)	kat-'to-li-ko
chalice	calice (m)	'ka-li-če
chapel	cappella	kap-'pel-la
choir	coro	—
Christianity	cristianesimo	cris-tya-'ne-zi-mo
• Christian	cristiano (-a)	cris-'tya-no
Christmas	Natale (m)	na-'ta-le
church	chiesa	'kye-za
• church candle	cero	'če-ro
clergy	clero	'kle-ro
cloister	chiostro	'kyos-tro
collection	colletta	kol-'let-ta

commandment	comandamento	*ko-man-da-'men-to*
communion	comunione (f)	*ko-mu-'nyo-ne*
confess	confessarsi	*kon-fes-'sar-si*
confession	confessione (f)	*kon-fes-'syo-ne*
• **confessional box**	confessionale (m)	*kon-fes-syo-'na-le*
confirmation	cresima	*'kre-zi-ma*
congregation	congregazione (f)	*kon-gre-ga-'tsyo-ne*
convent	convento	*kon-'ven-to*
cross	croce (f)	*'kro-če*
• **(to) cross oneself**	farsi* il segno della croce	*'far-si il 'se-nyo del-la 'kro-če*
crucifix	crocifisso	*kro-či-'fis-so*
cult	culto	*'kul-to*
deacon, deaconess	diacono (-essa)	*di-'a-'ko-no*
deadly sin	peccato mortale	*mor-'ta-le*
denomination	confessione (f)	*kon-fes-'syo-ne*
devil	diavolo	*'dya-vo-lo*
devotion	devozione (f)	*de-vo-'styo-ne*
• **devout**	devoto	*de-'vo-to*
Dominican	domenicano	*do-me-ni-'ka-no*
Easter	Pasqua	*'pas-kwa*
ecclesiastic	ecclesiastico	*ek-kle-zi-'as-ti-ko*
Eucharist	Eucarestia (Eucaristia)	*eu-ka-res-'ti-a*
evangelist	evangelista (m/f)	*e-van-je-'lis-ta*
Exodus	Esodo	*'e-zo-do*
faith	fede (f)	*'fe-de*
• **faithful**	fedele (m/f)	*fe-'de-le*
fast	digiuno	*di-'ju-no*
Franciscan	francescano	*fran-čes-'ka-no*
God	Dio	*'di-o*
	Signore	*si-'nyo-re*
Good Friday	Venerdì Santo	*ve-ner-'di 'san-to*
Gospel	Vangelo	*van-'je-lo*
Hail Mary	Ave Maria	*a-ve ma-'ri-a*
heaven, paradise	paradiso	*pa-ra-'di-zo*
Hebrew, Jewish	ebreo (-a)	*e-'bre-o*
hell	inferno	*in-fer-no*
Hinduism	Induismo	*in-du-'izmo*
• **Hindu**	indù (m/f)	*in-'du*
Holy Ghost	Santo Spirito	*'san-to 'spi-ri-to*
Holy Trinity	Santa Trinità	*'san-ta tri-ni-'ta*
homily	omelia	*o-me-'li-a*
host	ostia	*'os-tya*
hymn	inno	*'in-no*
	cantico	*'kan-ti-ko*
incense	incenso	*in-'čen-so*
Islam	Islam (m)	—
• **Islamic**	islamico (-a)	*iz-'la-mi-ko*
Jesuit	gesuita (m) (gesuiti, pl)	*je-zu-'i-ta*

Jesus Christ	Gesù Cristo	je-'zu 'kris-to
Judaism	giudaismo	ju-da-'iz-mo
(to) kneel	inginocchiarsi	in-ji-nok-'kyar-si
Koran	Corano	ko-'ra-no
lay person, secular	laico	'lai-ko
Lent	Quaresima	kwa-'re-zi-ma
liturgy	liturgia	li-tur-'ji-a
Madonna, Virgin Mary	Madonna	ma-'don-na
martyrdom	martirio	mar-'ti-ryo
• martyr	martire (m/f)	'mar-ti-re
Mass	messa	'mes-sa
minister	ministro	mi-'nis-tro
missionary	missionario (-a)	mis-syo-'na-ryo
monastery	monastero	mo-nas-'te-ro
monk	monaco	'mo-na-ko
Mormon	mormone (m/f)	mor-'mo-ne
mosque	moschea	mos-'ke-a
Muslim	musulmano (-a)	mu-sul-'ma-no
mysticism	misticismo	mis-ti-'čiz-mo
• mystic	mistico	'mis-ti-ko
myth	mito	—
nun, sister	suora	'swo-ra
order	ordine (m)	'or-di-ne
Our Father	Paternostro	pa-ter-'nos-tro
paganism	paganesimo	pa-ga-'ne-zi-mo
• pagan	pagano (-a)	pa-'ga-no
papacy	papato	pa-'pa-to
parable	parabola	pa-'ra-bo-la
parish	parrocchia	par-'rok-kya
• parish priest	parroco	'par-ro-ko
• parishioner	parrocchiano (-a)	par-rok-'kya-no
penance	penitenza	pe-ni-'ten-tsa
pew	banco di chiesa	'ban-ko di 'kye-za
pilgrim	pellegrino (-a)	pel-le-'gri-no
pilgrimage	pellegrinaggio	pel-le-gri-'naj-jo
pontiff	pontefice	pon-'te-fi-če
pope	papa (m)	—
prayer	preghiera	pre-'gye-ra
• (to) pray	pregare	pre-'ga-re
preaching, sermon	predica	'pre-di-ka
• (to) preach	predicare	pre-di-'ka-re
• preacher	predicatore (-trice)	pre-di-ka-'to-re
pride	superbia	su-'per-bya
priest	prete (m)	'pre-te
Protestantism	protestantesimo	pro-tes-tan-'te-zi-mo
• Protestant	protestante (m/f)	pro-tes-'tan-te
pulpit	pulpito	'pul-pi-to
purgatory	purgatorio	pur-ga-'to-ryo
rabbi	rabbino	rab-'bi-no

religion	religione (f)	re-li-'jo-ne
• **religious**	religioso	re-li-'jo-zo
rite	rito	—
rosary	rosario	ro-'za-ryo
sacrament	sacramento	sa-kra-'men-to
sacred	sacro	—
Sacred Scripture	Sacra Scrittura	'sa-kra skrit-'tu-ra
sacrifice	sacrificio	sa-kri-'fi-čo
sacrilege	sacrilegio	sa-kri-'le-jo
sacristan	sagrestano	sa-gres-'ta-no
sect	setta	—
sermon	sermone (m)	ser-'mo-ne
shamanism	sciamanismo	ša-ma-'niz-mo
• **shaman**	sciamano	ša-'ma-no
shrine, sanctuary	santuario	san-tu-'a-ri-o
sin	peccato	pek-'ka-to
• **(to) sin**	peccare	pek-'ka-re
• **sinner**	peccatore (-trice)	pek-ka-'to-re
soul	anima	'a-ni-ma
synagogue	sinagoga	si-na-'go-ga
temple	tempio	'tem-pyo
theology	teologia	te-o-lo-'ji-a
• **theologian**	teologo (-a)	te-'o-lo-go
vestry	sagrestia	sa-gres-'ti-a
vice, bad habit	vizio	'vi-tsyo
virtue	virtù (f, inv)	vir-'tu
vow	voto	—
worship	adorazione (f)	a-do-ra-'tsyo-ne
Zionism	sionismo	si-o-'niz-mo
• **Zionist**	sionista (m/f)	si-o-'nis-ta

E. CHARACTER AND SOCIAL TRAITS

absent-minded	distratto	dis-'trat-to
active	attivo	at-'ti-vo
adaptable	adattabile	a-dat-'ta-bi-le
affable	affabile	af-'fa-bi-le
affectionate	affettuoso	af-fet-'two-zo
affluent	benestante	be-nes-'tan-te
aggressive	aggressivo	ag-gres-'si-vo
altruist	altruista	al-tru-'is-ta
ambitious	ambizioso	am-bi-'tsyo-zo
annoying, unpleasant	antipatico	an-ti-'pa-ti-ko
anxious	ansioso	an-'syo-zo
arrogant	arrogante	ar-ro-'gan-te
artistic	artistico	ar-'tis-ti-ko
astute, bright	astuto	as-'tu-to
attentive	attento	at-'ten-to
audacious, bold	audace	au-'da-ce

bad, mean	cattivo	*kat-'ti-vo*
bigoted	bigotto	*bi-'got-to*
bothersome, irksome	noioso	*no-'yo-zo*
brash, bold	sfacciato	*sfač-'ča-to*
brilliant	brillante	*bril-'lan-te*
broad-minded	di ampie vedute	*'am-pye ve-'du-te*
brusque	brusco	*'brus-ko*
calm	calmo	*'kal-mo*
carefree	spensierato	*spen-sye-'ra-to*
careful	cauto	*'kau-to*
careless	spericolato	*spe-ri-ko-'la-to*
character	carattere (m)	*ka-'rat-te-re*
charming, fascinating	affascinante	*af-fa-ši-'nan-te*
competent, skilled	competente	*kom-pe-'ten-te*
conformist	conformista	*kon-for-'mis-ta*
conscientious	coscienzioso	*ko-šen-'tsyo-zo*
corrupt	corrotto	*kor-'rot-to*
courageous	coraggioso	*ko-raj-'jo-zo*
courteous	cortese	*kor-'te-ze*
cowardly	codardo	*ko-'dar-do*
crazy	pazzo	*'pa-tso*
	matto	*'mat-to*
creative	creativo	*kre-a-'ti-vo*
critical	critico	*'kri-ti-ko*
cruel	crudele	*kru-'de-le*
cultured	colto	*'kol-to*
delicate	delicato	*de-li-'ka-to*
depressed	depresso	*de-'pres-so*
desperate	disperato	*dis-pe-'ra-to*
diligent	diligente	*di-li-'jen-te*
diplomatic	diplomatico	*di-plo-'ma-ti-ko*
disgusted	disgustato	*diz-gus-'ta-to*
dishonest	disonesto	*di-zo-'nes-to*
disinterested	disinteressato	*di-zin-te-res-'sa-to*
downtrodden	avvilito	*av-vi-'li-to*
dynamic	dinamico	*di-'na-mi-ko*
egoist, self-centered	egoista	*e-go-'is-ta*
elegant	elegante	*e-le-'gan-te*
eloquent	eloquente	*e-lo-'kwen-te*
energetic	energico	*e-'ner-ji-ko*
envious	invidioso	*in-vi-'dyo-zo*
erudite	erudito	*e-ru-'di-to*
extraordinary	straordinario	*stra-or-di-'na-ryo*
extroverted	estroverso	*es-tro-'ver-so*
faithful	fedele	*fe-'de-le*
fearful	timoroso	*ti-mo-'ro-zo*
flexible	flessibile	*fles-'si-bi-le*
friendly	socievole	*so-'če-vo-le*

frivolous	frivolo	*'fri-vo-lo*
funny	buffo	—
fussy	fastidioso	*fas-ti-'dyo-zo*
generous	generoso	*je-ne-'ro-zo*
gentle	gentile	*jen-'ti-le*
gloomy	malinconico	*ma-lin-'ko-ni-ko*
good (at heart)	buono	*'bwo-no*
graceful	grazioso	*gra-'tsyo-zo*
greedy	avaro	*a-'va-ro*
grumpy	scorbutico	*skor-'bu-ti-ko*
happy	felice	*fe-'li-če*
	allegro	*al-'le-gro*
hard-working	laborioso	*la-bo-'ryo-zo*
hateful	odioso	*o-'dyo-so*
honest	onesto	*o-'nes-to*
humanity	umanità (f, inv)	*u-ma-ni-'ta*
humble	umile	*'u-mi-le*
idealist	idealista	*i-de-a-'lis-ta*
ignorant	ignorante	*i-nyo-'ran-te*
ill-mannered	maleducato	*me-le-du-'ka-to*
imaginative	immaginativo	*im-ma-ji-na-'ti-vo*
impatient	impaziente	*im-pa-'tsyen-te*
impetuous	impetuoso	*im-pe-'two-zo*
impressionable	impressionabile	*im-pres-syo-'na-bi-le*
imprudent	imprudente	*im-pru-'den-te*
impudent	impudente	*im-pu-'den-te*
impulsive	impulsivo	*im-pul-'si-vo*
incompetent	incompetente	*in-kom-pe-'ten-te*
inconsiderate	incosciente	*in-ko-šen-te*
incorruptible	incorruttibile	*in-kor-rut-'ti-bi-le*
indecisive	indeciso	*in-de-či-zo*
independent	indipendente	*in-di-pen-'den-te*
indifferent	indifferente	*in-dif-fe-'ren-te*
indigent	indigente	*in-di-'jen-te*
individualist	individualista	*in-di-vi-dwa-'lis-ta*
inept, unfortunate	disgraziato	*diz-gra-'tsya-to*
infallible	infallibile	*in-fal-'li-bi-le*
ingenious	ingegnoso	*in-je-'nyo-zo*
ingenuous, naive	ingenuo	*in-'je-nu-o*
insensitive	insensibile	*in-sen-'si-bi-le*
insistent, unrelenting	insistente	*in-sis-'ten-te*
insolent	insolente	*in-so-'len-te*
intellectual	intellettuale	*in-tel-let-'twa-le*
intelligent	intelligente	*in-tel-li-'jen-te*
introverted	introverso	*in-tro-'ver-so*
irascible	irascibile	*i-ra-ši-bi-le*
irksome	irritante	*ir-ri-'tan-te*
ironic	ironico	*i-'ro-ni-ko*

irrational	irrazionale	*ir-ra-tsyo-'na-le*
irresponsible	irresponsabile	*ir-res-pon-'sa-bi-le*
irreverent	irriverente	*ir-ri-ve-'ren-te*
jealous	geloso	*je-'lo-zo*
jovial	gioviale	*jo-'vya-le*
joyous	gioioso	*jo-'yo-zo*
kindness	gentilezza	*jen-ti-'le-tsa*
lazy	pigro	*'pi-gro*
liar	bugiardo	*bu-'jar-do*
likable	piacevole	*pya-'če-vo-le*
lively	vivace	*vi-'va-če*
loving	amoroso	*a-mo-'ro-zo*
malicious	malizioso	*ma-li-'tsyo-zo*
merit, worth	merito	*'me-ri-to*
meritorious	meritevole	*me-ri-'te-vo-le*
meticulous	meticoloso	*me-ti-ko-'lo-zo*
mischievous	capriccioso	*ka-prič-'čo-zo*
morose	scontroso	*skon-'tro-zo*
narrow-minded	di vedute ristrette	*ve-'du-te ris-'tret-te*
neat	ordinato	*or-di-'na-to*
negligent	negligente	*ne-gli-'jen-te*
nervous	nervoso	*ner-'vo-zo*
nonconformist	anticonformista	*an-ti-kon-for-'mis-ta*
obstinate	ostinato	*os-ti-'na-to*
obtuse	ottuso	*ot-'tu-zo*
optimist	ottimista	*ot-ti-'mis-ta*
original	originale	*o-ri-ji-'na-le*
patient	paziente	*pa-'tsyen-te*
perfectionist	perfezionista	*per-fe-tsyo-'nis-ta*
personality	personalità (f, inv)	*per-so-na-li-'ta*
pessimist	pessimista	*pes-si-'mis-ta*
picky, fastidious	pignolo	*pi-'nyo-lo*
pleasant, nice	simpatico	*sim-'pa-ti-ko*
politeness, courtesy	cortesia	*kor-te-'zi-a*
poor	povero	*'po-ve-ro*
possessive	possessivo	*pos-ses-'si-vo*
precise	preciso	*pre-'či-zo*
presumptuous	presuntuoso	*pre-zun-'two-zo*
pretentious	pretenzioso	*pre-ten-'tsyo-zo*
proud, haughty	orgoglioso	*or-go-'lyo-zo*
prudent	prudente	*pru-'den-te*
prudish, prim	pudico	*'pu-di-ko*
punctilious	puntiglioso	*pun-ti-'lyo-zo*
pure	puro	—
quarrelsome	litigioso	*li-ti-'jo-zo*
quiet	quieto	*'kwye-to*
rational	razionale	*ra-tsyo-'na-le*
realistic	realista	*re-a-'lis-ta*
reasonable	ragionevole	*ra-jo-'ne-vo-le*

English	Italian	Pronunciation
rebellious	ribelle	*ri-'bel-le*
reckless	temerario	*te-me-'ra-ryo*
refined	raffinato	*raf-fi-'na-to*
reserved	riservato	*ri-zer-'va-to*
rich	ricco	*'rik-ko*
romantic	romantico	*ro-'man-ti-ko*
rough	rozzo	*'ro-tso*
rude	rude	*'ru-de*
ruthless	spietato	*spye-'ta-to*
sad	triste	*'tris-te*
sarcastic	sarcastico	*sar-'kas-ti-ko*
satisfied	soddisfatto	*sod-dis-'fat-to*
scoundrel	briccone (-a)	*brik-'ko-ne*
seductive	seducente	*se-du-'čen-te*
self-confident, sure	sicuro	*si-'ku-ro*
self-sufficient	autosufficiente	*au-to-suf-fi-'čen-te*
sensible	sensato	*sen-'sa-to*
sensitive	sensibile	*sen-'si-bi-le*
sentimental	sentimentale	*sen-ti-men-'ta-le*
serene	sereno	*se-'re-no*
serious	serio	*'se-ryo*
severe	severo	*se-'ve-ro*
show-off	sfarzoso	*sfar-'tso-zo*
shrewd	perspicace	*per-spi-'ka-če*
shy, timid	timido	*'ti-mi-do*
silly	sciocco	*'šok-ko*
simple	semplice	*'sem-pli-če*
sloppy, disorganized	disorganizzato	*diz-or-ga-ni-'dza-to*
snobbish	altezzoso	*al-te-'tso-zo*
strong	forte	*'for-te*
stubborn	testardo	*tes-'tar-do*
stupid	stupido	*'stu-pi-do*
stuttering	balbuziente	*bal-bu-'tsyen-te*
sullen	cupo	*'ku-po*
superstitious	superstizioso	*su-per-sti-'tsyo-zo*
sweet	dolce	*'dol-ce*
tender	tenero	*'te-ne-ro*
tired	stanco	*'stan-ko*
tough	duro	—
toughness	durezza	*du-'re-tsa*
traditional	tradizionale	*tra-di-tsyo-'na-le*
tranquil, calm, serene	tranquillo	*tran-'kwil-lo*
unhappy	scontento	*skon-'ten-to*
unsatisfied	insoddisfatto	*in-sod-dis-'fat-to*
untidy	disordinato	*diz-or-di-'na-to*
vain	vanitoso	*va-ni-'to-zo*
vengeful	vendicativo	*ven-di-ka-'ti-vo*
versatile	versatile	*ver-'sa-ti-le*
virtuous	virtuoso	*vir-'two-zo*

voluble	volubile	vo-'lu-bi-le
vulnerable	vulnerabile	vul-ne-'ra-bi-le
weak	debole	'de-bo-le
well-mannered	educato	e-du-'ka-to
whimsical	capriccioso	ka-prič-'čo-zo
wily, sly	furbo	—
wise	saggio	'saj-jo
witty, spirited	spiritoso	spi-ri-'to-zo
worried	preoccupato	pre-ok-ku-'pa-to
zealous	zelante	dze-'lan-te

F. BASIC PERSONAL INFORMATION

> For jobs and professions, see §38a

address	indirizzo	in-di-'ri-tso
• **avenue**	corso	'kor-so
• **square**	piazza	'pya-tsa
• **street**	via	'vi-a
	strada	'stra-da
• **(to) live somewhere**	abitare	a-bi-'ta-re
	vivere*	'vi-ve-re
• **house number**	numero di casa	'nu-me-ro di 'ka-za
• **downtown**	in centro	'čen-tro
• **in the city**	in città	čit-'ta
• **in the country(side)**	in campagna	kam-'pa-nya
• **in the suburbs**	in periferia	pe-ri-fe-'ri-a
• **on...Street, number...**	in via...numero...	'vi-a 'nu-me-ro
• **with friends**	presso amici	'pres-so a-'mi-ci
• **with one's parents**	con i genitori	je-ni-'to-ri
• **forwarding address**	recapito	re-'ka-pi-to
(to) be of...origin	essere* d'origine...	'es-se-re do-'ri-ji-ne
(to) be from	essere* di	—
birth	nascita	'na-ši-ta
• **date of birth**	data di nascita	—
• **place of birth**	luogo di nascita	'lwo-go
career	carriera	kar-'rye-ra
citizenship	cittadinanza	čit-ta-di-'nan-tsa
education (level)	titolo di studio	'ti-to-lo di 'stu-dyo
• **(to) go to school**	andare* (ess) a scuola	an-'da-re a 'skwo-la
• **(to) finish school**	finire (isc) la scuola	fi-'ni-re
• **university degree**	laurea	'lau-re-a
• **diploma**	diploma	di-'plo-ma
• **high school diploma**	certificato di maturità	cer-ti-fi-'ka-to di ma-tu-ri-'ta

• **graduate**	laureato (-a) (*university*)	*lau-re-'a-to*
	diplomato (-a)	*di-plo-'ma-to*
	(*high school*)	
employment	lavoro	*la-'vo-ro*
• **employer**	datore di lavoro	*da-'to-re di la-'vo-ro*
• **employee**	dipendente (m/f)	*di-pen-'den-te*
identity	identità (f, inv)	*i-den-ti-'ta*
• **identification**	identificazione (f)	*i-den-ti-fi-ka-'tsyo-ne*
interests, hobbies	interessi (m, pl)	*in-te-'res-si*
job	mestiere (m)	*mes-'tye-re*
marital status	stato civile	*'sta-to či-'vi-le*
• **marriage**	matrimonio	*ma-tri-'mo-nyo*
• **married**	sposato (-a)	*spo-'za-to*
• **unmarried**	celibe (m)	*'če-li-be*
	nubile (f)	*'nu-bi-le*
• **separated**	separato	*se-pa-'ra-to*
• **divorced**	divorziato (-a)	*di-vor-'tsya-to*
• **single**	single (inv)	—
military service	servizio militare	*ser-'vi-tsyo mi-li-'ta-re*
name	nome (m)	*'no-me*
• **first name**	nome (m)	—
• **surname**	cognome (m)	*ko-'nyo-me*
• **nickname**	soprannome (m)	*so-pran-'no-me*
• **My name is**	Mi chiamo …	*mi 'kya-mo*
• **signature**	firma	—
• **(to) sign**	firmare	*fir-'ma-re*
nationality	nazionalità (f, inv)	*na-tsyo-na-li-'ta*
• **origin**	origine (f)	*o-'ri-ji-ne*
personal information	dati anagrafici	*'da-ti a-na-'gra-fi-či*
phone number	numero di telefono	*'nu-me-ro di te-'le-fo-no*
• **area code**	prefisso	*pre-'fis-so*
profession	professione (f)	*pro-fes-'syo-ne*
• **professional**	professionista (m/f)	*pro-fes-syo-'nis-ta*
references	referenze (f, pl)	*re-fe-'ren-tse*
residence	residenza	*re-zi-'den-tsa*
	domicilio	*do-mi-'či-lyo*
• **(to) reside**	risiedere	*ri-'sye-de-re*
title	titolo	*'ti-to-lo*
• **Accountant**	Ragioniere (-a)	*ra-jo-'nye-re*
• **Doctor**	Dottore (-essa)	*dot-'to-re*
• **Draftsperson**	Geometra (m/f)	*je-'o-me-tra*
• **Engineer**	Ingegnere (m/f)	*in-je-'nye-re*
• **Lawyer**	Avvocato (m/f)	*av-vo-'ka-to*
• **Miss, Ms.**	Signorina	*si-nyo-'ri-na*
• **Mr.**	Signore	*si-'nyo-re*
• **Mrs., Ms.**	Signora	*si-'nyo-ra*
• **Professor**	Professore (-essa)	*pro-fes-'so-re*
• **Reverend**	Reverendo	*re-ve-'ren-do*

widower, widow	vedovo	've-do-vo
	vedova	—
work	lavoro	la-'vo-ro
• **(to) work**	lavorare	la-vo-'ra-re
• **work experience**	esperienze lavorative	es-pe-'ryen-tse la-vo-ra-'ti-ve

12. THE BODY

A. PARTS, LIMBS, ORGANS, AND SYSTEMS

Achilles tendon	tallone di Achille	tal-'lo-ne di a-'kil-le
adenoids	adenoidi (f, pl)	'a-de-noy-'di
adrenaline	adrenalina	a-dre-na-'li-na
alimentary canal	tubo digestivo	'tu-bo di-jes-'ti-vo
ankle	caviglia	ka-'vi-lya
anus, bottom	ano	—
arm	braccio (braccia, f, pl)	'brač-čo
armpit	ascella	a-šel-la
artery	arteria	ar-'te-rya
back	schiena	'skye-na
beard	barba	—
belly	pancia	'pan-ča
belly button	ombelico	om-be-'li-ko
bladder	vescica	ve-'ši-ka
blood	sangue (m)	'san-gwe
• **blood group**	gruppo sanguigno	'grup-po san-'gwi-nyo
• **blood pressure**	pressione del sangue	pres-'syo-ne
• **blood vessel**	vaso sanguigno	'va-zo san-'gwi-nyo
body	corpo	—
bone	osso (ossa, f, pl)	—
brain	cervello	cer-'vel-lo
breast	seno	'se-no
brow, forehead	fronte (f)	'fron-te
calf	polpaccio	pol-'pač-čo
cardiovascular system	sistema cardiovascolare	sis-'te-ma kar-dyo-vas-ko-'la-re
cartilage	cartilagine (f)	kar-ti-'la-ji-ne
cell	cellula	'čel-lu-la
cheek	guancia	'gwan-ča
• **cheekbone**	zigomo	'dzi-go-mo
chest	petto	'pet-to
chin	mento	'men-to
complexion	carnagione (f)	kar-na-'jo-ne
diaphragm	diaframma	di-a-'fram-ma
dimple	fossetta	fos-'set-ta
disc	disco	'dis-ko
ear	orecchio	o-'rek-kyo
• **eardrum**	timpano	'tim-pa-no
elbow	gomito	'go-mi-to

English	Italian	Pronunciation
esophagus	esofago	*e-'zo-fa-go*
eye	occhio	*'ok-kyo*
• eyebrow	sopracciglio (sopracciglia, f, pl)	*so-prač-'či-lyo*
• eyelash	ciglio (ciglia, f, pl)	*'či-lyo*
• eyelid	palpebra	*'pal-pe-bra*
face	faccia	*'fač-ča*
finger, toe	dito (dita, f, pl)	*'di-to*
• fingernail	unghia	*'un-gya*
• little finger	(dito) mignolo	*('di-to) 'mi-nyo-lo*
• index finger	indice (m)	*'in-di-če*
• middle finger	(dito) medio	*('di-to) 'me-dyo*
• ring finger	(dito) anulare	*('di-to) a-nu-'la-re*
• thumb	pollice (m)	*'pol-li-če*
fist	pugno	*'pu-nyo*
flesh	carne (f)	*'kar-ne*
foot	piede (m)	*'pye-de*
forearm	avambraccio	*a-vam-'brač-čo*
frame	ossatura	*os-sa-'tu-ra*
gall bladder	cistifellea	*cis-ti-'fel-lea*
gland	ghiandola	*'gyan-do-la*
guts	ventre (m)	*'ven-tre*
hair (bodily)	peli	*'pe-li*
hair (head)	capelli (m, pl)	*ka-'pel-li*
hand	mano (f) (mani, pl)	*'ma-no*
head	testa	*'tes-ta*
heart	cuore (m)	*'kwo-re*
• heartbeat	battito del cuore	*'bat-ti-to*
heel	tallone (m)	*tal-'lo-ne*
hip	anca	*'an-ka*
immune system	sistema immunitario	*sis-'te-ma im-mu-ni-'ta-ryo*
intestine, bowel	intestino	*in-tes-'ti-no*
jaw	mandibola	*man-'di-bo-la*
• jawbone	mascella	*ma-'šel-la*
joint	articolazione (f)	*ar-ti-ko-la-'tsyo-ne*
kidney	rene (m)	*'re-ne*
knee	ginocchio (ginocchia, f, pl)	*ji-'nok-kyo*
leg	gamba	*'gam-ba*
limb	arto	*'ar-to*
lip	labbro (labbra, f, pl)	*'lab-bro*
liver	fegato	*'fe-ga-to*
lung	polmone (m)	*pol-'mo-ne*
lymphatic system	sistema linfatico	*sis-'te-ma lin-'fa-ti-ko*
membrane	membrana	*mem-'bra-na*
mouth	bocca	*'bok-ka*
muscle	muscolo	*'mus-ko-lo*
nape	nuca	*'nu-ka*

neck	collo	'kol-lo
nerve	nervo	'ner-vo
nervous system	sistema nervoso	sis-'te-ma ner-'vo-zo
nipple	capezzolo	ka-'pe-tso-lo
nose	naso	'na-zo
• nostril	narice (f)	na-'ri-če
organ	organo	'or-ga-no
palate	palato	pa-'la-to
palm	palma	'pal-ma
pancreas	pancreas (m, inv)	—
pelvis	pelvi (f, inv)	'pel-vi
pimple	foruncolo	fo-'run-ko-lo
pore	poro	—
pupil	pupilla	pu-'pil-la
respiratory system	sistema respiratorio	sis-te-ma res-pi-ra-'to-ryo
rib	costola	'kos-to-lo
saliva	saliva	sa-'li-va
scalp	cuoio capelluto	'kwo-yo ka-pel-'lu-to
shin	stinco	'stin-ko
shoulder	spalla	'spal-la
shoulder blade	scapola	'ska-po-la
skeleton	scheletro	'ske-le-tro
skin	pelle (f)	'pel-le
skull	cranio	'kra-ni-o
sole	pianta del piede	'pyan-ta del 'pye-de
spine	spina dorsale	'spi-na dor-'sa-le
spit	sputo	'spu-to
spleen	milza	'mil-tsa
stomach	stomaco	'sto-ma-ko
tendon	tendine (m)	'ten-di-ne
thigh	coscia	'ko-ša
throat	gola	—
tissue	tessuto	tes-'su-to
tongue	lingua	'lin-gwa
tonsils	tonsille (f, pl)	ton-'sil-le
torso, trunk	torso	'tor-so
urinary tract	apparato urinario	ap-pa-'ra-to 'u-ri-'na-ryo
vein	vena	—
vocal cord	corda vocale	'kor-da vo-'ka-le
waist	vita	'vi-ta
windpipe	trachea	tra-'ke-a
wrist	polso	'pol-so

B. PHYSICAL STATES AND ACTIVITIES

| (to) be cold | avere* freddo | a-'ve-re 'fred-do |
| (to) be hot | avere* caldo | a-'ve-re 'kal-do |

breath	respiro, fiato	res-'pi-ro, 'fia-to
• (to) breathe	respirare	res-pi-'ra-re
• breathing	respirazione (f)	res-pi-ra-'tsyo-ne
burp, belch	rutto	'rut-to
• (to) burp, belch	ruttare	rut-'ta-re
(to) choke	strozzarsi	stro-'tsar-si
cholesterol	colesterolo	ko-les-te-'ro-lo
dandruff	forfora	'for-fo-ra
(to) defecate	defecare	de-fe-'ka-re
digestion	digestione (f)	di-jes-'tyo-ne
digestive system	sistema digerente	sis-'te-ma di-je-'ren-te
(to) drink	bere*	'be-re
(to) eat	mangiare	man-'ja-re
(to) exhale	espirare	es-pi-'ra-re
(to) feel bad	sentirsi male	sen-'tir-si 'ma-le
(to) feel well	sentirsi bene	—
(to) get up	alzarsi	al-'tsar-si
health	salute (f)	sa-'lu-te
• healthy	sano	'sa-no
hunger	fame (f)	'fa-me
• (to) be hungry	avere* fame	—
(to) hurt	fare male a	—
(to) inhale	inspirare	ins-pi-'ra-re
lack of breath	senza fiato	'sen-tsa 'fya-to
(to) perceive	percepire (isc)	per-če-'pi-re
(to) rest, relax	riposarsi	ri-po-'zar-si
(to) run	correre*	'kor-re-re
sciatic nerve	nervo sciatico	'ner-vo 'šya-ti-ko
(to) sense, feel, smell	sentire	sen-ti-re
sick	malato	ma-'la-to
sleep	sonno	'son-no
• (to) be sleepy	avere* sonno	—
• (to) fall asleep	addormentarsi	ad-dor-men-'tar-si
• (to) sleep	dormire	dor-'mi-re
thirst	sete (f)	'se-te
• (to) be thirsty	avere* sete	—
tiredness, fatigue	fatica	fa-'ti-ka
• (to) be tired	essere* stanco	'es-se-re 'stan-ko
urine	urina	u-'ri-na
• (to) urinate	urinare	u-ri-'na-re
(to) wake up	svegliarsi	sve-'lyar-si
(to) walk	camminare	kam-mi-'na-re

C. HEARING

bang	colpo	'kol-po
(to) clash	cozzare	ko-'tsa-re
(to) crackle, squeak	scricchiolare	skri-kyo-'la-re

creak	cigolio	*či-go-'li-o*
• (to) creak	cigolare	*či-go-'la-re*
deafness	sordità (f, inv)	*sor-di-'ta*
• deaf	sordo	*'sor-do*
(to) echo	echeggiare	*e-kej-'ja-re*
(to) explode, blast	scoppiare	*skop-'pya-re*
(to) grate	grattugiare	*grat-tu-'ja-re*
(to) grind	sgretolare	*zgre-to-'la-re*
(to) hear, feel, sense	sentire	*sen-'ti-re*
• hearing	udito	*u-'di-to*
(to) hum	mormorare	*mor-mo-'ra-re*
(to) jingle, clink, jangle	tintinnare	*tin-tin-'na-re*
(to) listen	udire*	*u-'di-re*
• (to) listen to	ascoltare	*as-kol-'ta-re*
noise	rumore (m)	*ru-'mo-re*
• noisy	rumoroso	*ru-mo-'ro-zo*
rattle	sonaglio	*so-'na-'lyo*
(to) resonate	risuonare	*ri-'swo-'na-re*
(to) ring	suonare	*swo-'na-re*
(to) rustle	frusciare	*fru-'ša-re*
(to) shriek	squillare	*skwil-'la-re*
sound	suono	*'swo-no*
(to) splash	spruzzare	*spru-'tsa-re*
(to) squeal	strillare	*stril-'la-re*
(to) whistle	fischiare	*fis-'kya-re*

D. VISION

blindness	cecità (f, inv)	*če-či-'ta*
• blind	cieco	*'če-ko*
• (to) blind	accecare	*ač-če-'ka-re*
(to) blink	battere le palpebre	*'bat-te-re le 'pal-'pe-bre*
bright	brillante	*bril-'lan-te*
(to) cast a glance	gettare uno sguardo	*jet-'ta-re u-no 'zgwar-do*
clearness	chiarezza	*kya-'re-tsa*
• clear	chiaro	*'kya-ro*
contact lens	lenti a contatto	*'len-ti a kon-'tat-to*
cornea	cornea	*'kor-ne-a*
darkness	oscurità (f, inv)	*os-ku-ri-'ta*
• dark	scuro	*'sku-ro*
eyeglasses	occhiali (m, pl)	*ok-'kya-li*
(to) fade	sbiadire (isc)	*zbya-'di-re*
far-sighted	ipermetrope	*i-per-'me-tro-pe*
glance	sguardo	*'zgwar-do*
(to) glare at someone	fissare qualcuno	*fis-'sa-re kwal-'ku-no*
glimpse	occhiata fugace	*ok-'kya-ta fu-'ga-če*

(to) glow	risplendere	ris-'plen-de-re
illumination,	illuminazione (f)	il-lu-mi-na-'styo-ne
lens (of the eye)	lente (dell'occhio)	'len-te
long-sighted	presbite	'prez-bi-te
(to) look (at), watch	guardare	gwar-'da-re
• **(to) look around**	guardare in giro	'ji-ro
(to) peep, peer	sbirciare	zbir-'ča-re
reflection	riflesso	ri-'fles-so
(to) see	vedere*	ve-'de-re
(to) shine	brillare	bril-'la-re
short-sighted	miope	'mi-o-pe
sight	vista	'vis-ta
sight test	controllo della vista	kon-'trol-lo
(to) sparkle	scintillare	šin-til-'la-re
(to) stare	fissare	fis-'sa-re
(to) twinkle	luccicare	luč-či-'ka-re

E. TASTE, TOUCH, AND SMELL

acrid	acro	'a-kro
aroma	aroma	a-'ro-ma
bitter	aspro	'as-pro
delicate	delicato	de-li-'ka-to
delicious	squisito	skwi-'zito
fetid	fetido	'fe-ti-do
flavor	sapore (m)	sa-'po-re
	gusto	—
fragrance	fragranza	fra-'gran-tsa
fresh	fresco	'fres-ko
insipid	insipido	in-'si-pi-do
(to) itch	prudere	'pru-de-re
• **itchy**	pruriginoso	pru-ri-ji-'no-zo
knobby	nodoso	no-'do-zo
olfactory	olfattivo, olfattorio	ol-fat-'ti-vo
prickly	pungente	pun-'jen-te
putrid	putrido	'pu-tri-do
rough	ruvido	'ru-vi-do
salty	salato	sa-'la-to
scented	profumato	pro-fu-'ma-to
sense of smell	olfatto	ol-'fat-to
slippery	scivoloso	ši-vo-'lo-zo
smell, odor	odore (m)	o-'do-re
• **(to) smell**	odorare, annusare	o-do-'ra-re
smooth	liscio	'li-šo
soft	soffice, morbido	'sof-fi-če, 'mor-bi-do
sour	amaro	a-'ma-ro
spicy	piccante	pik-'kan-te
sticky	appiccicoso	ap-pi-či-'ko-zo

stiff	rigido	*'ri-ji-do*
stink	puzzo	*'pu-tso*
• **(to) stink**	puzzare	*pu'-tsa-re*
• **stinky**	puzzolente	*pu-tso-'len-te*
sweet	dolce	*'dol-ce*
taste	gusto	*'gus-to*
	sapore (m)	*sa-'po-re*
tasteless	sciocco	*'šok-ko*
touch	tatto	*'tat-to*
• **(to) touch**	toccare	*tok-'ka-re*

F. PERSONAL CARE

barber	barbiere (m)	*bar-'bye-re*
beautician	estetista (m/f)	*es-te-'tis-ta*
brush	spazzola	*'spa-tso-la*
• **(to) brush oneself**	spazzolarsi	*spa-tso-'lar-si*
clean	pulito	*pu-'li-to*
• **(to) clean oneself**	pulirsi	*pu-'lir-si*
comb	pettine (m)	*'pet-ti-ne*
• **(to) comb oneself**	pettinarsi	*pet-ti-'nar-si*
cosmetic	cosmetico	*kos-'me-ti-ko*
curls	ricci (m, pl)	*'rič-či*
• **curlers**	bigodini (m, pl)	*bi-go-'di-ni*
dirty	sporco	*'spor-ko*
(to) dry oneself	asciugarsi	*a-šu-'gar-si*
hairdresser	parrucchiere (-a)	*par-ruk-'kye-re*
hairdryer	asciugacapelli (inv)	*a-šu-ga-ka-'pel-li*
hygiene	igiene (f)	*i-'jye-ne*
• **hygienic**	igienico	*i-'jye-ni-ko*
makeup	trucco	*'truk-ko*
• **(to) put on makeup**	truccarsi	*truk-'kar-si*
manicure	manicure (f)	*ma-ni-'ku-re*
mascara	mascara (m, inv)	*mas-'ka-ra*
nail polish	smalto	*'zmal-to*
perfume	profumo	*pro-'fu-mo*
• **(to) put on perfume**	profumarsi	*pro-fu-'mar-si*
razor	rasoio	*ra-'zo-yo*
• **electric razor**	rasoio elettrico	*ra-'zo-yo e-'let-tri-ko*
scissors	forbici (f, pl)	*'for-bi-či*
shampoo	shampoo (m, inv)	—
(to) shave	farsi* la barba	—
soap	sapone (m)	*sa-'po-ne*
toothbrush	spazzolino da denti	*spa-tso-'li-no*
toothpaste	dentifricio	*den-ti-'fri-čo*
towel, handcloth	asciugamano	*a-šu-ga-'ma-no*
(to) wash oneself	lavarsi	*la-'var-si*
(to) wash one's hair	lavarsi i capelli	*la-'var-si i ka-'pel-li*

THE PHYSICAL, PLANT, AND ANIMAL WORLDS

13. THE PHYSICAL WORLD

A. THE UNIVERSE

astronomy	astronomia	*as-tro-no-'mi-a*
black hole	buco nero	*'bu-ko 'ne-ro*
comet	cometa	*ko-'me-ta*
cosmos	cosmo	*'koz-mo*
eclipse	eclissi (f, inv)	*e-'klis-si*
• **lunar eclipse**	eclissi lunare	*e-'klis-si lu-'na-re*
• **solar eclipse**	eclissi solare	*e-'klis-si so-'la-re*
galaxy	galassia	*ga-'las-sya*
• **gravity**	gravità (f, inv)	*gra-vi-'ta*
light	luce (f)	*'lu-če*
• **infrared light**	luce infrarossa	*in-fra-'ros-sa*
• **ultraviolet light**	luce ultravioletta	*ul-tra-vyo-'let-ta*
meteor	meteora	*me-'te-o-ra*
missile	missile (m)	*'mis-si-le*
moon	luna	*'lu-na*
• **full moon**	luna piena	*'lu-na 'pye-na*
• **moonbeam**	raggio lunare	*'raj-jo lu-'na-re*
orbit	orbita	*'or-bi-ta*
• **(to) orbit**	orbitare	*or-bi-'ta-re*
planet	pianeta (m) (pianeti, pl)	*pya-'ne-ta*
• **Earth**	Terra	*'ter-ra*
• **Jupiter**	Giove (m)	*'jo-ve*
• **Mars**	Marte (m)	*'mar-te*
• **Mercury**	Mercurio	*mer-'ku-ryo*
• **Neptune**	Nettuno	*net-'tu-no*
• **Pluto**	Plutone (m)	*plu-'to-ne*
• **Saturn**	Saturno	*sa-'tur-no*
• **Uranus**	Urano	*u-'ra-no*
• **Venus**	Venere (f)	*'ve-ne-re*
satellite	satellite (m)	*sa-'tel-li-te*

Idiomatic Expressions

(to) come to light	=	venire* (ess) alla luce
(to) shed light on	=	gettare luce su
(to) be in a bad mood	=	avere* la luna di traverso

space	spazio	*'spa-tsyo*
• space shuttle	navetta spaziale	*na-'vet-ta spa-'tsya-le*
star	stella	*'stel-la*
sun	sole	*'so-le*
• solar system	sistema (m) solare	*sis-'te-ma so-'la-re*
• sun ray	raggio solare	*'raj-jo so-'la-re*
• sunlight	luce solare	*'lu-če so-'la-re*
universe	universo	*u-ni-'ver-so*
world	mondo	*'mon-do*

B. THE ENVIRONMENT AND PHYSICAL FORMATIONS (COASTS, RIVERS, ETC.)

archipelago	arcipelago	*ar-či-'pe-la-go*
atmosphere	atmosfera	*at-mos-'fe-ra*
bay	baia	*'ba-ya*
beach	spiaggia	*'spyaj-ja*
boulder	macigno	*ma-'či-nyo*
cape	capo	*'ka-po*
cave	grotta	*'grot-ta*
channel	canale (m)	*ka-'na-le*
cliff	scogliera	*sko-'lye-ra*
coast, coastline	costa	*'kos-ta*
cove	insenatura	*in-se-na-'tu-ra*
crevasse	crepaccio	*kre-'pač-čo*
desert	deserto	*de-'zer-to*
earthquake	terremoto	*ter-re-'mo-to*
edge, bank	sponda	*'spon-da*
environment	ambiente (m)	*am-'byen-te*
estuary	estuario	*es-tu-'a-ryo*
farmland	terreno agrario	*ter-'re-no a-'gra-ryo*
field	campo	*'kam-po*
• field of grass	prato	*'pra-to*
flood	alluvione (f)	*al-lu-'vyo-ne*
foam	schiuma	*'skyu-ma*
forest	foresta	*fo-'res-ta*
	bosco	*'bos-ko*
grass	erba	*'er-ba*
gulf	golfo	*'gol-fo*
gully	burrone (m)	*bur-'ro-ne*
hill	collina	*kol-'li-na*
ice	ghiaccio	*'gyač-čo*
island	isola	*'i-zo-la*
lagoon	laguna	*la-'gu-na*
lake	lago	*'la-go*
land	terra	*'ter-ra*
landscape	paesaggio	*pa-e-'zaj-jo*
layer, stratum	strato	—

maritime	marittimo	*ma-'rit-ti-mo*
mount	monte (m)	*'mon-te*
mountain	montagna	*mon-'ta-nya*
• **mountain chain**	catena montuosa	*ka-'te-na mon-'two-za*
mud, silt	fango	*'fan-go*
• **muddy**	fangoso	*fan-'go-zo*
nature	natura	*na-'tu-ra*
• **natural**	naturale	*na-tu-'ra-le*
ocean	oceano	*o-'če-a-no*
• **Antarctic**	Antartico	*an-'tar-ti-ko*
• **Arctic**	Artico	*'ar-ti-ko*
• **Atlantic**	Atlantico	*at-'lan-ti-ko*
• **Pacific**	Pacifico	*pa-'ci-fi-ko*
pass	passo	*'pas-so*
peak	vetta	*'vet-ta*
pebble	ciottolo	*'čot-to-lo*
peninsula	penisola	*pe-'ni-zo-la*
plain	pianura	*pya-'nu-ra*
precipice	precipizio	*pre-či-'pi-tsyo*
promontory	promontorio	*pro-mon-'to-ryo*
reef	banco di scogli	*'ban-ko di 'sko-'lyi*
river	fiume (m)	*'fyu-me*
• **(to) flow**	scorrere*	*'skor-re-re*
• **river bank**	argine (m)	*'ar-ji-ne*
rock	roccia	*'roč-ča*
salt water	acqua di mare	*'ak-kwa di 'ma-re*
sand	sabbia	*'sab-bya*
sea	mare (m)	*'ma-re*
• **seabed**	fondo del mare	*'fon-do del 'ma-re*
slab, block	lastra	*'las-tra*
slope	pendio	*pen-'di-o*
steep	ripido	*'ri-pi-do*
stone	pietra	*'pye-tra*
	sasso	*'sas-so*
summit	cima	*'či-ma*
surf	cresta dell'onda	*'kres-ta del-'lon-da*
swamp	palude (f)	*pa-'lu-de*
tide	marea	*ma-'re-a*
tributary	affluente (m)	*af-flu-'en-te*
valley	valle (f)	*'val-le*
vegetation	vegetazione (f)	*ve-je-ta-'tsyo-ne*
volcano	vulcano	*vul-'ka-no*
• **eruption**	eruzione (f)	*e-ru-'tsyo-ne*
• **lava**	lava	—
waterfall	cascate (cascata)	*kas-'ka-te*
wave	onda	*'on-da*
whirlpool	gorgo	*'gor-go*
woods	bosco	*'bos-ko*

C. MATTER AND MATERIALS

acid	acido	*'a-či-do*
acrylic	acrilico	*a-'kri-li-ko*
air	aria	*'a-rya*
ammonia	ammoniaca	*am-mo-'ni-a-ka*
asbestos	amianto	*a-'myan-to*
asphalt	asfalto	*as-'fal-to*
atom	atomo	*'a-to-mo*
• **electron**	elettrone (m)	*e-let-'tro-ne*
• **neutron**	neutrone (m)	*neu-'tro-ne*
• **nucleus**	nucleo	*'nu-kle-o*
• **proton**	protone (m)	*pro-'to-ne*
boiling point	punto di ebollizione	*'pun-to di e-bol-li-'tsyo-ne*
brass	ottone (m)	*ot-'to-ne*
brick	mattone (m)	*mat-'to-ne*
• **bricklayer**	muratore (m)	*mu-ra-'to-re*
bronze	bronzo	*'bron-dzo*
burlap	tela di sacco	*'te-la di 'sak-ko*
calcium	calcio	*'kal-čo*
carbon (element)	carbonio	*kar-'bo-nyo*
carbon (solid), coal	carbone (m)	*kar-'bo-ne*
cardboard	cartone (m)	*kar-'to-ne*
cast iron	ghisa	*'gi-za*
chalk	gesso	*'jes-so*
chemical	chimico	*'ki-mi-ko*
• **chemistry**	chimica	*'ki-mi-ka*
chlorine	cloro	*'klo-ro*
clay	argilla	*ar-'jil-la*
cloth	stoffa	*'stof-fa*
compound	composto	*kom-'posto*
concrete. cement	cemento	*ce-'men-to*
copper	rame (m)	*'ra-me*
corduroy	fustagno	*fus-'ta-nyo*
cork	sughero	*'su-ge-ro*
cotton	cotone (m)	*ko-'to-ne*
ebony	ebano	*'e-ba-no*
elastic	elastico	*e-'las-ti-ko*
electrical	elettrico	*e-'let-tri-ko*
• **electricity**	elettricità (f, inv)	*e-let-tri-či-'ta*
enamel	smalto	*'zmal-to*
energy	energia	*e-ner-'ji-a*
ether	etere (m)	*'e-te-re*
felt	feltro	*'fel-tro*
fiber	fibra	*'fi-bra*
fiberglass	lana di vetro	*'la-na di 've-tro*
filter	filtro	—

fire	fuoco	'fwo-ko
flannel	flanella	fla-'nel-la
flint	selce (f)	'sel-če
freezing point	punto di congelamento	kon-je-la-'men-to
fuel	carburante (m)	kar-bu-'ran-te
gas	benzina	ben-'dzi-na
gauze	garza	'gar-dza
glass	vetro	've-tro
gold	oro	'o-ro
granite	granito	gra-'ni-to
gravel	ghiaia	'gya-ya
greenhouse effect	effetto serra	ef-'fet-to 'ser-ra
hardwood	legno duro	'le-nyo 'du-ro
heat	calore (m)	ka-'lo-re
hydrogen	idrogeno	i-'dro-je-no
industry	industria	in-'dus-trya
• industrial	industriale	in-dus-'trya-le
iodine	iodio	'yo-di-o
iron	ferro	—
knot	nodo	—
• knotty	nodoso	no-'do-zo
lace	pizzo	'pi-tso
lead	piombo	'pyom-bo
leather	pelle (f)	'pel-le
	cuoio	'kwo-yo
linen	lino	—
liquid	liquido	'li-kwi-do
magnesium	magnesio	ma-'nye-zi-o
mahogany	mogano	'mo-ga-no
marble	marmo	—
matter	materia	ma-'te-rya
mercury	mercurio	mer-'ku-ryo
metal	metallo	me-'tal-lo
microscope	microscopio	mi-kro-'sko-pyo
microwave	microonda	mi-kro-'on-da
mineral	minerale (m)	mi-ne-'ra-le
net	rete (f)	're-te
nickel	nichelio	ni-'ke-lyo
nitrogen	nitrogeno	ni-tro-je-no
organic	organico	or-'ga-ni-ko
• inorganic	inorganico	in-or-'ga-ni-ko
oxygen	ossigeno	os-'si-je-no
particle	particella	par-ti-'čel-la
petroleum	petrolio	pe-'tro-lyo
phosphate	fosfato	fos-'fa-to
physical	fisico	'fi-zi-ko
• physics	fisica	'fi-zi-ka
plaster	intonaco	in-'to-na-ko

plastic	plastica	'plas-ti-ka
platinum	platino	'pla-ti-no
pollution	inquinamento	in-kwi-na-'men-to
• (to) pollute	inquinare	in-kwi-'na-re
porcelain	porcellana	por-čel-'la-na
potassium	potassio	po-'tas-syo
pressure	pressione (f)	pres-'syo-ne
radiation	radiazione (f)	ra-dya-'tsyo-ne
• radioactive	radioattivo	ra-dyo-at-'ti-vo
resin	resina	're-zi-na
resistant	resistente	re-zis-'ten-te
rope	corda	'kor-da
rubber	gomma	'gom-ma
salt	sale	'sa-le
scale	bilancia	bi-'lan-ča
scrap iron	rottame (m)	rot-'ta-me
sheet metal	laminato	la-mi-'na-to
silk	seta	'se-ta
silver	argento	ar-jen-to
smoke	fumo	—
sodium	sodio	'so-dyo
solid	solido	'so-li-do
stainless steel	acciaio inossidabile	ač-'ča-yo in-os-si-'da-bi-le
steel	acciaio	ač-'ča-yo
straw	paglia	'pa-lya
string	spago	'spa-go
stuff	roba	'ro-ba
substance	sostanza	sos-'tan-tsa
sulfur	zolfo	'dzol-fo
synthetic	sintetico	sin-'te-ti-ko
tape	nastro	'nas-tro
tar	pece (f)	'pe-če
test tube	provetta	pro-'vet-ta
texture, textile	tessuto	tes-'su-to
thermometer	termometro	ter-'mo-me-tro
tin	latta	'la-ta
	stagno	'sta-nyo
vapor	vapore (m)	va-'po-re
velvet	velluto	vel-'lu-to
virgin wool	lana vergine	'la-na 'ver-ji-ne
water	acqua	'ak-kwa
wood	legno	'le-nyo
wool	lana	—
wrought iron	ferro battuto	'fer-ro bat-'tu-to

D. GEOGRAPHY

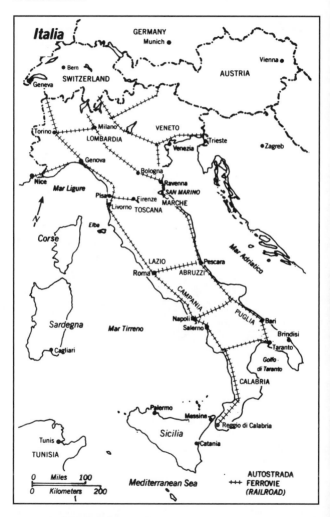

> For names of countries, cities, etc., see §30a-c

Antarctic Circle	Circolo Polare Antartico	*'čir-ko-lo po-'la-re an-tar-ti-ko*
Arctic Circle	Circolo Polare Artico	*'čir-ko-lo po-'la-re 'ar-ti-ko*
area	area	*'a-re-a*
atlas	atlante (m)	*at-'lan-te*
border (political)	frontiera (m)	*fron-'tye-ra*
climate	clima (m)	*'kli-ma*
compass	bussola	*'bus-so-la*
continent	continente (m)	*kon-ti-'nen-te*
• **continental**	continentale	*kon-ti-nen-ta-le*
country	paese (m)	*pa-'e-ze*
demographic	demografico	*de-mo-'gra-fi-ko*
east	est	—
• **eastern**	orientale	*o-ryen-'ta-le*
equator	equatore (m)	*e-kwa-'to-re*
geographical	geografico	*je-o-'gra-fi-ko*
• **geography**	geografia	*je-o-gra-'fi-a*
globe (planetary)	globo	—
globe (object)	mappamondo	*map-pa-'mon-do*
gulf	golfo	—
hemisphere	emisfero	*e-mis-'fe-ro*
latitude	latitudine (f)	*la-ti-'tu-di-ne*
longitude	longitudine (f)	*lon-ji-'tu-di-ne*
map	mappa	—
meridian	meridiano	*me-ri-'dya-no*
nation	nazione (f)	*na-'tsyo-ne*
• **national**	nazionale	*na-tsyo-'na-le*
north	nord	—
• **northeast**	nord-est	—
• **northern**	settentrionale	*set-ten-tryo-'na-le*
• **northwest**	nord-ovest	—
pole	polo	—
• **North Pole**	Polo Nord	—
• **South Pole**	Polo Sud	—
province	provincia	*pro-'vin-ča*
region	regione (f)	*re-'jo-ne*
south	sud	—
• **southeast**	sud-est	—
• **southern**	meridionale	*me-ri-dyo-'na-le*
• **southwest**	sud-ovest	—
state	stato	—

territory	territorio	*ter-ri-'to-ryo*
tropic	tropico	*'tro-pi-ko*
• Tropic of Cancer	Tropico del Cancro	*'tro-pi-ko del 'kan-kro*
• Tropic of Capricorn	Tropico del Capricorno	*'tro-pi-ko del ka-pri-'kor-no*
• tropical	tropicale	*tro-pi-'ka-le*
west	ovest	—
• western	occidentale	*oč-či-den-ta-le*
zone	zona	*'dzo-na*

Idiomatic Expressions

| It's a small world | = | Tutto il mondo è paese |

14. PLANTS

A. GENERAL VOCABULARY

agriculture	agricoltura	*a-gri-kol-'tu-ra*
bark	corteccia	*kor-'teč-ča*
barley	orzo	*'or-dzo*
(to) bloom	sbocciare	*zboč-'ča-re*
botanical	botanico	*bo-'ta-ni-ko*
• botany	botanica	*bo-'ta-ni-ka*
branch	ramo	—
bulb	bulbo	—
clay	argilla	*ar-'jil-la*
compost	miscela fertilizzante	*mi-'še-la fer-ti-li-'dzan-te*
corn	granturco	*gran-'tur-ko*
	mais (m, inv)	—
cultivation	coltivazione (f)	*kol-ti-va-'tsyo-ne*
• (to) cultivate	coltivare	*kol-ti-'va-re*
(to) dig	scavare	*ska-'va-re*
ditch	fossato	*fos-'sa-to*
dung	letame (m)	*le-'ta-me*
ear (of corn)	spiga	*'spi-ga*
fallow, uncultivated	incolto	*in-kol-to*
farmland	terreno agricolo	*ter-'re-no a-'gri-ko-lo*
fermentation	fermentazione (f)	*fer-men-ta-'tsyo-ne*
fertilizer	fertilizzante (m)	*fer-ti-li-'dzan-te*
flower	fiore (m)	*'fyo-re*
• (to) flower	fiorire (isc)	*fyo-'ri-re*

flower garden, flower bed	aiuola	a-'yuo-la
fodder	foraggio	fo-'raj-jo
foliage	fogliame (m)	fo-'lya-me
garden	giardino	jar-'di-no
garden seat	panchina	pan-'ki-na
gardener	giardiniere (-a)	jar-di-'nye-re
grain	grano	—
• granary	granaio	gra-'na-yo
greenhouse	serra	—
harvest	raccolta	rak-kol-ta
• (to) harvest	raccogliere*	rak-'ko-lye-re
hay	fieno	'fye-no
hedge	siepe (f)	'sye-pe
hoe	zappa	'dzap-pa
• (to) hoe	zappare	dzap-'pa-re
hose	tubo	—
• (to) hose	innaffiare	in-naf-'fya-re
irrigation	irrigazione (f)	ir-ri-ga-'tsyo-ne
lawn	prato (erboso)	'pra-to (er-'bo-zo)
• lawn mower	falciatrice (f)	fal-ča-'tri-če
leaf	foglia	'fo-lya
manure	concime (m)	kon-'či-me
meadow	prato	—
(to) mow, reap	falciare	fal-'ča-re
nursery	vivaio	vi-'va-yo
oats	avena	a-'ve-na
path	sentiero	sen-'tye-ro
petal	petalo	'pe-ta-lo
pest	parassita (m)	pa-ras-'si-ta
• pesticide	insetticida (m)	in-set-ti-'či-da
pitchfork	forcone (m)	for-'ko-ne
plant	pianta	'pyan-ta
• (to) plant	piantare	pyan-'ta-re
plow	aratro	a-'ra-tro
• (to) plow	arare	a-'ra-re
pollen	polline (m)	'pol-li-ne
(to) prune	potare	po-'ta-re
rake	rastrello	ras-'trel-lo
• (to) rake	rastrellare	ras-trel-'la-re
• (to) reap	mietere	'mye-te-re
ripe	maturo	ma-'tu-ro
root	radice (f)	ra-'di-če
rotten	marcio	'mar-čo
seed	seme (m)	'se-me
• (to) seed, sow	seminare	se-mi-'na-re
shovel, spade	vanga	'van-ga
sickle	falce (f)	'fal-če
slab	piastra	'pyas-tra

small garden	giardinetto	*jar-di-'net-to*
spade	vanga	—
species	specie (f)	*'spe-če*
spraying	polverizzazione (f)	*pol-ve-ri-dza-'tyo-ne*
sprinkler	spruzzatore (m)	*spru-tsa-'to-re*
stem	stelo	—
storage room, shed	ripostiglio	*ri-pos-'ti-lyo*
straw	paglia	*'pa-lya*
sundial	meridiana	*me-ri-'dya-na*
thorn	spina	—
(to) thresh	trebbiare	*treb-'bya-re*
(to) till	vangare	*van-'ga-re*
tree	albero	*'al-be-ro*
trimmer	potatore (delle piante)	*po-ta-'to-re*
trowel	cazzuola	*ka-'tswo-la*
trunk	tronco	*'tron-ko*
vegetable garden	orto	—
vine	vite (f)	*'vi-te*
vineyard	vigna	*'vi-nya*
weed	erbaccia	*er-'bač-ča*
(to) wilt	appassire (isc)	*ap-pas-'si-re*

B. FLOWERS

buttercup	ranuncolo	*ra-'nun-ko-lo*
camelia	camelia	*ka-'me-lya*
carnation	garofano	*ga-'ro-fa-no*
clematis	clematide (f)	*kle-'ma-ti-de*
cornflower	fiordaliso	*fyor-da-'li-zo*
cyclamen	ciclamino	*či-kla-'mi-no*
daffodil	trombone (m)	*trom-'bo-ne*
dahlia	dalia	*'da-lya*
daisy	margherita	*mar-ge-'ri-ta*
forget-me-not	miosotide (f)	*mi-o-'zo-ti-de*
geranium	geranio	*je-'ra-nyo*
gladiolus	gladiolo	*gla-'di-o-lo*
hyacinth	giacinto	*ja-'čin-to*
hydrangea	ortensia	*or-'ten-sya*
ivy	edera	*'e-de-ra*
lily	giglio	*'ji-lyo*
lily of the valley	mughetto	*mu-'get-to*
magnolia	magnolia	*ma-'nyo-lya*
marigold	calendola	*ka-'len-do-la*
mistletoe	vischio	*'vis-kyo*
nasturtium	nasturzio	*nas-'tur-tsyo*
nettle	ortica	*or-'ti-ka*
orchid	orchidea	*or-ki-'de-a*
pansy	viola del pensiero	*'vyo-la del pen-'sye-ro*

peony	peonia	*pe-'o-nya*
petunia	petunia	*pe-'tu-nya*
poppy	papavero	*pa-'pa-ve-ro*
primrose	primula	*'pri-mu-la*
rose	rosa	*'ro-za*
snowdrop	bucaneve (m, inv)	*bu-ka-'ne-ve*
sunflower	girasole (m)	*ji-ra-'so-le*
tulip	tulipano	*tu-li-'pa-no*
twig	ramoscello	*ra-mo-'šel-lo*
violet	viola	*'vyo-la*
wild rose	rosa selvatica	*'ro-za sel-'va-ti-ka*
wisteria	glicine (m)	*'gli-či-ne*

C. TREES

acorn	ghianda	*'gyan-da*
apple	melo	—
ash	frassino	*'fras-si-no*
beech	faggio	*'faj-jo*
birch	betulla	*be-'tul-la*
cherry	ciliegio	*či-'lye-jo*
chestnut	castagno	*kas-'ta-nyo*
cypress	cipresso	*ci-pres-so*
ebony	ebano	*'e-ba-no*
elm	olmo	—
evergreen	sempreverde (m)	*sem-pre-'ver-de*
fig	fico	*'fi-ko*
fir	abete (m)	*a-'be-te*
hazelnut	nocciolo	*noč-'čo-lo*
lemon	limone (m)	*li-'mo-ne*
maple	acero	*'a-če-ro*
oak	quercia	*'kwer-ča*
olive	olivo (ulivo)	*o-'li-vo*
orange	arancio	*a-'ran-čo*
palm	palma	—
peach	pesco	*'pes-ko*
pear	pero	—
pine	pino	—
poplar	pioppo	*'pyop-po*
sap	linfa	*'lin-fa*
sapling	alberello	*al-be-'rel-lo*
walnut	noce (m)	*'no-če*
willow, weeping willow	salice (m)	*'sa-li-če*
	salice piangente	*pyan-'jen-te*

D. FRUITS AND NUTS

| apple | mela | — |
| apricot | albicocca | *al-bi-'kok-ka* |

banana	banana	—
blueberry	mirtillo	*mir-'til-lo*
cherry	ciliegia	*či-'lye-ja*
chestnut	castagna	*kas-'ta-nya*
date	dattero	*'dat-te-ro*
fig	fico	*'fi-co*
fruit	frutta	*'frut-ta*
grapefruit	pompelmo	*pom-'pel-mo*
grapes	uva	*'u-va*
lemon	limone (m)	*li-'mo-ne*
mandarin orange	mandarino	*man-da-'ri-no*
melon	melone (m)	*me-'lo-ne*
olive	oliva	*o-'li-va*
orange	arancia	*a-'ran-ča*
peach	pesca	*'pes-ka*
peanut (as sold in the USA)	nocciolina americana	*noč-čo-'li-na a-me-re-'ka-na*
peanut (in general)	arachide (f)	*a-'ra-ki-de*
pear	pera	—
pineapple	ananas (m, inv)	—
pistachio	pistacchio	*pis-'tak-kyo*
plum	susina	*su-'zi-na*
prune	prugna	*'pru-nya*
raspberry	lampone (m)	*lam-'po-ne*
strawberry	fragola	*'fra-go-la*
walnut	noce (f)	*'no-če*
watermelon	anguria	*an-'gu-rya*

E. VEGETABLES AND GREENS

artichoke	carciofo	*kar-'čo-fo*
asparagus	asparagi (m, pl)	*as-'pa-ra-ji*
basil	basilico	*ba-'zi-li-ko*
bean	fagiolo	*fa-'jo-lo*
beet	barbabietola	*bar-ba-'bye-to-la*
broccoli	broccoli (m, pl)	*'brok-ko-li*
cabbage	cavolo	*'ka-vo-lo*
carrot	carota	*ka-'ro-ta*
cauliflower	cavolfiore (m)	*ka-vol-'fyo-re*
celery	sedano	*'se-da-no*
chick peas	ceci (m, pl)	*'če-či*
cucumber	cetriolo	*če-tri-'o-lo*
eggplant	melanzana	*me-lan-'dza-na*
fennel	finocchio	*fi-'nok-kyo*
garlic	aglio	*'a-lyo*
lentil	lenticchia	*len-'tik-kya*
lettuce	lattuga	*lat-'tu-ga*
lima bean	fava	—
mint	menta	—

mushroom	fungo	—
onion	cipolla	*či-'pol-la*
parsley	prezzemolo	*pre-'tse-mo-lo*
pea	pisello	*pi-'zel-lo*
pepper	peperone (m)	*pe-pe-'ro-ne*
potato	patata	*pa-'ta-ta*
pumpkin	zucca	*'dzuk-ka*
rosemary	rosmarino	*roz-ma-'ri-no*
rhubarb	rabarbaro	*ra-'bar-ba-ro*
salad	insalata	*in-sa-'la-ta*
spinach	spinaci (m, pl)	*spi-'na-či*
string bean	fagiolino	*fa-jo-'li-no*
tomato	pomodoro	*po-mo-'do-ro*
vegetables, greens	verdura	*ver-'du-ra*
zucchini	zucchine (f, pl)	*dzuk-'ki-ne*

15. THE ANIMAL WORLD

A. MAMMALS AND ANIMALS IN GENERAL

animal	animale (m)	*a-ni-'ma-le*
antelope	antilope (f)	*an-'ti-lo-pe*
antler, horn	corno (corna, pl)	*'kor-no*
ape, monkey	scimmia	*'šim-mya*
baboon	babbuino	*bab-'bwi-no*
badger	tasso	*'tas-so*
bat	pipistrello	*pi-pis-'trel-lo*
bear	orso	*'or-so*
beaver	castoro	*kas-'to-ro*
breeding	allevamento	*al-le-va-'men-to*
buffalo	bufalo	*'bu-fa-lo*
burrow, den	tana	—
bull	toro	—
camel	cammello	*kam-'mel-lo*
cat	gatto	*'gat-to*
• (to) hiss	sibilare	*si-bi-'la-re*
• kitten	gattino	*gat-'ti-no*
• (to) meow	miagolare	*mya-go-'la-re*
cow	mucca	*'muk-ka*
• calf	vitello	*vi-'tel-lo*
• (to) moo	muggire (isc)	*muj-'ji-re*
deer	cervo	*'čer-vo*
dog	cane (m)	*'ka-ne*
• (to) bark	abbaiare	*ab-ba-'ya-re*
• bulldog	mastino	*mas-'ti-no*
• female dog	cagna	*'ka-nya*
• German shepherd	cane lupo	*'ka-ne 'lu-po*
• guard dog	cane da guardia	*'ka-ne da 'gwar-dya*

• hound	cane da caccia	*'ka-ne da 'kač-ča*
• (to) howl	ululare	*u-lu-'la-re*
• kennel	canile (m)	*ka-'ni-le*
• poodle	barboncino	*bar-bon-'či-no*
• puppy	cucciolo	*'kuč-čo-lo*
donkey	asino	*'a-zi-no*
elephant	elefante (m)	*e-le-'fan-te*
• tusk	zanna	*'dzan-na*
farm	fattoria	*fat-to-'ri-a*
• barn	granaio	*gra-'na-yo*
• farmer	contadino (-a)	*kon-ta-'di-no*
• fence	recinto	*re-'čin-to*
giraffe	giraffa	*ji-'raf-fa*
goat	capra	*'ka-pra*
gorilla	gorilla (m, inv)	*go-'ril-la*
(to) graze	pascolare	*pas-ko-'la-re*
hamster	criceto	*kri-'če-to*
hare	lepre (f)	*'la-pre*
hedgehog	riccio	*'rič-čo*
hippopotamus	ippopotamo	*ip-po-'po-ta-mo*
horse	cavallo	*ka-'val-lo*
• hoof	zoccolo	*'dzok-ko-lo*
• (to) neigh	nitrire (isc)	*ni-'tri-re*
• mane	criniera	*kri-'nye-ra*
• mare	cavalla	*ka-'val-la*
hunter	cacciatore (-trice)	*kač-ča-'to-re*
• hunt	caccia	*'kač-ča*
hyena	iena	*'ye-na*
jackal	sciacallo	*ša-'kal-lo*
kangaroo	canguro	*kan-'gu-ro*
lamb	agnello	*a-'nyel-lo*
leopard	leopardo	*le-o-'par-do*
lion, lioness	leone (-essa)	*le-'o-ne*
• (to) roar	ruggire (isc)	*ruj-'ji-re*
livestock	bestiame (m)	*bes-'tya-me*
mammal	mammifero	*mam-'mi-fe-ro*
marmot	marmotta	*mar-'mot-ta*
mink	visone (m)	*vi-'zo-ne*
mole	talpa	*'tal-pa*
monkey	scimmia	*'šim-mya*
mouse	topo	—
mule	mulo	—
otter	lontra	—
ox	bue (buoi, pl)	*'bu-e*
panda	panda (m, inv)	—
panther	pantera	*pan-'te-ra*
pet	animale domestico	*a-ni-'ma-le do-'mes-ti-ko*

pig	maiale (m)	*ma-'ya-le*
• **sow**	scrofa	*'skro-fa*
polar bear	orso bianco	*'or-so 'byan-ko*
porcupine	porcospino	*por-ko-'spi-no*
rabbit	coniglio	*ko-'ni-lyo*
raccoon	procione (m)	*pro-'čo-ne*
ram	montone (m)	*mon-'to-ne*
rat	ratto	*'rat-to*
reindeer	renna	*'ren-na*
rhinoceros	rinoceronte (m)	*ri-no-če-'ron-te*
rodent	roditore (m)	*ro-di-'to-re*
seal	foca	*'fo-ka*
sea lion	leone marino	*le-'o-ne ma-'ri-no*
sheep	pecora	*'pe-ko-ra*
• **shepherd**	pastore (-a)	*pas-'to-re*
skunk	puzzola	*'pu-tso-la*
squirrel	scoiattolo	*sko-'yat-to-lo*
tail	coda	—
(to) tame	addomesticare	*ad-do-mes-ti-'ka-re*
tiger	tigre (f)	*'ti-gre*
trap	trappola	*'trap-po-la*
walrus	tricheco	*tri-'ke-ko*
whale	balena	*ba-'le-na*
wild boar	cinghiale (m)	*čin-'gya-le*
wolf	lupo	—
zebra	zebra	*'dze-bra*
zoo	zoo	*'dzo*
• **zoological**	zoologico	*dzo-o-'lo-ji-ko*
• **zoology**	zoologia	*dzo-o-lo-'ji-a*

B. BIRDS AND FOWL

beak	becco	*'bek-ko*
bird	uccello	*uč-'čel-lo*
• **bird of prey**	uccello rapace	*uč-'čel-lo ra-'pa-če*
birdcage	gabbia	*'gab-bya*
blackbird	merlo	—
brood	covata	*ko-'va-ta*
canary	canarino	*ka-na-'ri-no*
chaffinch	fringuello	*frin-'gwel-lo*
chick	pulcino	*pul-'či-no*
chicken, hen	gallina	*gal-'li-na*
crest	cresta	*'kres-ta*
crow	corvo	*'kor-vo*
cuckoo	cuculo	*ku-'ku-lo*
dove	colomba	*ko-'lom-ba*
duck	anatra (anitra)	*'a-na-tra*
eagle	aquila	*'a-kwi-la*

falcon	falcone (m)	*fal-'ko-ne*
feather	penna	—
flamingo	fenicottero	*fe-ni-'kot-te-ro*
goose	oca	*'o-ka*
hawk	falco	*'fal-ko*
homing pigeon	piccione (m)	*pič-'čo-ne*
kingfisher	martin pescatore	*mar-'tin pes-ka-'to-re*
lark	allodola	*al-'lo-do-la*
magpie	gazza	*'ga-dza*
migratory bird	uccello migratore	*uč-'čel-lo*
nest	nido	—
nightingale	usignolo	*u-zi-'nyo-lo*
ostrich	struzzo	*'stru-tso*
owl	gufo	—
parrot, budgie	pappagallo	*pap-pa-'gal-lo*
partridge	pernice (f)	*per-'ni-če*
peacock	pavone (m)	*pa-'vo-ne*
pelican	pellicano	*pel-li-'ka-no*
penguin	pinguino	*pin-'gwi-no*
pheasant	fagiano	*fa-'ja-no*
robin	pettirosso	*pet-ti-'ros-so*
rooster	gallo	*'gal-lo*
seagull	gabbiano	*gab-'bya-no*
sparrow	passero	*'pas-se-ro*
stork	cicogna	*či-'ko-nya*
swallow	rondine (f)	*'ron-di-ne*
swan	cigno	*'či-nyo*
turkey	tacchino	*tak-'ki-no*
turtle dove	tortora	*'tor-to-ra*
vulture	avvoltoio	*av-vol-'to-yo*
wing	ala (ali, pl)	—
woodpecker	picchio	*'pik-kyo*

Idiomatic Expressions

(to) line up	=	fare la coda
(to) kill two birds with one stone	=	pigliare due piccioni con una fava
(to) be very cold	=	fare un freddo da cani

C. FISH, REPTILES, AMPHIBIANS, AND MARINE MAMMALS

alligator	alligatore (m)	*al-li-ga-'to-re*
boa	serpente boa	*ser-'pen-te 'bo-a*
clam	vongola	*'von-go-la*

cobra	cobra (m, inv)	—
codfish	merluzzo	mer-'lu-tso
crab	granchio	'gran-kyo
crocodile	coccodrillo	kok-ko-'dril-lo
eel	anguilla	an-'gwil-la
fish	pesce (m)	'pe-še
• **fin, flipper**	pinna	'pin-na
• **(to) fish**	pescare	pes-'ka-re
• **fishing**	pesca	'pes-ka
• **fishing rod**	canna	'kan-na
• **gill**	branchia	'bran-kya
• **hook**	amo	—
• **scale**	scaglia	'ska-lya
frog	rana	—
• **(to) croak**	gracidare	gra-či-'da-re
goldfish	pesce rosso	'pe-še ros-so
herring	aringa	a-'rin-ga
jellyfish	medusa	me-'du-za
lizard	lucertola	lu-'čer-to-la
lobster	aragosta	a-ra-'gos-ta
mackerel	sgombro	'sgom-bro
mollusk, shellfish	mollusco	mol-'lus-ko
mullet	triglia	'tri-lya
mussel	cozza	'ko-tsa
octopus	polipo	'po-li-po
oyster	ostrica	'os-tri-ka
prawn, shrimp	gambero	'gam-be-ro
rattlesnake	serpente a sonagli	ser-'pen-te a so-'na-lyi
reptile	rettile (m)	'ret-ti-le
salmon	salmone (m)	sal-'mo-ne
sardine	sardina	sar-'di-na
scallop, shell	conchiglia	kon-'ki-lya
seahorse	cavalluccio marino	ka-val-'luč-čo ma-'ri-no
shark	squalo	'skwa-lo
shell	conchiglia	kon-'ki-lya
snake	serpente (m)	ser-'pen-te
sole	sogliola	'so-lyo-la
squid	calamaro	ka-la-'ma-ro
swordfish	pesce spada	'pe-še
tadpole	girino	ji-'ri-no
toad	rospo	'ros-po
trout	trota	'tro-ta
tuna	tonno	'ton-no
turtle, tortoise	tartaruga	tar-ta-'ru-ga
viper	vipera	'vi-pe-ra

D. INSECTS AND OTHER INVERTEBRATES

ant	formica	*for-'mi-ka*
• **ant hill**	formicaio	*for-mi-'ka-yo*
bedbug	cimice (f)	*'či-mi-če*
bee	ape (f)	*'a-pe*
• **(to) buzz**	ronzare	*ron-'dza-re*
• **hive**	alveare (m)	*al-ve-'a-re*
• **(to) sting**	pungere*	*'pun-je-re*
• **swarm**	sciame (m)	*'ša-me*
beetle	maggiolino	*maj-jo-'li-no*
butterfly	farfalla	*far-'fal-la*
caterpillar	bruco	*'bru-ko*
chrysalis	crisalide (f)	*kri-'sa-lide*
cockroach	scarafaggio	*ska-ra-'faj-jo*
cocoon	bozzolo	*'bo-tso-lo*
cricket	grillo	*'gril-lo*
dragonfly	libellula	*li-'bel-lu-la*
flatworm	verme (m)	*'ver-me*
flea	pulce (f)	*'pul-če*
glowworm	lucciola	*'luč-čo-la*
grasshopper	cavalletta	*ka-val-'let-ta*
hornet	calabrone (m)	*ka-la-'bro-ne*
housefly	mosca	*'mos-ka*
insect, bug	insetto	*in-'set-to*
ladybug	coccinella	*koč-či-'nel-la*
louse	pidocchio	*pi-'dok-kyo*
midge	moscerino	*mo-še-'ri-no*
mosquito	zanzara	*dzan-'dza-ra*
scorpion	scorpione (m)	*skor-'pyo-ne*
silk worm	baco da seta	*'ba-ko da 'se-ta*
spider	ragno	*'ra-nyo*
• **spiderweb**	ragnatela	*ra-nya-'te-la*
termite	termite (f)	*'ter-mi-te*
tick	zecca	*'dzek-ka*
wasp	vespa	*'ves-pa*
worm	verme (m)	*'ver-me*

COMMUNICATING, FEELING, AND THINKING

16. BASIC SOCIAL EXPRESSIONS

A. GREETINGS AND FAREWELLS

Adieu!	Addio!	*ad-'di-o*
Good afternoon, Hello!	Buon pomeriggio!	*bwon po-me-'rij-jo*
	Buona sera!	*'bwo-na 'se-ra*
	(later afternoon)	
Good evening, Hello!	Buona sera!	*'bwo-na 'se-ra*
Good luck, Best wishes!	Auguri!	*au-'gu-ri*
Good morning, Good day!	Buongiorno!	*bwon-'jor-no*
Good night!	Buona notte!	*'bwo-na 'not-te*
Good-bye!	Arrivederci! (fam)	*ar-ri-ve-'der-či*
	ArrivederLa! (pol)	*ar-ri-ve-'der-la*
greeting	saluto	*sa-'lu-to*
• **(to) greet**	salutare	*sa-lu-'ta-re*
Greetings, Hello!	Salve!	*'sal-ve*
Hi, Bye!	Ciao! (fam)	*ča-o*
How are you?	Come stai? (fam)	*'ko-me 'stai*
	Come sta? (pol)	*'ko-me sta*
How's it going?	Come va?	*'ko-me va*
• **Bad(ly)!**	Male!	*'ma-le*
• **Fine, Well!**	Bene!	*'be-ne*
• **Not bad!**	Non c'`e male!	*non če 'ma-le*
• **Quite well!**	Abbastanza bene!	*ab-bas-'tan-dza 'be-ne*
• **So, so!**	Così, così!	*ko-'zi ko-'zi*
• **Very well!**	Molto bene!	*'mol-to 'be-ne*
	Benissimo!	*be-'nis-si-mo*
Please give my regards, greetings to…	Ti prego di salutarmi… (fam)	*'pre-go sa-lu-'tar-mi*
	La prego di salutarmi… (pol)	—
See you!	Ci vediamo!	*či ve-'dya-mo*
See you later!	A più tardi!	*a pyu 'tar-di*
See you soon!	A presto!	*a 'pres-to*
See you Sunday!	A domenica!	*a do-'me-ni-ka*
(to) shake hands	dare* la mano	*'da-re la 'ma-no*
	stringere* la mano	*'strin-je-re*
• **handshake**	stretta di mano	*'stret-ta*

Alternative Spellings

Buon giorno	or	Buongiorno
Buona sera	or	Buonasera
Buona notte	or	Buonanotte

B. FORMS OF ADDRESS AND INTRODUCTIONS

A pleasure!	Piacere!	*pya-'če-re*
• The pleasure is mine!	Il piacere è mio!	—
(to) be on a first-name basis	darsi* del tu	—
(to) be on a formal basis	darsi* del Lei	—
(to) be seated	accomodarsi	*ak-ko-mo-'dar-si*
	sedersi*	*se-'der-si*
Be seated!	Accomodati! (fam)	*ak-'ko-ma-da-ti*
	Siediti! (fam)	*'sye-di-ti*
	Si accomodi! (pol)	*si ak-'ko-mo-di*
	Si sieda! (pol)	*si 'sye-da*
calling (business) card	biglietto da visita	*bi-'lyet-to da 'vi-zi-ta*
Come in!	Avanti!	*a-'van-ti*
	Prego!	*'pre-go*
Delighted!	Molto lieto! (m)	*'mol-to 'lye-to*
	Molto lieta! (f)	—
Happy to make your acquaintance	Felice di fare* la tua conoscenza (fam)	
	Felice di fare* la Sua conoscenza (pol)	*fe'li-če ko-no-'šen-tsa*
introduction	presentazione (f)	*pre-zen-ta-'tsyo-ne*
• (to) introduce	presentare	*pre-zen-'ta-re*
• (to) know someone	conoscere*	*ko-'no-še-re*
• Let me introduce you to...	Ti presento... (fam)	—
	Le presento... (pol)	
• May I introduce you to...?	Posso presentarti...? (fam)	—
	Ti posso presentare...? (fam)	
	Posso presentarLe...? (pol)	
	Le posso presentare...? (pol)	
Make yourself comfortable!	Si accomodi!	*si ak-'ko-mo-di*
(to) meet	conoscere*	*ko-'no-še-re*
• (to) run into	incontrare	*in-kon-'tra-re*
title	titolo	*'ti-to-lo*

• **Accountant**	Ragioniere (-a)	*ra-jo-'nye-re*
• **Doctor**	Dottore (-essa)	*dot-'to-re*
• **Draftsperson**	Geometra (m/f)	*je-'o-me-tra*
• **Engineer**	Ingegnere (m/f)	*in-je-'nye-re*
• **Lawyer**	Avvocato (m/f)	*av-vo-'ka-to*
• **Miss, Ms.**	Signorina	*si-nyo-'ri-na*
• **Mr.**	Signore	*si-'nyo-re*
• **Mrs., Ms.**	Signora	*si-'nyo-ra*
• **Professor**	Professore (-essa)	*pro-fes-'so-re*
• **Reverend**	Reverendo	*re-ve-'ren-do*
What's your name?	Come ti chiami? (fam)	*'ko-me ti 'kya-mi*
	Come si chiama? (pol)	—
• **My name is…**	Mi chiamo…	*mi 'kya-mo*
• **I'm…**	Sono…	—

C. EXCLAMATIONS AND VARIOUS PROTOCOLS (COMMANDING, BEING COURTEOUS, ETC.)

Are you crazy?	Ma sei pazzo (-a)? (fam)	*'pa-tso*
Attention!	Attenzione!	*at-ten-'tsyo-ne*
Be quiet!	Sta' zitto (-a)! (fam)	*'dzit-to*
	Stia zitto (-a)! (pol)	*'sti-a 'dzit-to*
Best wishes!	Auguri!	*au-'gu-ri*
Bless you!	Salute!	*sa-'lu-te*
Cheers!	Salute!	*sa-'lu-te*
	Cin cin!	*čin čin*
Congratulations!	Congratulazioni!	*kon-gra-tu-la-'tsyo-ni*
	Complimenti!	*kom-pli-'men-ti*
Curses! Damn (it)!	Maledizione!	*ma-le-di-'tsyo-ne*
Don't be stupid (silly)!	Non fare* lo stupido (-a)! (fam)	*'stu-pido*
	Non faccia lo stupido (-a)! (pol)	
Don't mention it!	Figurati! (fam)	*fi-'gu-ra-ti*
	Si figuri! (form)	*si fi-'gu-ri*
Don't talk nonsense!	Non dire* schiocchezze! (fam)	*šok-'ke-tse*
	Non dica schiocchezze! (pol)	
Excuse me!	Scusa! (fam)	*'sku-za*
	Scusi! (pol)	*'sku-zi*
	Mi scusi! (pol)	*mi 'sku-zi*
Excuse me (I need to get through)	Permesso!	*per-'mes-so*
Fantastic!	Fantastico!	*fan-'tas-ti-ko*
Good!	Bene!	*'be-ne*
Good luck!	Buona fortuna!	*'bwo-na for-tu-na*
	In bocca al lupo!	*in 'bok-ka al 'lu-po*

English	Italian	Pronunciation
Happy birthday!	Buon compleanno!	bwon kom-ple-'an-no
Happy Easter!	Buona Pasqua!	'bwo-na 'pas-kwa
Happy New Year!	Buon Anno!	bwon 'an-no
	Felice Anno Nuovo!	fe-'li-če an-no 'nwo-vo
Have a good holiday!	Buona vacanza!	'bwo-na va-'kan-dza
Have a good time!	Buon divertimento!	bwon di-ver-ti-'men-to
How lucky!	Che fortuna!	ke for-'tu-na
I wish!	Magari!	ma-'ga-ri
I'll be glad, happy to do it!	Lo farò con piacere!	pya-'če-re
I'm sorry!	Mi dispiace!	mi dis-'pya-če
If you don't mind, If you please...	Se non ti dispiace (fam)	dis-'pya-če
	Se non Le dispiace (pol)	
Incredible!	Incredibile!	in-kre-'di-bi-le
Interesting!	Interessante!	in-te-res-'san-te
It can't be!	Non è possibile!	pos-'si-bi-le
It doesn't matter!	Non importa!	im-'por-ta
Magnificent!	Magnifico!	ma-'nyi-fi-ko
Many thanks!	Grazie mille!	'gra-tsye 'mil-le
Marvelous!	Meraviglioso!	me-ra-vi-'lyo-zo
May I?	È permesso?	per-'mes-so
	Posso?	'pos-so
	Si può?	si 'pwo
May I help you?	Desideri? (fam)	de-'zi-de-ri
	Desidera? (pol)	—
Merry Christmas!	Buon Natale!	bwon na-'ta-le
No way!	Per carità!	per ka-ri-'ta
Please!	Per favore!	per fa-'vo-re
Ouch!	Ahi!	—
Quiet!	Silenzio!	si-'len-tsyo
Really?	Davvero?	dav-'ve-ro
Stay still!	Sta' fermo (-a)! (fam)	—
	Stia fermo (-a)! (pol)	—
Stop it! That's enough!	Basta!	—
Stupendous!	Stupendo!	stu-'pen-do
Thank God!	Grazie a Dio!	'gra-tsye
Thank you!	Grazie!	'gra-tsye
Thank you. It's very kind of you!	Grazie, molto gentile!	'gra-tsye 'mol-to jen-'ti-le
Too bad! Pity! A shame!	Peccato!	pek-'ka-to
Well done!	Bravo (-a)!	'bra-vo
What a bore!	Che noia!	ke 'no-ya
What a drag!	Che barba!	ke 'bar-ba
What a fool!	Che sciocco!	ke šok-ko
What a jam!	Che guaio!	ke 'gwa-yo
What a mess!	Che pasticcio!	ke pas-'tič-čo
	Che casino! (fam)	ke ka-'zi-no

What a nuisance!	Che seccatura!	*ke sek-ka-'tu-ra*
What a nice surprise!	Che bella sorpresa!	*ke 'bel-la sor-'pre-za*
Yah! Sure! There!	Ecco!	*'ek-ko*
You're welcome, Please, go ahead	Prego!	*'pre-go*

17. SPEAKING AND TALKING

A. SPEECH STYLES AND FUNCTIONS

advice	consiglio	*kon-'si-lyo*
• (to) advise	consigliare	*kon-si-'lya-re*
(to) affirm, remark	affermare	*af-fer-'ma-re*
(to) agree	essere* d'accordo	*'es-se-re dak-'kor-do*
(to) allude	alludere*	*al-'lu-de-re*
(to) announce	annunciare	*an-nun-'ča-re*
• announcement	annuncio	*an-'nun-čo*
answer	risposta	*ris-'pos-ta*
• (to) answer	rispondere*	*ris-'pon-de-re*
(to) argue, quarrel	litigare	*li-ti-'ga-re*
• argument	lite (f)	*'li-te*
(to) ask for	chiedere*	*'kye-de-re*
(to) beg to do something	pregare	*pre-'ga-re*
(to) call	chiamare	*kya-'ma-re*
(to) change the subject	cambiare soggetto	*kam-'bya-re soj-'jet-to*
(to) chat	chiacchierare	*kyak-kye-'ra-re*
(to) cheer, acclaim	acclamare	*ak-kla-'ma-re*
(to) communicate	comunicare	*ko-mu-ni-'ka-re*
• communication	comunicazione (f)	*ko-mu-ni-ka-'tsyo-ne*
(to) compare	paragonare	*pa-ra-go-'na-re*
• comparison	paragone (m)	*pa-ra-'go-ne*
(to) complain	lamentarsi	*la-men-'tar-si*
• complaint	lamentela	*la-men-'te-la*
(to) conclude	concludere*	*kon-'klu-de-re*
• conclusion	conclusione (f)	*kon-klu-'zyo-ne*
(to) confirm	confermare	*kon-fer-'ma-re*
(to) congratulate	congratulare	*kon-gra-tu-'la-re*
• congratulations	congratulazioni (f, pl)	*kon-gra-tu-la-'tsyo-ni*
(to) consult, look up	consultare	*kon-sul-'ta-re*
(to) contest, dispute	contestare	*kon-tes-'ta-re*
(to) contradict	contraddire*	*kon-trad-'di-re*
conversation	conversazione (f)	*kon-ver-sa-'tsyo-ne*
• (to) converse	conversare	*kon-ver-'sa-re*
(to) curse	maledire*	*ma-le-'di-re*
debate	dibattito	*di-'bat-ti-to*
• (to) debate	dibattere	*di-'bat-te-re*
(to) decipher	decifrare	*de-či-'fra-re*
(to) declare	dichiarare	*di-'kya-'ra-re*

(to) define	definire (isc)	de-fi-'ni-re
(to) deny	negare	ne-'ga-re
(to) describe	descrivere*	des-'kri-ve-re
• description	descrizione (f)	des-kri-'tsyo-ne
dialogue	dialogo	di-'a-lo-go
(to) disagree	non essere* d'accordo	non 'es-se-re dak-'kor-do
• disagreement	malinteso	ma-lin-'te-zo
(to) discuss, argue	discutere*	dis-'ku-te-re
• discussion, argument	discussione (f)	dis-kus-'syo-ne
eloquent	eloquente	e-lo-'kwen-te
(to) emphasize	sottolineare	sot-to-li-ne-'a-re
(to) ensure	assicurare	as-si-ku-'ra-re
excuse	scusa	'sku-za
• (to) excuse oneself	scusarsi	sku-'zar-si
(to) explain	spiegare	spye-'ga-re
• explanation	spiegazione (f)	spye-ga-'tsyo-ne
(to) express	esprimere*	es-'pri-me-re
• (to) express oneself	esprimersi*	es-'pri-mer-si
• expression	espressione (f)	es-pres-'syo-ne
gossip	pettegolezzo	pet-te-go-'le-tso
• (to) gossip	spettegolare	spet-'te-go-la-re
(to) guarantee	garantire (isc)	ga-ran-'ti-re
(to) hesitate	esitare	e-zi-'ta-re
• hesitation	esitazione (f)	e-zi-ta-'tsyo-ne
(to) identify	identificare	i-den-ti-fi-'ka-re
(to) imply	implicare	im-pli-'ka-re
(to) indicate	indicare	in-di-'ka-re
• indication	indicazione (f)	in-di-ka-'tsyo-ne
(to) inform	informare	in-for-'ma-re
• information	informazione (f)	in-for-ma-'tsyo-ne
(to) insinuate	insinuare	in-si-nu-'a-re
(to) interpret	interpretare	in-ter-pre-'ta-re
(to) interrogate	interrogare	in-ter-ro-'ga-re
(to) interrupt	interrompere*	in-ter-'rom-pe-re
• interruption	interruzione (f)	in-ter-ru-'tsyo-ne
(to) invite	invitare	in-vi-'ta-re
(to) jeer	fischiare	fis-'kya-re
(to) jest	scherzare	sker-'tsa-re
• jest, prank	scherzo	'sker-tso
joke (oral)	barzelletta	bar-dzel-'let-ta
• (to) tell a joke	raccontare una barzelletta	rak-kon-'ta-re u-na bar-dzel-'let-ta
(to) keep quiet	stare* zitto	'sta-re 'dzit-to
lecture	conferenza	kon-fe-'ren-dza
lie	bugia	bu-'ji-a
• (to) lie	dire* una bugia	'di-re u-na bu-'ji-a
loquacious	loquace	lo-'kwa-če

malicious gossip	maldicenza	*mal-di-'čen-dza*
(to) malign, speak badly of	malignare	*ma-li-'nya-re*
(to) mean	significare	*si-nyi-fi-'ka-re*
• meaning	significato	*si-nyi-fi-'ka-to*
(to) mention	menzionare	*men-tsyo-'na-re*
misunderstanding	fraintendimento	*fra-in-ten-di-'men-to*
(to) murmur	mormorare	*mor-mo-'ra-re*
(to) note	notare	*no-'ta-re*
(to) object	obiettare	*o-byet-'ta-re*
(to) offend	offendere*	*of-'fen-de-re*
oral	orale	*o-'ra-le*
order	ordine (m)	*'or-di-ne*
• (to) order	ordinare	*or-di-'na-re*
outspoken	schietto	*'skyet-to*
(to) praise	lodare	*lo-'da-re*
(to) pray	pregare	*pre-'ga-re*
• prayer	preghiera	*pre-'gye-ra*
(to) preach	predicare	*pre-di-'ka-re*
promise	promessa	*pro-'mes-sa*
• (to) promise	promettere*	*pro-'met-te-re*
(to) pronounce	pronunciare	*pro-nun-'ča-re*
• pronunciation	pronuncia	*pro-'nun-ča*
(to) propose, suggest	proporre*	*pro-'por-re*
(to) put forward	avanzare	*a-van-'tsa-re*
(to) raise one's voice	alzare la voce	*al-'tsa-re la 'vo-če*
(to) read between the lines	leggere* tra le righe	*'lej-je-re tra le 'ri-ge*
(to) recommend	raccomandare	*rak-ko-man-'da-re*
(to) refer	riferire (isc)	*ri-fe-'ri-re*
(to) repeat	ripetere	*ri-'pe-te-re*
• repetition	ripetizione (f)	*ri-pe-ti-'tsyo-ne*
(to) reply	rispondere*	*ris-'pon-de-re*
report	relazione (f)	*re-la-'tsyo-ne*
• (to) report	riferire (isc)	*ri-fe-'ri-re*
(to) reproach	rimproverare	*rim-pro-ve-'ra-re*
(to) request	richiedere*	*ri-'kye-de-re*
• request	richiesta	*ri-'kyes-ta*
rumor	diceria	*di-če-'ria*
• Rumor has it that…	Corre voce che…	*'kor-re 'vo-če ke*
(to) say, tell	dire*	*'di-re*
shout	grido	—
• (to) shout	gridare	*gir-'da-re*
silence	silenzio	*si-'len-tsyo*
• silent	silenzioso	*si-len-'tsyo-zo*
(to) speak, talk	parlare	*par-'la-re*
• speech, talk	discorso	*dis-'kor-so*
(to) spread gossip	seminare zizzania	*se-mi-'na-re dzi-'dza-nya*
(to) state, affirm, maintain	asserire (isc)	*as-se-'ri-re*
• statement	affermazione (f)	*af-fer-ma-'tsyo-ne*

story	storia	'sto-rya
• (to) tell a story	raccontare	rak-kon-'ta-re
(to) suggest	suggerire (isc)	suj-je-'ri-re
(to) summarize	riassumere*	ri-as-'su-me-re
• summary	riassunto	ri-as-'sun-to
(to) swear, curse	bestemmiare	bes-tem-'mya-re
(to) swear, avow	giurare	ju-'ra-re
talk, speech	discorso	dis-'kor-so
(to) tell (a story), recount	raccontare	rak-kon-'ta-re
(to) tell a joke	raccontare una	rak-kon-'ta-re u-na
	barzelletta	bar-dzel-'let-ta
(to) testify, vouch	testimoniare	tes-ti-mo-'nya-re
(to) thank	ringraziare	rin-gra-'tsya-re
threat	minaccia	mi-'nač-ča
• (to) threaten	minacciare	mi-nač-'ča-re
(to) toast	brindare	brin-'da-re
• toast	brindisi (m, inv)	'brin-di-zi
(to) translate	tradurre*	tra-'dur-re
• translation	traduzione (f)	tra-du-'tsyo-ne
(to) uphold, maintain	sostenere*	sos-te-'ne-re
vocabulary	vocabolario	vo-ka-bo-'la-ryo
(to) warn	avvertire	av-ver-'ti-re
• warning	avvertimento	av-ver-ti-'men-to
(to) whine	piagnucolare	pya-nyu-ko-'la-re
(to) whisper	sussurrare	sus-sur-'ra-re
witty	spiritoso	spi-ri-'to-zo
word	parola	pa-'ro-la
(to) yawn	sbadigliare	zba-di-'lya-re
(to) yell, scream	urlare	ur-'la-re

B. USEFUL EXPRESSIONS IN CONVERSATIONS

(to) be right	avere* ragione	a-'ve-re ra-'jo-ne
(to) be wrong	avere* torto	a-'ve-re 'tor-to
briefly	in breve	in 'bre-ve
by the way	a proposito	a pro-'po-zi-to
Go ahead, speak!	Di' pure! (fam)	'pu-re
	Dica pure! (pol)	—
How do you say…?	Come si dice…?	'ko-me si 'di-če
however	tuttavia	tut-ta-'vi-a
	comunque	ko-'mun-kwe
I didn't understand!	Non ho capito!	ka-'pi-to
I'm sure that…	Sono sicuro (-a) che…	si-'ku-ro
in my opinion	a mio parere	pa-'re-re
in my own opinion	secondo me	se-'kon-do
It seems that…	Sembra che…	'sem-bra ke
	Pare che…	'pa-re ke
It's necessary that…	È necessario che…	ne-čes-'sa-ryo ke
It's obvious that…	È ovvio che…	'ov-vyo ke

Common Gestures Used in Conversation

	Are you crazy?	Sei pazzo? (fam) È pazzo? (pol)	
	Come here!	Vieni qui (fam) Venga qui! (pol)	*'vye-ni kwi*
	Hello! (pol)	Buon giorno! etc.	
	Hi (fam)	Ciao!	

	Let me introduce you to . . .	Ti presento . . .
		  (fam)
		Le presento . . .
		  (pol)	

	No way!	Impossibile!!	*im-pos-'si-bi-le*

It's true!	È vero!	*'ve-ro*
• **It's not true!**	Non è vero!	—
Listen!	Senti! (fam)	*'sen-ti*
	Ascolta! (fam)	*as-'kol-ta*
	Senta! (pol)	—
	Ascolti! (pol)	—
now	ora	*'o-ra*
that is to say	cioè	*čo-'e*
	vale a dire	*va-le a -'di-re*

therefore	dunque	*'dun-kwe*
	quindi	*'kwin-di*
	allora	*al-'lo-ra*
to sum up	insomma	*in-'som-ma*
Who knows?	Chissà?	*kis-'sa*

18. THE TELEPHONE

A. TELEPHONES AND ACCESSORIES

amplifier	altoparlante (m)	*al-to-par-'lan-te*
answering machine	segreteria telefonica	*se-gre-te-'ri-a*
		te-le-'fo-ni-ka
cable	cavo	—
cell phone	cellulare (m)	*cel-lu-'la-re*
	telefonino	*te-le-fo-'ni-no*
digital	digitale	*di-ji-'ta-le*
earphone	auricolare (m)	*au-ri-ko-'la-re*
fax machine	fax (m)	—
intercom	citofono	*ci-'to-fo-no*
modem	modem (m)	—
operator	centralino	*cen-tra-'li-no*
outlet	presa	*'pre-za*
phone bill	bolletta del telefono	*bol-'let-ta del*
		te-'le-fo-no
phone book	elenco telefonico	*e-'len-ko te-le-'fo-ni-ko*
phone booth	cabina telefonica	*ka-'bi-na*
		te-le-'fo-ni-ka
phone card	scheda telefonica	*'ske-da te-le-'fo-ni-ka*
phone keyboard	tastiera del telefono	*tas-'tye-ra del*
		te-'le-fo-no
portable phone	telefono portatile	*te-'le-fo-no por-'ta-ti-le*
public phone	telefono pubblico	*te-'le-fo-no 'pub-bli-ko*
speaker	microfono	*mi-'kro-fo-no*
telecommunications	telecomunicazioni (f, pl)	*te-le-ko-mu-ni-ka-*
		'tsyo-ni
yellow pages	pagine gialle	*'pa-ji-ne 'jal-le*

B. USING THE TELEPHONE

1-800 number	numero verde	*'nu-me-ro 'ver-de*
(to) answer	rispondere*	*ris-pon-de-re*
area code	prefisso	*pre-'fis-so*
busy, occupied signal	occupato	*ok-ku-'pa-to*
collect call	telefonata a carico	*te-le-fo-'na-ta*
	del destinatario	*'ka-ri-ko del des-ti-*
		na-'ta-ryo
(to) dial the number	comporre* il numero	*kom-'por-re il 'nu-mero*
	fare* il numero	—

direct call	telefonata in	te-le-fo-na-ta in
	teleselezione	te-le-se-le-'tsyo-ne
distress phone line	telefono amico	te-'le-fo-no a-'mi-ko
free signal	libero	
(to) hang up	riattaccare il telefeono	ri-at-tak-'ka-re il
		te-'le-fo-no
information	informazioni (f, pl)	in-for-ma-'tsyo-ni
international call	telefonata internazionale	te-le-fo-'na-ta
		in-ter-na-tsyo-'na-le
local call	telefonata urbana	te-le-fo-'na-ta
		ur-'ba-na
long-distance call	telefonata interurbana	te-le-fo-'na-ta
		in-ter-ur-'ba-na
phone call	telefonata	te-le-fo-'na-ta
• Hello!	Pronto!	—
• I'm sorry, I've dialed	Scusi, ho sbagliato	'sku-zi o zba-'lya-to
the wrong number.	numero.	'nu-me-ro
• Is Mario in?	C'è Mario?	če 'ma-ryo
• Is Ms. Morelli in?	C'è la signora Morelli?	—
• (to) make a call	fare* una telefonata	'fa-re u-na
		te-le-fo-'na-ta
• May I speak with...?	Posso parlare con...?	—
• I would like to speak	Desidererei parlare	de-zi-de-re-'rei
with...	con...	
• The line is busy.	La linea è occupata.	'li-ne-a ok-ku-'pa-ta
• The line is free.	La linea è libera.	'li-ne-a 'li-be-ra
• This is...	Sono...	—
• Who is it?	Chi è?	ki 'e
• Who's speaking?	Chi parla?	ki 'par-la
phone line for reporting	telefono azzurro	te-'le-fo-no a-'dzur-ro
the abuse of children		
phone number	numero di telefono	'nu-me-ro di te-'le-fo-no
(to) ring	suonare	swo-'na-re
wrong number	numero sbagliato	'nu-me-ro zba-'lya-to

19. LETTER WRITING

A. FORMAL SALUTATIONS/CLOSINGS

Dear Madam or Sir...	Spettabile (Spett.le)	spet-'ta-bi-le
	Ditta...	
Dear Sir...	Egregio Signore...	egre-jo si-'nyo-re
Dear Madam...	Gentile Signora...	—
Greetings, regards...	Saluti...	sa-'lu-ti
To Whom It May	A Chi di Competenza...	kom-pe-'ten-dza
Concern...		
With cordial greetings...	Con i più cordiali	pyu kor-'dya-li sa-'lu-ti
	saluti...	

With kind wishes...	Un caro saluto...	—
Yours cordially...	Cordiali saluti...	kor-'dya-li sa-'lu-ti
Yours truly, sincerely...	Suo (Sua)...	—
	Distinti saluti...	—

Writing to a Company, Corporation, etc.

Dear Madam or Sir	Spettabile Ditta
To Whom It May Concern	A Chi di Competenza
Please accept...	La prego di accettare...

B. FAMILIAR SALUTATIONS/CLOSINGS

A hug...	Un abbraccio...	un ab-'bračˇ-čˇo
Affectionately...	Afettuosamente...	
Dear John...	Caro Giovanni...	—
Dear Mary...	Cara Maria...	—
Dearest John...	Carissimo Giovanni...	—
Dearest Mary...	Carissima Maria...	—
Give my regards to...	Tanti saluti a ...	'tan-ti sa-'lu-ti a
	Salutami...	sa-'lu-ta-mi
Greetings...	Saluti...	sa-'lu-ti
My dear John...	Mio caro Giovanni...	—
My dear Mary...	Mia cara Maria...	—
Yours...	Tuo (Tua)...	—

C. PARTS OF A LETTER/PUNCTUATION

body	contenuto	kon-te-'nu-to
boldface	grassetto	gras-'set-to
(to) center	centrare	čen-'tra-re
(to) clear, delete	annullare	an-nul-'la-re
closing	chiusa	'kyu-za
(to) copy	copiare	ko-'pya-re
date	data	—
(to) delete	cancellare	kan-čel-'la-re
draft	bozza	'bo-tsa
(to) duplicate	duplicare	du-pli-'ka-re
(to) enclose, attach	accludere*	ak-'klu-de-re
	allegare	al-le-'ga-re
• **enclosed, attached**	accluso	ak-'klu-zo
	allegato	al-le-'ga-to
(to) erase, delete	cancellare	kan-'čel-la-re
footnote	nota a piè di pagina	'no-ta a pye di 'pa-ji-na

Formal Letter

Luogo e data	Roma, 15 settembre 2012
Intestazione	Spettabile Ditta
Contenuto	scrivo per informarvi che ...
Chiusa	Con i più cordiali saluti
Firma	Alessandro De Grandi

Informal Letter

Luogo e data	Roma, 21 settembre 2012
Intestazione	Caro Marco
Contenuto	scrivo per dirti che ...
Chiusa	Un abbraccio
Firma	Sara

heading	intestazione (f)	in-tes-ta-'tsyo-ne
italics	corsivo	kor-'si-vo
place	luogo	'lwo-go
page	pagina	'pa-ji-na
• page set-up	impaginazione (f)	im-pa-ji-na-'tsyo-ne
punctuation	punteggiatura	pun-tej-ja-'tu-ra
• accent	accento	ač-'čen-to
• apostrophe	apostrofo	a-'pos-tro-fo
• asterisk	asterisco	as-te-'ris-ko
• colon	due punti	—
• comma	virgola	'vir-go-la
• dash	trattino	trat-'ti-no
• exclamation mark	punto esclamativo	es-kla-ma-'ti-vo
• lower-case character	carattere minuscolo	ka-'rat-te-re mi-'nus-ko-lo
• parenthesis, bracket	parentesi (f, inv)	pa-'ren-te-zi
• period	punto	—
• question mark	punto interrogativo	in-ter-ro-ga-'ti-vo
• quotation marks	virgolette (f, pl)	vir-go-'let-te

• **semicolon**	punto e virgola	*'pun-to e 'vir-go-la*
• **slash**	sbarra obliqua	*'zbar-ra o-'bli-kwa*
• **upper-case character**	carattere maiuscolo	*ka-'rat-te-re mi-'yus-ko-lo*
salutation	saluto epistolare	*sa-'lu-to e-pis-to-'la-re*
signature	firma	—
• **(to) sign**	firmare	*fir-'ma-re*
style	stile (m)	*'sti-le*
text	testo	*'tes-to*
• **character**	carattere (m)	*ka-'rat-te-re*
• **line**	riga	—
• **margin**	margine (m)	*'mar-ji-ne*
• **paragraph**	capoverso	*ka-po-'ver-so*
• **phrase**	frase (f)	*'fra-ze*
• **spelling**	ortografia	*or-to-gra-'fi-a*
underline	sottolineatura	*sot-to-li-ne-a-'tu-ra*

D. WRITING MATERIALS AND ACCESSORIES

adhesive tape	nastro adesivo	*'nas-tro a-de-'zi-vo*
ballpoint pen	biro (f, inv)	—
business card	biglietto da visita	*bi-'lyet-to da 'vi-zi-ta*
card, record, file	scheda	*'ske-da*
cartridge	cartuccia	*kar-'tuč-ča*
clip	grappetta	—
computer	computer	—
copy	copia	*'ko-pya*
draft	bozza	*'bo-tsa*
envelope	busta	—
eraser	gomma	—
glue	colla	—
highlighter	evidenziatore (m)	*e-vi-den-tsya-'to-re*
ink	inchiostro	*in-'kyos-tro*
invitation (to a wedding,		
baptism, and so on)	partecipazione (f)	*par-te-ci-pa-'tsyo-ne*
label	etichetta	*e-ti-'ket-ta*
letter	lettera	*'let-te-ra*
• **letter opener**	tagliacarte (m, inv)	*ta-lya-'kar-te*
• **letterhead**	carta intestata	*'kar-ta in-tes-'ta-ta*
Liquid Paper, White-out	bianchetto	*byan-'ket-to*
marker	pennarello	*pen-na-'rel-lo*
pad	taccuino	*tak-'kwi-no*
paper	carta	*'kar-ta*
• **official paper**	carta protocollo	*pro-to-'kol-lo*
pen	penna	—
photocopy shop	copisteria	*ko-pis-te-'ri-a*
photocopying machine,		
photocopier	fotocopiatrice (f)	*fo-to-ko-pya-'tri-če*

printer	stampante (f)	*stam-'pan-te*
punch	perforatrice (f)	*per-fo-ra-'tri-če*
ream of paper	risma di carta	*'riz-ma*
ring-binder	quaderno ad anelli	*kwa-'der-no ad a-'nel-li*
rubber band	elastico	*e-'las-ti-ko*
ruler	riga	—
scanner	scanner (m, inv)	—
scissors	forbici (f, pl)	*'for-bi-či*
sheet (of paper)	foglio	*'fo-lyo*
(to) shred	stracciare	*strač-'ča-re*
staple	graffa	*'graf-fa*
• **stapler**	cucitrice (f)	*ku-či-'tri-če*
string	spago	*'spa-go*
tack	puntina	*pun-'ti-na*
two copies	doppia copia	*'dop-pya 'ko-pya*
wastebasket	cestino	*čes-'ti-no*

For computer terminology, see section (f) below and §42b

E. MAILING

abroad	all'estero	*al-'les-te-ro*
address	indirizzo	*in-di-'ri-tso*
• **return address**	indirizzo del mittente	*mit-'ten-te*
airmail	posta aerea	*'pos-ta a-'e-re-a*
(to) attach, enclose	allegare	*al-le-'ga-re*
• **attached, enclosed**	allegato	*al-le-'ga-to*
business letter	lettera commerciale	*'let-te-ra kom-mer-'ča-le*
clerk (postal)	impiegato (-a)	*im-pye-'ga-to*
• **clerk's window**	sportello	*spor-'tel-lo*
confidential	confidenziale	*kon-fi-den-'tsya-le*
correspondence	corrispondenza	*kor-ris-pon-'den-tsa*
• **correspondent**	corrispondente (m/f)	*kor-ris-pon-'den-te*
(to) countersign	controfirmare	*kon-tro-fir-'ma-re*
• **countersignature**	controfirma	*kon-tro-'fir-ma*
courier	corriere (m)	*kor-'rye-re*
envelope	busta	—
express mail	posta celere	*'pos-ta 'če-le-re*
letter carrier	postino (-a)	*pos-'ti-no*
mail	posta	—
• **(to) mail**	spedire (isc)	*spe-'di-re*
mail delivery	distribuzione (f) della posta	*dis-tri-bu-'tsyo-ne*

mail truck	furgone (m) postale	*fur-'go-ne pos-'ta-le*
mail withheld for pick-up	fermo posta	—
mailbox	cassetta postale	*kas-'set-ta pos-'ta-le*
package	pacco	*'pak-ko*
packet	plico	*'pli-ko*
post office	ufficio postale	*uf-'fi-čo pos-'ta-le*
postage	affrancatura	*af-fran-ka-'tu-ra*
postal box	casella postale	*ka-'zel-la pos-'ta-le*
postal card	cartolina postale	*kar-to-'li-na pos-'ta-le*
postal check	assegno postale	*as-'se-nyo pos-'ta-le*
postal code	codice postale	*'ko-di-'če pos-'ta-le*
postal money order	vaglia (m) postale	*'va-lya pos-'ta-le*
postal package	pacco postale	*'pak-ko pos-'ta-le*
postal rate	tariffa postale	*ta-'rif-fa pos-'ta-le*
printed matter	stampe (f, pl)	*'stam-pe*
(to) put into a mailbox	imbucare	*im-bu-'ka-re*
(to) receive	ricevere	*ri-'če-ve-re*
receiver	destinatario	*des-ti-na-'ta-ryo*
registered mail	posta raccomandata	*'pos-ta rak-ko-man-'da-ta*
regular surface mail	posta ordinaria	*'pos-ta or-di-'na-rya*
reply	risposta	*ris-'pos-ta*
• (to) reply	rispondere*	*ris-'pon-de-re*
(to) send	spedire (isc)	*spe-'di-re*
sender	mittente (m/f)	*mit-'ten-te*
stamp	francobollo	*fran-ko-'bol-lo*
telegram	telegramma (m) (telegrammi, pl)	*te-le-'gram-ma*
time between the mailing and reception of mail	giro di posta	*'ji-ro*
(to) wait for	aspettare	*as-pet-'ta-re*
(to) write	scrivere*	*'skri-ve-re*

Envelope Address

> Signor(a) G. Ascoli
> Via Nazionale, 15
> 00135 Roma

F. E-MAIL AND THE INTERNET

| (to) click | cliccare | *klik-'ka-re* |
| comma | virgola | *'vir-go-la* |

cursor	cursore (m)	*kur-'so-re*
diskette	dischetto	*dis-'ket-to*
e-mail	posta elettronica	*'pos-ta e-let-'tro-ni-ka*
	e-mail (m, inv)	—
e-mail address	indirizzo e-mail	*in-di-'ri-tso*
• at (@)	chiocciola	*'kyoč-čo-la*
• dot	punto	—
hard drive	hard drive (inv)	—
hypertext	ipertesto	*i-per-'tes-to*
inputting on the screen	videoscrittura	*vi-de-o-skrit-'tu-ra*
interactive	interattivo	*in-ter-at-'ti-vo*
Internet	internet (m, inv)	—
Internet provider	provider (inv)	—
keyboard	tastiera	*tas-'tye-ra*
laptop computer	laptop (m, inv)	—
memory stick	chiavetta	*kya-'vet-ta*
mouse	mouse (m, inv)	—
(to) navigate	navigare	*na-vi-'ga-re*
peripherals	periferiche (f, pl)	*pe-ri-'fe-ri-ke*
(to) print	stampare	*stam-'pa-re*
• ink-jet printer	stampante a getto	*stam-'pan-te a 'jet-to*
	d'inchiostro	*din-'kyos-tro*
• laser printer	stampante laser	—
• printer	stampante (f)	—
(to) save	salvare	*sal-'va-re*
search	ricerca	*ri-'čer-ka*
server	server (m, inv)	—
space bar	barra spaziatrice	*'bar-ra spa-tsya-'tri-če*
tab	tabulatore (m)	*ta-bu-la-'to-re*
USB stick	chiavetta	*kya-'vet-ta*
user	utente (m/f)	*u-ten-te*
• user-friendly	di facile uso	*di 'fa-či-le 'u-zo*
website	sito (web)	—
word processing	trattamento di testi	*trat-ta-'men-to*

G. DIGITAL COMMUNICATIONS

Facebook	Facebook (m, inv)	—
• profile	profilo	—
mobile device	dispositivo mobile	*'mo-bi-le*
Skype	Skype (m, inv)	—
social media	i media sociali	—
text message	SMS (m, inv)	—
	messaggino	*mes-saj-'ji-no*
Twitter	Twitter (m, inv)	—

20. THE MEDIA

A. PRINT MEDIA

author	autore (-trice)	*au-'to-re*
book	libro	—
(to) cancel a subscription	annullare	*an-nul-'la-re*
	l'abbonamento	*lab-bo-na-'men-to*
(to) censor	censurare	*čen-su-'ra-re*
• **censorship**	censura	*čen-'su-ra*
column	rubrica	*ru-'bri-ka*
• **columnist, reporter**	cronista (m/f)	*kro-'nis-ta*
comic book	rivista a fumetti	*ri-'vis-ta a fu-'met-ti*
communiqué	comunicato stampa	*ko-mu-ni-'ka-to 'stam-pa*
contributor	collaboratore (-trice)	*kol-la-bo-ra-'to-re*
cover, dust jacket	copertina	*ko-per-'ti-na*
crime report	cronaca nera	*'kro-na-ka 'ne-ra*
critic	critico (-a)	*'kri-ti-ko*
crosswords	parole crociate	*pa-'ro-le kro-'ča-te*
daily newspaper	quotidiano	*kwo-ti-'dya-no*
(to) defame, libel	diffamare	*dif-fa-'ma-re*
(to) edit	redigere*	*re-'di-je-re*
• **editor**	redattore (-trice)	*re-dat-'to-re*
• **editorial**	articolo di fondo	*ar-'ti-ko-lo*
• **editorial offices, editing, editorial staff**	redazione (f)	*re-da-'tsyo-ne*
• **editor-in-chief**	caporedattore (-trice)	*ka-po-re-dat-'to-re*
fashion magazine	rivista di moda	*ri-'vis-ta di 'mo-da*
fiction, narrative	narrativa	*nar-ra-'ti-va*
film critic	critico del cinema	*'kri-ti-ko del 'či-ne-ma*
headline	titolo	*'ti-to-lo*
illustrated magazine	rivista illustrata	*ri-'vis-ta il-lus-'tra-ta*
index	indice (m)	*'in-di-če*
interview	intervista	*in-ter-'vis-ta*
journalist	giornalista (m/f)	*jor-na-'lis-ta*
kids' magazine	giornalino	*jor-na-'li-no*
local news	cronaca cittadina	*'kro-na-ka čit-ta-'di-na*
magazine	rivista	*ri-'vis-ta*
main story	titolo principale	*'ti-to-lo prin-či-'pa-le*
national press	stampa nazionale	*'stam-pa na-tsyo-'na-le*
news item, article, report	cronaca	*'kro-na-ka*
newspaper	giornale (m)	*jor-'na-le*
newsroom	sala di redazione	*re-da-'tsyo-ne*
note	nota	—
novel	romanzo	*ro-'man-dzo*
• **adventure**	d'avventura	*dav-ven-'tu-ra*
• **character**	personaggio	*per-so-'naj-jo*

• mystery, detective	giallo	'jal-lo
• plot	trama	—
periodical	periodico	pe-ri-'o-di-ko
play	rappresentazione (f)	rap-pre-zen-ta-'syo-ne
	teatrale	te-a-'tra-le
• comedy	commedia	kom-'me-dya
• drama	dramma	—
• tragedy	tragedia	tra-'je-dya
poem, poetry	poesia	poe-'zi-a
pornographic magazine	rivista pornografica	ri-'vis-ta por-no-'gra-fi-ka
press conference	conferenza stampa	kon-fe-'ren-dza 'stam-pa
press room	sala stampa	'sa-la 'stam-pa
press service, press agency	agenzia di stampa	a-jen-'tsi-a di 'stam-pa
(to) print	stampare	stam-'pa-re
• print (medium)	stampa	'stam-pa
• printing	tipografia	ti-po-gra-'fi-a
print run, circulation	tiratura	ti-ra-'tu-ra
proofs	prove (f, pl)	'pro-ve
(to) publish	pubblicare	pub-bli-'ka-re
• publisher	editore (m)	e-di-'to-re
puzzle section	enigmistica	e-nig-'mis-ti-ka
(to) read	leggere*	'lej-je-re
• readers	lettori (m, pl)	let-'to-ri
• definition	definizione (f)	de-fi-ni-'tsyo-ne
• dictionary	dizionario	di-tsyo-'na-ryo
• encyclopedia	enciclopedia	en-či-klo-pe-'di-a
report, news item, feature	cronaca	'kro-na-ka
report, reporting	servizio	ser-'vi-tsyo
review	recensione (f)	re-čen-'syo-ne
science fiction	fantascienza	fan-ta-'šen-tsa
soap-opera magazine	fotoromanzo	fo-to-ro-'man-dzo
special correspondent	inviato speciale	in-'vya-to spe-'ca-le
sports reporter	cronista sportivo	kro-'nis-ta spor-'ti-vo
(to) subscribe	abbonarsi	ab-bo-'nar-si
• subscription	abbonamento	ab-bo-na-'men-to
teen magazine	rivista per adolescenti	ri-'vis-ta per a-do-le-šen-ti
typographical error	errore tipografico	er-'ro-re ti-po-'gra-fi-ko
women's magazine	rivista femminile	ri-'vis-ta fem-mi-'ni-le

B. ELECTRONIC AND DIGITAL MEDIA

(to) air	mandare in onda	man-'da-re in 'on-da
announcer	annunciatore (-trice)	an-nun-ča-'to-re
antenna	antenna	an-'ten-na
audio receiver, tuner	sintonizzatore (m)	sin-to-ni-dza-'to-re

(to) be on the air	essere* in onda	*'es-se-re in 'on-da*
blog	blog (m, inv)	—
broadcast	trasmissione (f)	*traz-mis-'syo-ne*
• **(to) broadcast**	trasmettere*	*traz-'met-te-re*
• **cable television**	televisione via cavo	*te-le-vi-'zyo-ne*
cameraman	cameraman (m, inv)	—
channel	canale (m)	*ka-'na-le*
children's program	programma per bambini	*pro-'gram-ma per bam-'bi-ni*
closed-circuit television	televisione a circuito chiuso	*te-le-vi-'zyo-ne a čir-'kwi-to 'kyu-zo*
commercial	spot	—
commercial channel	canale commerciale	*ka-na-le kom-mer-ča-le*
compact disc, CD	compact disc CD	—
disc	disco	—
disc jockey	disc jockey	—
DVD	DVD (m, inv)	—
(to) go on the air	andare* in onda	*an-'da-re in 'on-da*
headphones	cuffie (f, pl)	*'kuf-fye*
	auricolari (m, pl)	*au-ri-ko-'la-ri*
high-definition television	televisione ad alta definizione	*te-le-vi-'zyo-ne ad 'al-ta de-fi-ni-'tsyo-ne*
Internet	Internet (m, inv)	—
live broadcast	trasmissione (f) in diretta	*traz-mis-'syo-ne*
live program	programma (m) dal vivo	*pro-'gram-ma dal 'vi-vo*
(to) make a connection	collegare	*kol-le-'ga-re*
microphone	microfono	*mi-'kro-fo-no*
news flash	notizia flash	*no-'ti-tsya*
on the air	in onda	—
optic cable	cavo ottico	*'ka-vo 'ot-ti-ko*
optic fiber	fibra ottica	*'fi-bra 'ot-ti-ka*
poll, rating	sondaggio	*son-'daj-jo*
portable radio	radio portatile	*'ra-dyo por-'ta-ti-le*
private channel	canale privato	*ka-'na-le pri-'va-to*
private television	televisione privata	*te-le-vi-'zyo-ne pri-'va-ta*
program	programma (m) (programmi, pl)	*pro-'gram-ma*
projector	proiettore (m)	*pro-yet-'to-re*
public channel	canale pubblico	*ka-'na-le 'pub-bli-ko*
public television	televisione pubblica	*te-le-vi-'zyo-ne 'pub-bli-ka*
radio	radio (m, inv)	*'ra-dyo*
• **radio broadcasting**	radiodiffusione (f)	*ra-dyo-dif-fu-'zyo-ne*
• **radio frequency**	banda a modulazione di frequenza	*'ban-da a mo-du-la-'tsyo-ne di fre-'kwen-tsa*
• **radio network**	rete radiofonica	*'re-te ra-dyo-'fo-ni-ka*

• radio news	giornale (m) radio	jor-'na-le 'ra-dyo
• radio station	stazione (f) radio	sta-'tsyo-ne 'ra-dyo
• radio wave	onda radiofonica	'on-da ra-dyo-'fo-ni-ka
recorder	registratore (m)	re-jis-tra-'to-re
remote control	telecomando	te-le-ko-'man-do
satellite dish	antenna parabolica	an-'ten-na pa-ra-'bo-li-ka
satellite television	televisione (f) via satellite	te-le-vi-'zyo-ne vi-a sa-'tel-li-te
serial, series	programma (m) a puntate	pro-'gram-ma a pun-'ta-te
short-wave	onde corte	'on-de -'kor-te
show	spettacolo	spet-'ta-ko-lo
speaker	cassa acustica	'kas-sa a-'kus-ti-ka
sports program	programma (m) di sport	pro-'gram-ma
talk show	talk show (m, inv)	—
tape	nastro	'nas-tro
television	televisione (f)	te-le-vi-'zyo-ne
• television broadcasting	telediffusione (f)	te-le-dif-fu-'zyo-ne
• television camera	telecamera	te-le-'ka-me-ra
• television direction booth	cabina di regia	ka-'bi-na di re-'ji-a
• television game show	telequiz (m, inv)	te-le-'kwidz
• television movie	telefilm (m, inv)	te-le-'film
• television network	rete televisiva	're-te te-le-vi-'zi-va
• television news	telegiornale (m)	te-le-jor-'na-le
• television report	telecronaca	te-le-'kro-na-ka
• television reporter	telecronista (m/f)	te-le-kro-'nis-ta
• television studio	studio televisivo	'stu-dyo te-le-vi-'zi-vo
(to) turn off	spegnere*	'spe-nye-re
(to) turn on	accendere*	ač-'čen-de-re
variety program	programma (m) di varietà	pro-'gram-ma di va-rye-'ta
via satellite	via satellite	'vi-a sa-'tel-li-te
video cassette	videocassetta	vi-de-o-kas-'set-ta
videodisc	videodisco	vi-de-o-'dis-ko
viewer	telespettatore (-trice)	te-le-spet-ta-'to-re
weather report	bollettino meteorologico	bol-let-'ti-no me-te-o-ro-'lo-ji-ko
webcast	trasmissione (f) web	—

C. ADVERTISING

advertisement	messaggio pubblicitario	mes-'saj-jo pub-bli-či-'ta-ryo
	réclame (f, inv)	
advertising	pubblicità (f, inv)	pub-bli-či-'ta

advertising agency	agenzia di pubblicità	a-jen-'tsi-a di pub-'bli-či-'ta
advertising break	spot pubblicitario	pub-bli-či-'ta-ryo
advertising campaign	campagna pubblicitaria	kam-'pa-nya pub-bli-či-'ta-rya
advertising sign	insegna pubblicitaria	in-'se-nya pub-bli-či-'ta-rya
brand, logo	marca	'mar-ka
	marchio	'mar-kyo
brochure	opuscolo	o-'pus-ko-lo
caption	leggenda	lej-'jen-da
coupon, voucher	buono	'bwo-no
cut-out coupon	tagliando	ta-'lyan-do
flier	dépliant (m, inv)	—
free	gratis	—
• free sample	campione (m) omaggio	kam-'pyo-ne
jingle	jingle (m, inv)	—
logo	logo	—
poster	cartellone pubblicitario	kar-tel-'lo-ne pub-bli-či-'ta-ryo
radio advertising	pubblicità radiofonica	pub-bli-či-'ta ra-dyo-'fo-ni-ka
sample	campione (m)	kam-'pyo-ne
slogan	slogan (m, inv)	—
sponsor	sponsor (m, inv)	—
• sponsoring	sponsorizzazione (f)	spon-so-ri-dza-'tsyo-ne
television advertising	pubblicità televisiva	pub-bli-či-'ta te-le-vi-'zi-va

21. FEELINGS

A. MOODS, ATTITUDES, EMOTIONS

affection	affetto	af-'fet-to
(to) agree	essere* d'accordo	'es-se-re dak-'kor-do
anger	rabbia	'rab-bya
• angry	arrabbiato	ar-rab-'bya-to
anxiety	ansia	'an-sya
• anxious	ansioso	an-'syo-zo
(to) argue	litigare	li-ti-'ga-re
• argument	lite (f)	'li-te
(to) assure	assicurare	as-si-ku-'ra-re
attitude	atteggiamento	at-tej-ja-'men-to
bad mood	cattivo umore	kat-'ti-vo u-'mo-re
bad-tempered	irascibile	i-ra-'ši-bi-le
bawdy	volgare	vol-'ga-re
(to) be ashamed	vergognarsi	ver-go-'nyar-si
(to) be down	essere* giù	'es-se-re ju

(to) be up	essere* su	—
(to) become bored	annoiarsi	*an-no-'yar-si*
benefactor	benefattore (-trice)	*be-ne-fat-'to-re*
bitter	amaro	*a-'ma-ro*
boastful	vanaglorioso	*va-na-glo-'ryo-zo*
bored	annoiato	*an-no-'ya-to*
• boredom	noia	*'no-'ya*
braggart	spaccone (-a)	*spak-'ko-ne*
captivating	accattivante	*ak-kat-ti-'van-te*
cautious	cauto	*'kau-to*
ceremonious	cerimonioso	*če-ri-mo-'nyo-zo*
charity	carità (f, inv)	*ka-ri-'ta*
cheeky, cocky	sfacciato	*sfač-'ča-to*
(to) complain	lamentarsi	*la-men-'tar-si*
• complaint	lamentela	*la-men-'te-la*
conceited	pieno di sé	*'pye-no*
contact	contatto	*kon-'tat-to*
cordial	cordiale	*kor-'dya-le*
cordiality	cordialità (f, inv)	*kor-dya-li-'ta*
correct, proper	corretto	*kor-'ret-to*
(to) cry	piangere*	*'pyan-je-re*
• crying	pianto	*'pyan-to*
(to) dare	osare	*o-'za-re*
decency	decenza	*de-'čen-tsa*
• decent	decente	*de-'čen-te*
decorum	decoro	*de-'ko-ro*
deferent	deferente	*de-fe-'ren-te*
degenerate	degenerato	*de-je-ne-'ra-to*
depraved	depravato	*de-pra-'va-to*
depressed	depresso	*de-'pres-so*
• depression	depressione (f)	*de-pres-'syo-ne*
desperate	disperato	*dis-pe-'ra-to*
• desperation	disperazione (f)	*dis-pe-ra-'tsyo-ne*
devout	devoto	*de-'vo-to*
direct	diretto	*di-'ret-to*
(to) disappoint	deludere*	*de-'lu-de-re*
• disappointed	deluso	*de-'lu-zo*
(to) disagree	non essere* d'accordo	*non 'es-se-re dak-'kor-do*
• disagreement	disaccordo	*diz-ak-'kor-do*
• (to) be against	essere* contrario	*'es-se-re kon-'tra-ryo*
(to) disgust	disgustare	*diz-gus-'ta-re*
• disgust	disgusto	*diz-'gus-to*
dishonorable	disonorevole	*diz-o-no-'re-vo-le*
dissatisfaction	insoddisfazione (f)	*in-sod-dis-fa-'tsyo-ne*
• dissatisfied	insoddisfatto	*in-sod-dis-'fat-to*
dissolute	dissoluto	*dis-so-'lu-to*
docile	docile	*'do-či-le*

eager	desideroso	*de-zi-de-'ro-zo*
effective	efficace	*ef-fi-'ka-če*
efficient	efficiente	*ef-fi-'čen-te*
egoism	egoismo	*e-go-'iz-mo*
enchanting	incantevole	*in-kan-'te-vo-le*
(to) encourage	incoraggiare	*in-ko-raj-'ja-re*
• **encouraged**	incoraggiato	*in-ko-raj-'ja-to*
(to) enjoy oneself, have fun	divertirsi	*di-ver-'tir-si*
erotic	erotico	*e-'ro-ti-ko*
estimable	stimabile	*sti-'ma-bi-le*
evasive	evasivo	*e-va-'zi-vo*
fanatic	fanatico	*fa-'na-ti-ko*
fear	paura	*pa-'u-ra*
• **(to) fear, be afraid**	avere* paura (di)	—
• **fearful**	pauroso	*pau-'ro-zo*
(to) feel like	avere* voglia di	*a-'ve-re 'vo-lya*
feeling	sensibilità (f, inv)	*sen-si-bi-li-'ta*
fierce	violento	*vyo-'len-to*
	feroce	*fe-'ro-če*
(to) flatter	lusingare	*lu-zin-'ga-re*
• **flattery**	lusinga	*lu-'zin-ga*
frenetic	frenetico	*fre-'ne-ti-ko*
friendship	amicizia	*a-mi-'či-tsya*
fun, enjoyment	divertimento	*di-ver-ti-'men-to*
funny	curioso	*ku-'ryo-zo*
furious	furioso	*fu-'ryo-zo*
generosity	generosità (f, inv)	*je-ne-ro-zi-'ta*
gentility, politeness	gentilezza	*jen-ti-'le-tsa*
good mood	buon umore	*bwon u-'mo-re*
grateful	grato	—
gullible	semplice	*'sem-pli-če*
happiness	felicità (f, inv)	*fe-li-či-'ta*
• **happy**	felice	*fe-'li-če*
	allegro	*al-'le-gro*
hard-headed	cocciuto	*koč-'ču-to*
haughty	altezzoso	*al-te-'tso-zo*
(to) have patience, be patient	avere* pazienza	*a-'ve-re pa-'tsyen-tsa*
hesitant	restio	*res-'ti-o*
honorable	onorevole	*o-no-'re-vo-le*
hope	speranza	*spe-'ran-dza*
• **(to) hope**	sperare	*spe-'ra-re*
humor	umorismo	*u-mo-'riz-mo*
hypocrite	ipocrita (m/f)	*i-'po-kri-ta*
• **hypocritical**	ipocrita	—
idle	ozioso	*o-'tsyo-zo*
immoral	immorale	*im-mo-'ra-le*

indecent	indecente	*in-de-'čen-te*
indifference	indifferenza	*in-dif-fe-'ren-dza*
• **indifferent**	indifferente	*in-dif-fe-'ren-te*
indolent	indolente	*in-do-'len-te*
inferiority	inferiorità (f, inv)	*in-fe-ryo-ri-'ta*
intrepid	intrepido	*in-'tre-pi-do*
ironic	ironico	*i-'ro-ni-ko*
joy	gioia	*'jo-ya*
lascivious	lascivo	*la-'ši-vo*
laudable	lodevole	*lo-'de-vo-le*
(to) laugh	ridere*	*'ri-de-re*
• **laughter**	risata	*ri-'za-ta*
(to) let off steam	sfogarsi	*sfo-'gar-si*
lethargic	letargico	*le-'tar-ji-ko*
level-headed	equilibrato	*e-kwi-li-'bra-to*
lewd	indecente	*in-de-'čen-te*
libidinous	libidinoso	*li-bi-di-'no-zo*
light-hearted	allegro	*al-'le-gro*
litigious	litigioso	*li-ti-'jo-zo*
lusty	lussurioso	*lus-su-'ryo-zo*
magnanimity	magnanimità (f, inv)	*ma-nya-ni'-mi-ta*
• **magnanimous**	magnanimo	*ma-'nya-ni-mo*
malleable	malleabile	*mal-le-'a-bi-le*
maniacal	maniaco	*ma-'ni-a-ko*
mean-minded	meschino	*mes-'ki-no*
mediocre	mediocre	*me-'dyo-kre*
• **mediocrity**	mediocrità (f, inv)	*me-dyo-kri-'ta*
merciful	pietoso	*pye-'to-zo*
merciless	spietato	*spye-'ta-to*
mischievous	malizioso	*ma-li-'tsyo-zo*
mocking, derisive	beffardo	*bef-'far-do*
modest	modesto	*mo-'des-to*
mood	umore (m)	*u-'mo-re*
• **moody**	lunatico	*lu-'na-ti-ko*
moralistic	moralistico	*mo-ra-'lis-ti-ko*
naughty, saucy	spinto	—
noisy	chiassoso	*kyas-'so-zo*
nosy	ficcanaso	*fik-ka-'na-zo*
obedient	ubbidiente	*ub-bi-'dyen-te*
obsequious	ossequioso	*os-se-kwi-'o-zo*
oddball	bizzarro	*bi-'dzar-ro*
passion	passione (f)	*pas-'syo-ne*
patience	pazienza	*pa-'tsyen-tsa*
• **(to) have patience**	avere* pazienza	—
perfidious	perfido	*'per-fi-do*
perverted	pervertito	*per-ver-'ti-to*
philanthropic	filantropico	*fi-lan-'tro-pi-ko*
• **philanthropy**	filantropia	*fi-lan-tro-'pi-a*
playful	giocoso	*jo-'ko-zo*

pleased, happy, content	contento	*kon-'ten-to*
pompous	pomposo	*pom-'po-zo*
(to) praise	elogiare	*e-lo-'ja-re*
presentable	presentabile	*pre-zen-'ta-bi-le*
presumptuous	presuntuoso	*pre-zun-'two-zo*
provocative	provocante	*pro-vo-'kan-te*
quality	qualità (f, inv)	*kwa-li-'ta*
relief	sollievo	*so-'lye-vo*
respectful	rispettoso	*ris-pet-'to-zo*
restless	irrequieto	*ir-re-'kwye-to*
roughness, rudeness	rudezza	*ru-'de-tsa*
sarcastic	sarcastico	*sar-'kas-ti-ko*
sardonic	sardonico	*sar-'do-ni-ko*
satisfaction	soddisfazione (f)	*sod-dis-fa-'tsyo-ne*
• **satisfied**	soddisfatto	*sod-dis-'fat-to*
scheming	intrigante	*in-tri-'gan-te*
scoundrel	scellerato	*šel-le-'ra-to*
scrupulous	scrupoloso	*skru-po-'lo-zo*
sensitive	sensibile	*sen-'si-bi-le*
• **sensitivity**	sensibilità (f, inv)	*sen-si-bi-li-'ta*
sensuous, sensual	sensuale	*sen-'swa-le*
servile	servizievole	*ser-vi-'tsye-vo-le*
sexy	sexy	—
shame	vergogna	*ver-'go-nya*
• **shameful**	vergognoso	*ver-go-'nyo-zo*
• **shameless**	svergognato	*zver-go-'nya-to*
silly	sciocco	*'šok-ko*
sincere	sincero	*sin-'če-ro*
slouch	fannullone (-a)	*fan-nul-'lo-ne*
(to) smile	sorridere*	*sor-'ri-de-re*
• **smile**	sorriso	*sor-'ri-zo*
smug	compiaciuto	*kom-pya-'cu-to*
sober	sobrio	*'so-bryo*
sociable	socievole	*so-'če-vo-le*
sorrow	dolore (m)	*do-'lo-re*
spendthrift	spilorcio	*spi-'lor-čo*
spontaneity	spontaneità (f, inv)	*spon-ta-nei-'ta*
• **spontaneous**	spontaneo	*spon-'ta-ne-o*
steadfast	costante	*kos-'tan-te*
strict	severo	*se-'ve-ro*
strong desire	voglia	*'vo-lya*
sulky	scontroso	*skon-'tro-zo*
sullen	tetro	*te-'tro*
sure, certain	sicuro	*si-'ku-ro*
(to) surprise	sorprendere*	*sor-'pren-de-re*
• **surprise**	sorpresa	*sor-'pre-za*
• **surprised**	sorpreso	*sor-'pre-zo*
sympathetic	comprensivo	*kom-pren-'si-vo*
• **sympathy**	comprensione (f)	*kom-pren-'syo-ne*

tenacious	tenace	*te-'na-če*
tenderness	tenerezza	*te-ne-'re-tsa*
thankfulness	gratitudine (f)	*gra-ti-'tu-di-ne*
tolerance	tolleranza	*tol-le-'ran-tsa*
• **tolerant**	tollerante	*tol-le-'ran-te*
touchy, over-sensitive	permaloso	*per-ma-'lo-zo*
troublemaker	attaccabrighe (m/f, inv)	*at-tak-ka-'bri-ge*
(to) trust	fidarsi (di)	*fi-'dar-si*
• **trust, faith**	fiducia	*fi-du-ča*
unbearable	insopportabile	*in-sop-por-'ta-bi-le*
unfaithful	infedele	*in-fe-'de-le*
unflustered	pacato	*pa-'ka-to*
ungrateful	ingrato	*in-'gra-to*
unscrupulous	senza scrupoli	*'sen-tsa 'skru-po-li*
upset, angry	adirato	*a-di-'ra-to*
vagabond	vagabondo	*va-ga-'bon-do*
vileness, baseness	viltà (f, inv)	*vil-'ta*
volatile	mutevole	*mu-'te-vo-le*
voracious	vorace	*vo-'ra-če*
vulgar	volgare	*vol-'ga-re*
• **vulgarity**	volgarità (f, inv)	*vol-ga-ri-'ta*
well-disciplined	disciplinato	*di-ši-pli-'na-to*
whimsical	estroso	*es-'tro-zo*
worried	preoccupato	*pre-ok-ku-'pa-to*
worthy	meritorio	*me-ri-'to-ryo*

Colloquial Expressions (Familiar)

Come off it!	Ma va!
Come on!	Su! Dai!
Cut it out!	Piantala!
Damn it!	Accidenti!
Get lost!	Vattene!
Go to the Devil!	Va' al diavolo!
No way!	Macché!
Yuch!	Che schifo!

B. LIKES AND DISLIKES

(to) accept	accettare	*ač-čet-'ta-re*
• **acceptable**	accettabile	*ač-čet-'ta-bi-le*
• **unacceptable**	inaccettabile	*in-ač-čet-'ta-bi-le*
approval	approvazione (f)	*ap-pro-va-'tsyo-ne*
• **(to) approve**	approvare	*ap-pro-'va-re*
(to) be fond of (something)	essere* appassionato di	*'es-se-re ap-pas-syo-'na-to*

(to) detest	detestare	de-tes-'ta-re
disgust	disgusto	diz-'gus-to
• disgusted	disgustato	diz-gus-'ta-to
dislike	antipatia	an-ti-pa-'ti-a
• (to) dislike	non piacere* (ess)	non pya-'ce-re
hatred	odio	'o-dyo
• (to) hate	odiare	o-'dya-re
I can't stand...	Non sopporto...	—
kiss	bacio	'ba-čo
• (to) kiss	baciare	ba-'ča-re
(to) like	piacere* (ess) a	pya-'če-re
• liking	simpatia	sim-pa-'ti-a
love	amore (m)	a-'mo-re
• (to) love	amare	a-'ma-re
mediocre	mediocre	me-'dyo-kre
pleasant	piacevole	pya-'če-vo-le
• unpleasant	spiacevole	spya-'če-vo-le
(to) prefer	preferire (isc)	pre-fe-'ri-re

Tip on Using the Verb Piacere

When saying that you like something, translate the English expression into your mind as "to be pleasing to" and then follow the word order in the formula below.

EXPRESSION	TRANSLATE MENTALLY TO ...	ITALIAN EXPRESSION
I like that book	"To me is pleasing that book"	*Mi piace quel libro*
We like those books	"To us are pleasing those books"	*Ci piacciono quei libri*

C. EXPRESSIONS

Are you joking?	Scherzi? (fam)	'sker-tsi
	Scherza? (pol)	—
Be careful!	Attento (-a)!	at-'ten-to
Enough!	Basta!	—
Fortunately!	Per fortuna!	—
I don't believe it!	Non ci credo!	či 'kre-do
I don't feel like...	Non mi va di...	—
	Non ho voglia di...	'vo-lya
	Non mi sento di...	—

I wish!	Magari!	ma-'ga-ri
I'm serious!	Dico sul serio!	'di-ko sul 'se-ryo
I'm sorry!	Mi dispiace!	mi dis-'pya-če
Impossible!	Impossibile!	im-pos-'si-bi-le
It doesn't matter!	Non importa!	im-'por-ta
Oh my!	Mamma mia!	—
Poor man!	Poveretto!	po-ve-'ret-to
Poor woman!	Poveretta!	po-ve-'ret-ta
Quiet!	Silenzio!	si-'len-tsyo
Really?	Davvero?	dav-'ve-ro
Shut up!	Zitto (-a)!	'dzit-to
Thank goodness!	Meno male!	'me-no 'ma-le
Too bad!	Peccato!	pek-'ka-to
Ugh!	Uffa!	—
Unbelievable!	Incredibile!	in-kre-'di-bi-le
Unfortunately!	Purtroppo!	pur-'trop-po
What a bore!	Che barba!	ke 'bar-ba
	Che noia!	ke 'no-ya

22. THOUGHT

A. THE MIND

belief	credenza	kre-'den-tsa
complicated	complicato	kom-pli-'ka-to
concept	concetto	kon-'čet-to
concrete	concreto	kon-'kre-to
conscience	coscienza	ko-šen-dza
• conscientious	coscienzioso	ko-šen-'tsyo-zo
creative	creativo	kre-a-'ti-vo
• creativity	creatività (f, inv)	kre-a-ti-vi-'ta
difficult	difficile	di-'fi-či-le
doubt	dubbio	'dub-byo
• doubtful	dubbioso	dub-'byo-zo
dream	sogno	'so-nyo
easy	facile	'fa-či-le
existence	esistenza	ez-is-'ten-dza
forgetful	smemorato	zme-mo-'ra-to
hypothesis	ipotesi (f, inv)	i-'po-te-zi
idea	idea	i-'de-a
ignorance	ignoranza	i-nyo-'ran-tsa
• ignorant	ignorante	i-nyo-'ran-te
imagination, fantasy	immaginazione (f)	im-ma-ji-na-'tsyo-ne
	fantasia	fan-ta-'zi-a
ingenious	ingegnoso	in-je-'nyo-zo
• ingenuity	ingegno	in-'je-nyo
intelligence	intelligenza	in-tel-li-'jen-tsa
• intelligent	intelligente	in-tel-li-'jen-te

interest	interesse (m)	*in-te-'res-se*
• interesting	interessante	*in-te-res-'san-te*
judgment, wisdom	giudizio	*ju-'di-tsyo*
knowledge	conoscenza	*ko-no-šen-tsa*
• knowledgeable	ben informato	*ben in-for-'ma-to*
logic	logica	*'lo-ji-ka*
memory	memoria	*me-'mo-rya*
mind	mente (f)	*'men-te*
opinion	opinione (f)	*o-pi-'nyo-ne*
problem	problema (m)	*pro-'ble-ma*
	(problemi, pl)	
reason	ragione (f)	*ra-'jo-ne*
reflection	riflessione (f)	*ri-fles-'syo-ne*
sensible	sensato	*sen-'sa-to*
simple	semplice	*'sem-pli-če*
thought	pensiero	*pen-'sye-ro*
wisdom	sapienza	*sa-'pyen-dza*
wrongfulness	torto	—

B. THINKING

(to) be interested in	interessarsi di	*in-te-res-'sar-si*
(to) be right	avere* ragione	*a-'ve-re ra-'jo-ne*
(to) be wrong	avere* torto	*'tor-to*
(to) believe	credere	*'kre-de-re*
(to) conceive	concepire (isc)	*kon-če-'pi-re*
(to) convince	convincere*	*kon-'vin-če-re*
(to) demonstrate	dimostrare	*di-mos-'tra-re*
(to) dissuade	dissuadere*	*dis-swa-'de-re*
(to) doubt	dubitare	*du-bi-'ta-re*
(to) dream	sognare	*so-'nya-re*
(to) exist	esistere (ess)	*e-'zis-te-re*
(to) forget	dimenticare	*di-men-ti-'ka-re*
(to) imagine	immaginare	*im-ma-ji-'na-re*
(to) judge	giudicare	*ju-di-'ka-re*
(to) know	sapere*	*sa-'pe-re*
	conoscere*	*ko-'no-še-re*
(to) learn	imparare	*im-pa-'ra-re*
(to) memorize	memorizzare	*me-mo-ri-'dza-re*
(to) persuade	persuadere*	*per-swa-'de-re*
(to) reason	ragionare	*ra-jo-'na-re*
(to) reflect	riflettere	*ri-'flet-te-re*
(to) remember	ricordare	*ri-kor-'da-re*
(to) solve a problem	risolvere* un problema	*ri-'zol-ve-re un pro-'ble-ma*
(to) study	studiare	*stu-'dya-re*
(to) think	pensare	*pen-'sa-re*
(to) understand	capire (isc)	*ka-'pi-re*

DAILY LIFE

23. AT HOME

A. ROOMS, PARTS OF THE HOUSE, AND TYPES OF HOUSES

arch, archway	arco	'ar-ko
	arcata	ar-'ka-ta
attic	attico	'at-ti-ko
balcony	balcone (m)	bal-'ko-ne
banister	balaustra	ba-la-'us-tra
basement	scantinato	skan-ti-'na-to
bathroom	bagno	'ba-nyo
bathtub	vasca	'vas-ka
bedroom	camera (da letto)	'ka-me-ra
blind	avvolgibile (m)	av-vol-'ji-bi-le
burglar alarm	allarme (m) antifurto	al-'lar-me an-ti-'fur-to
ceiling	soffitto	sof-'fit-to
chimney	camino	ka-'mi-no
clothes closet	guardaroba (m, inv)	gwar-da-'ro-ba
clothes rack	attaccapanni (m, inv)	at-tak-ka-'pan-ni
corridor	corridoio	kor-ri-'do-yo
dining room	sala da pranzo	'pran-dzo
door	porta	'por-ta
• **doorbell**	campanello	kam-pa-'nel-lo
• **door knob**	maniglia	ma-'ni-lya
• **hinge**	cardine (m)	'kar-di-ne
• **jamb**	stipite (m)	'sti-pi-te
estate, villa, large home	villa	—
façade	facciata	fač-'ča-ta
fan	ventilatore (m)	ven-ti-la-'to-re
faucet	rubinetto	ru-bi-'net-to
fixture, installation	impianto	im-'pyan-to
floor	pavimento	pa-vi-'men-to
• **floor tile**	piastrella	pyas-'trel-la
forecourt	cortile (m)	kor-'ti-le
foundations	fondamenta (f, pl)	fon-da-'men-ta
garage	garage (m, inv)	—
garden	giardino	jar-'di-no
gutter	grondaia	gron-'da-ya
handle	manico	'ma-ni-ko
handrail	ringhiera	rin-'gye-ra

English	Italian	Pronunciation
house	casa	'ka-za
• dwelling	abitazione (f)	a-bi-ta-'tsyo-ne
hut, beach house	capanno	ka-'pan-no
kitchen	cucina	ku-'či-na
landing	pianerottolo	pya-ne-'rot-to-lo
living room	salotto	sa-'lot-to
	soggiorno	soj-'jor-no
loft	soffitta	sof-'fit-ta
mailbox	cassetta delle lettere	kas-'set-ta del-le 'let-te-re
medicine chest	armadietto dei medicinali	ar-'ma-dyet-to dei me-di-či-na-li
mirror	specchio	'spek-kyo
paneling	pannello	pan-'nel-lo
pantry	dispensa	dis-'pen-sa
partition, wall	parete (f)	pa-'re-te
patio	terrazza	ter-'ra-tsa
porch	veranda	ve-'ran-da
prefab	casa prefabbricata	'ka-za pre-fab-bri-'ka-ta
property	proprietà (f, inv)	pro-prye-'ta
roof	tetto	—
room	stanza	'stan-dza
shingle	tegola	'te-go-la
shower	doccia	'doč-ča
shutter, blind	persiana	per-'sya-na
• shutter, leaf	battente (m)	bat-'ten-te
sink	lavandino	la-van-'di-no
sliding door	porta scorrevole	'por-ta skor-'re-vo-le
small villa, cottage home	villino	vil-'li-no
spy-hole	spioncino	spi-on-'či-no
stained-glass window	vetrata dipinta	ve-'tra-ta di-'pin-ta
stairs	scala	'ska-la
• step	gradino	gra-'di-no
storage space	deposito	de-'po-zi-to
switch (light)	interruttore (m)	in-ter-rut-'to-re
terrace	terrazza	ter-'ra-tsa
toilet	bagno	'ba-nyo
• toilet (bowl)	gabinetto	ga-bi-'net-to
towel rack	portasciugamani (m, inv)	por-ta-šu-ga-'ma-ni
veranda	veranda	ve-'ran-da
wall	muro (mura, f, pl)	—
washbasin	lavabo	la-'va-bo
window	finestra	fi-'nes-tra
• window ledge, sill	davanzale (m)	da-van-'tsa-le
• window frame	telaio	te-'la-yo
wine cellar	cantina	kan-'ti-na

B. FURNITURE, DECORATION, APPLIANCES, AND COMMON HOUSEHOLD ITEMS

armchair	poltrona	*pol-'tro-na*
bag	sacco	*'sak-ko*
basket	cesta	*'čes-ta*
bathroom scale	pesapersone (m, inv)	*pe-za-per-'so-ne*
bed	letto	*'let-to*
• bedsheet (sheets)	lenzuolo (lenzuola, f, pl)	*len-'tswo-lo*
• bedding	biancheria da letto	*byan-ke-'ri-a da 'let-to*
• bedside table	comodino	*ko-mo-'di-no*
• bedspread	copriletto	*ko-pri-'let-to*
• blanket	coperta	*ko-'per-ta*
bookcase	libreria	*li-bre-'ri-a*
• bookshelf	scaffale (m)	*skaf-'fa-le*
box, tin	scatola	*'ska-to-la*
broom	scopa	*'sko-pa*
brush	spazzola	*'spa-tso-la*
cabinet	armadietto	*ar-ma-'dyet-to*
cart, movable tray	carrello	*kar-'rel-lo*
chair	sedia	*'se-dya*
cleaning cloth	straccio	*'strač-čo*
clothes dryer	asciugatrice (f)	*a-šu-ga-'tri-če*
clothes hanger	attaccapanni (m, inv)	*at-tak-ka-'pan-ni*
cooker, stove	cucina	*ku-'či-na*
cover, covering	fodera	*'fo-de-ra*
cupboard	armadio	*ar-'ma-dyo*
curtain	tenda	—
cushion	cuscino	*ku-'ši-no*
decor, decoration	arredamento	*ar-re-da-'men-to*
dish cloth	strofinaccio per i piatti	*stro-fi-'nač-čo*
dishwasher	lavastoviglie (m/f, inv)	*la-va-sto-'vi-lye*
doormat	stuoia d'entrata	*'stwo-ya den-'tra-ta*
drawer	cassetto	*kas-'set-to*
dresser, sideboard	credenza	*kre-'den-dza*
dressing table	toilette (f, inv)	—
dust pan	paletta per la spazzatura	*pa-'let-ta per la spa-tsa-'tu-ra*
dustbin	pattumiera	*pat-tu-'mye-ra*
duster	piumino	*pyu-'mi-no*
extension cord	filo di prolungamento	*'fi-lo di pro-lun-ga-'men-to*
fitted carpet	moquette (f, inv)	—
folding chair	sedia pieghevole	*'se-dya pye-'ge-vo-le*
freezer	congelatore (m)	*kon-je-la-'to-re*
funnel	imbuto	*im-'bu-to*
furniture	mobili (m, pl)	*'mo-bi-li*
garbage bin	cestino dei rifiuti	*čes-'ti-no dei ri-'fyu-ti*

glass cabinet	vetrina	*ve-'tri-na*
heater	termosifone (m)	*ter-mo-si-'fo-ne*
high chair	seggiolone (m)	*sej-jo-'lo-ne*
hook	gancio	*'gan-čo*
household soap	sapone (m) di Marsiglia	*sa-'po-ne di mar-'si-lya*
ironing board	tavola da stiro	*'ta-vo-la da 'sti-ro*
kitchen scales	bilancia	*bi-'lan-ča*
kitchen shelf	mensola	*'men-so-la*
lamp	lampada	*'lam-pa-da*
large garbage can	bidone (m)	*bi-'do-ne*
laundry	biancheria	*byan-ke-'ri-a*
• laundry basket	cesta del bucato	*čes-ta del bu-'ka-to*
mattress	materasso	*ma-te-'ras-so*
microwave oven	forno a microonde	*'for-no a mi-kro-'on-de*
mop	scopa a stracci	*'sko-pa a 'strač-či*
oven	forno	—
piece of furniture	mobile (m)	*'mo-bi-le*
pillow	cuscino	*ku-'ši-no*
• pillowcase	federa	*'fe-de-ra*
quilt	trapunta	*tra-'pun-ta*
recliner	sedia a sdraio	*'se-dya a 'zdra-yo*
refrigerator	frigorifero	*fri-go-'ri-fe-ro*
rocking chair	sedia a dondolo	*'se-dya a 'don-do-lo*
rug	tappeto	*tap-'pe-to*
sewing machine	macchina per cucire	*'mak-ki-na per ku-'či-re*
shelf	ripiano	*ri-'pya-no*
shopping bag	sacchetto della spesa	*sak-'ket-to del-la 'spe-za*
soap-dish	portasapone (m, inv)	*por-ta-sa-'po-ne*
sofa, divan	divano	*di-'va-no*
steam iron	ferro da stiro	*'fer-ro da 'sti-ro*
stool	sgabello	*zga-'bel-lo*
stove (kitchen)	cucina	*ku-'či-na*
• stove element	fornello	*for-'nel-lo*
stove (heating)	stufa	*'stu-fa*
table lamp	lampada da tavolo	*'lam-pa-da da 'ta-vo-lo*
toilet paper	carta igienica	*'kar-ta i-'je-ni-ka*
towel	asciugamano	*a-šu-ga-'ma-no*
upholstery	tappezzeria	*tap-pe-tse-'ri-a*
vacuum cleaner	aspirapolvere (m, inv)	*as-pi-ra-'pol-ve-re*
wall painting	quadro	*'kwa-dro*
washing machine	lavatrice (f)	*la-va-'tri-če*
water-heater	riscaldatore (m) dell'acqua	*ris-kal-da-'to-re del-'lak-kwa*
wax	cera	*'če-ra*
writing desk	scrivania	*skri-va-'ni-a*

C. KITCHENWARE AND MEALTIME OBJECTS

baby bottle	biberon (m, inv)	bi-be-'ron
beaker, tumbler	coppa	'kop-pa
blade	lama	—
blender	frullatore	frul-la-'to-re
bottle	bottiglia	bot-'ti-lya
• bottled	imbottigliato	im-bot-ti-'lya-to
• bottle opener	cavatappi (m, inv)	ka-va-'tap-pi
bowl	scodella	sko-'del-la
bread basket	cesta del pane	'čes-ta del 'pa-ne
bread knife	coltello da pane	kol-'tel-lo da 'pa-ne
carafe, decanter	caraffa	ka-'raf-fa
casserole	casseruola	kas-se-'rwo-la
chopping (butcher's) knife	coltello da macellaio	kol-'tel-lo da ma-čel-'la-yo
chopping board	tagliere (m)	ta-'lye-re
coffee pot	bricco del caffè	'brik-ko del kaf-'fe
colander	colino	ko-'li-no
cooking pot	pentola	'pen-to-la
cork cap	tappo di sughero	'tap-po di 'su-ge-ro
cup	tazza	'ta-tsa
cutlery	posate (f, pl)	po-'za-te
dessert dish	coppa da dessert	'kop-pa
dessert fork	forchettina	for-ket-'ti-na
dish	piatto	'pyat-to
drinking can	lattina	lat-'ti-na
drinking glass	bicchiere (m)	bik-'kye-re
egg-beater	frullino	frul-'li-no
fork	forchetta	for-'ket-ta
fruit bowl	fruttiera	frut-'tye-ra
frying pan	padella	pa-'del-la
grater	grattugia	grat-'tu-ja
jug	brocca	'brok-ka
kettle	pentolino	pen-to-'li-no
knife	coltello	kol-'tel-lo
ladle	mestolo	'mes-to-lo
masher	pestello	pes-'tel-lo
milk jug	brocca del latte	'brok-ka del 'lat-te
mincer	tritacarne (m)	tri-ta-'kar-ne
mortar	mortaio	mor-'ta-yo
mug	boccale (m)	bok-'ka-le
napkin	tovagliolo	to-va-'lyo-lo
nutcracker	schiaccianoci (m, inv)	skyač-ča-'no-či
pan	padella	pa-'del-la
pepper container	pepiera	pe-'pye-ra
plate-rack	scolapiatti (m, inv)	sko-la-'pyat-ti

pot	pentola	'pen-to-la
	casseruola	kas-se-'rwo-la
	tegame (m)	te-'ga-me
potato masher	schiacciapatate (m, inv)	skyač-ča-pa-'ta-te
potato peeler	pelapatate (m, inv)	pe-la-pa-'ta-te
pressure cooker, steamer	pentola a pressione	'pen-to-la a pres-'syo-ne
salad bowl	insalatiera	in-sa-la-'tye-ra
salt container	saliera	sa-'lye-ra
saucepan	casseruola	kas-se-'rwo-la
saucer	piattino	pyat-'ti-no
spoon	cucchiaio	kuk-'kya-yo
sugar bowl	zuccheriera	dzuk-ke-'rye-ra
tablecloth	tovaglia	to-'va-lya
teacup	tazzina	tat-'tsi-na
teapot	teiera	te-'ye-ra
teaspoon	cucchiaino	kuk-kya-'yi-no
tinfoil	stagnola	sta-'nyo-la
tray, trolley	vassoio	vas-'so-yo
utensil	utensile (m)	u-ten-'si-le
vase	vaso	'va-zo
water glass	bicchiere da acqua	bik-'kye-re da 'ak-kwa
wine glass	bicchiere da vino	bik-'kye-re da 'vi-no
wooden spoon	cucchiaio di legno	kuk-'kya-yo di 'le-nyo

D. SERVICES, TOOLS, AND MAINTENANCE

air conditioning	aria condizionata	'a-rya kon-di-tsyo-'na-ta
adapter	adattatore (m)	a-dat-ta-'to-re
(to) blow a fuse	fare* saltare una valvola	'val-vo-la
bolt	bullone (m)	bul-'lo-ne
• (to) bolt down	bullonare	bul-lo-'na-re
chisel	cesello	če-'zel-lo
clamp	morsetto	mor-'set-to
drill	trapano	'tra-pa-no
electric outlet	presa (elettrica)	'pre-za
electricity	elettricità (f, inv)	e-let-tri-či-'ta
file	lima	'li-ma
flashlight, battery	pila	'pi-la
(to) furnish one's home	ammobiliare la casa	am-mo-bi-'lya-re la 'ka-za
fuse	valvola	'val-vo-la
gas	gas (m, inv)	—
gloss paint, varnish	lacca	'lak-ka
hammer	martello	mar-'tel-lo
hardware	ferramenta (f, pl)	fer-ra-'men-ta
heating	riscaldamento	ris-kal-da-'men-to

insulation	isolante (m)	*i-zo-'lan-te*
light bulb	lampadina	*lam-pa-'di-na*
light, power	luce (f)	*'lu-če*
mallet	mazza	*'ma-tsa*
masking tape	nastro isolante	*'nas-tro i-zo-'lan-te*
nail	chiodo	*'kyo-do*
• (to) nail	inchiodare	*in-kyo-'da-re*
paint	vernice (f)	*ver-'ni-če*
• (to) paint	imbiancare	*im-byan-'ka-re*
• paint brush	pennello	*pen-'nel-lo*
• wet paint	vernice fresca	*ver-'ni-če 'fres-ka*
plane	pialla	*'pyal-la*
pliers, tongs, tweezers	pinze (f, pl)	*'pin-tse*
plug	spina	*'spi-na*
plumbing	sistema idraulico	*sis-'te-ma i-'drau-li-ko*
roller	rullo	*'rul-lo*
sandpaper	carta vetrata	*'kar-ta ve-'tra-ta*
saw	sega	*'se-ga*
screw	vite (f)	*'vi-te*
• (to) screw	avvitare	*av-vi-'ta-re*
• screwdriver	cacciavite (m, inv)	*kač-ča-'vi-te*
• (to) unscrew	svitare	*zvi-'ta-re*
stove air vent	cappa	*'kap-pa*
tool	attrezzo	*at-'tre-tso*
wallpaper	carta da parati	*'kar-ta da pa-'ra-ti*
wire	filo	*'fi-lo*
• wiring	impianto elettrico	*im-'pyan-to e-'let-tri-ko*
wrench	chiave (f) inglese	*'kya-ve in-'gle-ze*

E. APARTMENTS

apartment	appartamento	*ap-par-ta-'men-to*
• apartment building	palazzo (di appartamenti)	*pa-'lat-tso*
building	edificio	*e-di-'fi-čo*
condominium	condominio	*kon-do-'mi-nyo*
elevator	ascensore (m)	*a-šen-'so-re*
entrance	ingresso	*in-'gres-so*
eviction	sfratto	*'sfrat-to*
exit	uscita	*u-'ši-ta*
• emergency exit	uscita di sicurezza	*si-ku-'re-tsa*
flight of stairs	rampa	*'ram-pa*
floor level	piano	*'pya-no*
ground floor	pianterreno	*pyan-ter-'re-no*
intercom	citofono	*či-'to-fo-no*
lease	contratto d'affitto	*kon-'trat-to daf-'fit-to*
lodger, renter, tenant	affittuario (-a)	*af-fit-'twa-ryo*
main door of a building	portone (m)	*por-'to-ne*
remodeling, renovation	rimodernamento	*ri-mo-der-na-'men-to*

rent	affitto	*af-'fit-to*
• overdue rental	morosità (f, inv)	*mo-ro-zi-'ta*
• (to) rent	affittare	*af-fit-'ta-re*
repair	riparazione	*ri-pa-ra'-zyo-ne*
staircase, stairwell	scale (f, pl)	*'ska-le*
tenant	inquilino (-a)	*in-kwi-'li-no*
waste-disposal	eliminazione (f) dei rifiuti	*e-li-mi-na-'tsyo-ne*

F. MISCELLANEOUS VOCABULARY

at home	a casa	*a 'ka-za*
(to) build	costruire (isc)	*kos-tru-'i-re*
(to) buy	comprare	*kom-'pra-re*
(to) clean	pulire (isc)	*pu-'li-re*
(to) clear the table	sparecchiare	*spa-rek-'kya-re*
(to) flush	tirare lo sciacquone	*šyak'-kwo-ne*
(to) house	alloggiare	*al-loj-'ja-re*
(to) live in	abitare	*a-bi-'ta-re*
householder, house owner	proprietario (-a)	*pro-prye-'ta-ryo*
(to) iron	stirare	*sti-'ra-re*
key	chiave (f)	*'kya-ve*
(to) move	traslocare	*traz-lo-'ka-re*
• moving (residence)	trasloco	*traz-'lo-ko*
nanny, housekeeper	governante (f)	*go-ver-'nan-te*
occupant, householder	residente (m/f)	*re-zi-'den-te*
(to) sell	vendere	*'ven-de-re*
(to) set the table	apparecchiare	*ap-pa-rek-'kya-re*
(to) wash	lavare	*la-'va-re*
• (to) wash dishes	lavare i piatti	*'pyat-ti*

24. EATING AND DRINKING

A. MEALS, EATING, PREPARATIONS, AND MENUS

appetizer	antipasto	*an-ti-'pas-to*
baked	al forno	*al 'for-no*
banquet	banchetto	*ban-'ket-to*
bitter, sour	amaro	*a-'ma-ro*
(to) boil	bollire	*bol-'li-re*
breakfast	prima colazione	*ko-la-'tsyo-ne*
• (to) have breakfast	fare* colazione	—
breast (chicken, turkey, etc.)	petto	—
broiled	arrostito	*ar-ros-'ti-to*
chop, cutlet	cotoletta	*ko-to-'let-ta*
(to) cook	cucinare	*ku-či-'na-re*

course, dish	piatto	'pyat-to
• first course	primo piatto	—
• second course	secondo piatto	—
cuisine	cucina	ku-'či-na
(to) cut	tagliare	ta-'lya-re
dinner	cena	'če-na
• (to) have dinner	cenare	če-'na-re
filet	filetto	fi-'let-to
food	cibo	'či-bo
French fries	patatine fritte	pa-ta-'ti-ne 'frit-te
fried	fritto	'frit-to
• (to) fry	friggere*	'frij-je-re
grilled	alla griglia	al-la 'gri-lya
juicy	succoso	suk-'ko-zo
leg (chicken, turkey, etc.)	coscia	'ko-ša
lunch	pranzo	'pran-dzo
• (to) have lunch	pranzare	pran-'dza-re
meal	pasto	'pas-to
menu	menù (m, inv)	me-'nu
mild	tiepido	'tye-pi-do
mixed salad	insalata mista	in-sa-'la-ta 'mis-ta
(to) peel	sbucciare	sbuč-'ča-re
platter	piatto misto	'pyat-to 'mis-to
• portion, helping	porzione (f)	por-'tsyo-ne
(to) pour	versare	ver-'sa-re
rare (meat)	al sangue	al 'san-gwe
ripe	maturo	ma-'tu-ro
roast	arrosto	ar-'ros-to
rotten	marcio	'mar-čo
salad	insalata	in-sa-'la-ta
salty	salato	sa-'la-to
side dish	contorno	kon-'tor-no
skin	pelle (f)	'pel-le
(to) slice	affettare	af-fet-'ta-re
snack	spuntino	spun-'ti-no
• (to) have a snack	fare* uno spuntino	—
sour	amaro	a-'ma-ro
spicy, hot	piccante	pik-'kan-te
steak	bistecca	bis-'tek-ka
(to) stir, mix	girare	ji-'ra-re
(to) stuff	farcire (isc)	far-'či-re
sweet	dolce	'dol-če
tasty	gustoso	gus-'to-zo
well-done	ben cotto	ben 'kot-to
with sauce	al sugo	al 'su-go

B. PASTAS, SOUPS, AND RICE

broth	brodo	*'bro-do*
cannelloni	cannelloni (m, pl)	*kan-nel-'lo-ni*
dumplings	gnocchi (m, pl)	*'nyok-ki*
fettuccine	fettuccine (f, pl)	*fet-tuč-'či-ne*
lasagna	lasagne (f, pl)	*la-'za-nye*
macaroni	maccheroni (m, pl)	*mak-ke-'ro-ni*
minestrone soup	minestrone (m)	*mi-nes-'tro-ne*
pasta	pasta	—
ravioli	ravioli (m, pl)	—
rice	riso	*'ri-zo*
rice with vegetables	risotto	*ri-'zot-to*
sauce	sugo	*'su-go*
	salsa	*'sal-sa*
soup	minestra	*mi-'nes-tra*
soup (thick)	zuppa	*'dzup-pa*
spaghetti	spaghetti (m, pl)	—

C. BREAD, GRAINS, PASTRIES, AND SWEETS

barley	orzo	*'or-dzo*
biscuit, cookie	biscotto	*bis-'kot-to*
bread	pane (m)	*'pa-ne*
breadstick	grissino	*gris-'si-no*
cake, pie	torta	*'tor-ta*
candy	caramella	*ka-ra-'mel-la*
chocolate candy	cioccolatino	*čok-ko-la-'ti-no*
corn	granturco	*gran-'tur-ko*
	mais (m, inv)	—
cracker	cracker (m, inv)	—
dessert	dessert (m, inv)	—
	dolce	*'dol-če*
flour	farina	*fa-'ri-na*
grain	grano	*'gra-no*
honey	miele (m)	*'mye-le*
marmalade, jam	marmellata	*mar-mel-'la-ta*
oat	avena	*a-'ve-na*
pudding	budino	*bu-'di-no*
sandwich (bun)	panino	*pa-'ni-no*
sandwich (flat)	tramezzino	*tra-me-'dzi-no*
whole-wheat bread	pane integrale	*'pa-ne in-te-'gra-le*

D. MEAT AND POULTRY

bacon	pancetta	*pan-'čet-ta*
beef	manzo	*'man-dzo*
chicken	pollo	*'pol-lo*

cold cuts	affettati (m, pl)	*af-fet-'ta-ti*
duck	anatra	*'a-na-tra*
ham	prosciutto	*pro-šut-to*
lamb	agnello	*a-'nyel-lo*
liver	fegato	*'fe-ga-to*
meat	carne (f)	*'kar-ne*
pork	maiale (m)	*ma-'ya-le*
salami sausage	salame (m)	*sa-'la-me*
sausage	salsiccia	*sal-'sič-ča*
turkey	tacchino	*tak-'ki-no*
veal	vitello	*vi-'tel-lo*

E. FISH, SEAFOOD, AND SHELLFISH

anchovy	acciuga	*ač-'ču-ga*
clam	vongola	*'von-gola*
cod	merluzzo	*mer-'lu-tso*
• dried cod	baccalà (m, inv)	*bak-ka-'la*
eel	anguilla	*an-'gwil-la*
fish	pesce (m)	*'pe-še*
herring	aringa	*a-'rin-ga*
lobster	aragosta	*a-ra-'gos-ta*
mussels	cozze (f, pl)	*'ko-tse*
oyster	ostrica	*'os-tri-ka*
prawn	scampo	*'skam-po*
salmon	salmone (m)	*sal-'mo-ne*
sardine	sardina	*sar-'di-na*
seafood	frutti di mare	*'frut-ti di 'ma-re*
shellfish	crostacei (m, pl)	*kros-'ta-če-i*
shrimp	gambero	*'gam-be-ro*
sole	sogliola	*'so-lyo-la*
squid	calamaro (m, pl)	*ka-la-'ma-ro*
trout	trota	*'tro-ta*
tuna	tonno	*'ton-no*

F. VEGETABLES AND GREENS

artichoke	carciofo	*kar-'čo-fo*
asparagus	asparagi (m, pl)	*as-'pa-ra-ji*
bean	fagiolo	*fa-'jo-lo*
beet	barbabietola	*bar-ba-'bye-to-la*
broccoli	broccoli (m, pl)	*'brok-ko-li*
cabbage	cavolo	*'ka-vo-lo*
carrot	carota	*ka-'ro-ta*
cauliflower	cavolfiore (m)	*ka-vol-'fyo-re*
celery	sedano	*'se-da-no*
chick peas	ceci (m, pl)	*'če-ci*
cucumber	cetriolo	*če-tri-'o-lo*

eggplant	melanzana	*me-lan-'dza-na*
fennel	finocchio	*fi-'nok-kyo*
lentil	lenticchia	*len-'tik-kya*
lettuce	lattuga	*lat-'tu-ga*
lima bean	fava	*'fa-va*
mushroom	fungo	*'fun-go*
olive	oliva	*o-'li-va*
onion	cipolla	*či-'pol-la*
pea	pisello	*pi-'zel-lo*
pepper	peperone (m)	*pe-pe-'ro-ne*
potato	patata	*pa-'ta-ta*
pumpkin	zucca	*'dzuk-ka*
radish	ravanello	*ra-va-'nel-lo*
rhubarb	rabarbaro	*ra-'bar-ba-ro*
spinach	spinaci	*spi-'na-či*
string bean	fagiolino	*fa-jo-'li-no*
tomato	pomodoro	*po-mo-'do-ro*
vegetables, greens	verdura	*ver-'du-ra*
zucchini	zucchine (f, pl)	*dzuk-'ki-ne*

G. FRUITS AND NUTS

apple	mela	*'me-la*
apricot	albicocca	*al-bi-'kok-ka*
banana	banana	*ba-'na-na*
blueberry	mirtillo	*mir-'til-lo*
cherry	ciliegia	*či-'lye-ja*
chestnut	castagna	*kas-'ta-nya*
citrus	cedro	*'če-dro*
date	dattero	*'dat-te-ro*
fig	fico	*'fi-ko*
fruit	frutta	*'frut-ta*
fruit salad	macedonia di frutta	*ma-če-'do-nya*
grapefruit	pompelmo	*pom-'pel-mo*
grapes	uva	*'u-va*
lemon	limone (m)	*li-'mo-ne*
mandarin orange	mandarino	*man-da-'ri-no*
melon	melone (m)	*me-'lo-ne*
orange	arancia	*a-'ran-ča*
peach	pesca	*'pes-ka*
peanut (salted)	nocciolina americana	*noč-čo-'li-na a-me-ri-'ka-na*
peanut (in general)	arachide (f)	*a-'ra-ki-de*
pear	pera	*'pe-ra*
pineapple	ananas (m, inv)	*a-na-'nas*
pistachio	pistacchio	*pis-'tak-kyo*
plum	susina	*su-'zi-na*
prune	prugna	*'pru-nya*

raspberry	lampone (m)	*lam-'po-ne*
strawberry	fragola	*'fra-go-la*
walnut	noce (f)	*'no-če*
watermelon	anguria	*an-'gu-rya*

H. DAIRY PRODUCTS, EGGS, AND RELATED FOODS

butter	burro	*'bur-ro*
cheese	formaggio	*for-'maj-jo*
cream	crema	*'kre-ma*
dairy product	latticino	*lat-ti-'či-no*
egg	uovo (uova, f, pl)	*'wo-vo*
ice cream	gelato	*je-'la-to*
milk	latte (m)	*'lat-te*
omelet	frittata	*frit-'ta-ta*
whipping cream	panna montata	*'pan-na mon-'ta-ta*
yogurt	yogurt	—

I. SPICES AND CONDIMENTS

anise	anice (m)	*'a-ni-če*
basil	basilico	*ba-'zi-li-ko*
cinnamon	cannella	*kan-'nel-la*
garlic	aglio	*'a-lyo*
ginger	zenzero	*'dzen-dzero*
herb	erba	*'er-ba*
mint	menta	*'men-ta*
oil	olio	*'o-lyo*
oregano	origano	*o-'ri-ga-no*
parsley	prezzemolo	*pre-'tse-mo-lo*
pepper	pepe (m)	*'pe-pe*
rosemary	rosmarino	*roz-ma-'ri-no*
saffron	zafferano	*dzaf-fe-'ra-no*
salt	sale (m)	*'sa-le*
spice	spezia	*'spe-tsya*
sugar	zucchero	*'dzuk-'ke-ro*
vanilla	vaniglia	*va-'ni-lya*
vinegar	aceto	*a-'če-to*

J. DRINKS AND BEVERAGES

alcoholic beverage	bevanda alcolica	*be-'van-da al-'ko-lika*
beer	birra	*'bir-ra*
• draft beer	birra alla spina	*'bir-ra al-la 'spi-na*
beverage, soft drink	bibita	*'bi-bi-ta*
cappuccino	cappuccino	*kap-puč-'či-no*
chamomile tea	camomilla	*ka-mo-'mil-la*

coffee	caffè (m, inv)	*'kaf-'fe*
• with a drop of milk	caffè macchiato	*mak-'kya-to*
• with a drop of alcohol	caffè corretto	*kor-'ret-to*
• with espresso coffee	caffè espresso	*es-'pres-so*
• long	caffè lungo	*'lun-go*
• short coffee (concentrated)	caffè ristretto	*ris-'tret-to*
drink, beverage	bevanda	*be-'van-da*
juice	succo	*'suk-ko*
lemonade	limonata	*li-mo-'na-ta*
liqueur	liquore (m)	*li-'kwo-re*
mineral water	acqua minerale	*'ak-kwa mi-ne-'ra-le*
• carbonated	gassata	*gas-'sa-ta*
	frizzante	*fri-'dzan-te*
• non-carbonated	liscia	*'li-ša*
orangeade	aranciata	*a-ran-'ča-ta*
tea	tè	—
whiskey	whiskey (m, inv)	—
• with ice, on the rocks	col ghiaccio	*'gyač-čo*
wine	vino	—

Italian Coffee

cappuccino	cappuccino
coffee with milk	caffellatte
expresso	espresso
long	lungo
regular	normale
short, concentrated	ristretto
with a drop of alcohol	corretto
with a drop of milk	macchiato

K. AT THE TABLE

bottle	bottiglia	*bot-'ti-lya*
cup	tazza	*'tat-tsa*
drinking glass	bicchiere (m)	*bik-'kye-re*
fork	forchetta	*for-'ket-ta*
knife	coltello	*kol-'tel-lo*
napkin	tovagliolo	*to-va-'lyo-lo*
paper cup	bicchiere di carta	*bik-'kye-re di 'kar-ta*
plate	piatto	*'pyat-to*
saucer	piattino	*pyat-'ti-no*
spoon	cucchiaio	*kuk-'kya-yo*
table	tavolo	*'ta-vo-lo*
tablecloth	tovaglia	*to-'va-lya*

tableware	posate (f, pl)	po-'za-te
teaspoon	cucchiaino	kuk-kya-'yi-no
toothpick	stuzzicadenti (m, inv)	stu-tsi-ka-'den-ti
tray	vassoio	vas-'so-yo
water bottle	bottiglia da acqua	bot-'ti-lya da 'ak-kwa

Table Manners

Cheers!	Cin, cin!
	Salute!
Eat up!	Buon appetito!

L. DINING OUT

For menu items see above §24a, and for various food choices, see §24b-j

bartender	barista (m/f)	ba-'ris-ta
bill, check	conto	'kon-to
cafeteria	mensa	'men-za
cover charge	coperto	ko-'per-to
pizza parlor	pizzeria	pi-tse-'ri-a
price	prezzo	'pret-tso
• fixed price	prezzo fisso	'pret-tso 'fis-so
reservation	prenotazione (f)	pre-no-ta-'tsyo-ne
• reserved	riservato	ri-zer-'va-to
restaurant (formal)	ristorante (m)	ris-to-'ran-te
restaurant (informal)	trattoria	trat-to-'ri-a
service	servizio	ser-'vi-tsyo
snack bar	snack bar	—
tip	mancia	'man-ča
• (to) tip	dare* la mancia	—
waiter, waitress	cameriere (-a)	ka-me-'rye-re
wine list	lista dei vini	—

M. BUYING FOOD AND DRINK

bread store, bakery	panificio	pa-ni-'fi-čo
butcher shop	macelleria	ma-čel-le-'ri-a
creamery	cremeria	kre-me-'ri-a
dairy shop, milk store	latteria	lat-te-'ri-a
delicatessen	salumeria	sa-lu-me-'ri-a
fish shop	pescheria	pes-ke-'ri-a

food store	negozio di alimentari	*ne-'go-tsyo di a-li-men-'ta-ri*
health food store	negozio dietetico	*ne-'go-tsyo di-e-'te-ti-ko*
hypermarket	ipermercato	*i-per-mer-'ka-to*
ice cream parlor	gelateria	*je-la-te-'ri-a*
pastry shop	pasticceria	*pas-tič-če-'ri-a*
produce, fruit vendor	fruttivendolo	*frut-ti-'ven-do-lo*
store	negozio	*ne-'go-tsyo*
supermarket	supermercato	*su-per-mer-'ka-to*
wine shop	enoteca	*e-no-'te-ka*

N. RELATED VOCABULARY

appetizing	appetitoso	*ap-pe-ti-'to-zo*
(to) be hungry	avere* fame	*a-'ve-re 'fa-me*
(to) be thirsty	avere* sete	*a-'ve-re 'se-te*
cheap	a buon mercato	*a bwon mer-'ka-to*
	economico	*e-ko-'no-mi-ko*
(to) cost	costare (ess)	*kos-'ta-re*
(to) drink	bere*	*'be-re*
(to) eat	mangiare	*man-'ja-re*
expensive	caro	—
(to) order	ordinare	*or-di-'na-re*
recipe	ricetta	*ri-'čet-ta*
(to) serve	servire	*ser-'vi-re*
(to) shop for food	fare* la spesa	*'fa-re la 'spe-za*
slice	fetta	*'fet-ta*
• (to) slice	affettare	*af-fet-'ta-re*
(to) take out	portare via	*por-ta-re 'vi-a*
(to) toast	brindare	*brin-'da-re*

25. SHOPPING

A. GENERAL VOCABULARY

antique shop	negozio dell'antiquariato	*ne-'go-tsyo del'lan-ti-kwa-'rya-to*
bag	sacco	*'sak-ko*
	sacchetto	*sak-'ket-to*
bar code	codice (m) a barre	*'ko-di-če a 'bar-re*
bar-code reader	lettore elettronico	*let-'to-re e-let-'tro-ni-ko*
bill	fattura	*fat-'tu-ra*
brand	marca	*'mar-ka*
	marchio	*'mar-kyo*
(to) bring	portare	*por-'ta-re*
(to) buy	comprare	*kom-'pra-re*
cash register	cassa	*'kas-sa*
• cashier	cassiere (-a)	*kas-'sye-re*

change (money)	resto	—
closing (time)	chiusura	*kyu-'zu-ra*
competition	concorrenza	*kon-kor-'ren-tsa*
(to) cost	costare (ess)	*kos-'ta-re*
• costly, expensive	costoso	*kos-'to-zo*
• How much does it cost?	Quanto costa?	*'kwan-to 'kos-ta*
• How much does it come to?	Quanto viene?	*'kwan-to 'vye-ne*
• How much is it?	Quanto è?	—
counter	banco	*'ban-ko*
customer	cliente (m/f)	*kli-'en-te*
• clientele	clientela	*kli-en-'te-la*
delivery	consegna	*kon-'se-nya*
• home delivery	consegna a domicilio	*kon-'se-nya a do-mi-'či-lyo*
department	reparto	*re-'par-to*
department store	grande magazzino	*ma-ga-'dzi-no*
display, exhibition	mostra	—
entrance	entrata	*en-'tra-ta*
(to) exchange	cambiare	*kam-'bya-re*
exit	uscita	*u-'ši-ta*
flea market	mercato delle pulci	*mer-'ka-to*
gift	regalo	*re-'ga-lo*
kiosk, booth	chiosco	*'kyos-ko*
label, price tag	etichetta	*e-ti-'ket-ta*
(to) lack	mancare (ess)	*man-'ka-re*
merchandise	merce (f)	*'mer-če*
newsstand	edicola	*e-'di-ko-la*
online shopping	comprare online	—
opening (times)	apertura	*a-per-'tu-ra*
(to) pack	imballare	*im-bal-'la-re*
package	pacco	*'pak-ko*
• small package	pacchetto	*pak-'ket-to*
(to) pay	pagare	*pa-'ga-re*
	carta bancaria	*'kar-ta ban-'ka-rya*
• cash	in contanti	*kon-'tan-ti*
• check	assegno	*as-'se-nyo*
• credit card	carta di credito	*'kre-di-to*
price	prezzo	*'pre-tso*
• discount	sconto	*'skon-to*
• expensive	caro	—
• fixed price	prezzo fisso	*'pre-tso 'fis-so*
• inexpensive	a buon mercato	*a bwon mer-'ka-to*
	economico	*e-ko-'no-mi-ko*
• price list	tariffa dei prezzi	*ta-rif-fa dei 'pre-tsi*
• price tag	etichetta	*e-ti-'ket-ta*
• reduced price	prezzo ridotto	*'pre-tso ri-dot-to*

product	prodotto	*pro-'dot-to*
• **range of products**	gamma di prodotti	*'gam-ma di pro-'dot-ti*
purchase	acquisto	*ak-'kwis-to*
queue, lineup	fila	—
	coda	—
receipt	scontrino	*skon-'tri-no*
refund	rimborso	*rim-'bor-so*
retail	al dettaglio	*al det-'ta-lyo*
• **retail price**	prezzo al dettaglio	*'pre-tso al det-'ta-lyo*
(to) return, bring back	restituire (isc)	*res-ti-tu-'i-re*
sale	saldo	—
• **for sale**	in vendita	*in 'ven-di-ta*
• **on (liquidation) sale**	in svendita	*in 'zven-di-ta*
• **on sale**	in saldo	*in 'sal-do*
• **(to) sell**	vendere	*'ven-de-re*
sample	campione (m)	*kam-'pyo-ne*
shop	negozio	*ne-'go-tsyo*
• **(to) shop**	fare* delle compere	*'fa-re del-le 'kom-pe-re*
• **shop window**	vetrina	*ve-'tri-na*
• **shopkeeper**	negoziante (m/f)	*ne-go-'tsyan-te*
store	negozio	*ne-'go-tsyo*
• **closed**	chiuso	*'kyu-zo*
• **closing time**	chiusura	*kyu-'zu-ra*
• **open**	aperto	*a-'per-to*
• **opening time**	apertura	*a-per-'tu-ra*
• **store chain**	catena di negozi	*ka-'te-na di ne-'go-tsyi*
• **store clerk**	commesso (-a)	*kom-'mes-so*
• **store window**	vetrina	*ve-'tri-na*
• **times (a store is open)**	orario	*o-'ra-ryo*
(to) take	prendere*	*'pren-de-re*
warehouse	magazzino	*ma-ga-'dzi-no*
wholesale	all'ingrosso	*al-lin-'gros-so*
• **wholesale price**	prezzo all'ingrosso	*'pre-tso*
(to) wrap	incartare	*in-kar-'ta-re*

Idiomatic Expression

> **It costs an arm and a leg!** = Costa un occhio della testa!

B. HARDWARE

battery	pila	—
	batteria	*bat-te-'ri-a*
bolt	bullone (m)	*bul-'lo-ne*
chisel	cesello	*če-'zel-lo*
clamp	morsetto	*mor-'set-to*

drill	trapano	'tra-pa-no
electric outlet	presa (elettrica)	'pre-za
file	lima	—
flashlight	pila	—
fuse	valvola	'val-vo-la
hammer	martello	mar-'tel-lo
hardware	ferramenta (f, pl)	fer-ra-'men-ta
hardware store	negozio di ferramenta	ne-'go-tsyo fer-ra-'men-ta
insulation	isolante (m)	i-zo-'lan-te
light bulb	lampadina	lam-pa-'di-na
• fluorescent	fluorescente	flwuor-eš-'en-te
• neon	al neon	—
mallet	mazza	'ma-tsa
masking tape	nastro isolante	'nas-tro i-zo-'lan-te
nail	chiodo	'kyo-do
paint	vernice (f)	ver-'ni-če
plane	pialla	'pyal-la
pliers, tongs, tweezers	pinze (f, pl)	'pin-tse
	tenaglie (f, pl)	te-'na-lye
plug	spina	—
punch	punzone (m)	pun-'tso-ne
roller	rullo	—
sandpaper	carta vetrata	'kar-ta ve-'tra-ta
saw	sega	'se-ga
screw	vite (f)	'vi-te
screwdriver	cacciavite (m, inv)	kač-ča-'vi-te
shovel	pala	—
tool	attrezzo	at-'tre-tso
transformer	trasformatore (m)	tras-for-ma-'to-re
wallpaper	carta da parati	'kar-ta da pa-'ra-ti
wire	filo	—
wrench	chiave (f) inglese	'kya-ve in-'gle-ze

C. STATIONERY, COMPUTER, AND OFFICE SUPPLIES

adhesive tape	nastro adesivo	'nas-tro a-de-'zi-vo
ballpoint pen	penna a sfera, biro (f, inv)	—
briefcase	cartella	kar-'tel-la
business card	biglietto da visita	bi-'lyet-to da 'vi-zi-ta
calculator	calcolatrice (f)	kal-ko-la-'tri-če
calendar	calendario	ka-len-'da-ryo
cartridge	cartuccia	kar-'tuč-ča
CD-ROM	CD-ROM (m, inv)	—
color monitor	monitor, schermo a colori	'sker-mo
compatible software	software compatibile	kom-pa-'ti-bi-le
computer	computer (m, inv)	—

copy shop	copisteria	*ko-pis-te-'ri-a*
diskette	dischetto	*dis-'ket-to*
envelope	busta	—
eraser	gomma	—
file folder	cartella	*kar-'tel-la*
filing card, filing folder	scheda	*'ske-da*
glue	colla	*'kol-la*
highlighter	evidenziatore (m)	*e-vi-den-tsya-'to-re*
ink	inchiostro	*in-'kyos-tro*
ink-jet printer	stampante a getto	*stam-'pan-te a 'jet-to*
	d'inchiostro	*din-'kyos-tro*
keyboard	tastiera	*tas-'tye-ra*
label	etichetta	*e-ti-'ket-ta*
laptop computer	computer portatile	*por-'ta-ti-le*
	laptop (m, inv)	—
laser printer	stampante laser	*stam-'pan-te*
letterhead	carta intestata	*'karta in-tes-'ta-ta*
Liquid Paper, White-out	bianchetto	*byan-'ket-to*
marker	penrarello	*pen-na-'rel-lo*
modem	modem (m, inv)	—
mouse	mouse (m, inv)	—
notice board	tabella	*ta-'bel-la*
office supplies	forniture (f, inv)	*for-ni-'tu-re per uf-*
	per ufficio	*'fi-čo*
pad	taccuino	*tak-'kwi-no*
paper	carta	—
pen	penna	—
pencil, crayon	matita	*ma-'ti-ta*
photocopying machine,	fotocopiatrice (f)	*fo-to-ko-pya-'tri-če*
planner	agenda	*a-'jen-da*
printer	stampante (f)	*stam-'pan-te*
punch	perforatrice (f)	*per-fo-ra-'tri-če*
ream of paper	risma di carta	*'riz-ma*
ring-binder	quaderno ad anelli	*kwa-'der-no ad a-'nel-li*
rubber band	elastico	*e-'las-ti-ko*
ruler	riga	—
scanner	scanner (m, inv)	—
scissors	forbici	*'for-bi-či*
sheet (of paper)	foglio	*'fo-lyo*
staple	punto metallico	*'pun-to me-'tal-li-ko*
stapler	cucitrice (f)	*ku-či-'tri-če*
stationery store	cartoleria	*kar-to-le-'ri-a*
string	spago	*'spa-go*
tack	puntina	*pun-'ti-na*
toner	toner (m, inv)	—
wrapping paper	carta da pacchi	*'pak-ki*
writing pad	blocco	*'blok-'ko*
• small writing pad	blocchetto	*blok-'ket-to*

D. PHOTOGRAPHY/CAMERAS

camera	macchina fotografica	*'mak-ki-na fo-to-'gra-fi-ka*
• **video, movie camera**	cinepresa	*či-ne-'pre-za*
• **digital camera**	macchina fotografica digitale	*di-ji-'ta-le*
dark room	camera oscura	*'ka-me-ra os-'ku-ra*
digital photography, digital photograph	fotografia digitale	*fo-to-gra-'fi-a di-ji-'ta-le*
film	pellicola	*pel-'li-ko-la*
focus	fuoco	*'fwo-ko*
• **(to) focus**	mettere* a fuoco	*'met-te-re a 'fwo-ko*
image	immagine (f)	*im-'ma-ji-ne*
lens	lente (f)	*'len-te*
negative	negativo	*ne-ga-'ti-vo*
objective lens	obiettivo	*o'byet-'ti-vo*
photograph	foto (m, inv)	—
	fotografia	*fo-to-gra-'fi-a*
photographer	fotografo (-a)	*fo-'to-gra-fo*
photographic shot	ripresa fotografica	*ri-'pre-za fo-to-'gra-fi-ka*
photo-sensitive	fotosensibile	*fo-to-sen-'si-bi-le*
push button (on a camera)	scatto	*'skat-to*
roll of film	rullino	*rul-'li-no*
slide	diapositiva	*di-a-po-zi-'ti-va*
tripod	treppiede (m, inv)	*trep-'pye-de*
unfocussed	sfocato	*sfo-'ka-to*
video disc	videodisco	*vi-de-o-'dis-ko*
viewer (of a camera), scope	mirino	*mi-'ri-no*
zoom	zoom (m, inv)	—

E. TOBACCO

cigar	sigaro	*'si-ga-ro*
cigarette	sigaretta	*si-ga-'ret-ta*
lighter	accendino	*ač-čen-'di-no*
match	fiammifero	*fyam-'mi-fe-ro*
pipe	pipa	—
(to) smoke	fumare	*fu-'ma-re*
tobacco	tabacco	*ta-'bak-ko*
tobacconist	tabaccaio	*ta-bak-'ka-yo*

F. COSMETICS/TOILETRIES

anti-wrinkle cream	crema antirughe	*'kre-ma an-ti-'ru-ge*
bath oil	olio da bagno	*'o-lyo da 'ba-nyo*
bath salts	sali da bagno	*'sa-li da 'ba-nyo*

blade	lametta da barba	*la-'met-ta da 'bar-ba*
brush	spazzola	*'spa-tso-la*
cologne	acqua di Colonia	*'ak-kwa di ko-'lo-nya*
comb	pettine (m)	*'pet-ti-ne*
cosmetic	cosmetico	*koz-'me-ti-ko*
cosmetic, perfume shop	profumeria	*pro-fu-me-'ri-a*
cream, lotion	crema	*'kre-ma*
curler	bigodino	*bi-go-'di-no*
deodorant	deodorante (m)	*de-o-do-'ran-te*
electric razor	rasoio elettrico	*ra-'zo-yo e-'let-tri-ko*
eyeliner	matita per gli occhi	*ma-'ti-ta per lyi 'ok-ki*
eye shadow	mascara (m, inv)	*mas-'ka-ra*
face powder	cipria	*'či-prya*
facial cream	crema per il viso	*'kre-ma per il 'vi-zo*
hair cream	brillantina	*bril-lan-'ti-na*
hairdryer	asciugacapelli (m, inv)	*a-šu-ga-ka-'pel-li*
hairnet	retina	*re-'ti-na*
hair remover	crema depilatoria	*'kre-ma de-pi-la-'to-ria*
hair-dye	tinta	*'tin-ta*
hairpin	fermaglio	*fer-'ma-lyo*
hairspray	lacca (per capelli)	*'lak-ka*
hand cream	crema per le mani	*'kre-ma per le 'ma-ni*
lipstick	rossetto	*ros-'set-to*
lotion	lozione (f)	*lo-'tsyo-ne*
makeup	trucco	*'truk-ko*
manicure	manicure (f)	*ma-ni-'ku-re*
mascara	mascara (m, inv)	*mas-'ka-ra*
moisturizer	crema idratante	*'kre-ma i-dra-'tan-te*
nail file	lima per unghie	*'li-ma per 'un-gye*
nail polish	smalto	*'zmal-to*
perfume	profumo	*pro-'fu-mo*
razor	rasoio	*ra-'zo-yo*
shampoo	shampoo (m, inv)	—
shaving cream	crema da barba	*'kre-ma da 'bar-ba*
soap	sapone (m)	*sa-'po-ne*
talc, talcum powder	talco	*'tal-ko*
toiletries	articoli da toilette	*ar-'ti-ko-li*
tweezers	pinzette (f, pl)	*pin-'tset-te*
wig, hair piece	parrucca	*par-'ruk-ka*

G. LAUNDRY

buckle	fibbia	*'fib-bya*
button	bottone (m)	*bot-'to-ne*
clean	pulito	*pu-'li-to*
clothes	abiti (m, pl)	*'a-bi-ti*
clothes basket	cestino del bucato	*čes-'ti-no del bu-'ka-to*
clothespin	molletta	*mol-'let-ta*

collar	colletto	*kol-'let-to*
delicate, soft	delicato	*de-li-'ka-to*
detergent	detergente	*de-ter-'jen-te*
dirty	sporco	*'spor-ko*
dry cleaner	lavanderia a secco	*la-van-de-'ri-a a 'sek-ko*
fabric	tessuto	*tes-'su-to*
fiber	fibra	*'fi-bra*
flannel	flanella	*fla-'nel-la*
fly, zipper	cerniera	*čer-'nye-ra*
heavy	pesante	*pe-'zan-te*
hole	buco	*'bu-ko*
iron	ferro da stiro	*'fer-ro da 'sti-ro*
• **(to) iron**	stirare	*sti-'ra-re*
• **ironed**	stirato	*sti-'ra-to*
lace	pizzo	*'pit-tso*
laundry	lavanderia	*la-van-de-'ri-a*
• **launderette**	lavanderia automatica	*la-van-de-'ri-a au-to-'ma-ti-ka*
light	leggero	*lej-'je-ro*
linen	lino	—
long	lungo	—
loose-fitting	largo	—
material	stoffa	—
(to) mend	rammendare	*ram-men-'da-re*
nylon	nailon (m, inv)	—
pair	paio (paia, f, pl))	*'pa-yo*
pocket	tasca	*'tas-ka*
polyester	poliestere (m)	*po-li-'es-te-re*
rag	cencio	*'čen-čo*
rough	rozzo	*'rot-tso*
(to) sew	cucire	*ku-'či-re*
short	corto	*'kor-to*
size (of clothes)	taglia	*'ta-lya*
sleeve	manica	*'ma-ni-ka*
small	piccolo	*'pik-ko-lo*
smooth	liscio	*'li-šo*
soap powder	sapone (m) in polvere	*sa-'po-ne*
sporty	sportivo	*spor-'ti-vo*
spot, stain	macchia	*'mak-kya*
starch	amido	*'a-mi-do*
stitch	punto	—
striped	a righe	*a 'ri-ge*
tight	stretto	*'stret-to*
tight-fitting	aderente	*a-de-'ren-te*
transparent	trasparente	*tras-pa-'ren-te*
(to) wash	lavare	*la-'va-re*
• **washable**	lavabile	*la-'va-bi-le*
woolen	lana	—

H. PHARMACY/DRUGSTORE

adhesive bandage	cerotto	*če-'rot-to*
antibiotic	antibiotico	*an-ti-bi-'o-ti-ko*
aspirin	aspirina	*as-pi-'ri-na*
barbiturate	barbiturico	*bar-bi-'tu-ri-ko*
condom	preservativo	*pre-ser-va-'ti-vo*
contraceptive	contracettivo	*kon-trač-čet-'ti-vo*
• contraceptive pill	pillola anticoncezionale	*'pil-lo-la an-ti-kon-če-tsyo-'na-le*
cortisone	cortisone (m)	*kor-ti-'zo-ne*
cough syrup	sciroppo contro la tosse	*ši-'rop-po 'kon-tro la 'tos-se*
covering, bandage	benda	*'ben-da*
cream	crema	*'kre-ma*
crutch	stampella	*stam-'pel-la*
dosage	posologia	*po-zo-lo-'ji-a*
dressing	fascia	*'fa-ša*
drop	goccia	*'goč-ča*
expectorant	espettorante (m)	*es-pet-to-'ran-te*
eyedrop	collirio	*kol-'li-ryo*
first aid	pronto soccorso	*'pron-to sok-'kor-so*
injection, needle	iniezione (f)	*i-nye-'tsyo-ne*
	puntura	*pun-'tu-ra*
insulin	insulina	*in-su-'li-na*
laxative	purga	*'pur-ga*
magnesium citrate	citrato di magnesio	*či-'tra-to*
medicine	medicina	*me-di-'či-na*
ointment	pomata	*po-'ma-ta*
painkiller	analgesico	*a-nal-'je-zi-ko*
palliative	palliativo	*pal-lya-'ti-vo*
pastille	pasticca	*pas-'tik-ka*
penicillin	penicillina	*pe-ni-čil-'li-na*
pharmaceutical	farmaco	*'far-ma-ko*
pharmacist	farmacista (m/f)	*far-ma-'čis-ta*
• pharmacy, drugstore	farmacia	*far-ma-'či-a*
phial	fiala	*'fya-la*
pill	pillola	*'pil-lo-la*
prescription	ricetta medica	*ri-čet-ta 'me-di-ka*
rubber gloves	guanti di gomma	*'gwan-ti di 'gom-ma*
sedative	sedativo	*se-da-'ti-vo*
sleeping pill	sonnifero	*son-'ni-fe-ro*
sling	bendaggio	*ben-'daj-jo*
sodium bicarbonate	bicarbonato di sodio	*bi-kar-bo-'nā-to di 'so-dyo*
sodium citrate	citrato di sodio	*či-'tra-to*
suppository	supposta	*sup-'pos-ta*
tablet	compressa	*kom-'pres-sa*

thermometer	termometro	*ter-'mo-me-tro*
tincture of iodine	tintura di iodio	*tin-'tu-ra di 'yo-dyo*
tonic	tonico	*'to-ni-ko*
tranquilizer	calmante (m)	*kal-'man-te*
vitamin	vitamina	*vi-ta-'mi-na*

I. JEWELRY

artificial	artificiale	*ar-ti-fi-'ča-le*
bracelet	braccialetto	*brač-ča-'let-to*
brooch	spilla	*'spil-la*
carat	carato	*ka-'ra-to*
chain	catena	*ka-'te-na*
coral	corallo	*ko-'ral-lo*
diamond	diamante (m)	*dya-'man-te*
earring	orecchino	*o-rek-'ki-no*
emerald	smeraldo	*zme-'ral-do*
engagement ring	anello di fidanzamento	*a-'nel-lo di fi-dan-dza-'men-to*
false	falso	—
(to) fix, repair	riparare	*ri-pa-'ra-re*
gemstone	brillante (m)	*bril-'lan-te*
gold	oro	—
gold ring	anello d'oro	—
jewel	gioiello	*jo-'yel-lo*
jewelry store, jeweler	gioielleria	*jo-yel-le-'ri-a*
locket, medal	medaglia	*me-'da-lya*
necklace	collana	*kol-'la-na*
nuptial, wedding ring	fede (f)	*'fe-de*
opal	opale (m)	*o-'pa-le*
pearl	perla	—
pendant	pendente	*pen-'den-te*
precious	prezioso	*pre-'tsyo-zo*
ring	anello	*a-'nel-lo*
ruby	rubino	*ru-'bi-no*
sapphire	zaffiro	*dzaf-'fi-ro*
silver	argento	*ar-'jen-to*
silver ring	anello d'argento	*a-'nel-lo dar-'jen-to*
topaz	topazio	*to-'pa-tsyo*
watch	orologio	*o-ro-'lo-jo*
• **band**	cinghietta	*čin-'gyet-ta*
• **dial**	quadrante (m)	*kwa-'dran-te*
• **hand**	lancetta	*lan-'čet-ta*
• **men's watch**	orologio da uomo	*'wo-mo*
• **quartz watch**	orologio al quarzo	*'kwar-tso*
• **spring**	molla	*'mol-la*

• watchmaker	orologiaio	o-ro-lo-'ja-yo
• wind	caricare	ka-ri-'ka-re
• women's watch	orologio da donna	'don-na
• wristwatch	orologio da polso	'pol-so
wedding-ring	fede (f)	'fe-de

J. MUSIC AND VIDEO

band	gruppo	'grup-po
	complesso	kom-'ples-so
blues	blues (m, inv)	—
chamber music	musica da camera	'mu-zi-ka da 'ka-me-ra
classical music	musica classica	'mu-zi-ka 'klas-si-ka
compact disc	compact disc (m, inv)	—
composer	compositore (-trice)	kom-po-zi-'to-re
• composition	composizione (f)	kom-po-zi-'tsyo-ne
concert, concerto	concerto	kon-'čer-to
conservatory	conservatorio	kon-ser-va-'to-ryo
dance music	musica da ballo	'mu-zi-ka da 'bal-lo
DVD	DVD (m, inv)	—
folk music	musica folk	'mu-zi-ka
folklorist music	musica folcloristica	'mu-zi-ka fol-klo-'ris-ti-ka
instrument	strumento	stru-'men-to
jazz	jazz (m, inv)	—
light music	musica leggera	'mu-zi-ka lej-'je-ra
melody	melodia	me-lo-'di-a
music	musica	'mu-zi-ka
music stand	portamusica (m, inv)	por-ta-'mu-zi-ka
musician	musicista (m/f)	mu-zi-'čis-ta
note	nota	—
opera	opera	—
orchestra	orchestra	or-'kes-tra
orchestra conductor	direttore (-trice) (d'orchestra)	di-ret-'to-re
performer	interprete (m/f)	in-'ter-pre-te
player, musician	suonatore (-trice)	swo-na-'to-re
rap	rap (m, inv)	—
rhythm	ritmo	—
rock music	musica rock	'mu-zi-ka
score	spartito	spar-'ti-to
singer	cantante (m/f)	kan-'tan-te
song	canzone (f)	kan-'tso-ne
symphony	sinfonia	sin-fo-'ni-a
tone	tono	—
tune, aria	aria	—
video camera	videocamera	vi-de-o-'ka-me-ra
video recorder	videoregistratore (m)	vi-de-o-re-jis-tra-'to-re
videocassette	videocassetta	vi-de-o-kas-'set-ta

K. CLOTHING AND APPAREL

apron	grembiule (m)	*grem-'byu-le*
bathrobe	accappatoio	*ak-kap-pa-'to-yo*
blouse	camicetta	*ka-mi-'čet-ta*
bra	reggiseno	*rej-ji-'se-no*
cap	berretto	*ber-'ret-to*
clothes (in general)	abbigliamento	*ab-bi-'lya-'men-to*
• **clothing store**	negozio di abbigliamento	*ne-'go-tsyo*
• **men's clothing store**	abbigliamento maschile	*mas-'ki-le*
• **women's clothing store**	abbigliamento femminile	*fem-mi-'ni-le*
coat	cappotto	*kap-'pot-to*
• **fur coat**	pelliccia	*pel-'lič-ča*
dress, clothing, suit	vestito	*ves-'ti-to*
	abito	*'a-bi-to*
dressing room	cabina	*ka-'bi-na*
evening attire	abito, vestito da sera	*'a-bi-to ves-'ti-to*
fashion	moda	—
garment	indumento	*in-du-'men-to*
glove	guanto	*'gwan-to*
handkerchief	fazzoletto	*fat-tso-'let-to*
hat	cappello	*kap-'pel-lo*
• **felt hat**	cappello di feltro	*'fel-tro*
• **hood**	cappuccio	*kap-'puč-čo*
• **straw hat**	cappello di paglia	*'pa-lya*
jacket	giacca	*'jak-ka*
• **dinner jacket**	smoking (m, inv)	—
• **double-breasted jacket**	giacca a doppio petto	*'jak-ka a 'dop-pyo* *'pet-to*
• **single-breasted jacket**	giacca a un petto	—
• **sports jacket**	giacca sportiva	*spor-'ti-va*
knickers	calzoni (m, pl)	*kal-'tso-ni*
lingerie, underclothing	biancheria (intima)	*byan-ke-'ri-a*
nightdress	camicia da notte	*ka-'mi-ča da -'not-te*
overcoat	soprabito	*so-'pra-bi-to*
pajamas	pigiama (m)	*pi-'ja-ma*
pants	pantaloni (m, pl)	*pan-to-'lo-ni*
• **ski pants**	pantaloni da sci	*ši*
pantyhose, tights	collant (m, inv)	*kol-'lant*
raincoat	impermeabile (m)	*im-per-me-'a-bi-le*
shawl	mantello	*man-'tel-lo*
shirt	camicia	*ka-'mi-ča*
shorts	pantaloncini (m, pl)	*pan-ta-lon-'či-ni*
skirt	gonna	—
• **pleated skirt**	gonna a pieghe	*'pye-ge*

suit	vestito	ves-'ti-to
	abito	'a-bi-to
• men's suit	abito, vestito da uomo	'wo-mo
• suit (complete), set	completo	kom'-ple-to
• women's suit	abito, vestito da donna	—
sweater	maglia	'ma-lya
	maglione (m)	ma-lyo-ne
swimming cap	cuffia da bagno	'kuf-fya
swimming suit	costume (m) da bagno	kos-'tu-me da 'ba-nyo
• two-piece suit	costume (m) a due pezzi	'pe-tsi
• swimming trunks	pantaloncini (m, pl) da bagno	pan-ta-lon-'či-ni da 'ba-nyo
tailor	sarto (-a)	—
T-shirt	T-shirt (f)	
tie	cravatta	kra-'vat-ta
• bow tie	farfalla	far-'fal-la
underpants, underwear	mutande (f, pl)	mu-'tan-de
undershirt	canottiera	ka-not-'tye-ra
underskirt	sottoveste (f)	sot-to-'ves-te
vest	gilè (m, inv)	ji-'le
wedding dress	abito, vestito da sposa	'a-bi-to ves-'ti-to da 'spo-za
wedding suit (men)	abito, vestito da sposo	'a-bi-to ves-'ti-to da 'spo-zo
wind-breaker	giacca a vento	'jak-ka a 'ven-to
women's suit	tailleur (m, inv)	—

L. DESCRIBING CLOTHING AND RELATED VOCABULARY

beautiful	bello	'bel-lo
big	grande	'gran-de
buckle	fibbia	'fib-bya
button	bottone (m)	bot-'to-ne
checkered	a scacchi	'skak-ki
collar	colletto	kol-'let-to
cotton	cotone	ko-'to-ne
cuff-links	gemelli (m, pl)	je-'mel-li
delicate, soft	delicato	de-li-'ka-to
dirty	sporco	'spor-ko
(to) dress, get dressed	vestirsi	ves-'tir-si
elegant	elegante	e-le-'gan-te
(to) enlarge	allargare	al-lar-'ga-re
evening	da sera	—
fabric	tessuto	tes-'su-to
fiber	fibra	'fi-bra
heavy	pesante	pe-'zan-te
hole	buco	'bu-ko

in style	di moda	—
It looks bad on you.	Ti sta male.	—
It looks good on you.	Ti sta bene.	—
lace	pizzo	'pi-tso
(to) lengthen	allungare	al-lun-'ga-re
light	leggero	lej-'je-ro
linen	lino	—
long	lungo	—
loose-fitting	largo	'lar-go
made-to-measure suit	abito, vestito su misura	'a-bi-to ves-'ti-to su mi-'zu-ra
material	stoffa	—
nylon	nailon	—
(to) put on (clothes)	mettersi*	'met-ter-si
rag	cencio	'čen-čo
(to) sew	cucire	ku-'či-re
short	corto	'kor-to
(to) shorten	accorciare	ak-kor-'ča-re
sleeve	manica	'ma-ni-ka
small	piccolo	'pik-ko-lo
smooth	liscio	'li-šo
sporty	sportivo	spor-'ti-vo
spot	macchia	'mak-kya
stitch	punto	—
string	filo	—
striped	a righe	'ri-ge
(to) take off (clothes)	spogliarsi	spo-'lyar-si
tight	stretto	'stret-to
(to) tighten	stringere*	'strin-je-re
tight-fitting	aderente	a-de-'ren-te
(to) try on	provarsi	pro-'var-si
	provare	pro-'va-re
ugly	brutto	'brut-to
(to) undress	spogliarsi	spo-'lyar-si
(to) wear	indossare	in-dos-'sa-re
woolen	di lana	—

M. FOOTWEAR

boot	stivale (m)	sti-'va-le
footwear	calzatura	kal-tsa-'tu-ra
gym shoes	scarpe (f, pl) da ginnastica	'skar-pe da jin-'nas-ti-ka
heel	tacco	'tak-ko
• flat-heeled	con tacco piatto	'pyat-to
• high-heeled	con tacco alto	—
• low-heeled	con tacco basso	—

leather shoes	scarpe (f, pl) di cuoio	*'kwo-yo*
men's shoes	scarpe (f, pl) da uomo	*'wo-mo*
(to) put on (shoes)	mettersi* (le scarpe)	*'met-ter-si*
sandal	sandalo	*'san-da-lo*
shoe	scarpa	*'skar-pa*
shoe horn	calzascarpe (m, inv)	*kal-tsa-'skar-pe*
shoe repair (shop)	calzolaio	*kal-tso-'la-yo*
shoe size	numero (di scarpa)	*'nu-me-ro*
shoe store	negozio di scarpe	*ne'go-tsyo di 'skar-pe*
shoelace	stringa	*'strin-ga*
slipper	pantofola	*pan-'to-fo-la*
sock	calzino	*kal-'tsi-no*
sole	suola	*'swo-la*
stocking	calza	*'kal-tsa*
suede shoes	scarpe (f, pl) di camoscio	*ka-'mo-šo*
(to) take off (shoes)	togliersi* (le scarpe)	*'to-lyer-si*
tennis shoes	scarpe (f, pl) da tennis	—
women's shoes	scarpe (f, pl) da donna	—

N. BOOKS, MAGAZINES, AND NEWSPAPERS

anthology	antologia	*an-to-lo-'ji-a*
appendix	appendice (f)	*ap-pen-'di-če*
atlas	atlante (m)	*at-'lan-te*
author	autore (-trice)	*au-'to-re*
autobiography	autobiografia	*au-to-bi-o-gra-'fi-a*
biography	biografia	*bi-o-gra-'fi-a*
book	libro	—
bookstore	libreria	*li-bre-'ri-a*
catalogue	catalogo	*ka-'ta-lo-go*
chapter	capitolo	*ka-'pi-to-lo*
character	personaggio	*per-so-'naj-jo*
collection	raccolta	*rak-'kol-ta*
comedy	commedia	*kom-'me-dya*
comic book	rivista a fumetti	*ri-'vis-ta a fu-'met-ti*
cover, dust jacket	copertina	*ko-per-'ti-na*
criticism	critica	*'kri-ti-ka*
crosswords	parole crociate	*pa-'ro-le kro-'ča-te*
daily newspaper	quotidiano	*kwo-ti-'dya-no*
diary	diario	*di-'a-ryo*
dictionary	dizionario	*di-tsyo-'na-ryo*
dissertation	dissertazione (f)	*dis-ser-ta-'tsyo-ne*
drama	dramma (m) (drammi, pl)	—
encyclopedia	enciclopedia	*en-či-klo-pe-'di-a*
episode	episodio	*e-pi-'so-dyo*

essay	saggio	'saj-jo
fable	favola	'fa-vo-la
fairy tale	fiaba	'fya-ba
fashion magazine	rivista di moda	ri-'vis-ta
fiction, narrative	narrativa	nar-ra-'ti-va
genre	genere (m)	'je-ne-re
guidebook	guida	'gwi-da
illustrated magazine	rivista illustrata	ri-'vis-ta il-lus-'tra-ta
index	indice (m)	'in-di-če
interview	intervista	in-ter-'vis-ta
kids' magazine	giornalino	jor-na-'li-no
(to) leaf through	sfogliare	sfo-'lya-re
legend	leggenda	lej-'jen-da
library	biblioteca	bib-lyo-'te-ka
line, verse	verso	—
literacy	alfabetismo	al-fa-be-'tiz-mo
• illiteracy	analfabetismo	an-al-fa-be-'tiz-mo
• illiterate person	analfabeta (m/f)	an-al-fa-'be-ta
literature	letteratura	let-te-ra-'tu-ra
magazine	rivista	ri-'vis-ta
memoirs	memorie (f, pl)	me-'mo-rye
mystery, detective, spy work	giallo	'jal-lo
myth	mito	—
• mythology	mitologia	mi-to-lo-'ji-a
narrative	narrativa	nar-ra-'ti-va
narrator	narratore (-trice)	nar-ra-'to-re
newspaper	giornale (m)	jor-'na-le
novel	romanzo	ro-'man-dzo
• novelist	romanziere (-a)	ro-man-'dzye-re
• novelistic	romanzesco	ro-man-'dzes-ko
ode	ode (f)	'o-de
parody	parodia	pa-ro-'di-a
periodical	periodico	pe-ri-'o-di-ko
photo-romance	fotoromanzo	fo-to-ro-'man-dzo
play	rappresentazione (f) teatrale	rap-pre-zen-ta-'tsyo-ne te-a-'tra-le
• playwright	commediografo (-a)	kom-me-'dyo-gra-fo
plot	trama	'tra-ma
poetry	poesia	po-e-'zi-a
• poet	poeta (-essa)	po-'e-ta
• poetics	poetica	po-'e-ti-ka
• poem	poesia	po-e-'zi-a
pornographic magazine	rivista pornografica	ri-'vis-ta por-no-'gra-fi-ka
preface	prefazione (f)	pre-fa-'tsyo-ne
press	stampa	'stam-pa
prose	prosa	'pro-za

(to) publish	pubblicare	*pub-bli-'ka-re*
publisher	editore (m)	*e-di-'to-re*
puzzle section	enigmistica	*e-nig-'mis-ti-ka*
(to) read	leggere*	*'lej-je-re*
• **reader**	lettore (-trice)	*let-'to-re*
• **reading**	lettura	*let-'tu-ra*
recipe book	libro di ricette	*ri-'čet-te*
reference book	libro di consultazione	*kon-sul-ta-'tsyo-ne*
satire	satira	*'sa-ti-ra*
scene	scena	*'še-na*
science fiction	fantascienza	*fan-ta-'šen-tsa*
short story	novella	*no-'vel-la*
sonnet	sonetto	*so-'net-to*
stanza	strofa	*'stro-fa*
style	stile (m)	*'sti-le*
• **stylistics**	stilistica	*sti-'lis-ti-ka*
table of contents	indice (m) delle materie	*'in-di-če del-le ma-'te-rye*
tale	racconto	*rak-'kon-to*
teen magazine	rivista per adolescenti	*ri-'vis-ta*
text	testo	—
textbook	libro di testo	—
theme	tema (m) (temi, pl)	—
thriller	thriller (m inv)	—
title (of a book)	titolo	*'ti-to-lo*
treatise	trattato	*trat-'ta-to*
volume	volume (m)	*vo-'lu-me*
women's magazine	rivista femminile	*ri-'vis-ta fem-mi-'ni-le*
writer	scrittore (-trice)	*skrit-'to-re*
writing	scrittura	*skrit-'tu-ra*

26. BANKING AND COMMERCE

A. BANKING, FINANCES, AND INSURANCE

account	conto bancario	*'kon-to ban-'ka-ryo*
• **(to) close an account**	chiudere* un conto	*'kyu-de-re*
• **current account**	conto corrente	*kor-'ren-te*
• **(to) open an account**	aprire* un conto	*a-'pri-re*
annuity	rendita	*'ren-di-ta*
ATM	bancomat (m, inv)	—
bank	banca	*'ban-ka*
• **branch**	filiale (f) di una banca	*fi-'lya-le di u-na 'ban-ka*
• **head office**	sede (f) centrale	*'se-de čen-'tra-le*
• **(to) work in a bank**	lavorare in banca	*la-vo-'ra-re in 'ban-ka*
bank book	libretto bancario	*li-'bret-to ban-'ka-ryo*
bank clerk	impiegato (-a) di banca	*im-pye-'ga-to 'ban-ka*

bank code	codice (m) bancario	'ko-di-če ban-'ka-ryo
bank money order	vaglia (m, inv) bancario	'va-lya ban-'ka-ryo
bank receipt	ricevuta	ri-če-'vu-ta
bank worker	bancario (-a)	ban-'ka-ryo
banking executive	banchiere (-a)	ban-'kye-re
bill, banknote	banconota	ban-ko-'no-ta
	biglietto di banca	bi-'lyet-to
• large bill	banconota di grosso taglio	ban-ko-'no-ta di 'gros-so 'ta-lyo
• small bill	banconota di piccolo taglio	ban-ko-'no-ta di 'pik-ko-lo 'ta-lyo
blank endorsement	girata in bianco	ji-'ra-ta in 'byan-ko
bond	obbligazione (f)	ob-bli-ga-'tsyo-ne
budget, balance	bilancio	bi-'lan-čo
capital	capitale (m)	ka-pi-'ta-le
cash	contanti (m, pl)	kon-'tan-ti
• cashier, teller	cassiere (-a)	kas-'sye-re
check	assegno	as-'se-nyo
• (to) cash a check	incassare un assegno	in-kas-'sa-re un as-'se-nyo
• check book	libretto degli assegni	li-'bret-to de-lyi as-'se-nyi
• check clearing	compensazione (f) degli assegni	kom-pen-sa-'styo-ne de-'lyi as-'se-nyi
• (to) clear	compensare	kom-pen-'sa-re
• non-transferrable check	assegno barrato	as-'se-nyo bar-'ra-to
counterfeit money	moneta falsa	mo-'ne-ta 'fal-sa
credit	credito	'kre-di-to
• credit card	carta di credito	'kar-ta di 'kre-di-to
• credit institute, trust	istituto di credito	is-ti-'tu-to di 'kre-di-to
• credit limit	fido	'fi-do
• credit transfer	bonifico	bo-'ni-fi-ko
currency value	valuta	va-'lu-ta
debit, bill, debt	debito	'de-bi-to
deficit	deficit (m, inv)	de-fi-'čit
deposit	versamento	ver-sa-'men-to
• (to) deposit	versare	ver-'sa-re
• deposit slip	modulo di versamento	'mo-du-lo di ver-sa-'men-to
devaluation	svaluta	zva-'lu-ta
• (to) devalue	svalutare	zva-lu-'ta-re
discount	sconto	'skon-to
• discount rate	tasso di sconto	'tas-so
draft, promissory note	cambiale (f)	kam-'bya-le
e-banking	e-banking (m, inv)	—
endorsement	girata	ji-'ra-ta
• (to) endorse	avallare	a-val-'la-re

euro	euro (m, inv)	'eu-ro
exchange	cambio	'kam-byo
• (to) exchange	cambiare	kam-'bya-re
financier	finanziere (m)	fi-nan-'tsye-re
form (to fill out)	modulo	'mo-du-lo
funding	finanziamento	fi-nan-tsya-'mento
income	reddito	'red-di-to
inflation	inflazione (f)	in-fla-'tsyo-ne
• deflation	deflazione (f)	de-fla-'tsyo-ne
• inflation rate	tasso d'inflazione	'tas-so din-fla-'tsyo-ne
• recession	recessione (f)	re-ces-'syo-ne
insurance	assicurazione (f)	as-si-ku-ra-'tsyo-ne
• accident insurance	assicurazione contro gli infortuni	as-si-ku-ra-'tsyo-ne 'kon-tro lyi in-for-'tu-ni
• anti-theft insurance	assicurazione contro il furto	'fur-to
• fire insurance	assicurazione contro l'incendio	in-'čen-dyo
• insurable	assicurabile	as-si-ku-'ra-bi-le
• insurance company	società d'assicurazione	so-če-'ta
• insurance policy	polizza d'assicurazione	'po-li-tsa
• (to) insure	assicurare	as-si-ku-'ra-re
• insured person	assicurato (-a)	as-si-ku-'ra-to
• life insurance	assicurazione sulla vita	—
interest	interesse (m)	in-te-'res-se
• compound interest	interesse composto	kom-'pos-to
• interest rate	tasso d'interesse	'tas-so
• simple interest	interesse semplice	'sem-pli-če
(to) invest	investire	in-ves-'ti-re
• investment	investimento	in-ves-ti-'men-to
liability, loan	ipoteca	i-po-'te-ka
loan	prestito	'pres-ti-to
loose change	spiccioli (m, pl)	'spič-čo-li
manager	direttore (-trice)	di-ret-'to-re
money	denaro	de-'na-ro
	soldi (m, pl)	'sol-di
mortgage	mutuo	'mu-two
• house mortgage	mutuo fondiario	fon-'dya-ryo
• (to) open up a mortgage	accendere* un mutuo	ač-'čen-de-re
• (to) pay off a mortgage	estinguere* un mutuo	es-'tin-gwe-re
(to) pay	pagare	pa-'ga-re
• (to) pay off	saldare	sal-'da-re
• payment	pagamento	pa-ga-'men-to
• payment on delivery	pagamento a pronta cassa	pa-ga-'men-to a 'pron-ta 'kas-sa
online banking	banca online	—

portfolio	portafoglio	*por-ta-'fo-lyo*
rate	tasso	*'tas-so*
safe	cassaforte (f)	*kas-sa-'for-te*
safety deposit box	cassetta di	*kas-'set-ta di*
	sicurezza	*si-ku-'re-tsa*
(to) save	risparmiare	*ris-par-'mya-re*
• savings	risparmi	*ris-'par-mi*
• savings book	libretto di risparmio	*li-'bret-to*
signature	firma	—
• (to) sign	firmare	*fir-'ma-re*
• signatory, signer	firmatario (-a)	*fir-ma-'ta-ryo*
stock, share	azione (f)	*a-'tsyo-ne*
• stock market	borsa valori	*'bor-sa va-'lo-ri*
surplus	eccedente (m)	*eč-če-'den-te*
tax	tassa	—
• taxable income	imponibile (m)	*im-po-'ni-bi-le*
• tax collector	esattore (-trice)	*e-zat-'to-re*
teller	cassiere (-a)	*kas-'sye-re*
• teller's window	sportello	*spor-'tel-lo*
traveler's check	traveler's check	—
withdrawal	prelevamento	*pre-le-va-'men-to*
• (to) withdraw	prelevare	*pre-le-'va-re*
• authorized	prelevamento	*pre-le-va-'men-to*
withdrawal	autorizzato	*auto-ri-'dza-to*
• automatic	prelevamento	
withdrawal	automatico	*au-to-'ma-ti-ko*

B. COMMERCE

amount	ammontare (m)	*ammon-'ta-re*
balancing the books	compensazione (f)	*kom-pen-sa-'tsyo-ne*
bankruptcy	bancarotta	*ban-ka-'rot-ta*
claim	rivendicazione (f)	*ri-ven-di-ka-'tsyo-ne*
(to) compensate	indennizzare	*in-den-ni-'dza-re*
competition	concorrenza	*kon-kor-'ren-dza*
credit letter	lettera di credito	*'let-te-ra di 'kre-di-to*
damages	danni (m, pl)	*'dan-ni*
deal	affare (m)	*af-'fa-re*
deduction	detrazione (f)	*de-tra-'tsyo-ne*
expenses	spese (f, pl)	*'spe-ze*
• expenses (business)	uscite (f, pl)	*u-'ši-te*
(to) export	esportare	*es-por-'ta-re*
fall in prices	ribasso dei prezzi	*ri-'bas-so dei 'pre-tsi*
(to) finance	finanziare	*fi-nan-'tsya-re*
gain	guadagno	*gwa-'da-nyo*
• gains, profits	entrate (f, pl)	*en-'tra-te*
import	importare	*im-por-'ta-re*
interest loan	prestito a interesse	*'pres-ti-to a in-te-'res-se*

large loan	prestito ingente	'pres-ti-to in-'jen-te
laws of the marketplace	leggi del mercato	'lej-ji del mer-'ka-to
legal tender	corso	—
liability	responsabilità (f, inv)	res-pon-sa-bi-li-'ta
liquidation	liquidazione (f)	li-kwi-da-'tsyo-ne
• (to) liquidate	liquidare	li-kwi-'da-re
loaner, creditor	creditore (m)	kre-di-'to-re
loss	perdita	'per-di-ta
lump sum	somma forfettaria	'som-ma for-fet-'ta-rya
market price	prezzo di mercato	'pre-tso di mer-'ka-to
personal income tax	imposta sul reddito	im-'pos-ta sul 'red-di-to
	delle persone fisiche	del-le per'so-ne 'fi-zi-ke
public debt	debito pubblico	'de-bi-to 'pub-bli-ko
quotation	quotazione (f)	kwo-ta-'tsyo-ne
• (to) quote	quotare	kwo-'ta-re
(stock price)		
realty tax	imposta sugli immobili	im-pos-ta su-lyi
		im-'mo-bi-li
rise in prices	rialzo dei prezzi	ri-'al-tso dei 'pre-tsi
sales tax	IVA (f. inv)	—
tax payment	prelievo d'imposta	pre-'lye-vo
• taxation office	ufficio delle imposte	uf-'fi-čo de-le im-'pos-te
treasurer	tesoriere (-a)	te-zo-'rye-re
yield	rendimento	ren-di-'men-to

27. GAMES AND SPORTS

A. GAMES, HOBBIES, AND PHYSICAL FITNESS

acrobat	acrobata (m/f)	a-'kro-ba-ta
bet	scommessa	skom-'mes-sa
• (to) bet	scommettere*	skom-'met-te-re
billiards	biliardo	bi-'lyar-do
• billiard ball	palla da biliardo	'pal-la
• billiard cue	stecca da biliardo	'stek-ka
• billiard table	tavolo da biliardo	'ta-vo-lo
bingo	tombola	'tom-bo-la
• bingo card	cartella della tombola	kar-'tel-la
charade	sciarada	ša-'ra-da
(to) cheat	imbrogliare	im-bro-'lya-re
• cheater	imbroglione (-a)	im-bro-'lyo-ne
• cheating	imbroglio	im-'bro-lyo
	truffa	'truf-fa
checkers	dama	—
• checker piece	pedina	pe-'di-na
chess	gioco degli scacchi	'jo-ko de-lyi 'skak-ki
circus	circo	'čir-ko
• clown	pagliaccio	pa-'lyač-čo

Cards and Chess

ace	asso
clubs	bastoni (m, pl)
goblets	coppe (f, pl)
hearts	cuori (m, pl)
money	denari (m, pl)
queen of spades	donna di picche
clubs	fiori (m, pl)
hand	mano
spades	picche (f, pl)
diamonds	quadri (m, pl)
swords	spade (f, pl)
bishop	alfiere (m)
knight	cavallo
pawn	pedone (m)
king	re (m, inv)
queen	regina
chess board	scacchiera
chess piece, check	scacco
checkmate	scacco matto
rook	torre (f)

coin	moneta	*mo-'ne-ta*
• coin collecting	numismatica	*nu-miz-'ma-ti-ka*
collecting	collezionismo	*kol-le-tsyo-'niz-mo*
• collector	collezionista (m/f)	*kol-le-tsyo-'nis-ta*
concert	concerto	*kon-čer-to*
crosswords	parole crociate	*pa-'ro-le kro-'ča-te*
dice	dadi	*'da-di*
• die	dado	—
doll	bambola	*'bam-bo-la*
electric toy train	trenino elettrico	*tre-'ni-no e-'let-tri-ko*
embroidery	ricamo	*ri-'ka-mo*
• (to) embroider	ricamare	*ri-ka-'ma-re*
fishing	pesca	*'pes-ka*
• bait	esca	*'es-ka*
• (to) fish	pescare	*pes-'ka-re*
• hook	amo	—
• line	lenza	*'len-tsa*
• reel	mulinello	*mu-li-'nel-lo*
• rod	canna da pesca	*'kan-na da 'pes-ka*
game	gioco	*'jo-ko*
game of chance, gambling	gioco d'azzardo	*'jo-ko dad-'dzar-do*
gardening	giardinaggio	*jar-di-'naj-jo*
hide-and-seek	rimpiattino	*rim-pyat-'ti-no*

hobby	hobby (m, inv)	—
hoop	cerchio	'čer-kyo
horse-racing	ippica	'ip-pi-ka
hunting	caccia	'kač-ča
• (to) hunt, go hunting	cacciare	kač-'ča-re
instrument	strumento	stru-'men-to
• (to) play	suonare	swo-'na-re
jogging	jogging (m, inv)	—
kite	aquilone (m)	a-kwi-'lo-ne
(to) knit	lavorare a maglia	la-vo-'ra-re a 'ma-'lya
lawn bowling	bocce (f, pl)	'boč-če
(to) lose	perdere*	'per-de-re
magic tricks	giochi di prestigio	'jo-ki di pres-'ti-jo
• magician	prestigiatore (-trice)	pres-ti-ja-'to-re
marble	bilia	'bi-lya
parade	parata	pa-'ra-ta
pinball machine	flipper (m, inv)	—
(to) play (a game)	giocare	jo-'ka-re
• (to) play ball (soccer)	giocare al pallone	pal-'lo-ne
• (to) play skipping rope	saltare con la corda	sal-'ta-re kon la 'kor-da
playing card	carta da gioco	'kar-ta da 'jo-ko
pottery	arte della ceramica	'ar-te del-la ce-'ra-mi-ka
puppet theater	teatro dei burrattini	te-a-tro dei bur-rat-'ti-ni
• marionette	marionetta	ma-ryo-'net-ta
puzzle	enigma (m) (enigmi, pl)	e-'nig-ma
rebus	rebus (m, inv)	—
recreational activities	attività ricreative	at-ti-vi-'ta ri-kre-a-'ti-ve
relaxation	riposo	ri-'po-zo
• (to) relax	riposarsi	ri-po-'zar-si
riddle	indovinello	in-do-vi-'nel-lo
(to) sew	cucire	ku-'či-re
skateboard	skateboard (m, inv)	—
stamp collecting	filatelia	fi-la-te-'li-a
swings	altalena	al-ta-'le-na
toboggan, slide	slitta	'zlit-ta
toy	giocattolo	jo-'kat-to-lo
• toy car	macchinina	mak-ki-'ni-na
• toy soldier	soldatino	sol-da-'ti-no
(to) unwind	distendersi	dis-'ten-der-si
video game	videogioco	vi-de-o-'jo-ko
(to) walk	camminare	kam-mi-'na-re
(to) win	vincere*	'vin-če-re

B. SPORTS

aerobics	aerobica	ae-'ro-bi-ka
amateur	dilettante (m/f)	di-let-'tan-te
archery	tiro con l'arco	'ti-ro kon 'lar-ko

athlete	atleta (m/f)	*at-'le-ta*
ball	palla	*'pal-la*
• (to) catch (the ball)	prendere*	*'pren-de-re*
• (to) hit	battere	*'bat-te-re*
• (to) kick	calciare	*kal-'ča-re*
• (to) pass	passare	*pas-'sa-re*
• (to) pitch	lanciare	*lan-'ča-re*
• (to) throw	tirare	*ti-'ra-re*
baseball	baseball	—
• baseball diamond	diamante (m)	*dya-'man-te*
• bat	mazza	*'ma-tsa*
• catcher's mask	maschera	*'mas-ke-ra*
• chest protector	corazza	*ko-'rat-tsa*
• helmet	casco	*'kas-ko*
• mound	pedana di lancio	*pe-'da-na di 'lan-čo*
• pitcher	lanciatore (m)	*lan-ča-'to-re*
• runner	corridore (m)	*kor-ri-'do-re*
basketball	pallacanestro (f, inv)	*pal-la-ka-'nes-tro*
	basket (m, inv)	—
• ball	pallone (m)	*pal-'lo-ne*
• basket	canestro	*ka-'nes-tro*
bicycle racing	corsa ciclistica	*'kor-sa či-'klis-ti-ka*
boat	barca	*'bar-ka*
body-building	culturismo	*kul-tu-'riz-mo*
• (to) lift weights	sollevare pesi	*sol-le-'va-re 'pe-zi*
• weight lifting	sollevamento pesi	*sol-le-va-'men-to 'pe-zi*
bowling	bowling (m, inv)	—
• lawn bowling	bocce (f, pl)	*'boč-če*
• bowling ball	boccia	*'boč-ča*
• bowling alley	pista	*'pis-ta*
• bowling pin	birillo	*bi-ril-lo*
boxing	pugilato	*pu-ji-'la-to*
• boxer	pugile (m/f)	*'pu-ji-le*
• featherweight	peso piuma	*'pe-zo 'pyu-ma*
• heavyweight	peso massimo	*'pe-zo 'mas-si-mo*
• middleweight	peso medio	*'pe-zo 'me-dyo*
(to) break a record	battere un record	*'bat-te-re*
canoe	canoa	*ka-'no-a*
car race	corsa automobilistica	*'kor-sa au-to-mo-bi-'lis-ti-ka*
• car racing	automobilismo	*au-to-mo-bi-'liz-mo*
champion	campione (m)	*kam-'pyo-ne*
change room	spogliatoio	*spo-lya-'to-yo*
coach	allenatore (-trice)	*al-le-na-'to-re*
competition	agonismo	*a-go-'niz-mo*
• (to) compete	concorrere*	*kom-'kor-re-re*
cup	coppa	*'kop-pa*
cycling	ciclismo	*či-'kliz-mo*

defeat	sconfitta	*skon-'fit-ta*
• (to) defeat	sconfiggere*	*skon-'fij-je-re*
disc, puck	disco	—
diving	(gare di) tuffi	*'tuf-fi*
• (to) dive	tuffarsi	*tuf-'far-si*
• diver	tuffatore (-trice)	*tuf-fa-'to-re*
driver	automobilista (m/f)	*au-to-mo-bi-'lis-ta*
(to) eliminate	eliminare	*e-li-mi-'na-re*
elimination round	girone eliminatorio	*ji-'ro-ne e-li-mi-na-'to-ryo*
fencing	scherma	*'sker-ma*
• fencing suit	divisa	*di-'vi-za*
• mask	maschera	*'mas-ke-ra*
• sword	spada	—
	sciabola	*'ša-bo-la*
field	campo	—
finalist	finalista (m/f)	*fi-na-'lis-ta*
football (American)	football americano	*a-me-ri-'ka-no*
foot racing	corsa podistica	*'kor-sa po-'dis-ti-ka*
game, match	partita	*par-'ti-ta*
goal, score	gol (m, inv)	—
	rete (f)	*'re-te*
golf	golf (m, inv)	—
gymnastics	ginnastica	*jin-'nas-ti-ka*
• gymnasium	palestra	*pa-'les-tra*
• gymnast	ginnasta (m/f)	*jin-'nas-ta*
• (to) work out	fare* ginnastica	—
high jumping	salto in alto	*'sal-to in 'al-to*
hockey	hockey (m, inv)	—
• hockey rink	campo di ghiaccio	*'kam-po di 'gyač-čo*
• hockey stick	bastone (m)	*bas-'to-ne*
• puck	disco	—
• skate	pattino	*'pat-ti-no*
horse race	corsa ippica	*'kor-sa 'ip-pi-ka*
• horse racing	equitazione (f)	*e-kwi-ta-'tsyo-ne*
ice skating	pattinaggio su ghiaccio	*pat-ti-'naj-jo su 'gyač-čo*
in record time	a tempo di record	
javelin throwing	lancio del giavellotto	*'lan-čo del ja-vel-'lot-to*
• javelin	giavellotto	*ja-vel-'lot-to*
judo	judo (m, inv)	—
(to) jump	saltare	*sal-'ta-re*
• jumper	saltatore (-trice)	*sal-ta-'to-re*
• long jumping	salto in lungo	—
karate	karatè (m, inv)	—
knapsack	zaino	*'dzai-no*
lap, stage	tappa	—
motorcycling	motociclismo	*mo-to-ci-'kliz-mo*

mountain climbing	alpinismo	*al-pi-'niz-mo*
• climber	alpinista (m/f)	*al-pi-'nis-ta*
oar	remo	—
Olympic games	giochi Olimpici	*'jo-ki o-'lim-pi-či*
opponent	avversario (-a)	*av-ver-'sa-ryo*
parachuting	paracadutismo	*pa-ra-ka-du-'tiz-mo*
player	giocatore (-trice)	*jo-ka-'to-re*
playoffs, championship	campionato	*kam-pyo-'na-to*
point	punto	—
pole vaulting	salto con l'asta	—
(to) practice a sport	praticare uno sport	*pra-ti-'ka-re*
race, racing	corsa	—
• (to) run	correre*	*'kor-re-re*
• runner	corridore (-trice)	*kor-ri-'do-re*
record	record (m, inv)	—
referee	arbitro (-a)	*'ar-bi-tra*
rival	rivale (m/f)	*ri-'va-le*
roller skating	pattinaggio a rotelle	*pat-ti-'naj-jo a ro-'tel-le*
rope	corda	—
rowing, canoeing	canottaggio	*ka-not-'taj-jo*
sailing	vela	—
score	punteggio	*pun-'tej-jo*
• draw, tie	pareggio	*pa-'rej-jo*
• (to) draw	pareggiare	*pa-rej-'ja-re*
• final score	risultato finale	*ri-zul-'ta-to*
• (to) lose	perdere*	*'per-de-re*
• loser	perdente	*per'-den-te*
• loss	perdita	*'per-di-ta*
• outcome	esito	*'e-zi-to*
• win	vincita	*'vin-či-ta*
• (to) win	vincere*	*'vin-če-re*
• winner	vincitore (-trice)	*vin-či-'to-re*
(to) set a record	stabilire (isc) un record	*sta-bi-'li-re*
skating	pattinaggio	*pat-ti-'naj-jo*
• skate	pattino	*'pat-ti-no*
• (to) skate	pattinare	*pat-ti-'na-re*
• skater	pattinatore (-trice)	*pat-ti-na-'to-re*
skiing, ski	sci (m, inv)	*ši*
• crosscountry skiing	sci da fondo	—
• downhill skiing	discesa	*di-'še-za*
• (to) ski	sciare	*ši-'a-re*
• ski jumping	salto	*'sal-to*
• skier	sciatore (-trice)	*ši-a-'to-re*
• water skiing	sci nautico	*'nau-ti-ko*
soccer	calcio	*'kal-čo*
• goaltender	portiere (m)	*por-'tye-re*
• (to) kick	calciare	*kal-'ča-re*
• net	porta	—

• (to) pass	passare	*pas-'sa-re*
• penalty	rigore (m)	*ri-'go-re*
• play (action)	gioco	*'jo-ko*
	azione (f)	*a-'tsyo-ne*
• (to) save	parata	*pa-'ra-ta*
• (to) score	segnare	*se-'nya-re*
• (to) shoot, kick	tirare	*ti-'ra-re*
• shot, kick	tiro	*'ti-ro*
• soccer ball	pallone (m)	*pal-'lo-ne*
• soccer player	calciatore (-trice)	*kal-ča-'to-re*
• (to) tackle	contrastare	*kon-tras-'ta-re*
• sports event	gara	—
• sports fan	tifoso (-a)	*ti-'fo-zo*
• sporty, of sports	sportivo	*spor-'ti-vo*
squash	squash (m, inv)	—
stadium	stadio	*'sta-dyo*
standings	classifica	*klas-'si-fi-ka*
surfing	surfing (m, inv)	—
swimming	nuoto	*'nwo-to*
• (to) swim	nuotare	*nwo-'ta-re*
• swimmer	nuotatore (-trice)	*nwo-ta-'to-re*
• swimming pool	piscina	*pi-'ši-na*
target	bersaglio	*ber-'sa-lyo*
team	squadra	*'skwa-dra*
tennis	tennis (m, inv)	—
• tennis court	campo da tennis	—
• tennis player	tennista (m/f)	*ten-'nis-ta*
• tennis racket	racchetta	*rak-'ket-ta*
ticket	biglietto	*bi-'lyet-to*
tournament	tournée (f, inv)	—
track and field	atletica leggera	*at-'le-ti-ka lej-'je-ra*
• track	pista	—
training	allenamento	*al-le-na-'men-to*
• (to) train	allenarsi	*al-le-'nar-si*
• trainer, coach	allenatore (-trice)	*al-le-na-'to-re*
volleyball	pallavolo (f, inv)	*pal-la-'vo-lo*
water polo	pallanuoto (f, inv)	*pal-la-'nwo-to*
World Cup	Coppa del Mondo	—
wrestling	lotta	—
• (to) wrestle	lottare	*lot-'ta-re*
• wrestler	lottatore (-trice)	*lot-ta-'to-re*

28. THE ARTS

A. CINEMA

actor, actress	attore (-trice)	*at-'to-re*
adventure film	film d'avventura	*dav-ven-'tu-ra*

aisle	corridoio	*kor-ri-'do-yo*
animation	animazione (f)	*a-ni-ma-'tsyo-ne*
balcony (of a movie theater)	galleria	*gal-le-'ri-a*
box office	botteghino	*bot-te-'gi-no*
cartoon	cartone animato	*kar-'to-ne a-ni-'ma-to*
cinema	cinema (m, inv)	*'či-ne-ma*
cowboy movie	film western	—
detective movie	film poliziesco	*po-li-'tsyes-ko*
director	regista (m/f)	*re-'jis-ta*
documentary	documentario	*do-ku-men-'ta-ryo*
dubbed	doppiato	*dop-'pya-to*
• **dubbing**	doppiaggio	*dop-'pyaj-jo*
editing	montaggio	*mon-'taj-jo*
feature (film)	lungometraggio	*'lun-go-me-'traj-jo*
film, movie	film (m, inv)	—
footage	metraggio	*me-'traj-jo*
ground floor	platea	*pla-'te-a*
horror film	film dell'orrore	*or-'ro-re*
in slow motion	al rallentatore	*ral-len-ta-'to-re*
lobby	ridotto	*ri-'dot-to*
movie camera	cinepresa	*ci-ne-'pre-za*
movie star	stella del cinema	*'stel-la del 'či-ne-ma*
movie theater	cinema (m, inv)	*'či-ne-ma*
musical film	film musicale	*mu-zi-'ka-le*
mystery movie	film giallo	*'jal-lo*
performer	interprete (m/f)	*in-'ter-pre-te*
pornographic movie	film pornografico	*por-no-'gra-fi-ko*
premiere showing	prima visione	*'pri-ma vi-'zyo-ne*
producer	produttore (-trice)	*pro-dut-'to-re*
• **production**	produzione (m)	*pro-du-'tsyo-ne*
restricted	vietato ai minori	*vye-'ta-to ai mi-'no-ri*
row	fila	—
scenery	sceneggiatura	*še-nej-ja-'tu-ra*
science fiction movie	film di fantascienza	*fan-ta-'šen-tsa*
screen	schermo	*'sker-mo*
(to) shoot a movie	girare un film	*ji-'ra-re*
• **shooting on location**	riprese (f, pl) in esterni	*ri-'pre-ze*
short (film)	cortometraggio	*kor-to-me-'traj-jo*
shot	ripresa (cinematografica)	*ri-'pre-za*
sound technician	tecnico del suono	*'tek-ni-ko del 'swo-no*
sound track	colonna sonora	*ko-'lon-na so-'no-ra*
spy movie	film di spionaggio	*spyo-'naj-jo*
subtitle	sottotitolo	*sot-to-'ti-to-lo*
thriller	thriller (m, inv)	—
video cassette	videocassetta	*vi-de-o-kas-'set-ta*

B. VISUAL ARTS, SCULPTURE, ARCHITECTURE, AND PHOTOGRAPHY

abstract	astratto	*as-'trat-to*
(to) aim the lens	puntare l'obiettivo	*pun-'ta-re lo-byet-'ti-vo*
architecture	architettura	*ar-ki-tet-'tu-ra*
art	arte (f)	*'ar-te*
• art exhibition	mostra d'arte	*'mos-tra 'dar-te*
• art gallery	galleria d'arte	*gal-le-'ri-a*
• art museum	museo d'arte	*mu-'ze-o*
• artist	artista (m/f)	*ar-'tis-ta*
background	sfondo	*'sfon-do*
Baroque	Barocco	*ba-'rok-ko*
blueprint	copia cianografica	*'ko-'pya ča-no-'gra-fi-ka*
bronze sculpture	scultura in bronzo	*skul-'tu-ra in 'bron-dzo*
brush	pennello	*pen-nel-lo*
canvas	tela	*'te-la*
chiaroscuro	chiaroscuro	*kya-ro-'sku-ro*
chisel	cesello	*če-'zel-lo*
• (to) chisel	cesellare	*če-zel-'la-re*
Classicism	Classicismo	*klas-si-'čiz-mo*
dark room	camera oscura	*'ka-me-ra os-'ku-ra*
digital photography	fotografia digitale	*fo-to-gra-'fi-a di-ji-'ta-le*
drawing	disegno	*di-'ze-nyo*
easel	cavalletto (da pittore)	*ka-val-'let-to (da pit-'to-re)*
etching	disegno a matita	*di-'ze-nyo a ma-'ti-ta*
exhibition	mostra	—
fine arts	belle arti	*'be-le 'ar-ti*
(to) focus	mettere* a fuoco	*'met-te-re a 'fwo-ko*
foreground	primo piano	*'pri-mo 'pya-no*
(to) frame	inquadrare	*in-kwa-'dra-re*
freehand drawing	disegno a mano libera	*di-'ze-nyo a 'ma-no 'li-be-ra*
fresco painting	affresco	*af-'fres-ko*
geometric design	disegno geometrico	*di-'ze-nyo je-o-'me-tri-ko*
image	immagine (f)	*im-'ma-ji-ne*
Impressionism	Impressionismo	*im-pres-syo-'niz-mo*
landscape	paesaggio	*pa-e-'zaj-jo*
marble sculpture	scultura in marmo	*skul-'tu-ra in 'mar-mo*
masterpiece	capolavoro	*ka-po-la-'vo-ro*
model	modello	*mo-'del-lo*
movie camera	cinepresa	*ci-ne-'pre-za*
mural painting	pittura murale	*pit-'tu-ra mu-'ra-le*
negative	negativo	*ne-ga-'ti-vo*
nude	nudo	—
oil painting	pittura a olio	*pit-'tu-ra a 'o-lyo*

(to) paint	dipingere*	*di-'pin-je-re*
• painter	pittore (-trice)	*pit-'to-re*
• painting	dipinto	*di-'pin-to*
	quadro	*'kwa-dro*
palette	tavolozza	*ta-vo-'lo-tsa*
pastel	pastello	*pas-'tel-lo*
pedestal	piedistallo	*pye-di-'stal-lo*
photograph	fotografia	*fo-to-gra-'fi-a*
• photographer	fotografo (-a)	*fo-'to-gra-fo*
• photographic shot	ripresa fotografica	*ri-'pre-za fo-to-'gra-fi-ka*
portrait	ritratto	*ri-'trat-to*
pose	posa	*'po-za*
print, mold	stampa	—
Realism	Realismo	*re-a-'liz-mo*
relief	rilievo	*ri-'lye-vo*
Rococo	Rococò	—
Romanticism	Romanticismo	*ro-man-ti-'čiz-mo*
(to) sculpt	scolpire (isc)	*skol-'pi-re*
• sculptor, sculptress	scultore (-trice)	*skul-'to-re*
• sculpture	scultura	*skul-'tu-ra*
shade, nuance	sfumatura	*sfu-ma-'tu-ra*
sketch	schizzo	*'ski-tso*
slide	diapositiva	*di-a-po-zi-'ti-va*
statue	statua	*'sta-tu-a*
(to) trace	calcare	*kal-'ka-re*
tripod	treppiede (m, inv)	*trep-'pye-de*
visual arts	arti figurative	*'ar-ti fi-gu-ra-'ti-ve*
water color	acquerello	*ak-kwe-'rel-lo*
• water colorist	aquerellista (m/f)	*ak-kwe-rel-'lis-ta*
wax museum	museo delle cere	*mu-ze-o del-le 'če-re*
work of art	opera d'arte	*'o-pe-ra 'dar-te*

C. MUSIC/DANCE

accordion	fisarmonica	*fi-zar-'mo-ni-ka*
• accordionist	fisarmonicista (m/f)	*fi-zar-mo-ni-'čis-ta*
ballad	ballata	*bal-'la-ta*
ballet	balletto	*bal-'let-to*
ballroom	sala da ballo	*'sa-la da 'bal-lo*
band	gruppo	*'grup-po*
	complesso	*kom-'ples-so*
baritone	baritono	*ba-'ri-to-no*
base	basso	*'bas-so*
baton	bacchetta	*bak-'ket-ta*
(to) beat time	battere il tempo	*'bat-te-re*
brass instruments	ottoni	*ot'-to-ni*
• horn	corno	*'kor-no*
• horn player	cornista (m/f)	*kor-'nis-ta*

• **trombone**	trombone	*trom-'bo-ne*
• **trumpet**	tromba	
• **trumpeter**	trombettista (m/f)	*trom-bet-'tis-ta*
• **tuba**	tuba	*'tu-ba*
chamber music	musica da camera	*'mu-zi-ka da 'ka-me-ra*
chant	canto	—
choir	coro	—
chord	accordo	*ak-'kor-do*
classical music	musica classica	*'mu-zi-ka*
composer	compositore (-trice)	*kom-po-zi-'to-re*
• **composition**	composizione (f)	*kom-po-zi-'tsyo-ne*
concert, concerto	concerto	*kon-'cer-to*
conservatory	conservatorio	*kon-ser-va-'to-ryo*
contralto	contralto	*kon-'tral-to*
dance	ballo	—
• **(to) dance**	ballare	*bal-'la-re*
• **dance music**	musica da ballo	*'mu-zi-ka da 'bal-lo*
• **dancer**	ballerino (-a)	*bal-le-'ri-no*
disco	discoteca	*dis-ko-'te-ka*
duet	duetto	*du-'et-to*
fandango	fandango	*fan-'dan-go*
folk music	musica folk	*'mu-zi-ka*
	musica folcloristica	*'mu-zi-ka fol-klo-'ris-ti-ka*
harmony	armonia	*ar-mo-'ni-a*
hymn	inno	—
instrument	strumento	*stru-'men-to*
key	chiave (f)	*'kya-ve*
lullaby	ninna nanna	—
madrigal	madrigale (m)	*ma-dri-'ga-le*
masked ball	ballo in maschera	*'bal-lo in 'mas-ke-ra*
melody	melodia	*me-lo-'di-a*
music	musica	*'mu-zi-ka*
• **music stand**	portamusica (m, inv)	*por-ta-'mu-zi-ka*
• **musician**	musicista (m/f)	*mu-zi-'čis-ta*
• **musicologist**	musicologo (-a)	*mu-zi-'ko-lo-go*
note	nota	—
opera	opera	*'o-pe-ra*
orchestra	orchestra	*or-'kes-tra*
orchestra conductor	direttore (-trice)	*di-ret-'to-re*
organ	organo	*'or-ga-no*
• **organist**	organista (m/f)	*or-ga-'nis-ta*
percussion instruments	strumenti a percussione	*stru-'men-ti a per-kus-'syo-ne*
• **bass drum**	grancassa	*gran-'kas-sa*
• **cymbal**	piatto	*'pyat-to*
• **drum, tambourine**	tamburo	*tam-'bu-ro*
• **drummer**	batterista (m/f)	*bat-te-'ris-ta*

• set of drums	batteria	*bat-te-'ri-a*
• timpani	timpano	*'tim-pa-no*
piano	pianoforte (m), piano	*pya-no-'for-te*
• grand piano	piano a coda	—
• pianist	pianista (m/f)	*pya-'nis-ta*
• upright piano	piano verticale	*ver-ti-'ka-le*
(to) play	suonare	*swo-'na-re*
• play out of tune	stonare	*sto-'na-re*
• player	suonatore (-trice)	*swo-na-'to-re*
polka	polca	*'pol-ka*
pop music	musica popolare	*'mu-zi-ka po-po-'la-re*
(to) practice	esercitarsi	*e-zer-či-'tar-si*
quadrille, square dance	quadriglia	*kwa-'dri-lya*
quartet	quartetto	*kwar-'tet-to*
quintet	quintetto	*kwin-'tet-to*
rap	rap (m, inv)	—
rehearsal	prova	*'pro-va*
rhythm	ritmo	—
rock music	musica rock	*'mu-zi-ka*
rumba	rumba	—
scale	scala	—
score	spartito	*spar-'ti-to*
sextet	sestetto	*ses-'tet-to*
singer	cantante (m/f)	*kan-'tan-te*
solo	assolo	*as-'so-lo*
• soloist	solista (m/f)	*so-'lis-ta*
song	canzone (f)	*kan-'tso-ne*
soprano	soprano	*so-'pra-no*
string instruments	strumenti a corda	*stru-'men-ti a 'kor-da*
• bow	arco	—
• double bass	contrabbasso	*kon-trab-'bas-so*
• double bass player	contrabbassista (m/f)	*kon-trab-bas-'sis-ta*
• cello	violoncello	*vyo-lon-'čel-lo*
• cellist	violoncellista (m/f)	*vyo-lon-čel-'lis-ta*
• guitar	chitarra	*ki-'tar-ra*
• guitarist	chitarrista (m/f)	*ki-tar-'ris-ta*
• harp	arpa	—
• harpist	arpista (m/f)	—
• harpsichord	clavicembalo	*kla-vi-'čem-ba-lo*
• mandolin	mandolino	*man-do-'li-no*
• mandolin player	mandolinista (m/f)	*man-do-li-'nis-ta*
• string	corda	—
• viola	viola	*'vyo-la*
• viola player	violista (m/f)	*vyo-'lis-ta*
• violin	violino	*vyo-'li-no*
• violinist	violinista (m/f)	*vyo-li-'nis-ta*
symphony	sinfonia	*sin-fo-'ni-a*
tango	tango	—

tap dancing	tip tap (m, inv)	—
tarantella	tarantella	*ta-ran-'tel-la*
tenor	tenore (m)	*te-'no-re*
tone	tono	—
trio	trio	—
(to) tune	accordare	*ak-kor-'da-re*
tune, aria	aria	—
waltz	valzer (m, inv)	—
wind instruments	strumenti a fiato	*stru-'men-ti a 'fya-to*
• **bagpipes**	zampogne (f, pl)	*dzam-'po-nye*
• **bassoon**	fagotto	*fa-'got-to*
• **bassoonist**	fagottista (m/f)	*fa-got-'tis-ta*
• **clarinet**	clarinetto	*kla-ri-'net-to*
• **clarinettist**	clarinettista (m/f)	*kla-ri-net-'ti-sta*
• **flute**	flauto	*'flau-to*
• **flautist**	flautista (m/f)	*flau-'tis-ta*
• **oboe**	oboe (m)	*'o-bo-e*
• **oboist**	oboista (m/f)	*o-bo-'is-ta*
• **saxophone**	sassofono	*sas-'so-fo-no*
• **saxophonist**	sassofonista (m/f)	*sas-so-fo-'nis-ta*

D. LITERATURE

adventure	avventura	*av-ven-'tu-ra*
allegory	allegoria	*al-le-go-'ri-a*
anecdote	aneddoto	*a-'ned-do-to*
anthology	antologia	*an-to-lo-'ji-a*
appendix	appendice (f)	*ap-pen-'di-če*
author	autore (-trice)	*au-'to-re*
autobiography	autobiografia	*au-to-bi-o-gra-'fi-a*
ballad	ballata	*bal-'la-ta*
biography	biografia	*bi-o-gra-'fi-a*
catalogue	catalogo	*ka-'ta-lo-go*
chapter	capitolo	*ka-'pi-to-lo*
character	personaggio	*per-son-'aj-jo*
collection	raccolta	*rak-'kol-ta*
colorful, vivacious	vivace	*vi-'va-če*
comedy, play	commedia	*kom-'me-dya*
comics	fumetti (m, pl)	*fu-'met-ti*
compiler, editor of a volume	curatore (-trice)	*ku-ra-'to-re*
concise	conciso	*kon-'či-zo*
confusing	confusionario	*kon-fu-zyo-'na-ryo*
contrast	contrasto	*kon-'tras-to*
controversial, polemical	polemico	*po-'le-mi-ko*
criticism	critica	*'kri-ti-ka*
• **(to) criticize**	criticare	*kri-ti-'ka-re*
(to) deal with	trattare	*trat-'ta-re*

(to) develop	sviluppare	*zvi-lup-'pa-re*
diary	diario	*di-'a-ryo*
dictionary, lexicon	dizionario	*di-tsyo-'na-ryo*
doodle	scarabocchio	*ska-ra-'bok-kyo*
draft	bozza	*'bot-tsa*
drama	dramma (m) (drammi, pl)	—
elaborate	elaborato	*e-la-bo-'ra-to*
elegy	elegia	*e-le-'ji-a*
(to) emphasize	accentuare	*ač-čen-tu-'a-re*
encyclopedia	enciclopedia	*en-či-'klo-pe'di-a*
epigram	epigramma (m) (epigrammi, pl)	*e-pi-'gram-ma*
episode	episodio	*e-pi-'zo-dyo*
essay	saggio	*'saj-jo*
• essay-writing	saggistica	*saj-'jis-ti-ka*
(to) explain	spiegare	*spye-'ga-re*
fable	favola	*'fa-vo-la*
fairy tale	fiaba	*'fya-ba*
far-fetched, unusual	inconsueto	*in-kon-'swe-to*
(to) frame	inquadrare	*in-kwa-'dra-re*
genre	genere (m)	*'je-ne-re*
heavy	pesante	*pe-'zan-te*
hero, heroine	eroe (-ina)	*e-'ro-e*
(to) highlight	sottolineare	*sot-to-li-ne-'a-re*
image	immagine (f)	*im-'ma-ji-ne*
index	indice (m)	*'in-di-če*
irony	ironia	*i-ro-'ni-a*
laconic	laconico	*la-'ko-ni-ko*
legend	leggenda	*lej-'jen-da*
light	leggero	*lej-'je-ro*
line, verse	verso	—
literal	letterale	*let-te-'ra-le*
literature	letteratura	*let-te-ra-'tu-ra*
lively	animato	*a-ni-'ma-to*
manuscript	manoscritto	*ma-no-'skrit-to*
memoirs	memorie (f, pl)	*me-'mo-rye*
metaphor	metafora	*me-'ta-fo-ra*
motif	motivo	*mo-'ti-vo*
mystery, detective novel	giallo	*'jal-lo*
myth	mito	—
• mythology	mitologia	*mi-to-lo-'ji-a*
narration	narrazione (f)	*nar-ra-'tsyo-ne*
• narrative, fiction	narrativa	*nar-ra-'ti-va*
• narrator	narratore (-trice)	*nar-ra-'to-re*
novel	romanzo	*ro-'man-dzo*
• novelist	romanziere (-a)	*ro-man-'dzye-re*

ode	ode (f)	*'o-de*
ornate	adorno	*a-'dor-no*
(to) outline	tratteggiare	*trat-tej-'ja-re*
parody	parodia	*pa-ro-'di-a*
perspective, framework	ottica	*'ot-ti-ka*
plot	trama	—
poet	poeta (-essa)	*po-'e-ta*
• **poetics**	poetica	*po-'e-ti-ka*
• **poetry, poem**	poesia	*po-e-'zi-a*
(to) point out	segnalare	*se-nya-'la-re*
pompous	pomposo	*pom-'po-zo*
preface	prefazione (f)	*pre-fa-'tsyo-ne*
prose	prosa	*'pro-za*
publisher, publishing house	editore (m)	*e-di-'to-re*
quotation	citazione (f)	*či-ta-'tsyo-ne*
• **(to) quote**	citare	*či-'ta-re*
(to) read	leggere*	*'lej-je-re*
• **reader**	lettore (-trice)	*let-'to-re*
• **reading**	lettura	*let-'tu-ra*
review	recensione (f)	*re-čen-'syo-ne*
• **(to) review**	recensire (isc)	*re-čen-'si-re*
rhetoric	retorica	*re-'to-ri-ka*
royalty	diritto d'autore	*di-'rit-to dau-'to-re*
satire	satira	*'sa-ti-ra*
scene	scena	*'še-na*
science fiction	fantascienza	*fan-ta-'šen-tsa*
short story	novella	*no-'vel-la*
• **short-story writer**	novellista (m/f)	*no-vel-'lis-ta*
spicy	piccante	*pik-'kan-te*
style	stile (m)	*'sti-le*
• **stylistics**	stilistica	*sti-'lis-ti-ka*
symbolic	simbolico	*sim-'bo-li-ko*
• **symbolism**	simbolismo	*sim-bo-'liz-mo*
table of contents	indice (m) delle materie	*'in-di-če del-le ma-'te-rye*
tale	racconto	*rak-'kon-to*
terse, succinct	lapidario	*la-pi-'da-ryo*
text	testo	—
theme	tema (m) (temi, pl)	—
title (of a book)	titolo	*'ti-to-lo*
tragedy	tragedia	*tra-'je-dya*
volume	volume (m)	*vo-'lu-me*
work	opera	*'o-pe-ra*
(to) write	scrivere*	*'skri-ve-re*
• **writer**	scrittore (-trice)	*skrit-'to-re*
• **writing**	scrittura	*skrit-'tu-ra*

E. THEATER

act	atto	*'at-to*
• (to) act	recitare	*re-či-'ta-re*
• actor, actress	attore (-trice)	*at-'to-re*
applause	applauso	*ap-'plau-zo*
• (to) applaud	applaudire (isc)	*ap-plau-'di-re*
aside	a parte	—
audience	pubblico	*'pub-bli-ko*
(to) boo	fischiare	*fis-'kya-re*
character	personaggio	*per-son-'aj-jo*
• main character, protagonist	protagonista (m/f)	*pro-ta-go-'nis-ta*
comedy, play	commedia	*kom-'me-dya*
comic, comedian	comico (-a)	*'ko-mi-ko*
costume	costume (m)	*kos-'tu-me*
curtain	tenda	*'ten-da*
• curtains	sipario	*si-'pa-ryo*
dialogue	dialogo	*di-'a-lo-go*
director	regista (m/f)	*re-'jis-ta*
drama	dramma (m) (drammi, pl)	—
footlights	luci di ribalta	*'lu-či di ri-'bal-ta*
hero, heroine	eroe (-ina)	*e-'ro-e*
intermission	intervallo	*in-ter-'val-lo*
line (verbal)	battuta	*bat-'tu-ta*
main role	ruolo principale	*'rwo-lo prin-ci-'pa-le*
make-up	trucco	*'truk-ko*
monologue	monologo	*mo-'no-lo-go*
pantomime	pantomima	*pan-to-'mi-ma*
play	recita	*'re-či-ta*
• performance	messa in scena	*'še-na*
playwright	commediografo (-a)	*kom-me-'dyo-gra-fo*
plot	trama	—
program	programma (m)	*pro-'gram-ma*

Some Well-Known Italian Playwrights

Carlo Goldoni (1707–93)	*La Locandiera (1753)*
Luigi Pirandello (1867–1936)	*Sei personaggi in cerca d'autore (1921)*
Ugo Betti (1892–1953)	*Corruzione al palazzo di giustizia (1949)*
Dario Fo (1926–)	*Morte accidentale di un anarchico (1971)*

prompter	suggeritore (-trice)	*suj-je-ri-'to-re*
role	ruolo	*'rwo-lo*
scenario, background	scenario	*še-'na-ryo*
scene	scena	*'še-na*
• **scenery**	sceneggiatura	*še-nej-ja-'tu-ra*
script	copione (m)	*ko-'pyo-ne*
show	spettacolo	*spet-'ta-ko-lo*
skit	sketch (inv) comico	*'ko-mi-ko*
spotlights	riflettori (m, pl)	*ri-flet-'to-ri*
stage	palcoscenico	*pal-ko-'še-ni-ko*
star	stella	—
theater	teatro	*te-'a-tro*
tragedy	tragedia	*tra-'je-dya*
usher	maschera	*'mas-ke-ra*
wings (of a stage)	quinte (f, pl)	*'kwin-te*

29. HOLIDAYS/GOING OUT

A. HOLIDAYS/SPECIAL OCCASIONS

anniversary	anniversario	*an-ni-ver-'sa-ryo*
birthday	compleanno	*kom-ple-'an-no*
Christmas	Natale	*na-'ta-le*
Easter	Pasqua	*'pas-kwa*
Feast of the Assumption	Ferragosto	*fer-ra-'gos-to*
holidays	ferie (f, pl)	*'fe-rye*
name day	onomastico	*o-no-'mas-ti-ko*
New Year's Day	Capodanno	*ka-po-'dan-no*
New Year's Eve	Vigilia di Capodanno	*vi-'ji-lya di ka-po-'dan-no*
picnic	picnic (m, inv)	—
vacation	vacanza	*va-'kan-dza*
• **(to) go on vacation**	andare* (ess) in vacanza	—

B. GOING OUT

bar	bar (m, inv)	—
circus	circo	*'čir-ko*
• **clown**	pagliaccio	*pa-'lyač-čo*
concert	concerto	*kon-'čer-to*
dance	ballo	—
date	appuntamento	*ap-pun-ta-'men-to*
disco	discoteca	*dis-ko-'te-ka*
(to) enjoy oneself, have fun	divertirsi	*di-ver-'tir-si*
fortune teller	chiromante (f)	*ki-ro-'man-te*
(to) go out	uscire* (ess)	*u-'ši-re*
good time, enjoyment	divertimento	*di-ver-ti-'men-to*

ice cream	gelato	*je-'la-to*
• **ice cream parlor**	gelateria	*je-la-te-'ri-a*
invitation	invito	*in-'vi-to*
leisure	svago	*'zva-go*
movies	cinema (m, inv)	*'či-ne-ma*
night club	locale notturno	*lo-'ka-le not-'tur-no*
parade	parata	*pa-'ra-ta*
party, feast	festa	—
relaxation	riposo	*ri-'po-zo*
(to) remain	rimanere* (ess)	*ri-ma-'ne-re*
(to) return	ritornare (ess)	*ri-tor-'na-re*
show, performance	spettacolo	*spet-'ta-ko-lo*
(to) stroll	passeggiata	*pas-sej-'ja-ta*
target practice	tiro	—
theater	teatro	*te-'a-tro*
unwind	distendersi	*dis-'ten-der-si*
visit	visita	*'vi-zi-ta*
• **(to) visit**	visitare	*vi-zi-'ta-re*
walk, stroll	camminata	*kam-mi-'na-ta*
• **(to) walk**	camminare	*kam-mi-'na-re*

C. SPECIAL GREETINGS

Best wishes!	Auguri!	*au-'gu-ri*
Compliments!	Complimenti!	*kom-pli-'men-ti*
Congratulations!	Congratulazioni!	*kon-gra-tu-la-'tsyo-ni*
Happy Birthday!	Buon compleanno!	*bwon kom-ple-'an-no*
Happy New Year!	Buon anno!	
Have a good vacation!	Buona vacanza!	*'bwo-na va-'kan-dza*
Have fun!	Buon divertimento!	*bwon di-ver-ti-'men-to*
Merry Christmas!	Buon Natale!	*bwon na-'ta-le*

TRAVEL

30. CHOOSING A DESTINATION

A. AT THE TRAVEL AGENCY

abroad	all'estero	al-'les-te-ro
brochure	opuscolo	o-'pus-ko-lo
bus tour	viaggio in pullman	'vyaj-jo in 'pul-man
charter flight	volo charter	—
class	classe (f)	'klas-se
• **economy class**	classe turistica	tu-'ris-ti-ka
• **first class**	prima classe	—
continent	continente (m)	kon-ti-'nen-te
country, nation	nazione (f)	na-'tsyo-ne
down-payment	caparra	ka-'par-ra
excursion, tour	gita	'ji-ta
guide	guida	'gwi-da
high season	alta stagione	'al-ta sta-'jo-ne
insurance	assicurazione (f)	as-si-ku-ra-'styo-ne
low season	bassa stagione	'bas-sa sta-'jo-ne
package tour	viaggio organizzato	'vyaj-jo
reservation	prenotazione (f)	pre-no-ta-'tsyo-ne
• **online reservation**	prenotazione (f) on-line	—
seaside area	zona balneare	'dzo-na bal-ne-'a-re
• **seaside vacation**	vacanza al mare	va-'kan-dza al 'ma-re
summer vacation	vacanze estive	va-'kan-dze es-'ti-ve
ticket	biglietto	bi-'lyet-to
• **(to) buy a travel ticket**	fare* il biglietto	—
• **by boat, by ship**	con la nave	'na-ve
• **by plane**	in aereo	a-'e-re-o
• **by train**	in treno	—
• **one-way ticket**	biglietto di andata	—
• **return ticket**	biglietto di andata e ritorno	—
tour	giro	'ji-ro
tourism	turismo	tu-'riz-mo
• **tourist**	turista (m/f)	tu-'ris-ta
(to) travel	viaggiare	vyaj-'ja-re
• **travel agency**	agenzia di viaggi	a-jen-'tsi-a di 'vyaj-ji
• **travel agent**	agente (m/f) di viaggio	a-'jen-te di 'vyaj-jo
trip, journey	viaggio	'vyaj-jo
• **Have a nice trip!**	Buon viaggio!	—
• **(to) take a trip**	fare* un viaggio	—

vacation	vacanza	*va-'kan-dza*
• **vacation in the mountains**	vacanze in montagna	*mon-'ta-nya*
• **winter vacation**	vacanze invernali	*in-ver-'na-li*

B. COUNTRIES AND CONTINENTS

Abyssinia	Abissinia	*ab-is-'si-nya*
Afghanistan	Afghanistan (m)	—
Africa	Africa	
Albania	Albania	*al-ba-'ni-a*
Algeria	Algeria	*al-je-'ri-a*
America	America	*a-'me-ri-ka*
• **Latin America**	America Latina	—
• **North America**	America del Nord	—
• **South America**	America del Sud	—
Argentina	Argentina	—
Armenia	Armenia	—
Asia	Asia	*'a-zia*
Australia	Australia	—
Austria	Austria	—
Bangladesh	Bangladesh (m)	—
Belgium	Belgio	*'bel-jo*
Bolivia	Bolivia	—
Bosnia	Bosnia	—
Brazil	Brasile (m)	*bra-'zi-le*
Bulgaria	Bulgaria	*bul-ga-'ri-a*
Cambodia	Cambogia	*kam-'bo-ja*
Canada	Canada	—
Caribbean	Caraibi (m, pl)	*ka-'ray-bi*
Chile	Cile (m)	*'či-le*
China	Cina	*'či-na*
Colombia	Colombia	—
Costa Rica	Costa Rica	—
Croatia	Croazia	*kro-'a-tsya*
Cuba	Cuba	—
Czech Republic	Repubblica Ceca	*re-'pub-bli-ka 'če-ka*
Denmark	Danimarca	*da-ni-'mar-ka*
Dominican Republic	Repubblica Dominicana	*re-'pub-bli-ka do-mi-ni-'ka-na*
Ecuador	Ecuador	—
Egypt	Egitto	*e-'jit-to*
El Salvador	El Salvador	—
England	Inghilterra	*in-gil-'ter-ra*
Eritrea	Eritrea	—
Estonia	Estonia	—
Ethiopia	Etiopia	*e-'tyo-pya*
Europe	Europa	*eu-'ro-pa*

Finland	Finlandia	*fin-'lan-dya*
France	Francia	*'fran-ča*
Georgia	Georgia	—
Germany	Germania	*jer-'ma-nya*
Great Britain	Gran Bretagna	*gran bre-'ta-nya*
Greece	Grecia	*'gre-ča*
Greenland	Groenlandia	*gro-en-'lan-dya*
Guatemala	Guatemala	—
Holland	Olanda	*o-'lan-da*
Honduras	Honduras (f)	—
Hungary	Ungheria	*un-ge-'ri-a*
India	India	—
Indonesia	Indonesia	—
Iran	Iran	—
Iraq	Iraq	—
Ireland	Irlanda	
Israel	Israele	*iz-ra-'e-le*
Italy	Italia	*i-'ta-li-a*
Jamaica	Giamaica	*ja-'may-ka*
Japan	Giappone (m)	*jap-'po-ne*
Jordan	Giordania	*jor-'da-nya*
Kenya	Kenya	—
Korea	Corea	*ko-'re-a*
Kuwait	Kuwait (m)	—
Laos	Laos (m)	—
Lebanon	Libano	*'li-ba-no*
Liberia	Liberia	—
Libya	Libia	—
Lithuania	Lituania	*li-tu-'a-ni-a*
Luxembourg	Lussemburgo	*lus-sem-'bur-go*
Macedonia	Macedonia	*ma-če-'do-nya*
Malaysia	Malaysia	—
Malta	Malta	—
Melanesia	Melanesia	—
Mexico	Messico	*'mes-si-ko*
Middle East	Medio Oriente	*'me-dyo o-'ryen-te*
Moldavia	Moldavia	—
Monaco	Monaco	—
Mongolia	Mongolia	—
Montenegro	Montenegro	—
Morocco	Marocco	*ma-'rok-ko*
Near East	Vicino Oriente	*vi-'či-no o-'ryen-te*
New Zealand	Nuova Zelanda	*'nwo-va dze-'lan-da*
Nicaragua	Nicaragua	—
Nigeria	Nigeria	—
Norway	Norvegia	*nor-'ve-ja*
Oceania	Oceania	*o-če-'a-nya*
Pakistan	Pakistan (m)	—

Paraguay	Paraguay (m)	—
Peru	Perù (m)	—
Philippines	Filippine (f, pl)	*fi-lip-'pi-ne*
Poland	Polonia	*po-'lo-nya*
Polynesia	Polinesia	—
Portugal	Portogallo	*por-to-'gal-lo*
Puerto Rico	Puerto Rico	—
Rumania	Romania	*ro-ma-'ni-a*
Russia	Russia	*'rus-sya*
San Marino	San Marino	—
Saudi Arabia	Arabia Saudita	*a-'ra-bya sau-'di-ta*
Scandinavia	Scandinavia	—
Scotland	Scozia	*'sko-tsya*
Senegal	Senegal (m)	—
Serbia	Serbia	—
Siberia	Siberia	—
Singapore	Singapore (m)	*sin-ga-'po-re*
Slovakia	Slovacchia	*zlo-'vak-kya*
Slovenia	Slovenia	*zlo-'ve-nya*
Somalia	Somalia	—
South Africa	Sud Africa	—
Spain	Spagna	*'spa-nya*
Sri Lanka	Sri Lanka	—
Sudan	Sudan	—
Sweden	Svezia	*'zve-tsya*
Switzerland	Svizzera	*'zvi-tse-ra*
Syria	Siria	—
Tanzania	Tanzania	—
Thailand	Tailandia	*tai-'lan-dya*
Tunisia	Tunisia	*tu-ni-'zi-a*
Turkey	Turchia	*tur-'ki-a*
Uganda	Uganda	—
United States	Stati Uniti (m, pl)	*'sta-ti u-'ni-ti*
Uruguay	Uruguay	—
Venezuela	Venezuela	—
Vietnam	Vietnam	—
Wales	Galles	*'gal-les*
Zambia	Zambia (m)	—

C. CITIES, PLACES, AND SITES

Adriatic	Adriatico	*a'dri-'a-ti-ko*
Alexandria	Alessandria	*a-les-'san-drya*
Alps	Alpi (f, pl)	*'al-pi*
• **alpine**	alpino	*al-'pi-no*
Amsterdam	Amsterdam	—
Apennines	Appennini (m, pl)	*ap-pen-'ni-ni*
Arno River	Arno	—

Formulas

to + country	in + *country*
to Italy	in Italia
to + city	a + *city*
to Rome	a Roma

Athens	Atene	*a-'te-ne*
• **Athenian**	ateniese	*a-te-'nye-ze*
Atlantic	Atlantico	*at-'lan-ti-ko*
Balkans	Balcani (m, pl)	*bal-'ka-ni*
Barcelona	Barcellona	*bar-čel-'lo-na*
Bari	Bari	—
Beijing	Pechino	*pe-'ki-no*
Belgrade	Belgrado	*bel-'gra-do*
Berlin	Berlino	*ber-'li-no*
Bologna	Bologna	—
Cairo	il Cairo	—
Catanzaro	Catanzaro	—
Caucasian	caucasico	*kau-'ka-zi-ko*
Corsica	Corsica	—
• **Corsican**	corso	—
Dolomites	Dolomiti (f, pl)	*do-lo-'mi-ti*
Edinburgh	Edinburgo	*e-din-'bur-go*
Elba	Elba	—
Etna	Etna	—
Florence	Firenze	*fi-'ren-dze*
French Riviera	Costa Azzurra	*'kos-ta a-'dzur-ra*
Geneva	Ginevra	*ji-'ne-vra*
Genoa	Genova	*'je-no-va*
Ivory Coast	Costa d'Avorio	*'kos-ta da-'vo-ryo*
Lisbon	Lisbona	*liz-'bo-na*
London	Londra	*'lon-dra*
Madrid	Madrid	—
Mediterranean	Mediterraneo	*me-dit-ter-'ra-ne-o*
Milan	Milano	*mi-'la-no*
Moscow	Mosca	*'mos-ka*
Naples	Napoli	*'na-po-li*
New York	New York	—
Pacific	Pacifico	*pa-'či-fi-ko*
Palermo	Palermo	—
Paris	Parigi	*pa-'ri-ji*
Perugia	Perugia	—

Pisa	Pisa	—
Po river	Po	—
Reggio Calabria	Reggio Calabria	'rej-jo ka-'la-brya
Rimini	Rimini	'ri-mi-ni
Rome	Roma	—
Siena	Siena	—
Tiber River	Tevere (m)	'te-ve-re
Turin	Torino	—
Tyrrenean Sea	Tirreno	tir-'re-no
Venice	Venezia	ve-'ne-tsya
Vesuvius	Vesuvio	ve-'zu-vyo
Vienna	Vienna	—

D. ITALIAN REGIONS

Abruzzi	Abruzzo	—
Alto Adige	Alto Adige	'a-di-je
Aosta	Aosta	—
Apulia	Puglia	'pu-lye
Calabria	Calabria	—
Campania	Campania	—
Emilia	Emilia Romagna	ro-'ma-nya
Friuli	Friuli	—
Latium	Lazio	'la-tsyo
Liguria	Liguria	—
Lombardy	Lombardia	lom-bar-'di-a
Lucania	Basilicata	Ba-'zi-li-ka-ta
Molise	Molise (m)	mo-'li-ze
Piedmont	Piemonte (m)	pye-'mon-te
Sardinia	Sardegna	sar-'de-nya
Sicily	Sicilia	si-'či-lya
Trentino Alto-Adige	Trentino Alto-Adige	tren-'ti-no 'al-to 'a-di-je
Tuscany	Toscana	tos-'ka-na
Umbria	Umbria	—
Venetia	Veneto	've-ne-to

E. NATIONALITIES

African	africano	a-fri-'ka-no
Albanian	albanese	al-ba-'ne-ze
Algerian	algerino	al-je-'ri-no
American	americano	a-me-ri-'ka-no
Arabic	arabo	'a-ra-bo
Argentinean	argentino	ar-jen-'ti-no
Armenian	armeno	ar-'me-no
Australian	australiano	aus-tra-'lya-no
Austrian	austriaco	aus-'tri-a-ko
Belgian	belga	'bel-ga

Pattern

All nationalities are given in the masculine form. *In general,* the language name is the same as the nationality.

tedesco	=	German nationality and language

but

canadese	=	Canadian
inglese/francese	=	Canada's two official languages

Bolivian	boliviano	*bo-li-'vya-no*
Bosnian	bosniaco	*boz-'ni-a-ko*
Brazilian	brasiliano	*bra-zi-'lya-no*
British	britannico	*bri-'tan-ni-ko*
Bulgarian	bulgaro	*'bul-ga-ro*
Cambodian	cambogiano	*kam-bo-'jano*
Canadian	canadese	*ka-na-'de-ze*
Cantonese	cantonese	*kan-to-'ne-ze*
Caribbean	caraibico	*ka-'ray-bi-ko*
Chilean	cileno	*či-'le-no*
Chinese	cinese	*či-'ne-ze*
Colombian	colombiano	*ko-lom-'bya-no*
Congolese	congolese	*kon-go-'le-ze*
Costa Rican	costaricano	*kos-ta-ri-'ka-no*
Croatian	croato	*kro-'a-to*
Cuban	cubano	*ku-'ba-no*
Czech	ceco	*če-ko*
Danish	danese	*da-'ne-ze*
Dominican	dominicano	*do-mi-ni-'ka-no*
Dutch	olandese	*o-lan-'de-ze*
Easterner, Oriental	orientale	*o-ryen-'ta-le*
Ecuadorian	ecuadoriano	*e-kwa-do-'rya-no*
Egyptian	egiziano	*e-ji-'tsya-no*
English	inglese	*in-'gle-ze*
Estonian	estone	*'es-to-ne*
Ethiopian	etiope	*e-'ti-o-pe*
European	europeo	*eu-ro-'pe-o*
Filipino	filippino	*fi-lip-'pi-no*
Finnish	finlandese	*fin-lan-'de-ze*
French	francese	*fran-'če-ze*
German	tedesco	*te-'des-ko*
Greek	greco	*'gre-ko*
Guatemalan	guatemalteco	*gwa-te-mal-'te-ko*

Haitian	haitiano	*ay-'tya-no*
Honduran	honduregno	*on-du-'renyo*
Hungarian	ungherese	*un-ge-'re-ze*
Indian	indiano	*in-'dya-no*
Indonesian	indonesiano	*in-do-ne-'zya-no*
Iranian	iraniano	*i-ra-'nya-no*
Iraqi	iracheno	*i-ra-'ke-no*
Irish	irlandese	*ir-lan-'de-ze*
Israeli	israeliano	*iz-ra-e-'lya-no*
Italian	italiano	*i-ta-'lya-no*
Jamaican	giamaicano	*ja-may-'ka-no*
Japanese	giapponese	*jap-po-'ne-ze*
Jordanian	giordano	*jor-'da-no*
Kenyan	keniano	*ke-'nya-no*
Korean	coreano	*ko-re-'a-no*
Kuwaiti	kuwaitiano	*ku-way-'tya-no*
Laotian	laoziano	*la-o-'tsya-no*
Lebanese	libanese	*li-ba-'ne-ze*
Liberian	liberiano	*li-be-'rya-no*
Libyan	libico	*'li-bi-ko*
Lithuanian	lituano	*li-'twa-no*
Luxembourger	lussemburghese	*lus-sem-bur-'ge-ze*
Macedonian	macedone	*ma-'če-do-ne*
Malaysian	malaysiano	*ma-lay-'sya-no*
Maltese	maltese	*mal-'te-ze*
Mexican	messicano	*mes-si-'ka-no*
Middle Easterner	mediorientale	*me-dyo-ryen-'ta-le*
Moldavian	moldavo	*mol-'da-vo*
Mongolian	mongolo	*'mon-go-lo*
Moroccan	marrocchino	*mar-rok-'ki-no*
New Zealander	neozelandese	*ne-o-dze-lan-'de-ze*
Nicaraguan	nicaraguense	*ni-ka-ra-'gwen-se*
Nigerian	nigeriano	*ni-je-'rya-no*
North American	nordamericano	*nord-a-me-ri-'ka-no*
Norwegian	norvegese	*nor-ve-'je-ze*
Pakistani	pachistano	*pa-kis-'ta-no*
Palestinian	palestinese	*pa-les-ti-'ne-ze*
Paraguayan	paraguaiano	*pa-ra-gwa-'ya-no*
Peruvian	peruviano	*pe-ru-'vya-no*
Polish	polacco	*po-'lak-ko*
Portuguese	portoghese	*por-to-'ge-ze*
Puerto Rican	portoricano	*por-to-ri-'ka-no*
Rumanian	rumeno	*ru-'me-no*
Russian	russo	*'rus-so*
Salvadoran	salvadoregno	*sal-va-do-'re-nyo*
Saudi	saudita	*sau-'di-ta*
Scandinavian	scandinavo	*skan-di-'na-vo*
Scottish	scozzese	*skot-'tse-ze*

Senegalese	senegalese	*se-ne-ga-'le-ze*
Serbian	serbo	*'ser-bo*
Siberian	siberiano	*si-be-'rya-no*
Singaporean	singaporiano	*sin-ga-po-'rya-no*
Slavic	slavo	*'zla-vo*
Slovak	slovacco	*zlo-'vak-ko*
Slovenian	sloveno	*zlo-'ve-no*
Somalian	somalo	*'so-ma-lo*
South African	sudafricano	*sud-a-fri-'ka-no*
South American	sudamericano	*sud-a-me-ri-'ka-no*
Spanish	spagnolo	*spa-'nyo-lo*
Sudanese	sudanese	*su-da-'ne-ze*
Swedish	svedese	*zve-'de-ze*
Swiss	svizzero	*'zvit-tse-ro*
Syrian	siriano	*si-'rya-no*
Thai	tailandese	*tay-lan-'de-ze*
Tunisian	tunisino	*tu-ni-'zi-no*
Turkish	turco	*'tur-ko*
Ugandan	ugandese	*u-gan-'de-ze*
Uruguayan	uruguaiano	*u-ru-gwa-'ya-no*
Venezuelan	venezuelano	*ve-ne-tswe-'la-no*
Vietnamese	vietnamita	*vyet-na-'mi-ta*
Welsh	gallese	*gal-'le-ze*
Westerner	occidentale	*oč-či-den-'ta-le*
Zambian	zambiano	*dzam-'bya-no*

31. PACKING AND GOING THROUGH CUSTOMS

baggage, luggage	bagaglio	*ba-'ga-lyo*
• hand luggage	bagaglio a mano	—
border	frontiera	*fron-'tye-ra*
citizenship	cittadinanza	*čit-ta-di-'nan-dza*
customs	dogana	*do-'ga-na*
• customs officer	doganiere (-a)	*do-ga-'nye-re*
(to) declare	dichiarare	*di-kya-'ra-re*
• nothing to declare	niente da dichiarare	*'nyen-te*
document	documento	*do-ku-'men-to*
duty tax	tassa	—
• (to) pay duty	pagare la dogana	*pa-'ga-re la do-'ga-na*
foreign currency	valuta straniera	*va-'lu-ta stra-'nye-ra*
foreigner	straniero (-a)	*stra-'nye-ro*
form (to fill out)	modulo	*'mo-du-lo*
identification document, proof of identity	carta d'identità	*'kar-ta di-den-ti-'ta*
nationality	nazionalità (f, inv)	*na-tsyo-na-li-'ta*
passport	passaporto	*pas-sa-'por-to*
• passport control	controllo passaporti	*kon-'trol-lo*
purse	borsa	—

suitcase	valigia	*va-'li-'ja*
tariff	tariffa	*ta-'rif-fa*
visa	visto	—
weight	peso	*'pes-zo*
• heavy	pesante	*pe-'zan-te*
• light	leggero	*lej-'je-ro*

32. TRAVELING BY AIR

A. IN THE TERMINAL

airline	linea aerea	*'li-ne-a a-'e-re-a*
airplane	aereo	*a-'e-re-o*
airport	aeroporto	*a-e-ro-'por-to*
boarding	imbarco	*im-'bar-ko*
• (to) board	salire* (ess) a bordo	*sa-'li-re*
• boarding pass	carta d'imbarco	*dim-'bar-ko*
check-in	accettazione (f)	*ač-čet-ta-'tsyo-ne*
	check-in (m)	—
connection	coincidenza	*ko-in-či-'den-tsa*
economy class	classe turistica	*'klas-se tu-'ris-ti-ka*
first class	prima classe	—
information counter,	banco	*ban-ko*
information desk	informazioni	
lost and found	ufficio oggetti smarriti	*uf-'fi-čo oj-'jet-ti*
		zmar-'ri-ti
no smoking	vietato fumare	*vye-'ta-to fu-'ma-re*
(to) pick up one's baggage	ritirare il bagaglio	*ri-ti-'ra-re il ba-'ga-lyo*
porter	assistente ai bagagli	*ba'-ga-lyi*
reservation	prenotazione (f)	*pre-no-ta-'tsyo-ne*
shuttle vehicle	navetta	*na-'vet-ta*
terminal	terminal (m, inv)	—
ticket	biglietto	*bi-'lyet-to*
• e-ticket	biglietto elettronico	*e-let-'tro-ni-ko*
ticket agent	bigliettaio (-a)	*bi-lyet-'ta-yo*
waiting room	sala d'aspetto	*'sa-la das-pet-to*

B. FLIGHT INFORMATION

arrival	arrivo	*ar-'ri-vo*
canceled	cancellato	*kan-čel-'la-to*
departure	partenza	*par-'ten-dza*
early	in anticipo	*an-'ti-či-po*
flight	volo	—
gate, exit	uscita	*u-'ši-ta*
international flight	volo internazionale	*in-ter-na-tsyo-'na-le*
late, delayed	in ritardo	*ri-'tar-do*
national, domestic flight	volo nazionale	*na-tsyo-'na-le*

on time	in orario	o-'ra-ryo
schedule, times board	orario	o-'ra-ryo
transit	transito	'tran-zi-to
• **transit passenger**	passeggero (-a) in transito	pas-sej-'je-ro

C. ON THE PLANE

cabin	cabina	ka-'bi-na
captain	comandante (m/f)	ko-man-'dan-te
copilot	copilota (m/f)	ko-pi-'lo-ta
crew	equipaggio	e-kwi-'paj-jo
flight attendant	assistente (m/f) di volo	as-sis-'ten-te
flying time	durata del volo	du-'ra-ta
headphones	auricolari (m, pl,)	au-ri-ko-'la-ri
(to) land	atterrare	at-ter-'ra-re
• **landing**	atterraggio	at-ter-'raj-jo
• **landing gear**	carrello	kar-'rel-lo
life jacket	salvagente (m, inv)	sal-va-'jen-te
motor	motore (m)	mo-'to-re
passenger	passeggero (-a)	pas-sej-'je-ro
pilot	pilota (m/f)	pi-'lo-ta
runway	pista	—
seat	posto	—
• **aisle**	corridoio	kor-ri-'do-yo
• **back of the seat**	schienale (m)	skye-'na-le
• **(to) buckle**	allacciare	al-lač-'ča-re
• **seat belt**	cintura di sicurezza	čin-'tu-ra si-ku-'ret-tsa
• **window**	finestrino	fi-nes-'tri-no
stopover	scalo	'ska-lo
(to) take off	decollare	de-kol-'la-re
• **take-off**	decollo	de-'kol-lo
time difference	fuso orario	'fu-zo o-'ra-ryo
toilet	toletta	to-'let-ta
tray	vassoio	vas-'so-yo
turbulence	turbolenza	tur-bo-'lendza
wing	ala	—

33. ON THE ROAD

A. DRIVING

accident	incidente (m)	in-či-'den-te
(to) brake	frenare	fre-'na-re
bridge	ponte (m)	'pon-te
corner (street)	angolo	'an-go-lo
city block	isolato	i-zo-'la-to

curve	curva	'kur-va
distance	distanza	dis-'tan-dza
(to) drive	guidare	gwi-'da-re
• driver	autista (m/f)	au-'tis-ta
	conducente (m/f)	kon-du-'cen-te
driver's license	patente (di guida)	pa-'ten-te
fine, traffic ticket	multa	
gas station	stazione (f) di servizio	sta-'tsyo-ne di ser-'vi-tsyo
• (to) change the oil	cambiare l'olio	kam-'bya-re 'lo-lyo
• (to) check the oil	controllare l'olio	kon-trol-'la-re 'lo-lyo
• (to) fill up	fare* il pieno	'fa-re il 'pye-no
• (to) fix	aggiustare	aj-jus-'ta-re
• gas	benzina	ben-'dzi-na
• gas attendant	benzinaio (-a)	ben-dzi-'na-yo
• mechanic	meccanico (-a)	mek-'ka-ni-ko
gears	marcia	'mar-ča
• (to) back up	fare* marcia indietro	in-'dye-tro
• (to) change gears	cambiare marcia	kam-'bya-re
• (to) go forward	fare* marcia avanti	a-'van-ti
(to) go through a red light	passare col rosso	pas-'sa-re
highway	autostrada	au-to-'stra-da
• highway police	polizia stradale	po-li-'tsi-a stra-'da-le
insurance card	carta verde	—
intersection	incrocio	in-'kro-čo
lane (traffic)	corsia	kor-'si-a
ownership papers	libretto di circolazione	li-'bret-to di čir-ko-la-'styo-ne
(to) park	parcheggiare	par-kej-'ja-re
• parking	parcheggio	par-'kej-jo
(to) pass	sorpassare	sor-pas-'sa-re
pedestrian	pedone (m)	pe-'do-ne
• pedestrian crosswalk	passaggio pedonale	pas-'saj-jo pe-do-'na-le
policeman, police woman	carabiniere (-a)	ka-ra-bi-'nye-re
	poliziotto (-a)	po-li-'tsyot-to
• traffic policeman	vigile (-essa)	'vi-ji-le
ramp	rampa	—
road map	mappa stradale	—
road sign	segnale stradale	se-'nya-le stra-'da-le
rush hour	ora di punta	—
speed	velocità (f, inv)	ve-lo-či-'ta
• (to) slow down	rallentare	ral-len-'ta-re
• (to) speed up	accelerare	ač-če-le-'ra-re
(to) start the car	mettere* in moto	'met-te-re
toll booth	casello (stradale)	ka-'zel-lo
(to) tow the car	rimorchiare la macchina	ri-mor-'kya-re la 'mak-ki-na
• towing	rimorchio	ri-'mor-kyo

traffic	traffico	*'traf-fi-ko*
• traffic jam	ingorgo	*in-'gor-go*
• traffic lights	semaforo	*se-'ma-fo-ro*
tunnel	galleria	*gal-'le-'ri-a*
	tunnel (m, inv)	—
turn	svolta	*'zvol-ta*
• left turn, exit left	svolta a sinistra	*si-'nis-tra*
• right turn, exit right	svolta a destra	*'des-tra*
• (to) turn	girare	*ji-'ra-re*
• (to) turn left	girare a sinistra	—
• (to) turn right	girare a destra	—

B. SIGNS

Bicycle path	Pista ciclabile	*či-'kla-bi-le*
Closed	Chiuso	*'kyu-zo*
Closed for holidays	Chiuso per ferie	*'fe-rye*
Emergency lane	Corsia d'emergenza	*kor-'si-a de-mer-'jen-dza*
Entrance	Ingresso	*in-gres-so*
Exit	Uscita	*u-'ši-ta*
Information	Informazioni	*in-for-ma-'tsyo-ni*
Lane reserved	Corsia preferenziale	*kor-'si-a pre-fe-ren-'tsya-le*
Level crossing	Passaggio a livello	*pas-'saj-jo a li-'vel-lo*
Limited parking	Sosta limitata	*li-mi-'ta-ta*
Merge	Confluenza	*kon-flu-'en-dza*
No entrance	Vietato l'ingresso	*vye-'ta-to lin-'gres-so*
No entry	Divieto di accesso	*di-'vye-to dač-'čes-so*
No exit	Vietata l'uscita	*vye-'ta-ta lu-'ši-ta*
No left turn	Divieto di svolta a sinistra	*di-'vye-to 'svol-ta a si-'nis-tra*
No parking	Sosta vietata	*vye-'ta-ta*
No passing	Divieto di sorpasso	*di-'vye-to di sor-'pas-so*
No right turn	Divieto di svolta a destra	*di-'vye-to di 'svol-ta*
No smoking	Vietato fumare	*vye-'ta-to fu-'ma-re*
No stopping	Divieto di fermata	*di-'vye-to di fer-'ma-ta*
No thoroughfare	Divieto di transito	*di-'vye-to di 'tran-zi-to*
No U-turn	Divieto di inversione a U	*di-'vye-to in-ver-'zyo-ne*
One way	Senso unico	*'sen-so 'u-ni-ko*
Open	Aperto	*a-'per-to*
Out of order	Fuori servizio	*'fwo-ri ser-'vi-tsyo*
Passing lane	Corsia di sorpasso	*kor-'si-a di sor-'pas-so*
Slippery when wet	Strada sdrucciolevole	*'stra-da zdruč-čo-'le-vo-le*
Speed limit	Limite di velocità	*'li-mi-te di ve-lo-či-'ta*
Stop	Stop	—

Common Road Signs

No U-turn

No passing

Border crossing

Traffic signal ahead

Speed limit

Traffic circle
(roundabout) ahead

Minimum speed limit

All traffic turns left

End of no passing zone

One-way street

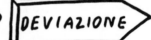

Detour

Danger ahead

Entrance to
expressway

Expressway ends

Common Road Signs

Guarded railroad crossing

Yield

Stop

Right of way

Dangerous intersection ahead

Gasoline (petrol) ahead

Parking

No vehicles allowed

Dangerous curve

Pedestrian crossing

Oncoming traffic has right of way

No bicycles allowed

No parking allowed

No entry

No left turn

Toll	Pedaggio	*pe-'daj-jo*
Tow-away zone	Zona rimozione	*'dzo-na ri'-mo-zyo-ne*
Underpass	Sottopassaggio	*sot-to-pas-'saj-jo*
Washroom	Toilette	—
	Servizi	*ser-'vi-zi*
Work in progress	Lavori in corso	*la-'vo-ri*
Yield	Precedenza	*pre-če-'den-dza*

C. THE CAR

air conditioning	aria condizionata	*'a-rya kon-di-tsyo-'na-ta*
back seat	sedile (m) posteriore	*se-'di-le pos-te-'ryo-re*
battery	batteria	*bat-te-'ri-a*
brake	freno	—
bumper	paraurti (inv)	*pa-ra-'ur-ti*
car body	carrozzeria	*kar-ro-tse-'ri-a*
car dealer(ship)	concessionario	*kon-čes-syo-'na-ryo*
car door	portiera	*por-'tye-ra*
car roof	tetto	*'tet-to*
car seat	sedile (m)	*se-'di-le*
car window	finestrino	*fi-nes-'tri-no*
carburetor	carburatore (m)	*kar-bu-ra-'to-re*
carpet	tappezzeria	*tap-pe-tse-'ri-a*
choke	valvola dell'aria	*'val-vo-la del-'la-rya*
clutch	frizione (f)	*fri-'tsyo-ne*
dashboard	cruscotto	*krus-'kot-to*
electric car	automobile elettrica (f)	*au-to-'mo-bi-le e-'let-ri-ka*
fender	parafango	*pa-ra-'fan-go*
filter	filtro	*'fil-tro*
front seat	sedile (m) anteriore	*se-'di-le an-te-'ryo-re*
gas pedal	acceleratore (m)	*ač-če-le-ra-'to-re*
gas tank	serbatoio	*ser-'ba-'to-yo*
gearshift	leva del cambio	*'le-va del -'kam-byo*
glove compartment	cassetto ripostiglio	*kas-'set-to ri-pos-'ti-lyo*
handle	maniglia	*ma-'ni-lya*
heater	aereatore (m)	*a-e-re-a-'to-re*
hood, bonnet	cofano	*'ko-fa-no*
horn	clacson (m, inv)	—
horse power	cilindrata	*či-lin-'dra-ta*
hybrid car	automobile ibrida (f)	*au-to-'mo-bi-la 'ib-ri-da*
jack	cric (m, inv)	—
license plate	targa	—
light	faro	—
luggage rack	portabagaglio (inv)	*por-ta-ba-'ga-lyo*
motor	motore (m)	*mo-'to-re*
• **fan**	ventola	*'ven-to-la*
• **gas pump**	pompa della benzina	*ben-'dzi-na*

• generator	dinamo (f, inv)	'di-na-mo
• piston	pistone (m)	pis-'to-ne
• sparkplug	candela	kan-'de-la
• valve	valvola	'val-vo-la
muffler	marmitta	mar-'mit-ta
oil	olio	'o-lyo
power brake	servofreno	ser-vo-'fre-no
power steering	servosterzo	ser-vo-'ster-tso
pump	pompa	—
radiator	radiatore (m)	ra-dya-'to-re
seat belt	cintura di sicurezza	čin-'tu-ra di si-ku-'re-tsa
side mirror	specchietto	spek-'kyet-to
signal light	luce (f) di posizione	'lu-če di po-zi-'tsyo-ne
speedometer	tachimetro	ta-'ki-me-tro
steering wheel	volante (m)	vo-'lan-te
tire	gomma	—
	pneumatico	pne-u-'ma-ti-ko
trunk	baule (m)	ba-'u-le
wheel	ruota	'rwo-ta
• spare wheel	ruota di scorta	'skor-ta
windshield	parabrezza (m, inv)	pa-ra-'bret-tsa
• wiper	tergicristallo	ter-ji-'kris-'tal-lo

D. CAR RENTAL

check-out vehicle conditions	condizioni del veicolo in uscita	kon-di-'tsyo-ni del ve-'i-ko-lo in u-'ši-ta
chip	scheggiatura	skej-ja-'tu-ra
dent	ammaccatura	am-mak-ka-'tu-ra
rate	tariffa	ta-'rif-fa
(to) rent	noleggiare	no-lej-'ja-re
• rental	noleggio	no-'lej-jo
• rental place	autonoleggio	au-to-no-'lej-jo
return vehicle conditions	condizioni del veicolo al rientro	kon-di-'tsyo-ni del ve-'i-ko-lo al ri-'en-tro
scratch	graffio	'graf-fyo
tear	squarcio	'skwar-co

34. TRANSPORTATION

ambulance	ambulanza	am-bu-'lan-dza
anchor	ancora	'an-ko-ra
automobile	automobile (f)	au-to-'mo-bi-le
	auto (f, inv)	—
bicycle	bicicletta	bi-či-'klet-ta
• brake	freno	'fre-no
• handlebar	manubrio	ma-'nu-bryo
• pedal	pedale (m)	pe-'da-le
• seat	sellino (m)	sel-'li-no

• spoke	raggio	'raj-jo
• tire	pneumatico	pne-u-'ma-ti-ko
bus	autobus (m, inv)	—
• bus driver	autista (m/f)	au-'tis-ta
• bus station, depot	capolinea (m)	ka-po-'li-ne-a
• courier bus, express	corriera	kor-'rye-ra
car	macchina	'mak-ki-na
• compact car	utilitaria	u-ti-li-'ta-rya
• rented car	macchina, auto noleggiata	no-lej-'ja-ta
• sports car	macchina, auto sportiva	spor-'ti-va
car-ferry	nave (f) traghetto	'na-ve tra-'get-to
commuter	pendolare (m/f)	pen-do-'la-re
compass	bussola	'bus-so-la
conductor	conduttore (-trice)	kon-dut-'to-re
connection	coincidenza	ko-in-či-'den-dza
driver (of a public vehicle)	conducente (m/f)	kon-du-'čen-te
ferry	traghetto	tra-'get-to
(to) hitchhike	fare* l'autostop	—
• hitchhiker	autostoppista (m/f)	au-to-stop-'pis-ta
(to) leave, depart	partire (ess)	par-'ti-re
• (to) miss (a bus)	perdere*	'per-de-re
life-jacket	giubbotto di salvataggio	jub-'bot-to di sal-va-'taj-jo
minivan	pulmino	pul-'mi-no
motor scooter	motorino	mo-to-'ri-no
motorcycle	motocicletta	mo-to-či-'klet-ta
oar	remo	—
paddle	pagaia	pa-'ga-ya
porthole	oblò (m, inv)	—
propeller	elica	'e-li-ka
public transport	trasporto pubblico	tras-'por-to 'pub-bli-ko
raft	zattera	'dzat-te-ra
railroad	ferrovia	fer-ro-'vi-a
• station	stazione (f) ferroviaria	sta-'tsyo-ne fero-ro-vi-'a-rya
schedule	orario	o-'ra-ryo
• arrival	arrivo	ar-'ri-vo
• canceled	cancellato	kan-čel-'la-to
• departure	partenza	par-'ten-dza
seat	posto	—
stop	fermata	fer-'ma-ta
subway	metropolitana	me-tro-po-li-'ta-na
• subway entrance	entrata della metropolitana	en-'tra-ta
• subway station	stazione (f) della metropolitana	sta-'tsyo-ne
ticket	biglietto	bi-'lyet-to

• e-ticket	biglietto elettronico	*e-let-'tro-ni-ko*
• ticket agent	bigliettaio (-a)	*bi-lyet-'ta-yo*
• ticket office, counter	biglietteria	*bi-lyet-te-'ri-a*
• ticket machine	biglietteria automatica	*au-to-'ma-ti-ka*
transportation	trasporto	*tras-'por-to*
tow truck	autosoccorso	*au-to-sok-'kor-so*
	autorimorchiatore (m)	*au-to-ri-mor-kya-'to-re*
train	treno	—
• coach	vagone (m)	*va-'go-ne*
• compartment	scompartimento	*skom-par-ti-'men-to*
• locomotive	locomotiva	*lo-ko-mo-'ti-va*
• railway	ferrovia	*fer-ro-'vi-a*
• sleeping coach	vagone (m) letto	—
• track	binario	*bi-'na-ryo*
• train station	stazione ferroviaria	*sta-tsyo-ne fer-ro-vi-'a-rya*
truck	camion (m, inv)	—
• fire truck	autopompa	*au-to-'pom-pa*
• garbage truck	autoimmondizie	*au-to-im-mon-'di-tsye*
van	furgone (m)	*fur-'go-ne*
vehicle	veicolo	*ve-'i-ko-lo*
(to) wait for	aspettare	*as-pet-'ta-re*

35. HOTELS

A. LODGING AND HOTELS

all-inclusive price	prezzo forfettario	*'pret-tso for-fet-'ta-ryo*
banquet	banchetto	*ban-'ket-to*
bed and breakfast	pensione (f)	*pen-'syo-ne*
bellhop	fattorino (-a)	*fat-to-'ri-no*
bill	conto	—
breakfast	prima colazione	*'pri-ma ko-la-'tsyo-ne*
• breakfast included	colazione compresa	*kom-'pre-za*
camping	campeggio	*kam-'pej-jo*
clerk	impiegato (-a)	*im-pye-'ga-to*
(to) complain	lamentarsi	*la-men-'tar-si*
• complaint	lamentela	*la-men-'te-la*
doorman, doorwoman	portiere (-a)	*por-'tye-re*
elevator	ascensore (m)	*a-šen-'so-re*
entrance	ingresso	*in-'gres-so*
exit	uscita	*u-'ši-ta*
floor	piano	—
foyer, lobby	atrio	*'a-tri-o*
ground floor	pianterreno	*pyan-ter-'re-no*
hostel	ostello	*os-'tel-lo*
hotel	albergo	*al-'ber-go*
• five-star hotel	albergo a cinque stelle	*'cin-kwe 'stel-le*

• hotel room	camera	'ka-me-ra
• luxury hotel	albergo di lusso	'lus-so
• modest hotel	albergo modesto	mo-'des-to
identification card	carta d'identità	i-den-ti-'ta
key	chiave (f)	'kya-ve
lodging, accommodations	alloggio	al-'loj-jo
luggage rack	portabagagli (m, inv)	por-ta-ba-'ga-lyi
lunch	pranzo	'pran-dzo
maid	cameriera	ka-me-'rye-ra
main door	portone (m)	por-'to-ne
manager	direttore (-trice)	di-ret-'to-re
message	messaggio	mes-'saj-jo
motel	motel (m, inv)	—
pool	piscina	pi-'ši-na
price	prezzo	'pret-tso
• high season	alta stagione	al-ta sta-'jo-ne
• low season	bassa stagione	'bas-sa sta-'jo-ne
• rate	tariffa	ta-'rif-fa
receipt	ricevuta	ri-če-'vu-ta
reservation	prenotazione (f)	pre-no-ta-'tsyo-ne
• (to) reserve	prenotare	pre-no-'ta-re
room	camera	'ka-me-ra
	stanza	'stan-dza
• double room	camera doppia	'ka-mera 'dop-pya
• single bed	camera singola	'sin-go-la
• with two beds	camera a due letti	—
• with double bed	camera matrimoniale	ma-tri-mo-'nya-le
services	servizi (m, pl)	ser-'vi-tsi
stairs	scale (f, pl)	'ska-le
view	veduta	ve-'du-ta
wake-up call	sveglia (telefonica)	'zve-lya

B. THE HOTEL ROOM

armchair	poltrona	pol-'tro-na
balcony	terrazza	ter-'ra-tsa
• sliding door	porta scorrevole	'por-ta skor-'re-vo-le
bath tub	vasca	—
bathroom	bagno	'ba-nyo
bed	letto	—
• double bed	letto matrimoniale	ma-tri-mo-'nya-le
bedside table	comodino	ko-mo-'di-no
blanket	coperta	ko-'per-ta
chest of drawers	cassettone (m)	kas-se-'to-ne
closet	armadio	ar-'ma-dyo
clothes hanger	attaccapanni (m, inv)	at-tak-ka-'pan-ni
curtain	tenda	'ten-da

dresser	comò (m, inv)	—
faucet	rubinetto	*ru-bi-'net-to*
lamp	lampada	*'lam-pa-da*
light	luce (f)	*'lu-če*
• **current**	corrente (f)	*kor-'ren-te*
• **switch**	interruttore (m)	*in-ter-rut-'to-re*
• **(to) turn off**	spegnere*	*'spe-nye-re*
• **(to) turn on**	accendere*	*ač-'čen-de-re*
(to) overlook	guardare su	*gwar-'da-re*
pillow	cuscino	*ku-'ši-no*
soap	sapone (m)	*sa-'po-ne*
shampoo	shampoo (m, inv)	—
sheets	lenzuola (f, pl)	*len-'tswo-la*
shower	doccia	*'doč-ča*
soap bar	saponetta	*sa-po-'net-ta*
sink, wash basin	lavabo	*la-'va-bo*
• **cold water**	acqua fredda	*'ak-kwa 'fred-da*
• **hot water**	acqua calda	*'kal-da*
thermostat	termostato	*ter-'mos-ta-to*
toilet paper	carta igienica	*'kar-ta i-'jye-ni-ka*
towel	asciugamano	*a-šu-ga-'ma-no*

36. ON VACATION

A. SIGHTSEEING

alley, lane	vicolo	*'vi-ko-lo*
amphitheater	anfiteatro	*an-fi-te-'a-tro*
amusement park	luna park (m, inv)	—
ancient monument	monumento storico	*mo-nu-'men-to 'sto-ri-ko*
art gallery (museum)	galleria d'arte	*gal-le-'ri-a 'dar-te*
	museo	*mu-'ze-o*
avenue, large road	corso	
barracks	caserma	*ka-'zer-ma*
basilica	basilica	*ba-'zi-li-ka*
bell tower	campanile (m)	*kam-pa-'ni-le*
botanical gardens	giardino botanico	*jar-'di-no bo-'ta-ni-ko*
bridge	ponte (m)	*'pon-te*
building	edificio	*e-di-'fi-čo*
bypass, highway	raccordo stradale	*rak-'kor-do stra-'da-le*
capital (of the country)	capitale (f)	*ka-pi-'ta-le*
capital town (of a region)	capoluogo	*ka-po-'lwo-go*
cathedral	cattedrale (f)	*kat-te-'dra-le*
chapel	cappella	*kap-'pel-la*
church	chiesa	*'kye-za*
city	città (f, inv)	*čit-'ta*
• **city hall**	municipio	*mu-ni-'či-pyo*
• **city map**	pianta della città	*'pyan-ta*

• city dweller, citizen	cittadino (-a)	čit-ta-'di-no
commuter	pendolare (m/f)	pen-do-'la-re
condominium	condominio	kon-do-'mi-nyo
courthouse	tribunale (m)	tri-bu-'na-le
district	quartiere (m)	kwar-'tye-re
downtown	centro	'čen-tro
(to) dwell, live in	abitare	a-bi-'ta-re
guide-book	guida	'gwi-da
gutter	fognatura	fo-nya-'tu-ra
intersection	incrocio	in-'kro-čo
kiosk	chiosco	'kyos-ko
law courts	palazzo di giustizia	pa-'lat-tso di jus-'ti-tsya
library	biblioteca	bib-lyo-'te-ka
(to) live (in a place)	vivere*	'vi-ve-re
monument	monumento	mo-nu-'men-to
museum	museo	mu-'ze-o
park	parco	'par-ko
parking meter	parchimetro	par-'ki-me-tro
pavement, sidewalk	marciapiede (m)	mar-ča-'pye-de
pedestrian crossing	passaggio pedonale	pas-'sajjo pe-do-'na-le
police station	questura	kwes-'tu-ra
public notices	affissioni pubbliche	af-fis-'syo-ni 'pub-bli-ke
railway crossing	passaggio a livello	pas-'saj-jo a li-'vel-lo
road, roadway, street	strada	—
souvenir shop	bottega dei souvenir	bot-'te-ga
square	piazza	'pya-tsa
stock exchange	borsa	—
street, road	via	—
tower	torre (f)	—
underpass	passaggio sotterraneo	pas-'saj-jo sot-ter-'ra-ne-o
urban dweller	urbano (-a)	ur-'ba-no
water fountain	fontana	fon-'ta-na
worksite	cantiere (m)	kan-'tye-re

B. GETTING OUT OF THE CITY

beach	spiaggia	'spyaj-ja
boat	barca	—
brook	ruscello	ru-'šel-lo
canoe	canoa	ka-'no-a
chairlift	seggiovia	sej-jo-'vi-a
countryside	campagna	kam-'pa-nya
crafts	artigianato	ar-ti-ja-'na-to
cruise	crociera	kro-'če-ra
deck chair	sedia a sdraio	'se-dya a 'zdra-yo
fishing	pesca	'pes-ka

footpath, trail	sentiero	*sen-'tye-ro*
(to) go sightseeing	andare* (ess) in giro	*an-'da-re in 'ji-ro*
highway	autostrada	*au-to-'stra-da*
in the country	in campagna	*kam-'pa-nya*
in the mountains	in montagna	*mon-'ta-nya*
lake	lago	—
motorway restaurant	autogrill (m, inv)	—
mountain boots	scarponi (m, pl)	*skar-'po-ni*
mountain climbing	alpinismo	*al-pi-'niz-mo*
on vacation	in vacanza	*va-'kan-dza*
river	fiume (m)	*'fyu-me*
scenic route	itinerario panoramico	*i-ti-ne-'ra-ryo*
sea	mare (m)	*'ma-re*
ski resort	campo di sci	*'kam-po di 'ši*
sleeping bag	sacco a pelo	*'sak-ko a -'pe-lo*
suburb	sobborgo	*sob-'bor-go*
• **suburbs, outskirts**	periferia	*per-i-fe-'ri-a*
suntan	abbronzatura	*ab-bron-dza-'tu-ra*
	tintarella	*tin-ta-'rel-la*
• **(to) get a suntan**	abbronzarsi	*ab-bron-'dzar-si*
tent	tenda	—
tourist information office	ufficio d'informazioni turistiche	*uf-'fi-čo din-for-ma-'tsyo-ni tu-'ris-ti-ke*
tourist place, sight-seeing place	posto di villeggiatura	*'pos-to di vil-lej-ja-'tu-ra*
town (hamlet), village	paese (m)	*pa-'e-ze*
town (market-town)	borgo	—
town (small city)	cittadina	*čit-ta-'di-na*
town council	comune (m)	*ko-'mu-ne*
village	villaggio	*vil-'laj-jo*

C. ASKING FOR DIRECTIONS

across	attraverso	*at-tra-'ver-so*
ahead	avanti	*a-'van-ti*
at the end of	in fondo a	—
at the top of	in cima a	*'či-ma*
back	indietro	*in-'dye-tro*
behind	dietro	*'dye-tro*
(to) cross	attraversare	*at-tra-ver-'sa-re*
down	giù	*ju*
east	est	—
• **to the east**	a est	—
(to) enter	entrare (ess)	*en-'tra-re*
everywhere	dappertutto	*dap-per-'tut-to*
(to) exit, go out	uscire* (ess)	*u-'ši-re*
far	lontano	*lon-'ta-no*
(to) follow	seguire	*se-'gwi-re*

(to) go	andare* (ess)	*an-'da-re*
(to) go down	scendere* (ess)	*'šen-de-re*
(to) go up	salire* (ess)	*sa-'li-re*
here	qui	*kwi*
in front of	di fronte a	—
inside	dentro	—
left	sinistra	*si-'nis-tra*
• **to the left**	a sinistra	—
near	vicino	*vi-'či-no*
north	nord	—
• **to the north**	a nord	—
outside	fuori	*'fwo-ri*
right	destra	—
• **to the right**	a destra	—
south	sud	—
• **to the south**	a sud	—
straight ahead	diritto (dritto)	*di-'rit-to*
west	ovest	*'o-vest*
• **to the west**	a ovest	—

Basic Formulas

Can you tell me where...?	=	Mi sa dire dove...?
How do you get to...?	=	Come si fa per andare a...?
Where is...?	=	Dov'è...?

SCHOOL AND WORK

37. SCHOOL

A. TYPES OF SCHOOLS AND GENERAL VOCABULARY

coed school	scuola mista	*'skwo-la 'mis-ta*
commercial school	istituto commerciale	*is-ti-'tu-to*
compulsory education	istruzione (f)	*is-tru-'tsyo-ne*
	obbligatoria	*ob-bli-ga-'to-rya*
conservatory	conservatorio	*kon-ser-va-'to-ryo*
course	corso	—
• **correspondence course**	corso per corrispondenza	*kor-ris-pon-'den-tsa*
daycare	asilo nido	*a-'zi-lo 'ni-do*
dean, chair of a faculty	preside (m/f) di facoltà	*'pre-zi-de di fa-kol-'ta*
(to) educate, instruct	istruire (isc)	*is-tru-'i-re*
• **education (as process)**	educazione (f)	*e-du-ka-'tsyo-ne*
• **education, instruction**	istruzione (f)	*is-tru-'tsyo-ne*
elementary school	scuola elementare	*'skwo-la*
evening course	corso serale	*'kor-so se-'ra-le*
evening school	scuola serale	*'skwo-la se-'ra-le*
faculty	facoltà (f, inv)	*fa-kol-'ta*
• **architecture**	facoltà di architettura	*ar-ki-tet-'tu-ra*
• **arts**	facoltà di lettere	*'let-te-re*
• **business and commerce**	facoltà di economia e commercio	*kom-'mer-čo*
• **engineering**	facoltà di ingegneria	*in-je-nye-'ria*
• **jurisprudence, law**	facoltà di giurisprudenza	*ju-ris-pru-'den-tsa*
• **medicine**	facoltà di medicina	*me-di-'či-na*
• **sciences**	facoltà di scienze	*'šen-tse*
grade	classe (f)	*'klas-se*
• **grade one**	prima	—
high school, lyceum	liceo	*li-'če-o*
• **art lyceum**	liceo artistico	*ar-'tis-ti-ko*
• **arts and letters**	liceo classico	*'klas-si-ko*
• **languages lyceum**	liceo linguistico	*lin-'gwis-ti-ko*
• **scientific lyceum**	liceo scientifico	*šen-'ti-fi-ko*
institute	istituto	*is-ti-'tu-to*
junior high school, middle school	scuola media	*'skwo-la 'me-dya*
kindergarten	asilo infantile	*a-'zi-lo in-fan-'ti-le*

Ministry of Public Education	Ministero della Pubblica Istruzione	—
nursery school	scuola materna	*'skwo-la ma-'ter-na*
primary school	scuola primaria	*'skwo-la pri-'ma-rya*
private school	scuola privata	*'skwo-la pri-'va-ta*
public school	scuola pubblica	*'skwo-la 'pub-bli-ka*
residential school (college)	collegio	*kol-'le-jo*
scholarship, grant	borsa di studio	*'bor-sa di 'stu-dyo*
• **scholarship holder**	borsista (m/f)	*bor-'sis-ta*
school	scuola	*'skwo-la*
school year	anno scolastico	*'an-no sko-'las-ti-ko*
secondary school	scuola secondaria	*'skwo-la se-kon-'da-rya*
specialization course	corso di specializzazione	*'kor-so di spe-ča-'li-dza-'tsyo-ne*
state school	scuola statale	*'skwo-la sta-'ta-le*
teacher training school	istituto magistrale	*is-ti-'tu-to ma-jis-'tra-le*
technical school, vocational school	istituto tecnico	*is-ti-'tu-to 'tek-ni-ko*
university	università (f, inv)	*u-ni-ver-si-'ta*
• **first year**	primo anno	—
• **second year**	secondo anno	—
university chair	cattedra	*'kat-te-dra*
upper school	scuola superiore	*'skwo-la su-pe-'ryo-re*

B. THE CLASSROOM

assignment book	agenda	*a-'jen-da*
ballpoint pen	biro (f, inv)	—
blackboard	lavagna	*la-'va-nya*
blackboard eraser	cancellino	*kan-čel-'li-no*
book	libro	—
calculator	calcolatrice (f)	*kal-ko-la-'tri-če*
• **pocket calculator**	calcolatrice tascabile	*tas-'ka-bi-le*
chalk	gesso	*'jes-so*
compass	compasso	*kom-'pas-so*
computer	computer (m, inv)	—
desk	banco	—
dictionary	dizionario	*di-tsyo-'na-ryo*
encyclopedia	enciclopedia	*en-či-klo-pe-'di-a*
eraser	gomma	—
glue, paste	colla	—
grammar book	grammatica	*gram-'ma-ti-ka*
highlighter	evidenziatore (m)	*e-vi-den-tsya-'to-re*
ink	inchiostro	*in-'kyos-tro*
knapsack. backpack	zaino	*'dzai-no*
laptop computer	laptop (m, inv)	—
manual	manuale (m)	*ma-'nwa-le*

map	cartina geografica	*kar-'ti-na je-o-'gra-fi-ka*
marker	pennarello	*pen-na-'rel-lo*
notebook, workbook	quaderno	*kwa-'der-no*
• ringed notebook	quaderno a anelli	*a-'nel-li*
• spiral notebook	quaderno a spirale	*spi-'ra-le*
overhead	lucido	*'lu-či-do*
• overhead projector	lavagna luminosa	*la-'va-nya lu-mi-'no-za*
paper	carta	*'kar-ta*
• carton paper	cartoncino	*kar-ton-'či-no*
• drawing paper	carta da disegno	*di-'ze-nyo*
• lined paper	carta a righe	*'ri-ge*
• squared paper	carta a quadretti	*kwa-'dret-ti*
projector	proiettore (m)	*pro-yet-'to-re*
protractor	goniometro	*go-'nyo-me-tro*
reading book	libro di lettura	*let-'tu-ra*
school bag	cartella	*kar-'tel-la*
textbook	libro di testo	—
writing desk	scrivania	*skri-va-'ni-a*

C. AREAS

cafeteria	mensa	—
campus	campus (inv)	—
classroom	aula	*'au-la*
gymnasium	palestra	*pa-'les-tra*
hallway	corridoio	*kor-ri-'do-yo*
laboratory	laboratorio	*la-bo-ra-'to-ryo*
library	biblioteca	*bib-lyo-'te-ka*
main office	segreteria	*se-gre-te-'ri-a*
office (of an instructor)	studio	*'stu-dyo*
school yard	cortile (m)	*kor-'ti-le*

D. PEOPLE

assistant	assistente (m/f)	*as-sis-'ten-te*
class (of students), grade	classe (f)	*'klas-se*
elementary school pupil	scolaro (-a)	*sko-'la-ro*
high school principal	preside (m/f) di liceo	*'pre-zi-de*
janitor	bidello (-a)	*bi-'del-lo*
librarian	bibliotecario (-a)	*bib-lyo-te-'ka-ryo*
non-teaching personnel	personale (m) non docente	*per-so-'na-le non do-'čen-te*
president of a university	rettore	*ret-'to-re*
principal	preside (m/f)	*'pre-zi-de*
pupil	alunno (-a)	*a-'lun-no*
schoolmate	compagno (-a)	*kom-'pa-nyo*
secretary	segretario (-a)	*se-gre-'ta-ryo*
self-learner	privatista	*pri-va-'tis-ta*

special education teacher	insegnante (m/f) di sostegno	*in-se-'nyan-te di sos-'te-nyo*
student	studente (-essa)	*stu-'den-te*
teacher, instructor	insegnante (m/f)	*in-se-'nyan-te*
• **elementary school**	maestro (-a)	*ma-'es-tro*
• **middle, high school**	professore (-essa)	*pro-fes-'so-re*
technician	tecnico (-a)	*'tek-ni-ko*

E. SUBJECTS

anatomy	anatomia	*a-na-to-'mi-a*
anthropology	antropologia	*an-tro-po-lo-'ji-a*
archeology	archeologia	*ar-ke-o-lo-'ji-a*
architecture	architettura	*ar-ki-tet-'tu-ra*
art	arte (f)	—
arts, humanities, letters	lettere (f, pl)	*'let-te-re*
astronomy	astronomia	*as-tro-no-'mi-a*
biology	biologia	*bi-o-lo-'ji-a*
botany	botanica	*bo-'ta-ni-ka*
chemistry	chimica	*'ki-mi-ka*
commerce	commercio	*kom-'mer-čo*
communication sciences	scienze della comunicazione	*'šen-dze del-la ko-mu-ni-ka-'tsyo-ne*
design	disegno	*di-'ze-nyo*
discipline	disciplina	*di-ši-'pli-na*
economics	economia	*e-ko-no-'mi-a*
engineering	ingegneria	*in-je-nye-'ri-a*
geography	geografia	*je-o-gra-'fi-a*
geometry	geometria	*je-o-me-'tri-a*
history	storia	*'sto-rya*
informatics, computer science	informatica	*in-for-'ma-ti-ka*
jurisprudence, law	giurisprudenza	*ju-ris-pru-'den-dza*
	legge (f)	*'lej-je*
languages	lingue (f, pl,)	*'lin-gwe*
linguistics	linguistica	*lin'-gwis-ti-ka*
literature	letteratura	*let-te-ra-'tu-ra*
mathematics	matematica	*ma-te-'ma-ti-ka*
medicine	medicina	*me-di-'či-na*
music	musica	*'mu-zi-ka*
philosophy	filosofia	*fi-lo-so-'fi-a*
physics	fisica	*'fi-zi-ka*
political science	scienze politiche	*'šen-dze po-'li-ti-ke*
psychiatry	psichiatria	*psi-ki-a-'tri-a*
psychology	psicologia	*psi-ko-lo-'ji-a*
science	scienza	*'šen-dza*
sociology	sociologia	*so-čo-lo-'ji-a*
statistics	statistica	*sta-'tis-ti-ka*

subject	materia	*ma-'te-rya*
trigonometry	trigonometria	*tri-go-no-me-'tri-a*
zoology	zoologia	*dzo-o-lo-'ji-a*

F. MISCELLANEOUS

ability	abilità (f, inv)	*a-bi-li-'ta*
admission test	prova d'ammissione	*dam-mis-'syo-ne*
answer	risposta	*ris-'pos-ta*
• **(to) answer**	rispondere*	*ris-'pon-de-re*
• **brief, short**	breve	—
• **long**	lunga	—
• **right**	corretta	*kor-'ret-ta*
• **wrong**	sbagliata	*zba-'lya-ta*
aptitude test	test d'attitudine	*dat-ti-'tu-di-ne*
assignment	compito	*'kom-pi-to*
(to) attend	frequentare	*fre-kwen-'ta-re*
• **attendance**	frequenza	*fre-'kwen-dza*
average	media	*'me-dya*
(to) be absent	essere* assente	*'es-se-re as-'sen-te*
(to) be present	essere* presente	*'es-se-re pre'zen-te*
(to) be promoted, pass	essere* promosso (-a)	*'es-se-re pro-'mos-so*
bibliography	bibliografia	*bib-li-o-gra-'fi-a*
bookmark	segnalibro	*se-nya-'li-bro*
catalogue	catalogo	*ka-'ta-lo-go*
class	classe (f)	*'klas-se*
• **class, lesson**	lezione (f)	*le-'tsyo-ne*
• **(to) have a class**	avere* lezione	—
• **(to) skip a class**	saltare una lezione	*sal-'ta-re*
composition	componimento	*kom-po-ni-'men-to*
computer-assisted learning	apprendimento tramite computer	*ap-pren-di-'men-to*
conference	convegno	*kon-'ve-nyo*
copy	copia	*'ko-pya*
• **good, final copy**	bella copia	—
• **rough copy, draft**	brutta copia	—
core subject	materia fondamentale	*ma-'te-rya fon-da-men-'ta-le*
curriculum	curriculum (m, inv)	—
degree	laurea	*'lau-re-a*
• **(to) get a degree**	laurearsi	*lau-re-'ar-si*
diploma	diploma (m) (diplomi, pl)	*di-'plo-ma*
• **(to) get a diploma**	diplomarsi	*di-plo-'mar-si*
drawing	disegno	*di-'ze-nyo*
• **(to) draw**	disegnare	*di-ze-'nya-re*
(to) drop out	abbandonare gli studi	*ab-ban-do-'na-re lyi 'stu-di*
educated	istruito	*is-tru-'i-to*

• education	istruzione (f)	*is-tru-'tsyo-ne*
(to) erase	cancellare	*kan-čel-'la-re*
error	errore (m)	*er-'ro-re*
evaluation, grading	valutazione (f)	*va-lu-ta-'tsyo-ne*
examination	esame (m)	*e-'za-me*
• entrance exam	esame d'ammissione	*dam-mis-'syo-ne*
• oral exam	esame orale	*o-'ra-le*
• (to) pass an exam	superare un esame	*su-pe-'ra-re*
• (to) take an exam	sostenere* un esame	*sos-te-'ne-re*
• written exam	esame scritto	*'skrit-to*
exercise	esercizio	*e-zer-'či-tsyo*
(to) fail	essere* bocciato	*'es-se-re boč-'ča-to*
• (to) fail (someone)	bocciare	*boč-'ča-re*
field (of study)	campo (di studio)	—
field trip	gita scolastica	*'ji-ta sko-'las-ti-ka*
grade, mark	voto	—
graph	grafico	*'gra-fi-ko*
group work	lavoro in gruppo	*la-'vo-ro*
(to) have a class, a lesson	avere* lezione	*a-'ve-re le-'tsyo-ne*
high school diploma	diploma (m) di	*di-'plo-ma di*
	maturità	*ma-tu-ri-'ta*
(to) learn	imparare	*im-pa-'ra-re*
• learning	apprendimento	*ap-pren-di-'men-to*
lesson, class	lezione (f)	*le-'tsyo-ne*
level of education	titolo di studio	*'ti-to-lo di 'stu-dyo*
(to) listen to	ascoltare	*as-kol-'ta-re*
(to) mark, correct	correggere*	*kor-'rej-je-re*
mistake	sbaglio	*'zba-lyo*
• (to) make mistakes	sbagliare	*zba-'lya-re*
note	appunto	*ap-'pun-to*
optional subject	materia opzionale	*ma-'te-rya op-tsyo-'na-le*
photocopy	fotocopia	*fo-to-'ko-pya*
• (to) photocopy	fotocopiare	*fo-to-ko-'pya-re*
physical education	educazione fisica	*e-du-ka-'tsyo-ne 'fi-zi-ka*
problem	problema (m) (problemi, pl)	*pro-'ble-ma*
• (to) solve a problem	risolvere* un problema	*'ri-zol-ve-re un pro-'ble-ma*
professional development	aggiornamento degli insegnanti	*aj-jor-na-'men-to de-lyi in-se-'nyan-ti*
professional development course	corso di formazione professionale	*'kor-so di for-ma-'tsyo-ne pro-fes-syo-'na-le*
quarter term	quadrimestre (m)	*kwa-dri-'mes-tre*
question	domanda	*do-'man-da*
• (to) ask a question	fare* una domanda	—
reading, reading passage	lettura	*let-'tu-ra*

• (to) read	leggere*	*'lej-je-re*
registration	iscrizione (f)	*is-kri-'tsyo-ne*
• **registration fee**	tassa d'iscrizione	*'tas-sa*
(to) repeat	ripetere	*ri-'pe-te-re*
report card	pagella	*pa-'jel-la*
review	ripasso	*ri-'pas-so*
• **(to) review**	ripassare	*ri-pas-'sa-re*
round table	tavola rotonda	*'ta-vo-la ro-'ton-da*
school fee, tuition	tassa scolastica	*'tas-sa sko-'las-ti-ka*
school registration	iscrizione (m) a scuola	*is-kri-'tsyo-ne a 'skwo-la*
self-taught	autodidatta (m/f)	*au-to-di-'dat-ta*
semester	semestre (m)	*se-'mes-tre*
seminar, workshop	seminario	*se-mi-'na-ryo*
(to) skip school,	marinare la scuola	*ma-ri-'na-re la 'skwo-la*
** play hooky**		
slide	diapositiva	*di-a-po-zi-'ti-va*
study	studio	—
• **(to) study**	studiare	*stu-'dya-re*
symposium	simposio	*sim-'po-zyo*
(to) take attendance	fare* l'appello	*ap-'pel-lo*
(to) teach	insegnare	*in-se-'nya-re*
teaching aids	materiale didattico	*ma-te-'rya-le di-'dat-ti-ko*
test	prova	—
thesis	tesi (f, inv)	*'te-zi*
• **(to) defend one's thesis**	discutere* la tesi	*dis-'ku-te-re*
training	formazione (f)	*for-ma-'tsyo-ne*
trimester	trimestre (m)	*tri-'mes-tre*
(to) write	scrivere*	*'skri-ve-re*

38. WORK AND THE BUSINESS WORLD

A. JOBS AND PROFESSIONS

accountant	contabile (m/f)	*kon-'ta-bi-le*
administration	amministrazione (f)	*am-mi-nis-tra-'tsyo-ne*
apprentice	apprendista (m/f)	*ap-pren-'dis-ta*
architect	architetto (-a)	*ar-ki-'tet-to*
auditor	revisore dei conti	*re-vi-'zo-re dei 'kon-ti*
baker	fornaio (-a)	*for-'na-yo*
barber	barbiere (-a)	*bar-'bye-re*
bookseller	libraio (-a)	*li-'bra-yo*
bricklayer	muratore (m)	*mu-ra-'to-re*
business consultant	consulente (m/f)	*kon-su-'len-te*
	commerciale	*kom-mer-'ča-le*
business person	persona d'affari	*per-'so-na daf-'fa-ri*
butcher	macellaio (-a)	*ma-čel-'la-yo*
carpenter	falegname (m/f)	*fa-le-'nya-me*

cashier	cassiere (-a)	*kas-'sye-re*
chartered accountant	commercialista (m/f)	*kom-mer-ča-'lis-ta*
chief executive	direttore (-trice) generale	*di-ret-'to-re je-ne-'ra-le*
cobbler, shoe-repairer	calzolaio (-a)	*kal-tso-'la-yo*
company lawyer	giurista (m/f) d'impresa	*ju-'ris-ta dim-'pre-za*
computer scientist	informatico (-a)	*in-for-'ma-ti-ko*
consultant	consulente (m/f)	*kon-su-'len-te*
cook	cuoco (-a)	*'kwo-ko*
customs officer	doganiere (-a)	*do-ga-'nye-re*
departmental manager	caporeparto	*ka-po-re-'par-to*
director, CEO	dirigente (m/f)	*di-ri-'jen-te*
doctor	medico	*'me-di-ko*
	dottore (-essa)	*dot-'to-re*
driver	autista (m/f)	*au-'tis-ta*
editor	redattore (-trice)	*re-dat-'to-re*
electrician	elettricista (m/f)	*e-let-tri-'čis-ta*
engineer	ingegnere (m/f)	*in-je-'nye-re*
farmer	contadino (-a)	*kon-ta-'di-no*
firefighter	vigile del fuoco	*'vi-ji-le del 'fwo-ko*
fishmonger	pescivendolo	*pe-ši-'ven-do-lo*
florist	fiorista (m/f)	*fyo-'ris-ta*
fruit vendor	fruttivendolo	*frut-ti-'ven-do-lo*
grocer	droghiere (-a)	*dro-'gye-re*
guard	guardiano (-a)	*gwar-'dya-no*
hairdresser	parrucchiere (-a)	*par-ruk-'kye-re*
house painter	imbianchino (-a)	*im-byan-'ki-no*
industrialist	industriale (m/f)	*in-dus-'trya-le*
jeweler	gioielliere (m/f)	*jo-yel-'lye-re*
job	mestiere (m)	*mes-'tye-re*
journalist	giornalista (m/f)	*jor-na-'lis-ta*
lawyer	avvocato (m/f)	*av-vo-'ka-to*
legal consultant	consulente (m/f) legale	*kon-su-'len-te le-'ga-le*
letter carrier	postino (-a)	*pos-'ti-no*
librarian	bibliotecario (-a)	*bib-lyo-te-'ka-ryo*
marriage counselor	consigliere (-a)	*kon-si-'lye-re*
	matrimoniale	*ma-tri-mo-'nya-le*
mechanic	meccanico (-a)	*mek-'ka-ni-ko*
midwife	levatrice (f)	*le-va-'tri-če*
nurse	infermiere (-a)	*in-fer-'mye-re*
occupation	occupazione (f)	*ok-ku-pa-'tsyo-ne*
oculist	oculista (m/f)	*o-ku-'lis-ta*
office worker	impiegato (-a)	*im-pye-'ga-to*
partner	socio (-a)	*'so-čo*
pharmacist	farmacista (m/f)	*far-ma-'čis-ta*
physical therapist	fisioterapista (m/f)	*fi-zyo-te-ra-'pis-ta*
pilot	pilota (m/f)	*pi-'lo-ta*
plasterer	intonacatore (-trice)	*in-to-na-ka-'to-re*
plumber	idraulico (m/f)	*i-'drau-li-ko*

policeman, policewoman	poliziotto (-a)	*po-li-'tsyot-to*
profession	professione (f)	*pro-fes-'syo-ne*
professional	professionista (m/f)	*pro-fes-syo-'nis-ta*
programmer	programmatore (-trice)	*pro-gram-ma-'to-re*
psychiatrist	psichiatra (m/f)	*psi-ki-'a-tra*
psychologist	psicologo (-a)	*psi-'ko-lo-go*
real-estate agent	agente immobiliare (m/f)	*a-'jen-te im-mo-bi-'lya-re*
sailor	marinaio (-a)	*ma-ri-'na-yo*
sales representative	agente commerciale (m/f)	*a-'jen-te kom-mer-'ča-le*
salesman, saleswoman	venditore (-trice)	*ven-di-'to-re*
scientist	scienziato (-a)	*šen-'tsya-to*
secretary	segretario (-a)	*se-gre-'ta-ryo*
social worker	assistente sociale (m/f)	*as-sis-'ten-te so-'ča-le*
soldier	soldato	*sol-'da-to*
speech therapist	logopedista (m/f)	*lo-go-pe-'dis-ta*
staff, personnel	personale (m)	*per-so-'na-le*
stockbroker	agente di cambio (m/f)	*a-'jen-te di 'kam-byo*
store clerk	commesso (-a)	*kom-'mes-so*
street sweeper	netturbino (-a)	*net-tur-'bi-no*
surgeon	chirurgo (-a)	*ki-'rur-go*
surveyor	geometra (m/f)	*je-'o-me-tra*
tailor	sarto (-a)	*'sar-to*
taxi driver	tassista (m/f)	*tas-'sis-ta*
teacher	insegnante (m/f)	*in-se-'nyan-te*
technical consultant	consulente tecnico (-a)	*kon-su-'len-te 'tek-ni-ko*
theatrical agent	agente teatrale	*a-'jen-te te-a-'tra-le*
upholsterer	tappezziere (-a)	*tap-pe-'tsye-re*
waiter, waitress	cameriere (-a)	*ka-me-'rye-re*
writer	scrittore (-trice)	*skrit-'to-re*

B. INTERVIEWING FOR A JOB

Name	nome (m)	*'no-me*
• surname	cognome (m)	*ko-'nyo-me*
• signature	firma	—
Address	indirizzo	*in-di-'rit-tso*
• street	via	—
• number	numero	*'nu-me-ro*
• city	città (f, inv)	*čit-'ta*
• postal code	codice (m) postale	*'ko-di-če pos-'ta-le*
Telephone Number	numero di telefono	*'nu-me-ro di te-'le-fo-no*
• area code	prefisso	*pre-'fis-so*
• e-mail address	e-mail	—
Date and Place of Birth	Data e luogo di nascita	*'lwo-go di 'na-ši-ta*
• date	data	—
• place	luogo	—

Age	Età	—
Sex	Sesso	—
• male	maschile	*'mas-kyle*
• female	femminile	*'fem-mi-nile*
Marital Status	Stato civile	*'sta-to či-'vi-le*
• divorced	divorziato (-a)	*di-vor-'tsya-to*
• married	sposato (-a)	*spo-'za-to*
• single	celibe (m)	*'če-li-be*
	nubile (f)	*'nu-bi-le*
• widowed	vedovo (-a)ʲ	*'ve-do-vo*
Nationality	Nazionalità (f, inv)	*na-tsyo-na-li-'ta*
Education	Istruzione (f)	*is-tru-'tsyo-ne*
educational qualifications, credentials	titoli di studio	*'ti-to-li*
• high school graduate	diplomato (-a)	*di-plo-'ma-to*
• university graduate	laureato (-a)	*lau-re-'a-to*
Profession	Professione (f)	*pro-fes-'syo-ne*
Qualifications	Qualifiche (f, pl)	*kwa-'li-fi-ke*
References	Referenze (f, pl)	*re-fe-'ren-dze*
Résumé	Curriculum vitae (m, inv)	—

C. THE OFFICE

adhesive tape	nastro adesivo	*'nas-tro a-de-'zi-vo*
answering machine	segreteria telefonica	*se-gre-te-'ri-a te-le-'fo-ni-ka*
at (@)	chiocciola	*'kyoč-čo-la*
business card	biglietto da visita	*bi-'lyet-to da -'vi-zi-ta*
calculator	calcolatrice (f)	*kal-ko-la-'tri-če*
calendar	calendario	*ka-len-'da-ryo*
carbon paper	carta carbone	*'kar-ta kar-'bo-ne*
card, record, file	scheda	*'ske-da*
cartridge	cartuccia	*kar-'tuč-ča*
CD-ROM	CD-ROM (m, inv)	—
clip	clip	—
compatible software	software (m, inv) compatibile	*kom-pa-'ti-bi-le*
computer	computer (m, inv)	—
copy	copia	*'ko-pya*
• (to) copy	copiare	*ko-'pya-re*
cursor	cursore (m)	*kur-'so-re*
directory	indirizzario	*in-di-ri-'tsya-ryo*
document	documento	*do-ku-'men-to*
• document cover	copertina	*ko-per-'ti-na*
draft	bozza	*'bot-tsa*
(to) duplicate	duplicare	*du-pli-'ka-re*

e-mail	e-mail	—
envelope	busta	—
fax	fax (m, inv)	—
file	archivio	*ar-'ki-vyo*
	scheda	*'ske-da*
• **(to) file away**	schedare	*ske-'da-re*
• **file folder**	cartella	*kar-'tel-la*
• **file name**	titolo del documento	*'ti-to-lo del do-ku-'men-to*
• **filing cabinet, box file**	schedario	*ske-'da-ryo*
(to) fill out	compilare	*kom-pi-'la-re*
format	format (m, inv)	—
• **(to) format**	formattare	*for-mat-'ta-re*
• **formatted**	formattato	*for-mat-'ta-to*
hard drive	hard drive	—
hardware	hardware (m, inv)	—
icon	icona	*i-'ko-na*
index	indice (m)	*'in-di-če*
ink	inchiostro	*in-'kyos-tro*
ink-jet printer	stampante (f) a getto d'inchiostro	*stam-'pan-te a 'jet-to din-'kyos-tro*
inputting on the screen	videoscrittura	*vi-de-o-skrit-'tu-ra*
• **(to) input**	digitare	*di-ji-'ta-re*
installation	installazione (f)	*in-stal-la-'tsyo-ne*
interactive	interattivo	*in-ter-at-'ti-vo*
intercom	citofono	*či-'to-fo-no*
Internet	Internet (m, inv)	—
justification	giustificazione (f)	*jus-ti-fi-ka-'tsyo-ne*
keyboard	tastiera	*tas-'tye-ra*
label	etichetta	*e-ti-'ket-ta*
laptop computer	laptop (m, inv)	—
laser printer	stampante (f) laser	*stam-'pan-te*
letterhead	carta intestata	*'kar-ta in-tes-'ta-ta*
Liquid Paper, White-out	bianchetto	*byan-'ket-to*
marker	pennarello	*pen-na-'rel-lo*
memory	memoria	*me-'mo-rya*
menu	menu (m, inv)	—
microprocessor	microprocessore (m)	*mi-kro-pro-ces-'so-re*
modem	modem (m, inv)	—
mouse	mouse (m, inv)	—
(to) navigate	navigare	*na-vi-'ga-re*
network	network (m, inv)	—
	rete (f)	*'re-te*
notice board	tabella	*ta-'bel-la*
office hours	orario d'ufficio	*o-'ra-ryo duf-'fi-čo*
• **office manager, boss**	capoufficio (capo)	*ka-po-uf-'fi-čo*
• **office personnel**	personale (m) d'ufficio	*per-so-'na-le*

• office supplies	forniture (f, pl) per ufficio	for-ni-'tu-re
online (online)	on-line	—
organization chart	organigramma (m)	or-ga-ni-'gram-ma
pad	taccuino	tak-'kwi-no
paper	carta	—
password	password (m, inv)	—
pen	penna	—
pencil, crayon	matita	ma-'ti-ta
permanent memory	memoria fissa	me-'mo-rya 'fis-sa
personal organizer	agenda	a-'jen-da
photocopier	fotocopiatrice (f)	fo-to-kopya-'tri-če
(to) print	stampare	stam-'pa-re
• printer	stampante (f)	stam-'pan-te
punch	perforatrice (f)	per-fo-ra-'tri-če
ruler	riga	—
sheet (of paper)	foglio	'fo-lyo
(to) shred	stracciare	strač-'ča-re
software	software (m, inv)	—
spreadsheet	foglio elettronico	'fo-lyo e-let-'tro-ni-ko
staple	punto metallico	'pun-to me-'tal-li-ko
• stapler	cucitrice (f)	ku-'či-'tri-če
string	spago	'spa-go
supply cupboard	armadietto delle forniture	ar-ma-'dyet-to del-le for-ni-'tu-re
systems analyst	analista (m/f) di sistemi	a-na-'lis-ta dei sis-'te-mi
tack	puntina	pun-'ti-na
teleconference	teleconferenza	te-le-kon-fe-'ren-tsa
terminal	terminal (m, inv)	—
toner	toner (m, inv)	—
(to) type in	digitare	di-ji-'ta-re
user	utente (m/f)	u-'ten-te
user-friendly	di facile uso	'fa-či-le 'u-zo
virtual	virtuale	vir-'twa-le
virus	virus (m, inv)	—
waiting room	sala d'aspetto	'sa-la das-'pet-to
wastebasket	cestino	čes-'ti-no
website	sito (web)	—
window	finestra	fi-'nes-tra
word processing	trattamento di testi	trat-ta-'men-to
workstation	stazione (f) di lavoro	sta-'tsyo-ne di la-'vo-ro
writing desk	scrivania	skri-va-'ni-a

D. EMPLOYMENT AND THE BUSINESS WORLD

accounting department	reparto della contabilità	re-'par-to del-la kon-ta-bi-li-'ta

advertising	pubblicità (f, inv)	*pub-bli-či-'ta*
annual leave	congedo annuale	*kon-'je-do an-'nwa-le*
applicant	candidato	*kan-di-'da-to*
appointment	appuntamento	*ap-pun-ta-'men-to*
bargaining, negotiations	trattative (f, pl)	*trat-ta-'ti-ve*
base salary	paga base	*'pa-ga 'ba-ze*
(to) be self-employed	lavorare in proprio	*la-vo-'ra-re in 'pro-pryo*
board of directors	consiglio d'amministrazione	*kon-'si-lyo dam-mi-nis-tra-'tsyo-ne*
branch	succursale (f)	*suk-kur-'sa-le*
break	pausa	*'pau-za*
budget	bilancio	*bi-'lan-čo*
• budget prediction	bilancio preventivo	*pre-ven-'ti-vo*
career	carriera	*kar-'rye-ra*
(to) chair a meeting	presiedere una riunione	*pre-'sye-de-re*
classified ad	piccola pubblicità	*'pik-ko-la pub-bli-či-'ta*
clientele	clientela	*kli-en-'te-la*
commerce, trade	commercio	*kom-'mer-čo*
company	ditta	—
company policy	politica aziendale	*po-'li-ti-ka a-dzyen-'da-le*
competition	concorrenza	*kon-kor-'ren-tsa*
• competitor	concorrente (m/f)	*kon-kor-'ren-te*
consumer	consumatore (-trice)	*kon-su-ma-'to-re*
consumer good	bene (m) di consumo	*'be-ne di kon-'su-mo*
consumer protection	tutela del consumatore	*tu-'te-la del kon-su-ma-'to-re*
contract	contratto	*kon-'trat-to*
corporation	società (f, inv)	*so-če-'ta*
cost price	prezzo di costo	*'pret-tso di 'kos-to*
customer	cliente (m/f)	*kli-'en-te*
delivery	consegna	*kon-'se-nya*
demonstration	manifestazione (f)	*ma-ni-fes-ta-'tsyo-ne*
discount	sconto	*'skon-to*
dividend	dividendo	*di-vi-'den-do*
(to) earn	guadagnare	*gwa-da-'nya-re*
employee	dipendente (m/f)	*di-pen-'den-te*
• blue-collar worker	operaio (-a)	*o-per-'a-yo*
• employer	datore di lavoro	*da-'to-re di la-'vo-ro*
• employment	lavoro	*la-'vo-ro*
• employment agency	agenzia di collocamento	*a-jen-'tsi-a di kol-lo-ka-'men-to*
• white-collar worker	impiegato (-a)	*im-pye-'ga-to*
factory	fabbrica	*'fab-bri-ka*
(to) fire	licenziare	*li-cen-'tsya-re*
• firing	licenziamento	*li-cen-tsya-'men-to*
firm, company	azienda	*a-'dsyen-da*
fixed wage	stipendio fisso	*sti-'pen-dyo 'fis-so*
franchise	appalto	*ap-'pal-to*

• franchiser	appaltatore (-trice)	*ap-pal-ta-'to-re*
general strike	sciopero generale	*'šo-pe-ro je-ne-'ra-le*
(to) get a job	procurarsi un lavoro	*pro-ku-'rar-si un la-'vo-ro*
(to) go on strike	scioperare	*šo-pe-'ra-re*
grievance	lamentela	*la-men-'te-la*
gross national product	prodotto nazionale lordo	*pro-'dot-to na-tsyo-'na-le 'lor-do*
gross profit	guadagno lordo	*gwa-'da-nyo 'lor-do*
head office	sede (f) principale	*'se-de prin-ci-'pa-le*
(to) hire	assumere*	*as-'su-me-re*
• hiring	assunzione (f)	*as-sun-'tsyo-ne*
income	reddito	*'red-di-to*
labor shortage	scarsezza di manodopera	*skar-'set-tsa di ma-no-'do-pe-ra*
labor surplus	eccesso di manodopera	*eč-'čes-so di ma-no-'do-pe-ra*
labor union	sindacato	*sin-da-'ka-to*
leave-of-absence	congedo	*kon-'je-do*
(to) lose one's job	perdere* il lavoro	*'per-de-re il la-'vo-ro*
lunch break	pausa mensa	*'pau-za 'men-sa*
management	direzione (f)	*di-re-'tsyo-ne*
	gestione (f)	*jes-'tyo-ne*
• management board	comitato direttivo	*ko-mi-'ta-to di-ret-'ti-vo*
• manager	direttore (-trice)	*di-ret-'to-re*
market	mercato	*mer-'ka-to*
• market research	ricerche (f, pl) di mercato (di marketing)	*ri-čer-'ke di mer-'ka-to*
merchandise	merce (f)	*'mer-če*
(to) merge	fondere*	*'fon-de-re*
monopoly	monopolio	*mo-no-'po-lyo*
multinational (company)	multinazionale (f)	*mul-ti-na-tsyo-'na-le*
net profit	guadagno netto	*gwa-'da-nyo 'net-to*
night work	lavoro notturno	*la-'vo-ro not-'tur-no*
occasional job	lavoro saltuario	*la-'vo-ro sal-'twa-ryo*
occupational hazard	rischio del mestiere	*'ris-kyo del mes-'tye-re*
(to) offer a job	offrire* un lavoro	*of-'fri-re un la-'vo-ro*
office	ufficio	*uf-'fi-čo*
overtime work	lavoro straordinario	*la-'vo-ro stra-or-di-'na- ryo*
partnership	partnership (m, inv)	—
pay	paga	—
pay claim	rivendicazione (f) salariale	*ri-ven-di-ka-'tsyo-ne sa-la-'rya-le*
pay day	giorno di paga	*'jor-no di 'pa-ga*
pension, retirement	pensione (f)	*pen-'syo-ne*
personality test	test psicologico	*psi-ko-'lo-ji-ko*

piece work	lavoro a cottimo	la-'vo-ro a 'kot-ti-mo
plant	stabilimento	sta-bi-li-'men-to
(to) privatize	privatizzare	pri-va-tid-'dza-re
probation period	tirocinio	ti-ro-'či-nyo
producer	produttore (m)	pro-dut-'to-re
• **product**	prodotto	pro-'dot-to
profit	profitto	pro-'fit-to
	guadagno	gwa-'da-nyo
• **profit margin**	margine (m) di guadagno	'mar-ji-ne
promotion	promozione (f)	pro-mo-'tsyo-ne
public relations office	ufficio pubbliche relazioni	uf-'fi-čo 'pub-bli-ke re-la-'tsyo-ni
(to) register a company	immatricolare un'azienda	im-ma-tri-ko-'la-re un-a-'dzyen-da
(to) retire	andare* (ess) in pensione	an-'da-re in pen-'syo-ne
second job, moonlighting	secondo lavoro	se-'kon-do la-'vo-ro
shift work	turno di lavoro	'tur-no di la-'vo-ro
starting wage	stipendio iniziale	sti-'pen-dyo i-ni-'tsya-le
stay-at-home job	lavoro a domicilio	la-'vo-ro a do-mi-'či-lyo
stock company, corporation	società (f, inv) per azioni	so-če-'ta per a-'tsyo-ni
• **stockholder**	azionista (m/f)	a-tsyo-'nis-ta
strike	sciopero	'šo-pe-ro
• **striker**	scioperante (m/f)	šo-pe-'ran-te
subsidiary	filiale (f)	fi-'lya-le
survey	sondaggio	son-'daj-jo
take-home pay	busta paga	—
takeover bid	offerta pubblica d'acquisto	of-'fer-ta 'pub-bli-ka dak-'kwis-to
tax on salary	imposta sul reddito	im-'pos-ta sul 'red-di-to
temporary work	lavoro temporaneo	la-'vo-ro tem-po-'ra-ne-o
unemployed	disoccupato	diz-ok-ku-'pa-to
• **unemployment**	disoccupazione (f)	diz-ok-ku-pa-'tsyo-ne
• **unemployment benefits**	cassa integrazione	'kas-sa in-te-gra-'tsyo-ne
union member	sindacalista (m/f)	sin-da-ka-'lis-ta
union negotiation	trattativa sindacale	trat-ta-'ti-va sin-da-'ka-le
wage, stipend	stipendio	sti-'pen-dyo
• **wage increase**	aumento di stipendio	au-'men-to di sti-'pen-dyo
warehouse	magazzino	ma-gad-'zi-no
work	lavoro	la-'vo-ro
• **(to) work**	lavorare	la-vo-'ra-re
work associate	collega (m/f)	kol-'le-ga
work contract	contratto di lavoro	kon-'trat-to di la-'vo-ro
working hours	orario di lavoro	o-'ra-ryo di la-'vo-ro

EMERGENCIES

39. REPORTING AN EMERGENCY

A. FIRE

alarm	allarme (m)	al-'lar-me
arson	incendio doloso	in-cen-dyo do-'lo-zo
• arsonist	piromane (m/f)	pi-'ro-ma-ne
building	edificio	e-di-'fi-čo
burn (on body)	ustione (f)	us-'tyo-ne
(to) burn	bruciare	bru-'ča-re
(to) call the fire department	chiamare i pompieri	kya-'ma-re i pom-'pye-ri
(to) catch fire	incendiarsi	in-cen-'dyar-si
danger	pericolo	pe-'ri-ko-lo
(to) destroy	distruggere*	dis-'truj-je-re
emergency exit	uscita di sicurezza (emergenza)	u-'ši-ta di si-ku-'ret-tsa
(to) escape, get out	uscire* (ess) fuori	u-'ši-re 'fwo-ri
(to) extinguish, put out	spegnere* il fuoco	'spe-nye-re il 'fwo-ko
fire	incendio	in-'čen-dyo
	fuoco	'fwo-ko
• Fire!	Al fuoco!	—
• fire extinguisher	estintore (m)	es-tin-'to-re
• firefighter	vigile del fuoco	'vi-ji-le
• fire hose	pompa	—
• fire hydrant	idrante (m)	i-'dran-te
• fire truck	autopompa	au-to-'pom-pa
fireproof	antincendio	an-tin-'čen-dyo
first aid	pronto soccorso	'pron-to sok-'kor-so
flame	fiamma	'fyam-ma
help	aiuto	a-'yu-to
• (to) help	aiutare	a-yu-'ta-re
• Help!	Aiuto!	—
• (to) give help	dare* aiuto	—
ladder	scala	'ska-la
out	fuori	'fwo-ri
• Everybody out!	Tutti fuori!	—
(to) protect	proteggere*	pro-'tej-je-re
(to) rescue	soccorrere*	sok-'kor-re-re
shout	grido	—
• (to) shout	gridare	gri-'da-re
siren	sirena	si-'re-na

| smoke | fumo | — |
| victim | vittima | *'vit-ti-ma* |

B. ROBBERY, ASSAULT, AND OTHER CRIMES

accomplice	complice (m)	*'kom-pliče*
(to) argue	litigare	*li-ti-'ga-re*
arrest	arresto	*ar-'res-to*
• (to) arrest	arrestare	*ar-res-'ta-re*
• arrest warrant	mandato di cattura	*man-'da-to di kat-'tu-ra*
assailant	aggressore (m)	*a-gres-'so-re*
assassin, murderer	assassino	*as-sas-'si-no*
assault, attack	aggressione (f)	*ag-res-'syo-ne*
• armed assault, attack	aggressione a mano armata	*ar-'ma-ta*
• (to) assault, attack	aggredire (isc)	*ag-gre-'di-re*
blackmail	ricatto	*ri-'kat-to*
• (to) blackmail	ricattare	*ri-kat-'ta-re*
bodyguard	guardia del corpo	*'gwar-dya del 'kor-po*
break and enter	scasso	*'skas-so*
bribe	bustarella	*bus-ta-'rel-la*
• bribery	corruzione (f)	*kor-ru-'tsyo-ne*
chief of police	commissario di polizia	*kom-mis-'sa-ryo di po-li-'tsi-a*
clue	indizio	*in-'di-tsyo*
conspiracy, frame-up	complotto	*kom-'plot-to*
coroner	magistrato (investigatore)	*ma-jis-'tra-to*
court-appointed lawyer	difensore d'ufficio	*di-fen-'so-re duf-'fi-čo*
crime	crimine (m)	*'kri-mi-ne*
• criminal	criminale (m/f)	*kri-mi-'na-le*
• criminal act	reato	*re-'a-to*
• criminal record	passato criminale	*pas-'sa-to kri-mi-'na-le*
defense lawyer	difensore	*di-fen-'so-re*
delinquency	delinquenza	*de-lin-'kwen-tsa*
description	descrizione (f)	*des-kri-'tsyo-ne*
DNA	DNA (m, inv)	—
drug pusher	spacciatore (m) di droga	*spač-ča-'tore*
• drug pushing	spaccio di droga	*'spač-čo*
• drug traffic	traffico di droga	*'traf-fi-ko*
• drug trafficker	trafficante di droga	*traf-fi-'kan-te*
• (to) push drugs	spacciare droga	*spač-'ča-re*
embezzlement	appropriazione indebita	*ap-pro-prya-tsyo-ne in-'de-bi-ta*
escape	evasione (f)	*e-va-'zyo-ne*
(to) fight	picchiarsi	*pik-'kyar-si*
fingerprint	impronta digitale	*im-'pron-ta di-ji-'ta-le*
firearm	arma da fuoco	*'ar-ma da 'fwo-ko*

forensics, forensic science	medicina legale	me-di-'či-na le-'ga-le
forgery	contraffazione (f)	kon-traf-fa-'tsyo-ne
• forger	contraffattore (-trice)	kon-traf-fat-'to-re
fraud	frode (f)	'fro-de
fugitive	evaso (-a)	e-'va-zo
(to) give oneself up	consegnarsi alla polizia	kon-se-'nyar-si al-la po-li-'tsi-a
gun	rivoltella	ri-vol-'tel-la
handcuffs	manette (f, pl)	ma-'net-te
hijacking	dirottamento	di-rot-ta-'men-to
• (to) hijack	dirottare	di-rot-'ta-re
hired killer	sicario	si-'ka-ryo
hostage	ostaggio (-a)	os-'taj-jo
informant	informatore (-trice)	in-for-ma-'to-re
infraction	infrazione (f)	in-fra-'tsyo-ne
injury, wound	ferita	fe-'ri-ta
• (to) injure, wound	ferire (isc)	fe-'ri-re
investigation	investigazione (f)	in-ves-ti-ga-'tsyo-ne
• investigator	investigatore (-trice)	in-ve-ti-ga-'to-re
juvenile delinquency	delinquenza minorile	de-lin-'kwen-tsa mi-no-'ri-le
• juvenile delinquent	delinquente minorile	de-lin-'kwen-te
kidnapping	sequestro	se-kwes-tro
• (to) kidnap	sequestrare	se-kwes-'tra-re
• kidnapper	sequestratore (m)	se-kwes-tra-'to-re
(to) kill	uccidere*	uč-'či-de-re
• killer	assassino	as-sas-'si-no
knife	coltello	kol-'tel-lo
legal assistance	assistenza legale	as-sis-'ten-dza le-'ga-le
loot	bottino	bot-'ti-no
manslaughter	omicidio	o-mi-'či-dyo
	preterintenzionale	pre-ter-in-ten-tsyo-'na-le
murder	assassinio	as-sas-'si-nyo
• (to) murder	uccidere*	uč-'či-de-re
• murderer	omicida (m/f)	o-mi-'či-da
outlaw	fuorilegge (m/f)	fwo-ri-'lej-je
patrol	pattuglia	pat-'tu-lya
• (to) patrol	pattugliare	pat-tu-'lya-re
perjury	falsa testimonianza	'fal-sa tes-ti-mo-'nyan-tsa
pickpocket	scippatore (-trice)	šip-pa-'to-re
• pocket-picking	scippo	'šip-po
pistol	pistola	pis-'to-la
police	polizia	po-li-'tsi-a
• police headquarters	commissariato	kom-mis-sa-'rya-to
• police officer	poliziotto (-a)	po-lit-'tsyot-to
• police station	questura	kwes-'tu-ra

• police van	furgone (m) della polizia	*fur-'go-ne*
premeditated crime	delitto premeditato	*de-'lit-to pre-me-di-'ta-to*
prisoner	detenuto (-a)	*de-te-'nu-to*
private detective	investigatore (-trice) privato (-a)	*in-ves-ti-ga-'to-re* *pri-'va-to*
questioning	interrogatorio	*in-ter-ro-ga-'to-ryo*
ransom	riscatto	*ris-'kat-to*
rape	violenza carnale	*vyo-'len-tsa kar-'na-le*
• (to) rape	violentare	*vyo-len-'ta-re*
• rapist	violentatore (m)	*vyo-len-ta-'to-re*
rifle	fucile (m)	*fu-'či-le*
robbery, burglary	rapina	*ra-'pi-na*
• armed robbery	rapina a mano armata	—
• (to) rob	rapinare	*ra-pi-'na-re*
• robber, burglar	rapinatore (-trice)	*ra-pi-na-'to-re*
scuffle	baruffa	*ba-'ruf-fa*
search	perquisizione (f)	*per-kwi-zi-'tsyo-ne*
• search warrant	mandato di perquisizione	*man-'da-to*
(to) shoot	sparare	*spa-'ra-re*
smuggling	contrabbando	*kon-trab-'ban-do*
(to) stab	pugnalare	*pu-nya-'la-re*
statement made to authorities	verbale (m)	*ver-'ba-le*
(to) steal	rubare	*ru-'ba-re*
tax evasion	frode (f) fiscale	*'fro-de fis-'ka-le*
thief	ladro (-a)	—
vandal	vandalo (-a)	*'van-da-lo*
• vandalism	vandalismo	*van-da-'liz-mo*
violence	violenza	*vyo-'len-tsa*
warrant	mandato	*man-'da-to*
weapon	arma	—

Useful Expressions

Help!	Aiuto!
Hurry! Come quickly!	Presto!
Fire!	Al fuoco!
Someone assaulted me!	Qualcuno mi ha aggredito (-a)!
Someone stole my...	Qualcuno mi ha rubato...!

C. TRAFFIC ACCIDENTS

accident	incidente (m)	*in-či-'den-te*
• **serious accident**	incidente grave	*'gra-ve*
• **traffic accident**	incidente stradale	*stra-'da-le*
ambulance	ambulanza	*am-bu-'lan-tsa*
	autoambulanza	*au-to-am-bu-'lan-tsa*
(to) be run over	essere* investito (-a)	*'es-se-re in-ves-'ti-to*
(to) bleed	sanguinare	*san-gwi-'na-re*
• **blood**	sangue (m)	*'san-gwe*
broken bone	osso rotto	*'os-so 'rot-to*
(to) bump	sbattere	*'zbat-te-re*
(to) collide, smash	scontrarsi	*skon-'trar-si*
• **collision, smash**	scontro	*'skon-tro*
crash	schianto	*'skyan-to*
• **(to) crash**	schiantarsi	*skyan-'tar-si*
doctor	medico	*'me-di-ko*
• **(to) get a doctor**	chiamare un medico	*kya-'ma-re*
first aid	pronto soccorso	*'pron-to sok-'kor-so*
• **antiseptic**	antisettico	*an-ti-'set-ti-ko*
• **bandage**	benda	*'ben-da*
• **gauze**	garza	*'gar-dza*
• **splint**	stecca	*'stek-ka*
• **tincture of iodine**	tintura di iodio	*tin-'tu-ra di 'yo-dyo*
Help!	Aiuto!	*a-'yu-to*
hospital	ospedale (m)	*os-pe-'da-le*
• **emergency**	pronto soccorso	*'pron-to sok-'kor-so*
• **X-rays**	raggi X	*'raj-ji*
police	polizia	*po-li-'tsi-a*
• **(to) call the police**	chiamare la polizia	*kya-'ma-re*
shock, bang	trauma (m) (traumi, pl)	—
wound, injury	ferita	*fe-'ri-ta*

40. MEDICAL CARE

A. AT THE DOCTOR'S

abortion	aborto	*a-'bor-to*
acne	acne (f)	—
acupuncture	agopuntura	*a-go-pun-'tu-ra*
addiction	dipendenza	*di-pen-'den-tsa*
adhesive bandage	cerotto	*če-'rot-to*
AIDS	AIDS (m, inv)	—
ailment	indisposizione (f)	*in-dis-po-zi-'tsyo-ne*
allergic	allergico	*al-'ler-ji-ko*
• **allergy**	allergia	*al-ler-'ji-a*
anemia	anemia	*a-ne-'mi-a*
• **anemic**	anemico	*a-'ne-mi-co*

anesthesia	anestesia	*a-nes-te-'zi-a*
• anesthetic	anestetico	*a-nes-'te-ti-ko*
ankle sprain	storta alla caviglia	*ka-'vi-lya*
antibiotic	antibiotico	*an-ti-bi-'o-ti-ko*
anxiety	ansietà	*an-sye-'ta*
appendicitis	appendicite (f)	*ap-pen-di-'či-te*
appointment	appuntamento	*ap-pun-ta-'men-to*
arrhythmia	aritmia	*a-rit-'mi-a*
arteriosclerosis	arteriosclerosi (f, inv)	*ar-te-ryo-skle-'ro-zi*
arthritis	artrite (f)	*ar-'tri-te*
aspirin	aspirina	*as-pi-'ri-na*
asthma	asma	*'az-ma*
athlete's foot	micosi (f, inv) dei piedi	*mi-'ko-zi*
autism	autismo	*au-'tiz-mo*
bacillus, bacterium	bacillo	*ba-'čil-lo*
backache	mal di schiena	*'skye-na*
(to) bandage	bendare	*ben-'da-re*
barbiturate	barbiturico	*bar-bi-'tu-ri-ko*
(to) be on call	essere* di turno	*'es-se-re di -'tur-no*
(to) become cured	guarire (isc)	*gwa-'ri-re*
(to) become ill	ammalarsi	*am-ma-'lar-si*
benign	benigno	*be-'ni-nyo*
bile	bile (f)	*'bi-le*
bite	morso	*'mor-so*
blister	vescica	*ve-'ši-ka*
blood	sangue (m)	*'san-gwe*
• blood test	analisi (f, inv) del sangue	*a-'na-'li-zi*
• blood transfusion	trasfusione (f) del sangue	*tras-fu-'zyo-ne*
(to) break a limb	fratturare un arto	*frat-tu-'ra-re*
bronchitis	bronchite (f)	*bron-'ki-te*
bruise	livido	*'li-vi-do*
cancer	cancro	*'kan-kro*
cataract	cateratta	*ka-te-'rat-ta*
catarrh	catarro	*ka-'tar-ro*
(to) catch a chill	prendere* freddo	*'pren-de-re 'fred-do*
cellulite	cellulite (f)	*čel-lu-'li-te*
chest infection	infezione (f) polmonare	*in-fe-'tsyo-ne pol-mo-'na-re*
chicken-pox	varicella	*va-ri-'čel-la*
chill, shiver	brivido	*'bri-vi-do*
cold	raffreddore (m)	*raf-fred-'do-re*
colitis	colite (f)	*ko-'li-te*
concussion	commozione (f) cerebrale	*kom-mo-'tsyo-ne če-re-'bra-le*
condom	preservativo	*pre-zer-va-'ti-vo*

constipation	stitichezza	*sti-ti-'ke-tsa*
contraceptive	contraccettivo	*kon-trač-čet-'ti-vo*
• contraceptive pill	pillola anticoncezionale	*'pil-lo-la an-ti-kon-če-tsyo-'na-le*
convalescence	convalescenza	*kon-va-le-'šen-dza*
corn, callus	callo	—
cortisone	cortisone (m)	*kor-ti-'zo-ne*
cough	tosse (f)	*'tos-se*
• (to) cough	tossire (isc)	*tos-'si-re*
• cough syrup	sciroppo contro la tosse	*ši-rop-po*
• coughing fit	colpo di tosse	*'kol-po di 'tos-se*
cream	crema	—
critical condition	grave stato	—
crutch	stampella	*stam-'pel-la*
cure	cura	—
• (to) cure	curare	*ku-'ra-re*
cyst	cisti (f, inv)	*'čis-ti*
dehydrated	disidratato	*di-si-dra-'ta-to*
• dehydration	disidratazione (f)	*di-si-dra-ta-'tsyo-ne*
depression	depressione (f)	*de-pres-'syo-ne*
dermatitis	dermatite (f)	*der-ma-'ti-te*
diabetes	diabete (m)	*di-a-'be-te*
(to) diagnose	diagnosticare	*di-a-nyos-ti-'ka-re*
• diagnosis	diagnosi (f, inv)	*di-'a-nyo-zi*
diarrhea	diarrea	*di-ar-'re-a*
diet	dieta	*'dye-ta*
discomfort	malessere (m)	*ma-'les-se-re*
disease	malattia	*ma-lat-'ti-a*
dislocated	slogato	*zlo-'ga-to*
• dislocation	slogatura	*zlo-ga-'tu-ra*
diuretic	diuretico	*di-u-'re-ti-ko*
dizziness	giramento di testa	*ji-ra-'men-to*
doctor	medico	*'me-di-co*
	dottore (-essa)	*dot-'to-re*
• doctor's office	gabinetto medico	*ga-bi-'net-to 'me-di-ko*
• family doctor	medico di famiglia	*fa-'mi-lya*
dosage	posologia	*po-zo-lo-'ji-a*
dressing	fascia	*'fa-ša*
drop	goccia	*'goč-ča*
drowsiness	sonnolenza	*son-no-'len-tsa*
drug addiction	tossicodipendenza	*tos-si-ko-di-pen-'den-tsa*
ear infection	otite (f)	*o-'ti-te*
electrocardiogram	elettrocardiogramma (m)	*e-let-tro-kar-dyo-'gram-ma*
embolism	embolia	*em-bo-'li-a*
epidemic	epidemia	*e-pi-de-'mi-a*
epileptic fit	crisi epilettica	*'kri-zi e-pi-'let-ti-ka*

estrogen	estrogeno	es-'tro-je-no
(to) examine	visitare	vi-zi-'ta-re
expectorant	espettorante (m)	es-pet-to-'ran-te
eye-drop	collirio	kol-'li-ryo
(to) faint	svenirsi*	zve-'nir-si
fainting spell	svenimento	zve-ni-'men-to
(to) feel nauseous	avere* la nausea	'nau-ze-a
fever, temperature	febbre (f)	'feb-bre
flu, influenza	influenza	in-flu-'en-dza
food poisoning	intossicazione (f)	in-tos-si-ka-'tsyo-ne
	alimentare	a-li-men-'ta-re
fracture	frattura	frat-'tu-ra
gallstones	calcoli biliari	'kal-ko-li bi-'lya-ri
(to) gargle	fare* gargarismi	gar-ga-'riz-mi
(to) get better	migliorare	mi-lyo-'ra-re
gonorrhea	gonorrea	gon-nor-'re-a
gynecologist	ginecologo (-a)	ji-ne-'ko-lo-go
• gynecology	ginecologia	ji-ne-ko-lo-'ji-a
(to) have…	avere*	a-'ve-re
• a backache	avere* mal di schiena	'skye-na
• a headache	avere* mal di testa	—
• a sore throat	avere* mal di gola	—
• a sore, upset stomach	avere* mal di stomaco	'sto-ma-ko
• a temperature	avere* la febbre	—
(to) heal	guarire	gwa-'ri-re
hearing aid	apparecchio acustico	ap-pa-'rek-kyo a-'kus-ti-ko
heart attack	infarto cardiaco	in-'far-to kar-'di-a-ko
heartburn	bruciore (m) di stomaco	bru-'čo-re di 'sto-ma-ko
hematoma	ematoma (m)	e-ma-'to-ma
hemorrhage, bleeding	emorragia	e-mor-raj-'ji-a
hernia	ernia	'er-nya
herpes	erpete (m)	'er-pe-te
high blood pressure	ipertensione (f)	i-per-ten-'syo-ne
HIV-positive	sieropositivo	sye-ro-po-zi-'ti-vo
homeopathy	omeopatia	o-me-o-pa-'ti-a
hormone	ormone (m)	or-'mo-ne
house call	visita domiciliare	'vi-zi-ta do-mi-či-'lya-re
incontinence	incontinenza	in-kon-ti-'nen-dza
indigestion	indigestione (f)	in-di-jes-'tyo-ne
infection	infezione (f)	in-fe-'tsyo-ne
• inflamed	infiammato	in-fyam-'ma-to
• inflammation	infiammazione (f)	in-fyam-ma-'tsyo-ne
injection, needle	puntura	pun-'tu-ra
injury	infortunio	in-for-'tu-nyo
insomnia	insonnia	in-'son-nya
insulin	insulina	in-su-'li-na

intensive care unit	sala di rianimazione	ri-a-ni-ma-'tsyo-ne
(to) itch	prudere	'pru-de-re
• itchiness	prurito	pru-'ri-to
kidney stone	calcolo renale	'kal-ko-lo re-'na-le
laryngitis	laringite (f)	la-rin-'ji-te
laxative	purga	—
lesion	lesione (f)	le-'zyo-ne
leukemia	leucemia	leu-če-'mi-a
magnesium citrate	citrato di magnesio	či-'tra-to di ma-'nye-zyo
(to) make an appointment	fissare un appuntamento	fis-'sa-re un ap-pun-ta-'men-to
malignant	maligno	ma-'li-nyo
measles, red measles	morbillo	mor-'bil-lo
	roseola	ro-'ze-o-la
medical checkup	visita di controllo	'vi-zi-ta di kon-'trol-lo
• medical examination	esame (m) medico	e-'za-me 'me-di-ko
menopause	menopausa	me-no-'pau-za
menstruation	mestruazione (f)	mes-tru-a-'tsyo-ne
miscarriage	aborto spontaneo	a-'bor-to spon-'ta-ne-o
mumps	orecchioni (m, pl)	o-rek-'kyo-ni
nausea	nausea	'nau-ze-a
nurse	infermiere (-a)	in-fer-'mye-re
obstetrician	ostetrico (-a)	os-'te-tri-ko
oculist, eye specialist	oculista (m/f)	o-ku-'lis-ta
ointment	pomata	po-'ma-ta
(to) operate	operare	o-pe-'ra-re
• operating room	sala operatoria	'sa-la o-pe-ra-'to-rya
• operation	intervento chirurgico	in-ter-'ven-to ki-'rur-ji-ko
optometrist	optometrista (m/f)	op-to-me-'tris-ta
orthopedic surgeon	chirurgo ortopedico	ki-'rur-go or-to-'pe-di-ko
pain	dolore (m)	do-'lo-re
• painful	doloroso	do-lo-'ro-zo
• painkiller	analgesico	a-nal-'je-zi-ko
pale	pallido	'pal-li-do
palliative	palliativo	pal-lya-'ti-vo
paralysis	paralisi (f, inv)	pa-'ra-li-zi
paramedic	paramedico	pa-ra-'me-di-ko
pastille	pasticca	pas-'tik-ka
pathologist	patologo (-a)	pa-'to-lo-go
patient	paziente (m/f)	pa-'tsyen-te
pediatrician	pediatra (m/f)	pe-di-'a-tra
penicillin	penicillina	pe-ni-čil-'li-na
pharmaceutical	farmaco	'far-ma-ko
• pharmacist	farmacista (m/f)	far-ma-'čis-ta
phial	fiala	'fya-la
pill	pillola	'pil-lo-la
plaster	ingessatura	in-jes-sa-'tu-ra
• plaster cast	fascia gessata	'fa-ša jes-'sa-ta

plastic surgeon	chirurgo estetico	*ki-'rur-go es-'te-ti-ko*
pneumonia	polmonite (f)	*pol-mo-'ni-te*
pregnancy	gravidanza	*gra-vi-'dan-dza*
• **pregnant**	incinta	*in-'čin-ta*
(to) prescribe	prescrivere*	*pre-'skri-ve-re*
• **prescription**	ricetta medica	*ri-'čet-ta 'me-di-ka*
(to) probe	sondare	*son-'da-re*
prognosis	prognosi (f, inv)	*'pro-nyo-zi*
psychiatrist	psichiatra (m/f)	*psi-ki-'a-tra*
psychosomatic	psicosomatico	*psi-ko-so-'ma-ti-ko*
psychotherapist	psicoterapista (m/f)	*psi-ko-te-ra-'pis-ta*
pulse	polso	*'pol-so*
pus	pus (m, inv)	—
radiography	radiografia	*ra-dyo-gra-'fi-a*
radiologist	radiologo (-a)	*ra-'dyo-lo-go*
rash	eruzione cutanea	*e-ru-'tsyo-ne ku-'ta-ne-a*
(to) recover	rimettersi*	*ri-met-ter-si*
redness	rossore (m)	*ros-'so-re*
(to) resuscitate	rianimare	*ri-a-ni-'ma-re*
rheumatism	reumatismo	*reu-ma-'tiz-mo*
rubber gloves	guanti di gomma	*'gwan-ti*
scar	cicatrice (f)	*či-ka-'tri-če*
scarlet fever	scarlattina	*skar-lat-'ti-na*
scurvy	scorbuto	*skor-'bu-to*
sedative	sedativo	*se-da-'ti-vo*
self-examination	autopalpazione (f)	*au-to-pal-pa-'tsyo-ne*
shingles	fuoco di Sant'Antonio	*'fwo-ko di sant-an-'to-nyo*
sick person	ammalato (-a)	*am-ma-'la-to*
• **sickly**	malaticcio	*ma-la-'tič-čo*
sinusitis	sinusite (f)	*si-nu-'zi-te*
sleeping pill	sonnifero	*son-'ni-fe-ro*
sling	bendaggio	*ben-'daj-jo*
sneeze	starnuto	*star-'nu-to*
• **(to) sneeze**	starnutire (isc)	*star-nu-'ti-re*
sodium bicarbonate	bicarbonato di sodio	*bi-kar-bo-'na-to di 'so-dyo*
spasm	spasimo	*'spa-zi-mo*
speech therapist	logopedista (m/f)	*lo-go-pe-'dis-ta*
sprain	distorsione (f)	*dis-tor-'syo-ne*
	storta	*'stor-ta*
squint	strabismo	*stra-'biz-mo*
stiff neck	torcicollo	*tor-či-'kol-lo*
• **stiffness**	rigidezza	*ri-ji-'det-tsa*
stitch	punto	—
stomachache	mal di stomaco	*'sto-ma-ko*
stone	calcolo	*'kal-ko-lo*
stress	stress (m, inv)	—

stretcher	barella	ba-'rel-la
stroke	ictus cerebrale	če-re-'bra-le
strong	forte	'for-te
sunstroke	colpo di sole	'kol-po di -'so-le
suppository	supposta	sup-'pos-ta
surgeon	chirurgo (-a)	ki-'rur-go
• surgery	chirurgia	ki-rur-'ji-a
• surgical appliance	protesi (f, inv)	'pro-te-zi
swab	tampone (m)	tam-'po-ne
sweat	sudore (m)	su-'do-re
• (to) sweat	sudare	su-'da-re
swelling	gonfiore (m)	gon'fyo-re
• (to) swell	gonfiare	gon'fya-re
• swollen	gonfio	'gon-fyo
symptom	sintomo	'sin-to-mo
syphilis	sifilide (f)	si-'fi-li-de
syringe	siringa	si-'rin-ga
tablet	compressa	kom-'pres-sa
(to) take one's temperature	misurare la febbre	mi-zu-'ra-re la 'feb-bre
tetanus	tetano	'te-ta-no
therapist	terapista (m/f)	te-ra-'pis-ta
• therapy	terapia	te-ra-'pi-a
thermometer	termometro	ter-'mo-me-tro
tincture of iodine	tintura di iodio	tin-'tu-ra di 'yo-dyo
tonic	tonico	'to-ni-ko
tonsillitis	tonsillite (f)	ton-sil-'li-te
tourniquet	laccio emostatico	'lač-čo
tranquilizer	calmante (m)	kal-'man-te
transplant	trapianto	tra-'pyan-to
tumor	tumore (m)	tu-'mo-re
ulcer	ulcera	'ul-če-ra
ultrasound	ecografia	e-ko-gra-'fi-a
unconscious	inconscio	in-'kon-šo
urologist	urologo (-a)	u-ro-lo-go
(to) vaccinate	vaccinare	vač-či-'na-re
• vaccination	vaccino	vač-'či-no
varicose vein	vena varicosa	've-na va-ri-'ko-za
vasectomy	vasectomia	va-zek-to-'mi-a
venereal disease	malattia venerea	ma-lat-'ti-a ve-'ne-re-a
virus	virus (m, inv)	—
• viral infection	infezione virale	in-fe-'tsyo-ne vi-'ra-le
visiting hours	ore di visita	'o-re di -'vi-zi-ta
vitamin	vitamina	vi-ta-'mi-na
vomit	vomito	'vo-mi-to
• (to) vomit	vomitare	vo-mi-'ta-re
waiting room	sala d'aspetto	'sa-la das-'pet-to
wart	verruca	ver-'ru-ka

weak	debole	*'de-bo-le*
wheelchair	sedia a rotelle	*'se-dya a ro-'tel-le*
whooping cough	pertosse (f)	*per-'tos-se*
(to) worsen, deteriorate	aggravarsi	*ag-gra-'var-si*
wound	ferita	*fe-'ri-ta*

B. AT THE DENTIST'S

anesthetic	anestetico	*a-nes-'te-ti-ko*
appointment	appuntamento	*ap-pun-ta-'men-to*
braces	apparecchio per denti	*ap-pa-'rek-kyo per i-'den-ti*
cavity, tooth decay	carie (f, inv)	*'ka-rye*
dental assistant	assistente (m/f)	*as-sis-'ten-te*
dentist	dentista (m/f)	*den-'tis-ta*
• at the dentist's	dal dentista	—
• dentist's office	gabinetto dentistico	*ga-bi-'net-to den-'tis-ti-ko*
drill	trapano	*'tra-pa-no*
false teeth, denture	dentiera	*den-'tye-ra*
(to) fill a tooth	impiombare un dente	*im-pyom-'ba-re*
• filling	piombatura	*pyom-ba-'tu-ra*
injection, needle	iniezione (f)	*in-ye-'tsyo-ne*
mouth	bocca	*'bok-ka*
• gums	gengive (f, pl)	*jen-'ji-ve*
• jaw	mandibola	*man-'di-bo-la*
• lip	labbro (labbra, f, pl)	*'lab-bro*
• Open!	Apra!	—
• palate	palato	*pa-'la-to*
• tongue	lingua	*'lin-gwa*
office hours	orario	*o-'ra-ryo*
orthodontist	ortodontista (m/f)	*or-to-don-'tis-ta*
plaque	placca dentaria	*'plak-ka den-'ta-rya*
(to) pull a tooth	estrarre* un dente	*es-'trar-re*
(to) rinse	sciacquarsi la bocca	*šak-'kwar-si la 'bok-ka*
tartar	tartaro	*'tar-ta-ro*
tooth	dente (m)	*'den-te*
• canine	canino	*ka-'ni-no*
• molar	molare (m)	*mo-'la-re*
• root	radice (f)	*ra-'di-če*
• tooth extraction	estrazione (f)	*es-tra-'tsyo-ne*
• wisdom tooth	dente del giudizio	*ju-'di-tsyo*
toothache	mal di denti	—
• (to) have a toothache	avere* mal di denti	—
toothpaste	dentifricio	*den-ti-'fri-čo*
X-rays	raggi X	*'raj-ji iks*

accusation	imputazione (f)	*im-pu-ta-'tsyo-ne*
• **(to) accuse**	accusare	*ak-ku-'za-re*
• **accused**	imputato (-a)	*im-pu-'ta-to*
(to) acquit	assolvere*	*as-'sol-ve-re*
(to) admit	ammettere*	*am-me-te-re*
attorney	avvocato (-essa)	*av-vo'-ka-to*
bail	cauzione (f)	*kau-'tsyo-ne*
(to) be on trial	essere* sotto processo	*'es-se-re 'sot-to pro-'čes-so*
(to) carry out a sentence	eseguire una sentenza	*e-ze-'gwi-re u-na sen-'ten-dza*
(to) charge	incolpare	*in-kol-'pa-re*
civil right	diritto civile	*di-'rit-to či-'vi-le*
closed-door hearing	udienza a porte chiuse	*u-'dyen-sza a 'por-te 'kyu-ze*
controversy	controversia	*kon-tro-'ver-sya*
(to) convince	convincere*	*kon-'vin-če-re*
court	tribunale (m)	*tri-bu-'na-le*
• **court for serious crimes**	corte (m) d'assise	*'kor-te das-'si-ze*
• **court for the administration of public funds**	corte (m) dei conti	—
• **court of appeal**	corte (m) d'appello	*dap-'pel-lo*
courtroom	aula del tribunale	*'au-la del tri-bu-'na-le*
• **courtroom hearing**	udienza in tribunale	*u-'dyen-tsa in tri-bu-'na-le*
criminal hearing	udienza penale	*u-'dyen-tsa pe-'na-le*
debate	dibattito	*di-'bat-ti-to*
• **(to) debate**	dibattere	*di-'bat-te-re*
(to) defend oneself	difendersi*	*di-'fen-der-si*
deferred sentence	sentenza di rinvio a giudizio	*sen-'ten-dza di rin-'vi-o a ju-'di-tsyo*
deposition, testimony	deposizione (f)	*de-po-zi-'tsyo-ne*
(to) detain	detenere*	*de-te-'ne-re*
detention	detenzione (f)	*de-ten-'tsyo-ne*
(to) disagree	non essere* d'accordo	*non-'es-se-re dak-'kor-do*
(to) discuss, argue	discutere*	*dis-'ku-te-re*
evidence	prove (f, pl)	*'pro-ve*
• **(to) examine the witness**	interrogare il testimone	*in-ter-ro-'ga-re il tes-ti-'mo-ne*
extradition	estradizione (f)	*es-tra-di-'tsyo-ne*
fault, guilt	colpa	—
freedom on bail	libertà (f, inv) su cauzione	*li-ber-'ta su kau-'tsyo-ne*

guilt	colpevolezza	*kol-pe-vo-'let-tsa*
• **guilty**	colpevole	*kol-'pe-vo-le*
hearing	udienza	*u-'dyen-tsa*
hostile party	parte avversa	*'par-te av-'ver-sa*
illegal	illegale	*il-le-'ga-le*
(to) imprison	incarcerare	*in-kar-če-'ra-re*
innocence	innocenza	*in-no-'čen-tsa*
• **innocent**	innocente	*in-no-'čen-te*
insufficient evidence	insufficienza di prove	*insuf-fi-'čen-'tsa di 'pro-ve*
(to) issue a sentence	pronunciare una sentenza	*pro-nun-'ča-re u-na sen-'ten-tsa*
judge	giudice (m/f)	*'ju-di-če*
• **(to) judge**	giudicare	*ju-di-'ka-re*
juror	giurato (-a)	*ju-'ra-to*
• **jury**	giuria	*ju-'ri-a*
justice	giustizia	*jus-'ti-tsya*
justice of the peace	giudice di pace	*'ju-di-če di 'pa-če*
law	legge (f)	*'lej-je*
lawsuit	querela	*kwe-'re-la*
lawyer	avvocato	*av-vo-'ka-to*
legal	legale	*le-'ga-le*
life imprisonment	ergastolo	*er-'gas-to-lo*
litigation, legal case	causa	*'kau-za*
• **(to) litigate**	fare* causa	—
magistrate	magistrato	*ma-jis-'tra-to*
(to) pay bail	versare la cauzione	*ver-'sa-re la kau-'tsyo-ne*
(to) persuade	persuadere*	*per-swa-'de-re*
plaintiff	querelante (m/f)	*kwe-re-'lan-te*
plea	supplica	*'sup-pli-ka*
• **(to) postpone, adjourn**	rimandare	*ri-man-'da-re*
power of attorney	procura	*pro-'ku-ra*
prison	prigione (f)	*pri-'jo-ne*
probation	libertà vigilata	*li-ber-'ta vi-ji-'la-ta*
proof	prova	—
public prosecutor	pubblico accusatore	*'pub-bli-ko ak-ku-za-'to-re*
(to) release on bail	rilasciare sotto cauzione	*ri-la-'ša-re sot-to kau-'tsyo-ne*
sentence	sentenza	*sen-'ten-tsa*
(to) sue	querelare	*kwe-re-'la-re*
summons	citazione (f)	*či-ta-'tsyo-ne*
supreme court	corte (f) di cassazione	*'kor-te di kas-sa-'tsyo-ne*
(to) testify	testimoniare	*tes-ti-mo-'nya-re*
testimony	testimonianza	*tes-ti-mo-'nyan-tsa*
trial	processo	*pro-'čes-so*
verdict	verdetto	*ver-det-to*
witness	testimone (m/f)	*tes-ti-'mo-ne*
• **eyewitness**	testimone oculare	*o-ku-'la-re*

THE CONTEMPORARY WORLD

42. SCIENCE AND TECHNOLOGY

A. TECHNOLOGY AND TELECOMMUNICATIONS

acoustics	acustica	*a-'kus-ti-ka*
antenna	antenna	*an-'ten-na*
audio	audio	*'au-dyo*
by cable	via cavo	—
distortion	distorsione (f)	*dis-tor-'syo-ne*
emission	emissione (f)	*e-mis-'syo-ne*
fee	tariffa	*ta-'rif-fa*
fidelity	fedeltà (f, inv)	*fe-del-'ta*
frequency	frequenza	*fre-'kwen-tsa*
interference	interferenza	*in-ter-fe-'ren-dza*
light signal	segnale luminoso	*se-'nya-le lu-mi-'no-zo*
message	messaggio	*mes-'saj-jo*
network	rete (f)	*'re-te*
optical reader	lettore ottico (m)	*let-to-re 'ot-ti-ko*
optics	ottica	*'ot-ti-ka*
real time	tempo reale	*re-'a-le*
reception	ricezione (f)	*ri-če-'tsyo-ne*
satellite	satellite (m)	*sa-'tel-li-te*
• satellite dish	antenna parabolica	*an-'ten-na pa-ra-'bo-li-ka*
sound signal	segnale sonoro	*se-'nya-le so-'no-ro*
subscription	abbonamento	*ab-bo-na-'men-to*
• subscription fee	canone (m) d'abbonamento	*'ka-no-ne*
technology	tecnologia	*tek-no-lo-'ji-a*
telecommunication	telecomunicazione (f)	*te-le-ko-mu-ni-ka-'tsyo-ne*
teleconference	teleconferenza	*te-le-kon-fe-'ren-dza*
transmission	trasmissione (f)	*traz-mis-'syo-ne*
video conference	videoconferenza	*vi-de-o-kon-fe-'ren-dza*
• video game	videogioco	*vi-de-o-'jo-ko*
• video telephone	videotelefono	*vi-de-o-te-'le-fo-no*
volume	volume (m)	*vo-'lu-me*
wavelength	lunghezza d'onda	*lun-'ge-tsa 'don-da*
wireless	senza fili	*'sen-tsa 'fi-li*

B. COMPUTERS, COMPUTER SCIENCE, AND THE INTERNET

(to) align	allineare	*al-li-ne-'a-re*
analog	analogico	*a-na-'lo-ji-ko*
animated image	immagine animata	*im-'ma-ji-ne a-ni-'ma-ta*
artificial intelligence	intelligenza artificiale	*in-tel-li-'jen-tsa ar-ti-fi-'ca-le*
automation	automazione (f)	*au-to-ma-'tsyo-ne*
byte	byte (m, inv)	—
cartridge	cartuccia	*kar-'tuč-ča*
CD reader, drive	lettore	*let-'to-re*
CD-ROM	CD-ROM (inv)	—
(to) center	centrare	*čen-'tra-re*
chip	chip (m, inv)	—
(to) clear, delete	annullare	*an-nul-'la-re*
(to) click	cliccare	*klik-'ka-re*
color monitor	schermo a colori	*'sker-mo a ko-'lo-ri*
command	comando	*ko-'man-do*
compatible	compatibile	*kom-pa-'ti-bi-le*
computer	computer (m, inv)	
computer science	informatica	*in-for-'ma-ti-ka*
computerization	computerizzazione (f)	*kom-pu-te-ri-tsa-'tsyo-ne*
(to) copy	copiare	*ko-'pya-re*
cursor	cursore (m)	*kur-'so-re*
datum, data	dato (sing.)	—
	dati (pl.)	—
• **data bank**	banca dati	—
• **data file**	file (m, inv) di dati	—
• **data processing**	elaborazione (f) dati	*e-la-bo-ra-'tsyo-ne*
(to) delete	cancellare	*kan-'čel-'la-re*
digital	digitale	*di-ji-'ta-le*
document	cartella (documento)	*kar-'tel-la*
(to) duplicate	duplicare	*du-pli-'ka-re*
editing	editing (m, inv)	—
electronic file	archivio elettronico	*ar-'ki-vyo e-let-'tro-ni-ko*
e-mail	e-mail	—
(to) erase, delete	cancellare	*kan-'cel-'la-re*
file	archivio	*ar-'ki-vyo*
	file (m, inv)	—
• **file manager**	file manager (m, inv)	—
• **file name**	titolo del documento	*'ti-to-lo del do-ku-men-to*
format	format (m, inv)	—
• **(to) format**	formattare	*for-mat-'ta-re*
• **formatted**	formattato	*for-mat-'ta-to*

grammar check	controllo della	kon-'trol-lo del-la
	grammatica	gram-'ma-ti-ka
graphic, graph	grafico	'gra-fi-ko
• **graphic interface**	interfaccia grafica	in-ter-'fač-ča
hard drive	hard drive	—
hardware	hardware (m, inv)	—
help command	comando help (m, inv)	ko-'man-do
	aiuto	a-'yu-to
hypertext	ipertesto	i-per-'tes-to
icon	icona	i-'ko-na
index	indice (m)	'in-di-če
information	informazione (f)	in-for-ma-'tsyo-ne
inputting on the screen	videoscrittura	vi-de-o-skrit-'tu-ra
installation	installazione (f)	in-stal-la-'tsyo-ne
integrated circuit	circuito integrato	čir-ku-'i-to in-te-'gra-to
interactive	interattivo	in-ter-at-'ti-vo
interface	interfaccia	in-ter-'fač-ča
Internet provider	provider (m, inv)	—
justification	giustificazione (f)	jus-ti-fi-ka-'tsyo-ne
keyboard	tastiera	tas-'tye-ra
keyword	parola chiave	pa-'ro-la 'kya-ve
laser printer	stampante (f) laser	stam-'pan-te
lock	bloccaggio	blok-'kaj-jo
margin	margine (m)	'mar-ji-ne
memory	memoria	me-'mo-rya
• **memory capacity**	capacità (f, inv) di	ka-pa-či-'ta
	memoria	
• **permanent memory**	memoria fissa	'fis-sa
• **RAM memory**	RAM	—
menu	menu (m, inv)	—
microprocessor	microprocessore (m)	mi-kro-pro-čes-'so-re
modem	modem (m, inv)	—
mouse	mouse (m, inv)	—
multimedia	multimedialità (f, inv)	mul-ti-me-dya-li-'ta
(to) navigate	navigare	na-vi-'ga-re
network	network (m, inv)	—
	rete (f)	—
online	on-line	—
optical reader	lettore ottico	let-'to-re 'ot-ti-ko
page set-up	impaginazione (f)	im-pa-ji-na-'tsyo-ne
peripheral	unità (f, inv) periferica	pe-ri-'fe-ri-ka
• **peripherals**	periferiche (f, pl)	pe-ri-'fe-ri-ke
personal organizer	agenda elettronica	a-'jen-da e-let-'tro-ni-ka
(to) print	stampare	stam-'pa-re
printer	stampante (f)	stam-'pan-te
program	programma (m)	pro-'gram-ma
	(programmi, pl)	
• **program instruction**	istruzione (f)	is-tru-'tsyo-ne

• **programmer**	programmatore (-trice)	*program-ma-'to-re*
• **program language**	linguaggio di programmazione	*lin-'gwaj-jo di pro-gram-ma-'tsyo-ne*
• **pirate program**	programma (m) pirata	*pro-'gram-ma pi-'ra-ta*
(to) put a space	interlineare	*in-ter-li-ne-'a-re*
(to) save	salvare	*sal-'va-re*
screen	schermo	*'sker-mo*
search	ricerca	*ri-'čer-ka*
server	server (m, inv)	—
(to) set up a page	impaginare	*im-pa-ji-'na-re*
software	software (m, inv)	—
space bar	barra spaziatrice	*'bar-ra spa-tsya-'tri-če*
spell check	controllo dell'ortografia	*kon-'trol-lo del-lor-to-gra-'fi-a*
spreadsheet	foglio elettronico	*'fo-lyo e-let-'tro-ni-ko*
(to) store	immagazzinare	*im-ma-ga-tsi-'na-re*
style	stile (m)	*'sti-le*
symbols table	tavola dei simboli	*'ta-vo-la dei 'sim-bo-li*
tab	tabulatore (m)	*ta-bu-la-'to-re*
• **(to) tab**	tabulare	*ta-bu-'la-re*
terminal	terminal (m, inv)	—
(to) type in	digitare	*di-ji-'ta-re*
underline	sottolineatura	*sot-to-li-ne-a-'tu-ra*
user	utente (m/f)	*u-'ten-te*
virtual	virtuale	*vir-'twa-le*
virus	virus (m, inv)	—
website	sito web	—
window	finestra	*fi-'nes-tra*
word processing	word processing	
work station	stazione (f) di lavoro	*sta-'tsyo-ne di la-'vo-ro*

C. COMPUTER FUNCTIONS AND COMMANDS

Attachment	Allegato	*al-le-'ga-to*
Back	Indietro	*in-'dye-tro*
Close	Chiudi	*'kyu-di*
Connect	Connetta	*kon-'net-ta*
Control	Controlla	*kon-'trol-la*
Copy	Copia	*'ko-pya*
Customize	Personalizza	*per-so-na-'li-dza*
Cut	Taglia	*'ta-lya*
Delete	Annulla	*an-nul-la*
Dialogue Window	Finestra di Dialogo	*fi-'nes-tra di di-'a-lo-go*
Edit	Modifica	*mo-'di-fi-ka*
Eliminate	Elimina	*e-'li-mi-na*
File	File	—
Find	Trova	*'tro-va*
Format	Formato	*for-'ma-to*

Forward	Avanti	*a-'van-ti*
Forward (e-mail)	Inoltra	*i-'nol-tra*
Go to	Vai a	
Incoming mail	Posta in arrivo	*'pos-ta in ar-'ri-vo*
Insert	Inserisci	*in-se-'ri-ši*
Layout	Layout	—
Menu	Menu	—
Message	Messaggio	*mes-'saj-jo*
Move	Sposta	—
Nicknames	Rubrica	*ru-'bri-ka*
Open	Apri	—
Options	Opzioni	*op-'tsyo-ni*
Outgoing mail	Posta in uscita	*u-'ši-ta*
Page layout	Impaginazione	*im-pa-ji-na-'tsyo-ne*
Password	Password	—
Paste	Incolla	*in-kol-la*
Preferences	Preferiti	*pre-fe-'ri-ti*
Print	Stampa	—
Remove	Rimuovi	*ri-'mwo-vi*
Reply	Rispondi	*ris-'pon-di*
Return	Invio	*in-'vi-o*
Save	Salva	—
Select	Seleziona	*se-le-'tsyo-na*
Send	Invia	*in-'vi-a*
Sent mail	Posta inviata	*in-'vya-ta*
Spell check	Controllo ortografia	*kon-'trol-lo or-to-gra-'fi-a*
Table	Tabella	*ta-'bel-la*
Tools	Strumenti	*stru-'men-ti*
Trashed mail	Posta eliminata	*e-li-mi-'na-ta*
Update	Aggiorna	*aj-'jor-na*
User name	Nome utente	*'no-me u-'ten-te*
View	Visualizza	*vi-zwa-'li-dza*
Window	Finestra	*fi-'nes-tra*

D. NEW TECHNOLOGIES AND MEDIA

blog	blog	—
downloading	downloading (m, inv)	—
	scaricare	—
Facebook	Facebook (m, inv)	—
Facebook profile	profilo	—
memory stick	chiavetta	*kya-'vet-ta*
mobile device	dispositivo mobile	*'mo-bi-le*
Skype	Skype (m, inv)	—
social media	i media sociali	—
text message	SMS (m, inv)	—
	messaggino	*mes-saj-'ji-no*

Twitter	Twitter (m, inv)	—
uploading	uploading (m, inv), caricare online	—
webcast	trasmissione web	—
website	sito web	—
YouTube	YouTube (m, inv)	—

43. POLITICS AND HISTORY

A. THE POLITICAL WORLD

administration	amministrazione (f)	*am-mi-nis-tra-'tsyo-ne*
agenda (of a meeting)	ordine del giorno	*'or-di-ne del 'jor-no*
assembly	assemblea	*as-sem-'ble-a*
ballot	scheda elettorale	*'ske-da e-let-to-'ra-le*
• **ballot box**	urna elettorale	*'ur-na*
• **balloting**	ballottaggio	*bal-lot-'taj-jo*
bicameral	bicamerale	*bi-ka-me-'ra-le*
bill (of the legislature)	disegno di legge	*di-'ze-nyo di 'lej-je*
cabinet	gabinetto	*ga-bi-'net-to*
• **cabinet head**	capo di gabinetto	—
• **cabinet meeting**	consiglio di gabinetto	*kon-'si-lyo*
(to) call (a meeting, etc.)	convocare	*kon-vo-'ka-re*
center (political)	di centro	*čen-tro*
chamber of representatives	camera dei deputati	*'ka-me-ra dei de-pu-'ta-ti*
citizen	cittadino (-a)	*čit-ta-'di-no*
• **citizenship**	cittadinanza	*čit-ta-di-'nan-dza*
civic duty	dovere civico	*do-'ve-re 'či-vi-ko*
civil affairs	affari civili	*af-'fa-ri či-'vi-li*
civil right	diritto civile	*di-'rit-to či-'vi-le*
civil servant	funzionario	*fun-tsyo-'na-ryo*
coalition	coalizione (f)	*ko-a-li-'tsyo-ne*
commission	commissione (f)	*kom-mis-'syo-ne*
commission of inquiry	commissione d'inchiesta	*din-'kyes-ta*
committee	comitato	*ko-mi-'ta-to*
communism	comunismo	*ko-mu-'niz-mo*
confederation	confederazione (f)	*kon-fe-de-ra-'tsyo-ne*
conservative	conservatore (-trice)	*kon-ser-va-'to-re*
constitution	costituzione (f)	*kos-ti-tu-'tsyo-ne*
consulate	consolato	*kon-so-'la-to*
council	consiglio	*kon-'si-lyo*
• **Council of Europe**	Consiglio d'Europa	—
• **council of ministers**	consiglio dei ministri	*mi-'nis-tri*
• **councilor**	consigliere (-a)	*kon-si-'lye-re*
country of origin	paese (m) d'origine	*pa-'e-ze do-'ri-ji-ne*
decentralization	decentramento	*de-čen-tra-'men-to*
decree	decreto	*de-'kre-to*

democracy	democrazia	de-mo-kra-'tsi-a
• democratic party	partito democratico	par-'ti-to de-mo-'kra-ti-ko
• democratic society	società democratica	so-če-'ta
demonstration	dimostrazione (f)	di-mos-tra-'tsyo-ne
economy	economia	e-ko-no-'mi-a
(to) elect	eleggere*	e-'lej-je-re
• elected representative	deputato (-a)	de-pu-'ta-to
• election	elezione (f)	e-le-'tsyo-ne
• electoral campaign	campagna elettorale	kam-'pa-nya e-let-to-'ra-le
embassy	ambasciata	am-ba-'ša-ta
euro	euro (m, inv)	—
executive	esecutivo	e-ze-ku-'ti-vo
external affairs	affari esteri	af-'fa-ri 'es-te-ri
federation	federazione (f)	fe-de-ra-'tsyo-ne
foreign country	paese straniero	pa-'e-ze stra-'nye-ro
(to) govern	governare	go-ver-'na-re
• government	governo	go-'ver-no
• government bond	buono del tesoro	'bwo-no del te-'zo-ro
• governmental	governativo	go-ver-na-'ti-vo
• head of government	capo del governo	'ka-po
• head of state	capo dello stato	—
ideology	ideologia	i-de-o-lo-'ji-a
imperialism	imperialismo	im-pe-rya-'liz-mo
inflation	inflazione (f)	in-fla-'tsyo-ne
internal affairs	affari interni	af-'fa-ri in-'ter-ni
judiciary	giudiziario	ju-di-'tsya-ryo
juridical, legal, authorized	giuridico	ju-'ri-di-ko
king	re (m, inv)	—
labor union	sindacato	sin-da-'ka-to
left-wing	di sinistra	si-'nis-tra
legislation	legislazione (f)	le-jis-la-'tsyo-ne
• legislative	legislativo	le-jis-la-'ti-vo
• legislature	legislatura	le-jis-la-'tu-ra
liberal	liberale	li-be-'ra-le
• liberal party	partito liberale	par-'ti-to
local agency	ente locale (m)	'en-te lo-'ka-le
mayor	sindaco	'sin-da-ko
minister	ministro	mi-'nis-tro
• ministry	ministero	mi-nis-'te-ro
monarchist party	partito monarchico	par-'ti-to mo-'nar-ki-ko
• monarchy	monarchia	mo-nar-'ki-a
motion	mozione (f)	mo'tsyo-ne
• abstention	astensione (f)	as-ten-'syo-ne
• against	sfavorevole	sfa-vo-'re-vo-le
• amendment	emendamento	e-men-da-'men-to

• in favor	favorevole	*fa-vo-'re-vo-le*
• passing	approvazione (f)	*ap-pro-va-'tsyo-ne*
municipal	municipale	*mu-ni-či-'pa-le*
national	nazionale	*na-tsyo-'na-le*
parliament	parlamento	*par-la-'men-to*
party	partito	*par-'ti-to*
platform	programma (m)	*pro-'gram-ma*
	elettorale	*e-let-to-'ra-le*
policy (in general)	politica	*po-'li-ti-ka*
politician	politico (m/f)	*po-li-ti-'ko*
poll	sondaggio	*son-'daj-jo*
power	potere (m)	*po-'te-re*
president	presidente (m/f)	*pre-zi-'den-te*
prime minister	primo ministro	*'pri-mo mi-'nis-tro*
prince	principe (m)	*'prin-či-pe*
princess	principessa	*prin-či-'pes-sa*
progressive party	partito progressista	*par-'ti-to pro-gres-'sis-ta*
protest	protesta	*pro-'tes-ta*
provincial	provinciale	*pro-vin-'ča-le*
queen	regina	*re-'ji-na*
(to) ratify	ratificare	*ra-ti-fi-'ka-re*
referendum	referendum (m)	—
reform	riforma	*ri-'for-ma*
regional	regionale	*re-jo-'na-le*
representation (political)	rappresentanza	*rap-pre-zen-'tan-dza*
republic	repubblica	*re-'pub-bli-ka*
republican party	partito repubblicano	*par-'ti-to re-pub-bli-'ka-no*
revolt, riot	rivolta	*ri-'vol-ta*
revolution	rivoluzione (f)	*ri-vo-lu-'tsyo-ne*
right to vote	diritto al voto	*di-'rit-to al 'vo-to*
right to work	diritto al lavoro	*di-'rit-to al la-'vo-ro*
right-wing	di destra	—
seat (political)	seggio	*'sej-jo*
security services	servizi di sicurezza	*ser-'vi-tsi*
senate	senato	*se-'na-to*
session	sessione (f)	*ses-'syo-ne*
sitting (of the house)	seduta	*se-'du-ta*
socialism	socialismo	*so-ča-'liz-mo*
• socialist party	partito socialista	*par-ti-to so-ča-'lis-ta*
speech	discorso	*dis-'kor-so*
statute	statuto	*sta-'tu-to*
task, duty	incarico	*in-'ka-ri-ko*
treasurer	tesoriere (-a)	*te-zo-'rye-re*
• treasury	tesoreria	*te-zo-re-'ri-a*
universal suffrage	suffragio universale	*suf-'fra-jo u-ni-ver-'sa-le*

(to) violate a right	violare un diritto	*vyo-'la-re un di-'rit-to*
vote	voto	—
• **(to) vote**	votare	*vo-'ta-re*
• **confidence vote**	fiducia	*fi-'du-ča*
• **non-confidence vote**	sfiducia	*sfi-'du-ča*

B. HISTORY

alliance	alleanza	*al-le-'an-tsa*
• **ally**	alleato	*al-le-'a-to*
ancient Greece	Antica Grecia	*an-'ti-ka 'gre-ča*
ancient Rome	Antica Roma	*an-'ti-ka 'ro-ma*
antiquity	antichità (f, inv)	*an-ti-ki-'ta*
archivist	archivista (m/f)	*ar-ki-'vis-ta*
Baroque	Barocco	*ba-'rok-ko*
century	secolo	*'se-ko-lo*
civil war	guerra civile	*'gwer-ra či-'vi-le*
Classicism	Classicismo	*klas-si-'čiz-mo*
curfew	coprifuoco	*ko-pri-'fwo-ko*
decade	decennio	*de-'čen-nyo*
decline	declino	*de-'kli-no*
defeat	sconfitta	*skon-'fit-ta*
defense	difesa	*di-'fe-za*
document	documento	*do-ku-'men-to*
Enlightenment	Illuminismo	*il-lu-mi-'niz-mo*
epoch	epoca	*'e-po-ka*
era	era	—
faction	fazione (f)	*fa-'tsyo-ne*
feudal	feudale	*fe-u-'da-le*
First World War	Prima Guerra Mondiale	*'pri-ma 'gwer-ra mon-'dya-le*
fossil	fossile (m)	*'fos-si-le*
Hellenic	ellenico	*el-'le-ni-ko*
history	storia	*'sto-rya*
• **historian**	storico (-a)	*'sto-ri-ko*
Industrial Revolution	Rivoluzione (f) Industriale	*ri-vo-lu-'tsyo-ne in-dus-'trya-le*
insurrection	insurrezione (f)	*in-sur-re-'tsyo-ne*
medieval	medioevale	*me-dyo-e-'va-le*
Middle Ages	Medioevo	*me-dyo-'e-vo*
paleontology	paleontologia	*pa-le-on-to-lo-'ji-a*
period	periodo	*pe-'ri-o-do*
plebeian	plebeo	*ple-'be-o*
prehistoric	preistorico	*pre-is-'to-ri-ko*
• **prehistory**	preistoria	*pre-is-'to-rya*
Renaissance	Rinascimento	*ri-na-ši-'men-to*
Roman Empire	Impero Romano	*im-pe-ro ro-'ma-no*
Romanticism	Romanticismo	*ro-man-ti-'čiz-mo*
ruin	rovina	*ro-'vi-na*

Second World War	Seconda Guerra	*se-'kon-da 'gwer-ra*
	Mondiale	*mon-'dya-le*
World War	Guerra Mondiale	*'gwer-ra mon-'dya-le*

44. CONTROVERSIAL ISSUES

A. THE ENVIRONMENT

air pollution	inquinamento	*in-kwi-na-'men-to*
	atmosferico	*at-mos-'fe-ri-ko*
biosystem	biosistema (m)	*bi-o-sis-'te-ma*
disposal, waste, discharge	scarico	*'ska-ri-ko*
energy	energia	*e-ner-'ji-a*
• **energy conservation**	conservazione (f)	*kon-ser-va-'tsyo-ne*
	dell'energia	
• **energy crisis**	crisi (f, inv) energetica	*'kri-zi e-ner-'je-ti-ka*
• **energy waste**	spreco d'energia	*'spre-ko*
environment	ambiente (f)	*am-'byen-te*
• **environmentalist**	ambientalista (m/f)	*am-byen-ta-'lis-ta*
fossil fuel	combustibile (m)	*kom-bus-'ti-bi-le*
natural resources	risorse naturali (f, inv)	*ri-'sor-se na-tu-'ra-li*
petroleum	petrolio	*pe-'tro-lyo*
pollution	inquinamento	*in-kwi-na-'men-to*
• **polluted**	inquinato	*in-kwi-'na-to*
radiation	radiazione (f)	*ra-dya-'tsyo-ne*
• **radioactive waste**	rifiuto radioattivo	*ri'fyu-to ra-dyo-at-*
		'ti-vo
sewage	acque di scarico	*'ak-kwe di 'ska-ri-ko*
• **sewage system**	fognatura	*fo-nya-'tu-ra*
solar energy	energia solare	*e-ner-'ji-a so-'la-re*
thermal energy	energia termica	*e-ner-'ji-a 'ter-mi-ka*
toxic	tossico	*'tos-si-ko*
waste	rifiuto	*ri-'fyu-to*
waste disposal	scarico delle	*'ska-ri-ko del-le*
	immondizie	*im-mon-'di-tsye*
water pollution	inquinamento delle	*in-kwi-na-'men-to*
	acque	*del-le 'ak-kwe*

B. SOCIAL ISSUES

abortion	aborto	*a-'bor-to*
AIDS	AIDS (m, inv)	—
alcohol	alcool (m, inv)	—
• **alcoholism**	alcolismo	*al-ko-'liz-mo*
(to) beg	mendicare	*men-di-'ka-re*
• **beggar**	mendicante (m/f)	*men-di-'kan-te*
censorship	censura	*čen-'su-ra*
death penalty	pena di morte	—
depressed area	zona depressa	*'dzo-na de-'pres-sa*

disadvantage	svantaggio	zvan-'taj-jo
ghetto	ghetto	—
health assistance	assistenza sanitaria	sa-ni-'ta-rya
homeless	senzatetto	sen-tsa-'tet-to
homosexuality	omosessualità (f, inv)	o-mo-ses-swa-li-'ta
legal assistance	assistenza legale	as-sis-'ten-tsa le-'ga-le
lesbian	lesbica	'lez-bi-ka
National Welfare Agency	Istituto Nazionale della Previdenza Sociale	is-ti-'tu-to na-tsyo-'na-le del-la pre-vi-'den-dza so-'ča-le
overpopulation	sovrappopolazione (f)	so-vrap-po-po-la-'tsyo-ne
pornography	pornografia	por-no-gra-'fi-a
poverty	povertà (f, inv)	po-ver-'ta
prostitution	prostituzione (f)	pros-ti-tu-'tsyo-ne
provision of welfare services	previdenza sociale	pre-vi-'den-tsa so-'ča-le
racism	razzismo	rat-'tsiz-mo
(to) receive benefits	ricevere assistenza sociale	ri-'če-ve-re as-sis-'ten-dza so-'ča-le
shelter	rifugio	ri-'fu-jo
social assistance, welfare	assistenza, previdenza sociale	as-sis-'ten-dza pre-vi-'den-dza so-ča-le

C. DRUGS

amphetamine	amfetamina	am-fe-ta-'mi-na
cocaine	cocaina	ko-ka-'i-na
(to) detoxify oneself, come clean	disintossicarsi	diz-in-tos-si-'kar-si
drug addict	tossicodipendente (m/f)	tos-si-ko-di-pen-'den-te
drug dependency, addiction	tossicodipendenza	tos-si-ko-di-pen-'den-tsa
drug pusher	spacciatore (-trice) di droga	spač-ča-'to-re
drug traffic	traffico degli stupefacenti	'traf-fi-ko de-lyi stu-pe-fa-'čen-ti
drugs	droga	—
(to) get out of drugs	uscire* (ess) dalla droga	u-'ši-re
hallucination, high	allucinazione (f)	al-lu-či-na-'tsyo-ne
hard drug	droga pesante	pe-'zan-te
heroin	eroina	e-ro-'i-na
marijuana	marijuana	—
needle	ago	—
overdose	overdose (m, inv)	—
soft drug	droga leggera	lej-'je-ra
syringe	siringa	si-'rin-ga
trip	trip (m, inv)	—

D. GLOBAL ISSUES

armed conflict	conflitto a fuoco	kon-'flit-to a 'fwo-ko
armistice	armistizio	ar-mi-'sti-tsyo
arms dealer	mercante d'armi	mer-'kan-te 'dar-mi
arms reduction	diminuzione (f) delle armi	di-mi-nu-'tsyo-ne del-le 'ar-mi
arms trade	mercato delle armi	mer-'ka-to del-le 'ar-mi
army	esercito	e-'zer-ci-to
attack	attacco	at-'tak-ko
automatic weapon	arma automatica	'ar-ma au-to-'ma-ti-ka
ballistic missile	missile balistico	'mis-si-le ba-'lis-ti-ko
biological war	guerra batteriologica	'gwer-ra bat-te-ryo-'lo-ji-ka
biological weapon	arma batteriologica	'ar-ma bat-te-ryo-'lo-ji-ka
bomb	bomba	'bom-ba
• **atomic bomb**	bomba atomica	a-'to-mika
• **hand bomb**	bomba a mano	—
• **molotov cocktail**	bomba molotov	—
• **smoke bomb**	bomba fumogena	fu-'mo-je-na
chemical war	guerra chimica	'gwer-ra 'ki-mi-ka
conflict	conflitto	kon-'flit-to
conventional weapon	arma convenzionale	'ar-ma kon-ven-tsyo-'na-le
disarmament	disarmo	diz-'ar-mo
emigrant	emigrante (m/f)	e-mi-'gran-te
• **emigration**	emigrazione (f)	e-mi-gra-'tsyo-ne
espionage	spionaggio	spyo-'naj-jo
• **spy**	spia	'spi-a
fight, struggle	lotta	—
grenade	granata	gra-'na-ta
guerrilla warfare	guerriglia	gwer-'ri-lya
headquarters	quartiere (m) generale	kwar-'tye-re je-ne-'ra-le
holy war	guerra santa	'gwer-ra 'san-ta
hostage	ostaggio	os-'taj-jo
human rights	diritti umani	di-'rit-ti u-'ma-ni
immigrant	immigrante (m/f)	im-mi-'gran-te
• **immigration**	immigrazione (f)	im-mi-gra-'tsyo-ne
missile	missile (m)	'mis-si-le
multiracial society	società (f, inv) multirazziale	so-če-'ta mul-ti-ra-'tsya-le
nerve gas	gas (m, inv) nervino	ner-'vi-no
peace	pace (f)	'pa-če
poison gas	gas (m, inv) tossico	'tos-si-ko
racism	razzismo	rat-'tsiz-mo
• **racist**	razzista (m/f)	rat-'tsis-ta

refugee	profugo (-a)	'pro-fu-go
• refugee camp	campo profughi	'kam-po 'pro-fu-gi
state of war	stato di guerra	'sta-to di 'gwer-ra
supplies	viveri (m, pl)	'vi-ve-ri
tank	carro armato	'kar-ro ar-'ma-to
tear gas	gas (m, inv) lacrimogeno	la-kri-'mo-je-no
terrorism	terrorismo	ter-ro-'riz-mo
• terrorist	terrorista (m/f)	ter-ro-'ris-ta
totalitarian	totalitario	to-ta-li-'ta-ryo
• totalitarianism	totalitarismo	to-ta-li-ta-'riz-mo
truce	tregua	'tre-gwa
United Nations	Nazioni Unite (f, pl)	na-'tsyo-ni u-'ni-te
visa	visto	—
war	guerra	'gwer-ra
weapon	arma	'ar-ma

E. EXPRESSING YOUR OPINION

according to me	secondo me	se-'kon-do me
as a matter of fact	anzi	'an-tsi
by the way	a proposito	a pro-'po-zi-to
for example	per esempio	per e-'zem-pyo
from my point of view	dal mio punto di vista	—
however	tuttavia	tut-ta-'vi-a
	comunque	ko-'mun-kwe
I believe that…	credo che…	—
I don't know if…	non so se…	—
I doubt that…	dubito che…	'du-bi-to
I think that…	penso che…	'pen-so
I would like to say that…	vorrei dire che…	'vor-'rey 'di-re
I'm not sure that…	non sono sicuro (-a) che…	si-'ku-ro
I'm sure that…	sono sicuro (-a) che…	si-'ku-ro
in conclusion	in conclusione	kon-klu-'zyo-ne
in my opinion	a mio avviso	av-'vi-zo
	a mio parere	pa-'re-re
it seems that…	sembra che…	'sem-bra
	pare che…	'pa-re
it's clear that…	è chiaro che…	'kya-ro
no	no	—
that is to say	cioè	čo-'e
	vale a dire	'va-le a 'di-re
there's no doubt that…	non c'è dubbio che…	non če 'dub-byo ke
therefore	allora	al-'lo-ra
	dunque	'dun-kwe
	quindi	'kwin-di
unless	a meno che	—
yes	sì	—

IRREGULAR VERBS

The following verbs used in this book have some irregularity in their conjugation. Only the irregular feature or tense is given here.

accadere (conjugated like **cadere**)

accendere
Past Participle   acceso
Past Absolute   (io) accesi, (tu) accendesti, (Lei) accese, (lui/lei)
                        accese, (noi) accendemmo, (voi) accendeste, (loro)
                        accesero

accludere (conjugated like **concludere**)

aggiungere (conjugated like **piangere**)

alludere (conjugated like **concludere**)

ammettere (conjugated like **mettere**)

andare
Present Indicative   (io) vado, (tu) vai, (Lei) va, (lui/lei) va, (noi) andiamo,
                        (voi) andate, (loro) vanno
Future   (io) andrò, (tu) andrai, (Lei) andrà, (lui/lei) andrà, (noi)
                        andremo, (voi) andrete, (loro) andranno
Conditional   (io) andrei, (tu) andresti, (Lei) andrebbe, (lui/lei)
                        andrebbe, (noi) andremmo, (voi) andreste, (loro)
                        andrebbero
Present Subjunctive   (io) vada (tu) vada, (Lei) vada, (lui/lei) vada, (noi)
                        andiamo, (voi) andiate, (loro) vadano
Imperative   (tu) va', (Lei) vada, (noi) andiamo, (voi) andate, (Loro)
                        vadano

apprendere (conjugated like **prendere**)

aprire
Past Participle   aperto

assolvere (conjugated like **risolvere**)

assumere

Past Participle	assunto
Past Absolute	(io) assunsi, (tu) assumesti, (Lei) assunse, (lui/lei) assunse, (noi) assumemmo, (voi) assumeste, (loro) assunsero

astrarre

Present Indicative	(io) astraggo, (tu) astrai, (Lei) astrae, (lui/lei) astrae, (noi) astraiamo, (voi) astraete, (loro) astraggono
Past Participle	astratto
Imperfect	(io) astraevo, (tu) astraevi, (Lei) astraeva, (lui/lei) astraeva, (noi) astraevamo, (voi) astraevate, (loro) astraevano
Past Absolute	(io) astrassi, (tu) astraesti, (Lei) astrasse, (lui/lei) astrasse, (noi) astraemmo, (voi) astraeste, (loro) astrassero
Present Subjunctive	(io) astragga, (tu) astragga, (Lei) astragga, (lui/lei) astragga, (noi) astraiamo, (voi) astraiate, (loro) astraggano
Imperfect Subjunctive	(io) astraessi, (tu) astraessi, (Lei) astraesse, (lui/lei) astraesse, (noi) astraessimo, (voi) astraeste, (loro) astraessero
Imperative	(tu) astrai, (Lei) astragga, (noi) astraiamo, (voi) astraete, (Loro) astraggano
Gerund	astraendo

attendere

Past Participle	atteso
Past Absolute	(io) attesi, (tu) attendesti, (Lei) attese, (lui/lei) attese, (noi) attendemmo, (voi) attendeste, (loro) attesero

avere

Present Indicative	(io) ho, (tu) hai, (Lei) ha, (lui/lei) ha, (noi) abbiamo, (voi) avete, (loro) hanno
Past Absolute	(io) ebbi, (tu) avesti, (Lei) ebbe, (lui/lei) ebbe, (noi) avemmo, (voi) aveste, (loro) ebbero
Future	(io) avrò, (tu) avrai, (Lei) avrà, (lui/lei) avrà, (noi) avremo, (voi) avrete, (loro) avranno
Conditional	(io) avrei, (tu) avresti, (Lei) avrebbe, (lui/lei) avrebbe, (noi) avremmo, (voi) avreste, (loro) avrebbero
Present Subjunctive	(io) abbia (tu) abbia, (Lei) abbia, (lui/lei) abbia, (noi) abbiamo, (voi) abbiate, (loro) abbiano
Imperative	(tu) abbi, (Lei) abbia, (noi) abbiamo, (voi) abbiate, (Loro) abbiano

avvenire (conjugated like **venire**)

benedire (conjugated like **dire**)

bere

Present Indicative	(io) bevo, (tu) bevi, (Lei) beve, (lui/lei) beve, (noi) beviamo, (voi) bevete, (loro) bevono
Past Participle	bevuto
Past Absolute	(io) bevvi (bevetti), (tu) bevesti, (Lei) bevve (bevette), (lui/lei) bevve (bevette), (noi) bevemmo, (voi) beveste, (loro) bevvero (bevettero)
Future	(io) berrò, (tu) berrai, (Lei) berrà, (lui/lei) berrà, (noi) berremo, (voi) berrete, (loro) berranno
Conditional	(io) berrei, (tu) berresti, (Lei) berrebbe, (lui/lei) berrebbe, (noi) berremmo, (voi) berreste, (loro) berrebbero
Present Subjunctive	(io) beva, (tu) beva, (Lei) beva, (lui/lei) beva, (noi) beviamo, (voi) beviate, (loro) bevano
Imperfect	(io) bevevo, (tu) bevevi, (Lei) beveva, (lui/lei) beveva, (noi) bevevamo, (voi) bevevate, (loro) bevevano
Imperative	(tu) bevi, (Lei) beva, (noi) beviamo, (voi) bevete, (Loro) bevano
Gerund	bevendo

cadere

Past Absolute	(io) caddi, (tu) cadesti, (Lei) cadde, (lui/lei) cadde, (noi) cademmo, (voi) cadeste, (loro) caddero
Future	(io) cadrò, (tu) cadrai, (Lei) cadrà, (lui/lei) cadrà, (noi) cadremo, (voi) cadrete, (loro) cadranno
Conditional	(io) cadrei, (tu) cadresti, (Lei) cadrebbe, (lui/lei) cadrebbe, (noi) cadremmo, (voi) cadreste, (loro) cadrebbero
Present Subjunctive	(io) cada, (tu) cada, (Lei) cada, (lui/lei) cada, (noi) cadiamo, (voi) cadiate, (loro) cadano

chiedere

Past Participle	chiesto
Past Absolute	(io) chiesi, (tu) chiedesti, (Lei) chiese, (lui/lei) chiese, (noi) chiedemmo, (voi) chiedeste, (loro) chiesero

chiudere

Past Participle	chiuso
Past Absolute	(io) chiusi, (tu) chiudesti, (Lei) chiuse, (lui/lei) chiuse, (noi) chiudemmo, (voi) chiudeste, (loro) chiusero

comporre (conjugated like **porre**)

comprendere (conjugated like **prendere**)

concludere

Past Participle	concluso
Past Absolute	(io) conclusi, (tu) concludesti, (Lei) concluse, (lui/lei) concluse, (noi) concludemmo, (voi) concludeste, (loro) conclusero

concorrere (conjugated like **correre**)

conoscere

Past Absolute	(io) conobbi, (tu) conoscesti, (Lei) conobbe, (lui/lei) conobbe, (noi) conoscemmo, (voi) conosceste, (loro) conobbero

contenere (conjugated like **tenere**)

contraddire (conjugated like **dire**)

convincere (conjugated like **vincere**)

convivere (conjugated like **vivere**)

correggere

Past Participle	corretto
Past Absolute	(io) corressi, (tu) correggesti, (Lei) corresse, (lui/lei) corresse, (noi) correggemmo, (voi) correggeste, (loro) corressero

correre

Past Participle	corso
Past Absolute	(io) corsi, (tu) corresti, (Lei) corse, (lui/lei) corse, (noi) corremmo, (voi) correste, (loro) corsero

crescere

Past Absolute	(io) crebbi, (tu) crescesti, (Lei) crebbe, (lui/lei) crebbe, (noi) crescemmo, (voi) cresceste, (loro) crebbero

cuocere

Past Participle	cotto
Past Absolute	(io) cossi, (tu) cocesti, (Lei) cosse, (lui/lei) cosse, (noi) cocemmo, (voi) coceste, (loro) cossero

dare

Present Indicative	(io) do, (tu) dai, (Lei) dà, (lui/lei) dà, (noi) diamo, (voi) date, (loro) danno
Past Participle	dato
Imperfect	(io) davo, (tu) davi, (Lei) dava, (lui/lei) dava, (noi) davamo, (voi) davate, (loro) davano
Past Absolute	(io) diedi, (tu) desti, (Lei) diede, (lui/lei) diede, (noi) demmo, (voi) deste, (loro) diedero

Future	(io) darò, (tu) darai, (Lei) darà, (lui/lei) darà, (noi) daremo, (voi) darete, (loro) daranno
Conditional	(io) darei, (tu) daresti, (Lei) darebbe, (lui/lei) darebbe, (noi) daremmo, (voi) dareste, (loro) darebbero
Present Subjunctive	(io) dia (tu) dia, (Lei) dia, (lui/lei) dia, (noi) diamo, (voi) diate, (loro) diano
Imperfect Subjunctive	(io) dessi, (tu) dessi, (Lei) desse, (lui/lei) desse, (noi) dessimo, (voi) deste, (loro) dessero
Imperative	(tu) da', (Lei) dia, (noi) diamo, (voi) date, (Loro) diano
Gerund	dando

darsi (conjugated like **dare**)

decidere

Past Participle	deciso
Past Absolute	(io) decisi, (tu) decidesti, (Lei) decise, (lui/lei) decise, (noi) decidemmo, (voi) decideste, (loro) decisero

deludere (conjugated like **concludere**)

deporre (conjugated like **porre**)

descrivere (conjugated like **scrivere**)

detenere (conjugated like **tenere**)

difendere

Past Participle	difeso
Past Absolute	(io) difesi, (tu) difendesti, (Lei) difese, (lui/lei) difese, (noi) difendemmo, (voi) difendeste, (loro) difesero

difendersi (conjugated like **difendere**)

diffondere

Past Participle	diffuso
Past Absolute	(io) diffusi, (tu) diffondesti, (Lei) diffuse, (lui/lei) diffuse, (noi) diffondemmo, (voi) diffondeste, (loro) diffusero

dipingere

Past Participle	dipinto
Past Absolute	(io) dipinsi, (tu) dipingesti, (Lei) dipinse, (lui/lei) dipinse, (noi) dipingemmo, (voi) dipingeste, (loro) dipinsero

dire

Present Indicative	(io) dico, (tu) dici, (Lei) dice, (lui/lei) dice, (noi) diciamo, (voi) dite, (loro) dicono
Past Participle	detto

Imperfect	(io) dicevo, (tu) dicevi, (Lei) diceva, (lui/lei) diceva, (noi) dicevamo, (voi) dicevate, (loro) dicevano
Past Absolute	(io) dissi, (tu) dicesti, (Lei) disse, (lui/lei) disse, (noi) dicemmo, (voi) diceste, (loro) dissero
Future	(io) dirò, (tu) dirai, (Lei) dirà, (lui/lei) dirà, (noi) diremo, (voi) direte, (loro) diranno
Conditional	(io) direi, (tu) diresti, (Lei) direbbe, (lui/lei) direbbe, (noi) diremmo, (voi) direste, (loro) direbbero
Present Subjunctive	(io) dica, (tu) dica, (Lei) dica, (lui/lei) dica, (noi) diciamo, (voi) diciate, (loro) dicano
Imperfect Subjunctive	(io) dicessi, (tu) dicessi, (Lei) dicesse, (lui/lei) dicesse, (noi) dicessimo, (voi) diceste, (loro) dicessero
Imperative	(tu) di', (Lei) dica, (noi) diciamo, (voi) dite, (Loro) dicano
Gerund	dicendo

discutere

Past Participle	discusso
Past Absolute	(io) discussi, (tu) discutesti, (Lei) discusse, (lui/lei) discusse, (noi) discutemmo, (voi) discuteste, (loro) discussero

dissuadere (conjugated like **persuadere**)

distruggere

Past Participle	distrutto
Past Absolute	(io) distrussi, (tu) distruggesti, (Lei) distrusse, (lui/lei) distrusse, (noi) distruggemmo, (voi) distruggeste, (loro) distrussero

dividere

Past Participle	diviso
Past Absolute	(io) divisi, (tu) dividesti, (Lei) divise, (lui/lei) divise, (noi) dividemmo, (voi) divideste, (loro) divisero

dovere

Present Indicative	(io) devo, (tu) devi, (Lei) deve, (lui/lei) deve, (noi) dobbiamo, (voi) dovete, (loro) devono
Future	(io) dovrò, (tu) dovrai, (Lei) dovrà, (lui/lei) dovrà, (noi) dovremo, (voi) dovrete, (loro) dovranno
Conditional	(io) dovrei, (tu) dovresti, (Lei) dovrebbe, (lui/lei) dovrebbe, (noi) dovremmo, (voi) dovreste, (loro) dovrebbero
Present Subjunctive	(io) deva (debba), (tu) deva (debba), (Lei) deva (debba), (lui/lei) deve (debba), (noi) dobbiamo, (voi) dobbiate, (loro) devano (debbano)

eleggere (conjugated like **leggere**)

emettere (conjugated like **mettere**)

espandere
Past Participle espanso
Past Absolute (io) espansi, (tu) espandesti, (Lei) espanse, (lui/lei) espanse, (noi) espandemmo, (voi) espandeste, (loro) espansero

esprimere
Past Participle espresso
Past Absolute (io) espressi, (tu) esprimesti, (Lei) espresse, (lui/lei) espresse, (noi) esprimemmo, (voi) esprimeste, (loro) espressero

esprimersi (conjugated like **esprimere**)

essere
Present Indicative (io) sono, (tu) sei, (Lei) è, (lui/lei) è, (noi) siamo, (voi) siete, (loro) sono
Past Participle stato
Imperfect (io) ero, (tu) eri, (Lei) era, (lui/lei) era, (noi) eravamo, (voi) eravate, (loro) erano
Past Absolute (io) fui, (tu) fosti, (Lei) fu, (lui/lei) fu, (noi) fummo, (voi) foste, (loro) furono
Future (io) sarò, (tu) sarai, (Lei) sarà, (lui/lei) sarà, (noi) saremo, (voi) sarete, (loro) saranno
Conditional (io) sarei, (tu) saresti, (Lei) sarebbe, (lui/lei) sarebbe, (noi) saremmo, (voi) sareste, (loro) sarebbero
Present Subjunctive (io) sia, (tu) sia, (Lei) sia, (lui/lei) sia, (noi) siamo, (voi) siate, (loro) siano
Imperfect Subjunctive (io) fossi, (tu) fossi, (Lei) fosse, (lui/lei) fosse, (noi) fossimo, (voi) foste, (loro) fossero
Imperative (tu) sii, (Lei) sia, (noi) siamo, (voi) siate, (Loro) siano

estinguere
Past Participle estinto
Past Absolute (io) estinsi, (tu) estinguesti, (Lei) estinse, (lui/lei) estinse, (noi) estinguemmo, (voi) estingueste, (loro) estinsero

estrarre (conjugated like **astrarre**)

fare
Present Indicative (io) faccio, (tu) fai, (Lei) fa, (lui/lei) fa, (noi) facciamo, (voi) fate, (loro) fanno
Past Participle fatto
Imperfect (io) facevo, (tu) facevi, (Lei) faceva, (lui/lei) faceva, (noi) facevamo, (voi) facevate, (loro) facevano

Past Absolute	(io) feci, (tu) facesti, (Lei) fece, (lui/lei) fece, (noi) facemmo, (voi) faceste, (loro) fecero
Future	(io) farò, (tu) farai, (Lei) farà, (lui/lei) farà, (noi) faremo, (voi) farete, (loro) faranno
Conditional	(io) farei, (tu) faresti, (Lei) farebbe, (lui/lei) farebbe, (noi) faremmo, (voi) fareste, (loro) farebbero
Present Subjunctive	(io) faccia, (tu) faccia, (Lei) faccia, (lui/lei) faccia, (noi) facciamo, (voi) facciate, (loro) facciano
Imperfect Subjunctive	(io) facessi, (tu) facessi, (Lei) facesse, (lui/lei) facesse, (noi) facessimo, (voi) faceste, (loro) facessero
Imperative	(tu) fa', (Lei) faccia, (noi) facciamo, (voi) fate, (Loro) facciano
Gerund	facendo

farsi (conjugated like **fare**)

fondere

Past Participle	fuso
Past Absolute	(io) fusi, (tu) fondesti, (Lei) fuse, (lui/lei) fuse, (noi) fondemmo, (voi) fondeste, (loro) fusero

friggere

Past Participle	fritto
Past Absolute	(io) frissi, (tu) friggesti, (Lei) frisse, (lui/lei) frisse, (noi) friggemmo, (voi) friggeste, (loro) frissero

indurre (conjugated like **riprodurre**)

interrompere (conjugated like **rompere**)

leggere

Past Participle	letto
Past Absolute	(io) lessi, (tu) leggesti, (Lei) lesse, (lui/lei) lesse, (noi) leggemmo, (voi) leggeste, (loro) lessero

maledire (conjugated like **dire**)

mettere

Past Participle	messo
Past Absolute	(io) misi, (tu) mettesti, (Lei) mise, (lui/lei) mise, (noi) mettemmo, (voi) metteste, (loro) misero

mettersi (conjugated like **mettere**)

morire

Present Indicative	(io) muoio, (tu) muori, (Lei) muore, (lui/lei) muore, (noi) moriamo, (voi) morite, (loro) muoiono
Past Participle	morto

Present Subjunctive   (io) muoia, (tu) muoia, (Lei) muoia, (lui/lei) muoia, (noi) moriamo, (voi) morite, (loro) muoiano

muovere
Past Participle   mosso
Past Absolute   (io) mossi, (tu) movesti, (Lei) mosse, (lui/lei) mosse, (noi) movemmo, (voi) moveste, (loro) mossero

muoversi (conjugated like **muovere**)

nascere
Past Participle   nato
Past Absolute   (io) nacqui, (tu) nascesti, (Lei) nacque, (lui/lei) nacque, (noi) nascemmo, (voi) nasceste, (loro) nacquero

offendere
Past Participle   offeso
Past Absolute   (io) offesi, (tu) offendesti, (Lei) offese, (lui/lei) offese, (noi) offendemmo, (voi) offendeste, (loro) offesero

offrire
Past Participle   offerto

ottenere (conjugated like **tenere**)

perdere
Past Participle   perso
Past Absolute   (io) persi, (tu) perdesti, (Lei) perse, (lui/lei) perse, (noi) perdemmo, (voi) perdeste, (loro) persero

persuadere
Past Participle   persuaso
Past Absolute   (io) persuasi, (tu) persuadesti, (Lei) persuase, (lui/lei) persuase, (noi) persuademmo, (voi) persuadeste, (loro) persuasero

piacere
Present Indicative   (io) piaccio, (tu) piaci, (Lei) piace, (lui/lei) piace, (noi) piacciamo, (voi) piacete, (loro) piacciono
Past Absolute   (io) piacqui, (tu) piacesti, (Lei) piacque, (lui/lei) piacque, (noi) piacemmo, (voi) piaceste, (loro) piacquero
Present Subjunctive   (io) piaccia, (tu) piaccia, (Lei) piaccia, (lui/lei) piaccia, (noi) piacciamo, (voi) piacciate, (loro) piacciano

piangere
Past Participle   pianto
Past Absolute   (io) piansi, (tu) piangesti, (Lei) pianse, (lui/lei) pianse, (noi) piangemmo, (voi) piangeste, (loro) piansero

porre

Present Indicative	(io) pongo, (tu) poni, (Lei) pone, (lui/lei) pone, (noi) poniamo, (voi) ponete, (loro) pongono
Past Participle	posto
Imperfect	(io) ponevo, (tu) ponevi, (Lei) poneva, (lui/lei) poneva, (noi) ponevamo, (voi) ponevate, (loro) ponevano
Past Absolute	(io) posi, (tu) ponesti, (Lei) pose, (lui/lei) pose, ponemmo, (voi) poneste, (loro) posero
Future	(io) porrò, (tu) porrai, (Lei) porrà, (lui/lei) porrà, (noi) porremo, (voi) porrete, (loro) porranno
Conditional	(io) porrei, (tu) porresti, (Lei) porrebbe, (lui/lei) porrebbe, (noi) porremmo, (voi) porreste, (loro) porrebbero
Present Subjunctive	(io) ponga, (tu) ponga, (Lei) ponga, (lui/lei) ponga, (noi) poniamo, (voi) poniate, (loro) pongano
Imperfect Subjunctive	(io) ponessi, (tu) ponessi, (Lei) ponesse, (lui/lei) ponesse, (noi) ponessimo, (voi) poneste, (loro) ponessero
Imperative	(tu) poni, (Lei) ponga, (noi) poniamo, (voi) ponete, (Loro) pongano
Gerund	ponendo

potere

Present Indicative	(io) posso, (tu) puoi, (Lei) può, (lui/lei) può, (noi) possiamo, (voi) potete, (loro) possono
Future	(io) potrò, (tu) potrai, (Lei) potrà, (lui/lei) potrà, (noi) potremo, (voi) potrete, (loro) potranno
Conditional	(io) potrei, (tu) potresti, (Lei) potrebbe, (lui/lei) potrebbe, (noi) potremmo, (voi) potreste, (loro) potrebbero
Present Subjunctive	(io) possa, (tu) possa, (Lei) possa, (lui/lei) possa, (noi) possiamo, (voi) possiate, (loro) possano

prendere

Past Participle	preso
Past Absolute	(io) presi, (tu) prendesti, (Lei) prese, (lui/lei) prese, (noi) prendemmo, (voi) prendeste, (loro) presero

prescrivere (conjugated like **scrivere**)

promettere (conjugated like **mettere**)

proporre (conjugated like **porre**)

proteggere

Past Participle	protetto
Past Absolute	(io) protessi, (tu) proteggesti, (Lei) protesse, (lui/lei) protesse, (noi) proteggemmo, (voi) proteggeste, (loro) protessero

pungere
Past Participle	punto
Past Absolute	(io) punsi, (tu) pungesti, (Lei) punse, (lui/lei) punse, (noi) pungemmo, (voi) pungeste, (loro) punsero

raccogliere
Present Indicative	(io) raccolgo, (tu) raccogli, (Lei) raccoglie, (lui/lei) raccoglie, (noi) raccogliamo, (voi) raccogliete, (loro) raccolgono
Past Participle	raccolto
Past Absolute	(io) raccolsi, (tu) raccogliesti, (Lei) raccolse, (lui/lei) raccolse, (noi) raccogliemmo, (voi) raccoglieste, (loro) raccolsero
Present Subjunctive	(io) raccolga, (tu) raccolga, (Lei) raccolga, (lui/lei) raccolga, (noi) raccogliamo, (voi) raccogliete, (loro) raccolgano
Imperative	(tu) raccogli, (Lei) raccolga, (noi) raccogliamo, (voi) raccogliete, (Loro) raccolgano

raggiungere
Past Participle	raggiunto
Past Absolute	(io) raggiunsi, (tu) raggiungesti, (Lei) raggiunse, (lui/lei) raggiunse, (noi) raggiungemmo, (voi) raggiungeste, (loro) raggiunsero

redigere
Past Participle	redatto
Past Absolute	(io) redassi, (tu) redigesti, (Lei) redasse, (lui/lei) redasse, (noi) redigemmo, (voi) redigeste, (loro) redassero

riassumere (conjugated like **assumere**)

richiedere (conjugated like **chiedere**)

ridere
Past Participle	riso
Past Absolute	(io) risi, (tu) ridesti, (Lei) rise, (lui/lei) rise, (noi) ridemmo, (voi) rideste, (loro) risero

ridurre (conjugated like **riprodurre**)

rimanere
Present Indicative	(io) rimango, (tu) rimani, (Lei) rimane, (lui/lei) rimane, (noi) rimaniamo, (voi) rimanete, (loro) rimangono
Past Participle	rimasto

Past Absolute	(io) rimasi, (tu) rimanesti, (Lei) rimase, (lui/lei) rimase, (noi) rimanemmo, (voi) rimaneste, (loro) rimasero
Future	(io) rimarrò, (tu) rimarrai, (Lei) rimarrà, (lui/lei) rimarrà, (noi) rimarremo, (voi) rimarrete, (loro) rimarranno
Conditional	(io) rimarrei, (tu) rimarresti, (Lei) rimarrebbe, (lui/lei) rimarrebbe, (noi) rimarremmo, (voi) rimarreste, (loro) rimarrebbero
Present Subjunctive	(io) rimanga, (tu) rimanga, (Lei) rimanga, (lui/lei) rimanga, (noi) rimaniamo, (voi) rimaniate, (loro) rimangano
Imperative	(tu) rimani, (Lei) rimanga, (noi) rimaniamo, (voi) rimanete, (Loro) rimangano

rimettere/rimettersi (conjugated like **mettere**)

riprodurre
Present Indicative	(io) riproduco, (tu) riproduci, (Lei) riproduce, (lui/lei) riproduce, (noi) riproduciamo, (voi) riproducete, (loro) riproducono
Past Participle	riprodotto
Imperfect	(io) riproducevo, (tu) riproducevi, (Lei) riproduceva, (lui/lei) riproduceva, (noi) riproducevamo, (voi) riproducevate, (loro) riproducevano
Past Absolute	(io) riprodussi, (tu) riproducesti, (Lei) riprodusse, (lui/lei) riprodusse, (noi) riproducemmo, (voi) riproduceste, (loro) riprodussero
Future	(io) riprodurrò, (tu) riprodurrai, (Lei) riprodurrà, (lui/lei) riprodurrà, (noi) riprodurremo, (voi) riprodurrete, (loro) riprodurranno
Conditional	(io) riprodurrei, (tu) riprodurresti, (Lei) riprodurrebbe, (lui/lei) riprodurrebbe, (noi) riprodurremmo, (voi) riprodurreste, (loro) riprodurrebbero
Present Subjunctive	(io) riproduca, (tu) riproduca, (Lei) riproduca, (lui/lei) riproduca, (noi) riproduciamo, (voi) riproduciate, (loro) riproducano
Imperfect Subjunctive	(io) riproducessi, (tu) riproducessi, (Lei) riproducesse, (lui/lei) riproducesse, (noi) riproducessimo, (voi) riproduceste, (loro) riproducessero
Imperative	(tu) riproduci, (Lei) riproduca, (noi) riproduciamo, (voi) riproducete, (Loro) riproducano
Gerund	riproducendo

riscuotere
Past Participle	riscosso
Past Absolute	(io) riscossi, (tu) riscotesti, (Lei) riscosse, (lui/lei) riscosse, (noi) riscuotemmo, (voi) riscoteste, (loro) riscossero

risolvere
Past Participle   risolto
Past Absolute   (io) risolsi, (tu) risolvesti, (Lei) risolse, (lui/lei) risolse, (noi) risolvemmo, (voi) risolveste, (loro) risolsero

rispondere
Past Participle   risposto
Past Absolute   (io) risposi, (tu) rispondesti, (Lei) rispose, (lui/lei) rispose, (noi) rispondemmo, (voi) rispondeste, (loro) risposero

rivolgersi
Past Participle   rivolto
Past Absolute   (io) mi rivolsi, (tu) ti rivolgesti, (Lei) si rivolse, (lui/lei) si rivolse, (noi) ci rivolgemmo, (voi) vi rivolgeste, (loro) si rivolsero

rompere
Past Participle   rotto
Past Absolute   (io) ruppi, (tu) rompesti, (Lei) ruppe, (lui/lei) ruppe, (noi) rompemmo, (voi) rompeste, (loro) ruppero

salire
Present Indicative   (io) salgo, (tu) sali, (Lei) sale, (lui/lei) sale, (noi) saliamo, (voi) salite, (loro) salgono
Present Subjunctive   (io) salga, (tu) salga, (Lei) salga, (lui/lei) salga, (noi) saliamo, (voi) saliate, (loro) salgano
Imperative   (tu) sali, (Lei) salga, (noi) saliamo, (voi) salite, (Loro) salgano

sapere
Present Indicative   (io) so, (tu) sai, (Lei) sa, (lui/lei) sa, (noi) sappiamo, (voi) sapete, (loro) sanno
Past Absolute   (io) seppi, (tu) sapesti, (Lei) seppe, (lui/lei) seppe, (noi) sapemmo, (voi) sapeste, (loro) seppero
Future   (io) saprò, (tu) saprai, (Lei) saprà, (lui/lei) saprà, (noi) sapremo, (voi) saprete, (loro) sapranno
Conditional   (io) saprei, (tu) sapresti, (Lei) saprebbe, (lui/lei) saprebbe, (noi) sapremmo, (voi) sapreste, (loro) saprebbero
Present Subjunctive   (io) sappia, (tu) sappia, (Lei) sappia, (lui/lei) sappia, (noi) sappiamo, (voi) sappiate, (loro) sappiano
Imperative   (tu) sappi, (Lei) sappia, (noi) sappiamo, (voi) sappiate, (Loro) sappiano

scegliere
Present Indicative   (io) scelgo, (tu) scegli, (Lei) sceglie, (lui/lei) sceglie, (noi) scegliamo, (voi) scegliete, (loro) scelgono

Past Participle	scelto
Past Absolute	(io) scelsi, (tu) scegliesti, (Lei) scelse, (lui/lei) scelse, (noi) scegliemmo, (voi) sceglieste, (loro) scelsero
Present Subjunctive	(io) scelga, (tu) scelga, (Lei) scelga, (lui/lei) scelga, (noi) scegliamo, (voi) scegliate, (loro) scelgano
Imperative	(tu) scegli, (Lei) scelga, (noi) scegliamo, (voi) scegliete, (Loro) scelgano

scendere

Past Participle	sceso
Past Absolute	(io) scesi, (tu) scendesti, (Lei) scese, (lui/lei) scese, (noi) scendemmo, (voi) scendeste, (loro) scesero

sciogliere

Past Participle	sciolto
Past Absolute	(io) sciolsi, (tu) sciogliesti, (Lei) sciolse, (lui/lei) sciolse, (noi) sciogliemmo, (voi) scioglieste, (loro) sciolsero

scommettere (conjugated like **mettere**)

sconfiggere

Past Participle	sconfitto
Past Absolute	(io) sconfissi, (tu) sconfiggesti, (Lei) sconfisse, (lui/lei) sconfisse, (noi) sconfiggemmo, (voi) sconfiggeste, (loro) sconfissero

scorrere (conjugated like **correre**)

scrivere

Past Participle	scritto
Past Absolute	(io) scrissi, (tu) scrivesti, (Lei) scrisse, (lui/lei) scrisse, (noi) scrivemmo, (voi) scriveste, (loro) scrissero

scuotere

Past Participle	scosso
Past Absolute	(io) scossi, (tu) scotesti, (Lei) scosse, (lui/lei) scosse, (noi) scotemmo, (voi) scoteste, (loro) scossero

sedersi

Present Indicative	(io) mi siedo, (tu) ti siedi, (Lei) si siede, (lui/lei) si siede, (noi) ci sediamo, (voi) vi sedete, (loro) si siedono
Present Subjunctive	(io) mi sieda, (tu) ti sieda, (Lei) si sieda, (lui/lei) si sieda, (noi) ci sediamo, (voi) vi sediate, (loro) si siedano
Imperative	(tu) siediti, (Lei) si sieda, (noi) sediamoci, (voi) sedetevi, (Loro) si siedano

sedurre (conjugated like **riprodurre**)

soccorrere (conjugated like **correre**)

sorprendere (conjugated like **prendere**)

sorridere (conjugated like **ridere**)

sostenere (conjugated like **tenere**)

sottrarre (conjugated like **estrarre**)

spargere

Past Participle	sparso
Past Absolute	(io) sparsi, (tu) spargesti, (Lei) sparse, (lui/lei) sparse, (noi) spargemmo, (voi) spargeste, (loro) sparsero

spegnere

Present Indicative	(io) spengo, (tu) spegni, (Lei) spegne, (lui/lei) spegne, (noi) spegniamo, (voi) spegnete, (loro) spengono
Past Participle	spento
Past Absolute	(io) spensi, (tu) spegnesti, (Lei) spense, (lui/lei) spense, (noi) spegnemmo, (voi) spegneste, (loro) spensero
Present Subjunctive	(io) spenga, (tu) spenga, (Lei) spenga, (lui/lei) spenga, (noi) spegniamo, (voi) spegniate, (loro) spengano
Imperative	(tu) spegni, (Lei) spenga, (noi) spegniamo, (voi) spegnete, (Loro) spengano

spingere (conjugated like **dipingere**)

stare

Present Indicative	(io) sto, (tu) stai, (Lei) sta, (lui/lei) sta, (noi) stiamo, (voi) state, (loro) stanno
Past Participle	stato
Imperfect	(io) stavo, (tu) stavi, (Lei) stava, (lui/lei) stava, (noi) stavamo, (voi) stavate, (loro) stavano
Past Absolute	(io) stetti, (tu) stesti, (Lei) stette, (lui/lei) stette, (noi) stemmo, (voi) steste, (loro) stettero
Future	(io) starò, (tu) starai, (Lei) starà, (lui/lei) starà, (noi) staremo, (voi) starete, (loro) staranno
Conditional	(io) starei, (tu) staresti, (Lei) starebbe, (lui/lei) starebbe, (noi) staremmo, (voi) stareste, (loro) starebbero
Present Subjunctive	(io) stia, (tu) stia, (Lei) stia, (lui/lei) stia, (noi) stiamo, (voi) stiate, (loro) stiano
Imperfect Subjunctive	(io) stessi, (tu) stessi, (Lei) stesse, (lui/lei) stesse, (noi) stessimo, (voi) steste, (loro) stessero
Imperative	(tu) sta', (Lei) stia, (noi) stiamo, (voi) state, (Loro) stiano
Gerund	stando

stringere
Past Participle stretto
Past Absolute (io) strinsi, (tu) stringesti, (Lei) strinse, (lui/lei) strinse, (noi) stringemmo, (voi) stringeste, (loro) strinsero

stringersi (conjugated like **stringere**)

svenirsi (conjugated like **venire**)

svolgere
Past Participle svolto
Past Absolute (io) svolsi, (tu) svolgesti, (Lei) svolse, (lui/lei) svolse, (noi) svolgemmo, (voi) svolgeste, (loro) svolsero

svolgersi (conjugated like **svolgere**)

tacere (conjugated like **piacere**)

tenere
Present Indicative (io) tengo, (tu) tieni, (Lei) tiene, (lui/lei) tiene, (noi) teniamo, (voi) tenete, (loro) tengono
Past Absolute (io) tenni, (tu) tenesti, (Lei) tenne, (lui/lei) tenne, (noi) tenemmo, (voi) teneste, (loro) tennero
Future (io) terrò, (tu) terrai, (Lei) terrà, (lui/lei) terrà, (noi) terremo, (voi) terrete, (loro) terranno
Conditional (io) terrei, (tu) terresti, (Lei) terrebbe, (lui/lei) terrebbe, (noi) terremmo, (voi) terreste, (loro) terrebbero
Present Subjunctive (io) tenga, (tu) tenga, (Lei) tenga, (lui/lei) tenga, (noi) teniamo, (voi) teniate, (loro) tengano
Imperative (tu) tieni, (Lei) tenga, (noi) teniamo, (voi) tenete, (Loro) tengano

tenersi (conjugated like **tenere**)

tingere (conjugated like **dipingere**)

tingersi (conjugated like **dipingere**)

togliersi (conjugated like **raccogliere**)

torcere
Past Participle torto
Past Absolute (io) torsi, (tu) torcesti, (Lei) torse, (lui/lei) torse, (noi) torcemmo, (voi) torceste, (loro) torsero

tradurre (conjugated like **riprodurre**)

trascorrere (conjugated like **correre**)
trasmettere (conjugated like **mettere**)

uccidere
Past Participle   ucciso
Past Absolute   (io) uccisi, (tu) uccidesti, (Lei) uccise, (lui/lei) uccise, (noi) uccidemmo, (voi) uccideste, (loro) uccisero

udire
Present Indicative   (io) odo, (tu) odi, (Lei) ode, (lui/lei) ode, (noi) udiamo, (voi) udite, (loro) odono
Present Subjunctive   (io) oda, (tu) oda, (Lei) oda, (lui/lei) oda, (noi) udiamo, (voi) udiate, (loro) odano
Imperative   (tu) oda, (Lei) oda, (noi) udiamo, (voi) udite, (Loro) odano

ungere
Past Participle   unto
Past Absolute   (io) unsi, (tu) ungesti, (Lei) unse, (lui/lei) unse, (noi) ungemmo, (voi) ungeste, (loro) unsero

uscire
Present Indicative   (io) esco, (tu) esci, (Lei) esce, (lui/lei) esce, (noi) usciamo, (voi) uscite, (loro) escono
Present Subjunctive   (io) esca, (tu) esca, (Lei) esca, (lui/lei) esca, (noi) usciamo, (voi) usciate, (loro) escano
Imperative   (tu) esci, (Lei) esca, (noi) usciamo, (voi) uscite, (Loro) escano

vedere
Past Participle   visto/veduto
Past Absolute   (io) vidi, (tu) vedesti, (Lei) vide, (lui/lei) vide, (noi) vedemmo, (voi) vedeste, (loro) videro
Future   (io) vedrò, (tu) vedrai, (Lei) vedrà, (lui/lei) vedrà, (noi) vedremo, (voi) vedrete, (loro) vedranno
Conditional   (io) vedrei, (tu) vedresti, (Lei) vedrebbe, (lui/lei) vedrebbe, (noi) vedremmo, (voi) vedreste, (loro) vedrebbero

venire
Present Indicative   (io) vengo, (tu) vieni, (Lei) viene, (lui/lei) viene, (noi) veniamo, (voi) venite, (loro) vengono
Past Participle   venuto
Past Absolute   (io) venni, (tu) venisti, (Lei) venne, (lui/lei) venne, (noi) venimmo, (voi) veniste, (loro) vennero
Future   (io) verrò, (tu) verrai, (Lei) verrà, (lui/lei) verrà, (noi) verremo, (voi) verrete, (loro) verranno
Conditional   (io) verrei, (tu) verresti, (Lei) verrebbe, (lui/lei) verrebbe, (noi) verremmo, (voi) verreste, (loro) verrebbero
Present Subjunctive   (io) venga, (tu) venga, (Lei) venga, (lui/lei) venga, (noi) veniamo, (voi) veniate, (loro) vengano

Imperative   (tu) vieni, (Lei) venga, (noi) veniamo, (voi) venite,
                   (Loro) vengano

vincere
Past Participle vinto
Past Absolute   (io) vinsi, (tu) vincesti, (Lei) vinse, (lui/lei) vinse, (noi)
                   vincemmo, (voi) vinceste, (loro) vinsero

vivere
Past Participle vissuto
Past Absolute   (io) vissi, (tu) vivesti, (Lei) visse, (lui/lei) visse, (noi)
                   vivemmo, (voi) viveste, (loro) vissero

volere
Present Indicative   (io) voglio, (tu) vuoi, (Lei) vuole, (lui/lei) vuole, (noi)
                       vogliamo, (voi) volete, (loro) vogliono
Past Absolute   (io) volli, (tu) volesti, (Lei) volle, (lui/lei) volle, (noi)
                       volemmo, (voi) voleste, (loro) vollero
Future   (io) vorrò, (tu) vorrai, (Lei) vorrà, (lui/lei) vorrà, (noi)
                       vorremo, (voi) vorrete, (loro) vorranno
Conditional   (io) vorrei, (tu) vorresti, (Lei) vorrebbe, (lui/lei)
                       vorrebbe, (noi) vorremmo, (voi) vorreste, (loro)
                       vorrebbero
Present Subjunctive (io) voglia, (tu) voglia, (Lei) voglia, (lui/lei) voglia,
                       (noi) vogliamo, (voi) vogliate, (loro) vogliano

ENGLISH-ITALIAN WORDFINDER

The following *Wordfinder* contains all the items used in this book. It will enable you to find the information you need quickly and efficiently. If all you want is the Italian equivalent of an entry word, you will find it here. If you also want pronunciation details and other kinds of information, the numbers(s) and letter(s) will tell you where to locate such information.

A

a, an   un, una, uno, un'   8b

a bit, little, some   un po'   8c

A hug...   Un abbraccio...   19a, 19b

a little   un po'   3b

a lot, much   molto, tanto   3b

A pleasure!   Piacere!   16b

ability   abilità, capacità   37f

abort   abortire   11c

abortion   aborto   11c, 40a, 44b

above   sopra   3c, 8f

above zero   sopra zero   6c

abroad   all'estero   19e, 30a

Abruzzi   Abruzzo   30d

abscissa   ascissa   2b

absent-minded   distratto   11e

abstention   astensione   43a

abstinence   astinenza   11d

abstract   astratto, 28b

Abyssinia   Abissinia   30b

accelerate   accelerare   3f

accent   accento   8a, 19c

accept   accettare   21b

acceptable   accettabile   21b

accident   incidente   33a, 39c

accident insurance   assicurazione contro gli infortuni   26a

accomplice   complice   39b

according to me   secondo me   44e

accordion   fisarmonica   28c

accordionist   fisarmonicista   28c

account   conto bancario   26a

accountant   contabile, ragioniere (-a)   11f, 16b, 38a

accounting department   reparto della contabilità   38d

accounting, bookkeeping   contabilità, ragioneria   1g

accusation   imputazione   41

accuse   accusare   41

accused   imputato (-a),   41

Achilles tendon   tallone di Achille   12a

acid   acido   13c

acne   acne   40a

acorn   ghianda   14c

acoustics   acustica   42a

acquaintance   conoscenza   10b

acquit   assolvere   41

acrid   acro   12e

acrobat   acrobata   27a

across   attraverso   3c, 36c

acrylic   acrilico   13c

act   atto, recitare   28e

active   attivo   8a, 11e

actor, actress   attore (-trice)   28a, 28e

acupuncture   agopuntura   40a

acute   acuto   2b

acute-angled   acutangolo   2a

adaptable   adattabile   11e

adapter   adattatore   23d

add   addizionare   1e

add on   aggiungere   1e

addiction   dipendenza   40a

addition   addizione   1e

address   indirizzo   11f, 19e, 38b

adenoids   adenoidi   12a

adhesive bandage   cerotto   25h, 40a

adhesive tape   nastro adesivo   19d, 25c, 38c

Adieu!   Addio!   16a

adjacent   adiacente   2b

adjective   aggettivo   8a

administration   amministrazione   38a, 43a

admission test   prova d'ammissione   37f

admit   ammettere   41

adolescence   adolescenza   11b

adolescent, teenager   adolescente   11b

adopt   adottare   11c

adoption   adozione   11c

adorable   adorabile   11a

adrenaline   adrenalina   12a

Adriatic   Adriatico   30c

adult   adulto   11b

adultery   adulterio   11c

adulthood, maturity   maturità   11b

adventure   avventura   20a, 28d

adventure film   film d'avventura   28a

adverb   avverbio   8a

advertisement   messaggio pubblicitario, réclame   20c

advertising   pubblicità   20c, 38d

advertising agency   agenzia di pubblicità   20c

advertising break   spot pubblicitario   20c

advertising campaign   campagna pubblicitaria   20c

advertising sign   insegna pubblicitaria   20c

advice   consiglio   17a

advise   consigliare   17a

aerobics   aerobica   27b

affable   affabile   11e

affection   affetto   21a

affectionate   affettuoso   11e

Affectionately   affettuosamente…   19b

affirm, remark   affermare   17a

affluent   benestante   11e

Afghanistan   Afghanistan   30b

Africa   Africa   30b

African   africano   30e

after   dopo   4c

afternoon   pomeriggio   4b

again   ancora (una volta), di nuovo   4c, 8j

against   sfavorevole   43a

age   età   11b, 38b

agenda (of a meeting)   ordine del giorno   43a

aggressive   aggressivo   11e

agile   agile   11a

agnostic   agnostico   11d

ago   fa   4c

agree   essere d'accordo   21a, 17a

agriculture   agricoltura   14a

ahead, forward   avanti   3c, 36c

AIDS   AIDS   40a, 44b

ailment   indisposizione   40a

aim the lens   puntare l'obiettivo   28b

air   aria, mandare in onda   6a, 13c, 20b

air conditioning   aria condizionata   23d, 33c

air pollution   inquinamento atmosferico   44a

airline   linea aerea   32a

airmail   posta aerea   19e

airplane   aereo, aereoplano   32a

airport   aeroporto   32a

aisle   corridoio   28a, 32c

alarm   allarme   39a

alarm clock   sveglia   4d

Albania   Albania   30b

Albanian   albanese   30e

alcohol   alcool, bevanda alcolica   44b

alcoholic beverage   bevanda alcolica   24j

alcoholism   alcolismo   44b

alert   sveglio   11a

Alexandria   Alessandria   30c

algebra algebra 1f, 1g
algebraic algebrico 1f
Algeria Algeria 30b
Algerian algerino 30e
algorithm algoritmo 1f
align allineare 42b
alimentary canal tubo digestivo 12a
alimony alimenti 11c
all day tutta la giornata 4b
all, everything tutto 3b
all-inclusive price prezzo forfettario 35a
allegory allegoria 28d
allergic allergico 40a
allergy allergia 40a
alley, lane vicolo 36a
alliance alleanza 43b
alligator alligatore 15c
allude alludere 17a
ally alleato 43b
almost quasi 8j
almost always quasi sempre 4c
almost, nearly circa, quasi 3b
alphabet alfabeto 8a
alpine alpino 30c
Alps Alpi 30c
already già 4c, 8j
also, too anche 8i, 8j
altar altare 11d
altar-boy chierichetto 11d
although benché, sebbene 8i
Alto Adige Alto Adige 30d
altruist altruista 11e
always sempre 4c
amateur dilettante 27b
ambitious ambizioso 11e
ambulance ambulanza, autoambulanza 34
amendment emendamento 43a
America America 30b
American americano 30e
ammonia ammoniaca 13c
among, between fra, tra 3c, 8f
amount ammontare 26b
at (@) chiocciola 19f, 38c
amphetamine amfetamina 44c

amphitheater anfiteatro 36a
amplifier altoparlante 18a
Amsterdam Amsterdam 30c
amusement park luna park 36a
analog analogico 42b
analytical geometry geometria analitica 1g
anatomy anatomia 37e
ancestor antenato 11c
anchor ancora 34
anchovy acciuga 24e
ancient Greece Antica Grecia 43b
ancient monument monumento storico 36a
ancient Rome Antica Roma 43b
and e 8i
anecdote aneddoto 28d
anemia anemia 40a
anemic anemico 40a
anesthesia anestesia 40a
anesthetic anestetico 40a, 40b
angel angelo 11d
anger rabbia 21a
angle angolo 2b
angry arrabbiato 21a
animal animale 15a
animated image immagine animata 42b
animation animazione 28a
anise anice 24i
ankle caviglia 12a
ankle sprain storta alla caviglia 40a
anniversary anniversario 11c, 29a
announce annunciare 17a
announcement annuncio 17a
announcer annunciatore (-trice) 20b
annoying, unpleasant antipatico 11e
annual leave congedo annuale 38d
annuity rendita 26a

anoint   ungere   11d

answer   risposta, rispondere   9a, 17a, 18b, 37f

answering machine   segreteria telefonica   18a, 38c

ant   formica   15d

ant hill   formicaio   15d

Antarctic   Antartico   13b

Antarctic Circle   Circolo Polare Antartico   13d

antelope   antilope   15a

antenna   antenna   20b, 42a

anterior, before   anteriore   4c

anthology   antologia   25n, 28d

anthropology   antropologia   37e

anti-theft insurance   assicurazione contro il furto   26a

anti-wrinkle cream   crema antirughe   25f

antibiotic   antibiotico   25h, 40a

antique shop   negozio dell'antiquariato   25a

antiquity   antichità   43b

antiseptic   antisettico   39c

antler, horn   corno   15a

anus, bottom   ano   12a

anxiety, anxiousness   ansia, ansietà   21a, 40a

anxious   ansioso   11e, 21a

Aosta   Aosta   30d

apartment   appartamento   23e

apartment building   palazzo (di appartamenti)   23e

ape, monkey   scimmia   15a

Apennines   Appennini   30c

apostrophe   apostrofo   19c

appendicitis   appendicite   40a

appendix   appendice   24a, 25n, 28d

appetizer   antipasto   24a

appetizing   appetitoso   24n

applaud   applaudire   28e

applause   applauso   28e

apple   mela   24g, 14d

apple tree   melo   14c

applicant   candidato   38d

appointment   appuntamento   38d, 40a, 40b

apprentice   apprendista   38a

approach   avvicinarsi a   3f

approval   approvazione   21b

approve   approvare   21b

approximately   approssimativamente   3b

apricot   albicocca   14d, 24g

April   aprile   5b

apron   grembiule   25k

aptitude test   test d'attitudine   37f

Apulia   Puglia   30d

Aquarius   Acquario   5d

Arabic   arabo   1d, 30e

arc   arco   2a

arch, archway   arco, arcata   23a

archbishop   arcivescovo   11d

archeology   archeologia   37e

archery   tiro con l'arco   27b

archipelago   arcipelago   13b

architect   architetto (-a)   38a

architecture   architettura   28b, 37e

architecture faculty   facoltà di architettura   37a

archivist   archivista   43b

Arctic   Artico   13b

Arctic Circle   Circolo Polare Artico   13d

Are you crazy?   Ma sei pazzo (-a)?   16c

Are you joking?   Scherzi? Scherza?   21c

area   area, superficie   3a, 13d

area code   prefisso   11f, 18b, 38c

Argentina   Argentina   30b

Argentinean   argentino   30e

argue   litigare   17a, 21a, 39b

argument   lite   17a, 21a

Aries   Ariete   5d

arithmetic   aritmetica   1f, 1g

arithmetical   aritmetico   1f

arithmetical operations   operazioni aritmetiche   1e

arm   braccio   12a

armchair poltrona 23b, 35b
armed assault, attack
aggressione a mano armata 39b
armed conflict conflitto a fuoco
44d
armed robbery rapina a mano
armata 39b
Armenia Armenia 30b
Armenian armeno 30e
armistice armistizio 44d
armpit ascella 12a
arms dealer mercante d'armi
44d
arms reduction diminuzione
delle armi 44d
arms trade mercato delle armi
44d
army esercito 44d
Arno River Arno 30c
aroma aroma 12e
arrest arresto, arrestare 39b
arrest warrant mandato di
cattura 39b
arrhythmia aritmia 40a
arrival arrivo 32b, 34
arrive arrivare 3f
arrogant arrogante 11e
arson incendio doloso 39a
arsonist piromane 39a
art arte 28b, 37e
art exhibition mostra d'arte
28b
art gallery galleria d'arte, museo
d'arte 28b, 36a
art lyceum liceo artistico 37a
arteriosclerosis arteriosclerosi
40a
artery arteria 12a
arthritis artrite 40a
artichoke carciofo 14e, 24f
article articolo 8a
artificial artificiale 25i
artificial insemination
fecondazione artificiale 11c
artificial intelligence intelligenza
artificiale 42b
artist artista 28b
artistic artistico 11e

arts and letters lyceum liceo
classico 37a
arts faculty facoltà di lettere
37a
arts, humanities, letters lettere
37e
as come 8i
as a matter of fact anzi 8j
as if come se 8i
as much as tanto...quanto 3b
as soon as appena 4c, 8i
asbestos amianto 13c
ascent salita, ascesa 3f
ash frassino 14c
Ash Wednesday Ceneri 11d
Asia Asia 30b
aside a parte 28e
ask a question fare una domanda
9, 37f
ask for chiedere 9a, 17a
asparagus asparagi 14e, 24f
asphalt asfalto 13c
aspirin aspirina 25h, 40a
assailant aggressore 39b
assassin, murderer assassino
39b
assault, attack aggressione,
aggredire 39b
assembly assemblea 43a
assignment compito 37f
assignment book agenda 37b
assistant assistente 37d
assure assicurare 21a
asterisk asterisco 19c
asthma asma 40a
astronomy astronomia 13a,
37e
astute, bright astuto 11e
at a, in 8f
At 1:00. All'una. 4a
At 2:00. Alle due. 4a
At 3:00. Alle tre. 4a
at home a casa 23f
at midnight a mezzanotte 4b
at night di notte, della notte 4b
at noon a mezzogiorno 4b
at the bottom in fondo 3c
at the dentist's dal dentista 40b

at the end of in fondo a 36c

at the same time allo stesso tempo 4c

At what time? A che ora? 4a

atheism ateismo 11d

atheist ateo 11d

Athenian ateniese 30c

Athens Atene 30c

athlete atleta 27b

athlete's foot micosi dei piedi 40a

athletic atletico 11a

Atlantic Atlantico 13b, 30c

atlas atlante 13d

ATM bancomat 26a

atmosphere atmosfera 6a, 13b

atmospheric conditions condizioni atmosferiche 6a

atom atomo 13c

atomic bomb bomba atomica 44d

atone for one's sins scontare i propri peccati 11d

attach, enclose allegare 19e

attached, enclosed allegato 19e

Attachment Allegato 42c

attack attacco 44d

attend frequentare 37f

attendance frequenza 37f

Attention! Attenzione! 16c

attentive attento 11e

attic attico 23a

attitude atteggiamento 21a

attorney avvocato (-essa) 41

attractive attraente 11a

audacious, bold audace 11e

audience pubblico 28e

audio audio 42a

audio receiver, tuner sintonizzatore 20b

auditor revisore dei conti 38a

August agosto 5b

aunt zia 10a

Australia Australia 30b

Australian australiano 30e

Austria Austria 30b

Austrian austriaco 30e

author autore (-trice) 20a, 25n

authorized withdrawal prelevamento autorizzato 26a

autism autismo 40a

autobiography autobiografia 25n, 28d

automatic weapon arma automatica 44d

automatic withdrawal prelevamento automatico 26a

automobile automobile, auto 34

autumn autunno 5c

avenue viale, corso 11f, 36a

average media 1f, 37f

average height altezza media 11a

avoid evitare 3f

away via 3c

axis asse 2b

B

baboon babbuino 15a

baby bottle biberon 11c, 23c

baby, child bambino (-a) 11b

bachelor scapolo (-a) 11c

bacillus, bacterium bacillo 40a

back (behind) dietro, indietro 3c, 36c, 42c

back (of the body) schiena 12a

back and forth avanti e indietro 3f

back of the seat schienale 32c

back seat sedile posteriore 33c

back up fare marcia indietro 33a

backache mal di schiena 40a

background sfondo 28b

backward indietro 3c

bacon pancetta 24d

bad male, malamente 8j, 16a

bad mood cattivo umore 21a

bad, mean cattivo 11e

bad-tempered irascibile 21a

badger tasso 15a

bag, sac sacco, sacchetto 3e, 23b, 25a

baggage, luggage bagaglio 31

bagpipes zampogne 28c

bail cauzione 41

bait esca 27a

baked al forno 24a

baker fornaio (-a) 38a

balance scale bilancia 3b

balancing the books compensazione 26b

balcony terrazza, balcone 23a, 35b

balcony (of a theater) galleria 28a

bald calvo 11a

baldness calvizie 11a

Balkans Balcani 30c

ball palla, pallone 27b

ballad ballata 28c, 28d

ballet balletto 28c

ballistic missile missile balistico 44d

ballot scheda elettorale 43a

ballot box urna elettorale 43a

balloting ballottaggio 43a

ballpoint pen biro 19d, 25c, 37b

ballroom sala da ballo 28c

banana banana 14d, 24g

band (watch) cinghietta 25i

band (musical) gruppo, complesso 25j, 28c

bandage benda, bendare 39c, 40a

bang colpo 12c

Bangladesh Bangladesh 30b

banister balaustra 23a

bank banca 26a

bank book libretto bancario 26a

bank card carta bancaria 25a

bank clerk impiegato (-a) di banca 26a

bank code codice bancario 26a

bank money order vaglia bancario 26a

bank receipt ricevuta 26a

bank worker bancario (-a) 26a

banking executive banchiere (-a) 26a

bankruptcy bancarotta 26b

banquet banchetto 24a, 35a

baptism battesimo 11d

baptismal font fonte battesimale 11d

baptistery battistero 11d

bar bar 29b

bar code codice a barre 25a

bar-code reader lettore elettronico 25a

barber barbiere (-a) 12f, 38a

barbiturate barbiturico 25h, 40a

Barcelona Barcellona 30c

bargaining, negotiations trattative 38d

Bari Bari 30c

baritone baritono 28c

bark (of a tree) corteccia, scorza 14a

bark (dog) abbaiare 15a

barley orzo 14a, 24c

barn granaio 15a

barometer barometro 6c

barometric pressure pressione barometrica 6c

Baroque Barocco 28b, 43b

barracks caserma 36a

barrel botte 3e

bartender barista 24l

base basso 28c

base salary paga base 38d

baseball baseball 27b

baseball diamond diamante 27b

basement scantinato 23a

basil basilico 14e, 24i

basilica basilica 36a

basket cesto, cestino, canestro 3e, 23b, 27b

basketball pallacanestro, basket 27b

bass drum grancassa 28c

bassoon fagotto 28c

bassoonist fagottista 28c
bat (baseball) mazza 27b
bat (mammal) pipistrello 15a
bath oil olio da bagno 25f
bath salts sali da bagno 25f
bathrobe accappatoio 25k
bathroom bagno 23a, 35b
bathroom scale pesapersone 23b
bathtub vasca 23a, 35b
baton bacchetta 28c
battery pila, batteria, 25b, 33c
bawdy volgare 21a
bay baia 13b
be about to stare per 4c
be absent essere assente 37f
be against essere contrario 21a
be ashamed vergognarsi 21a
be bad (awful) weather fare (essere) brutto, cattivo tempo 6a
be born nascere 11c
Be careful! Attento (-a)! 21c
be cold avere freddo, fare freddo 6a, 6b, 12b
be cool fare fresco 6a
be down essere giù 21a
be early essere in anticipo 4c
be enough bastare, essere abbastanza 3b
be equal to essere uguale a 1f
be equivalent to essere equivalente a 1f
be fond of (something) essere appassionato di 21b
be from essere di 11f
be good weather fare bel tempo, essere bel tempo 6a
be greater than essere maggiore di 1f
be hot avere caldo, fare caldo 6a, 6b, 12b
be hungry avere fame 12b, 24n
be in a bad mood avere la luna di traverso 13a
be in mourning essere in lutto 11c

be interested in interessarsi di 22b
be late essere in ritardo 4c
be less than essere minore di 1f
be mild essere mite 6a
be of…origin essere d'origine… 11f
be on a first-name basis darsi del tu 16b
be on a formal basis darsi del Lei 16b
be on call essere di turno 40a
be on the air essere in onda 20b
be on the point, verge of essere sul punto di 4c
be on time essere in orario 4c
be on trial essere sotto processo 41
be pregnant essere incinta 11c
be present essere presente 37f
be promoted, pass essere promosso 37f
be punctual essere puntuale 4c
Be quiet! Sta' zitto (-a)! Stia zitto (-a)! 16c
be right avere ragione 17b, 22b
be run over essere investito (-a) 39c
be seated accomodarsi, sedersi 16b
be self-employed lavorare in proprio 38d
be similar to essere simile a 1f
be sleepy avere sonno 12b
be slightly built avere un fisico debole 11a
be strongly built avere un fisico forte 11a
be sufficient essere sufficiente 3b
be thirsty avere sete 12b, 24n
be tired essere stanco 12b
be up essere su 21a
be very cold fare un freddo da cani 15b

be windy, blow wind   tirare vento   6a

be wrong   avere torto   17b, 22b

beach   spiaggia   13b, 36b

beak   becco   15b

beaker, tumbler   coppa   23c

bean   fagiolo   14e, 24f

bear (animal)   orso   15a

bear, put up with   sopportare   6b

beard   barba   12a

beat time   battere il tempo   28c

beautician   estetista   12f

beautiful, handsome   bello   11, 25l

beauty   bellezza   11a

beaver   castoro   15a

because   perché   8i

become bored   annoiarsi   21a

become cured   guarire   40a

become fat   ingrassare   11a

become friends   diventare amici, fare amicizia   10b

become ill   ammalarsi   40a

become old   invecchiarsi   11b

become small   impiccolire, rimpiccolire   3b

become thin   dimagrire   11a

bed   letto   23b, 35b

bed and breakfast   pensione   35a

bedbug   cimice   15d

bedsheet   lenzuolo   23b

bedding   biancheria da letto   23b

bedroom   camera (da letto)   23a

bedside table   comodino   23b, 35b

bedspread   copriletto   23b

bee   ape   15d

beech   faggio   14c

beef   manzo   24d

beer   birra   24j

beet   barbabietola   14e, 24f

beetle   maggiolino   15d

before   prima   4c

beg (alms)   mendicare   44b

beg to do something   pregare   17a

beggar   mendicante   44b

begin   cominciare   3f

behind   dietro   3c, 36c

Beijing   Pechino   30c

Belgian   belga   30e

Belgium   Belgio   30b

Belgrade   Belgrado   30c

belief   credenza   11d, 22a

believe   credere   11d, 22b

believer   credente   11d

bell tower   campanile   11d, 36a

bellhop   fattorino (-a)   35a

belly   pancia   12a

belly button   ombelico   12a

below   sotto   8f

below zero   sotto zero   6c

bend   piegare   3f

Benedictine   benedettino   11d

benefactor   benefattore (-trice)   21a

benign   benigno   40a

Berlin   Berlino   30c

beside, next to   accanto a   3c

best man   testimone (dello sposo)   11c

Best wishes!   Auguri!   16c, 29c

bet   scommessa, scommettere   27a

Better late than never!   Meglio tardi che mai!   4c

between   fra, tra   8f

beverage, soft drink   bibita   24j

beyond   oltre   3c

be...years old   avere...anni   11b

Bible   Bibbia   11d

bibliography   bibliografia   37f

bicameral   bicamerale   43a

bicycle   bicicletta   34

bicycle lane, path   pista ciclabile   33b

bicycle racing   corsa ciclistica   27b

big   grande, grosso   11a, 11b, 25l

bigoted   bigotto   11e

bile   bile   40a

bill (to pay)   conto, fattura   24l, 25a, 35a

bill (of the legislature)   disegno di
legge   43a
bill, banknote   banconota,
biglietto di banca   26a
billiard ball   palla da biliardo
27a
billiard cue   stecca da biliardo
27a
billiard table   tavolo da biliardo
27a
billiards   biliardo   27a
billionth   miliardesimo   1b
bingo   tombola   27a
bingo card   cartella della tombola
27a
biography   biografia   25n, 28d
biological war   guerra
batteriologica   44d
biological weapon   arma
batteriologica   44d
biology   biologia   37e
biosystem   biosistema   44a
birch   betulla   14c
bird   uccello   15b
bird of prey   uccello rapace   15b
birdcage   gabbia   15b
birth   nascita   11c, 11f
birth certificate   certificato di
nascita   11c
birth pains   doglie   11c
birthday   compleanno   11c, 29a
biscuit, cookie   biscotto   24c
bisector   bisettrice   2b
bishop   vescovo   11d
bite   morso   40a
bitter   aspro, amaro   12e, 21a,
24a
black   nero   7a
black hole   buco nero   13a
blackbird   merlo   15b
blackboard   lavagna   37b
blackboard eraser   cancellino
37b
blackmail   ricatto, ricattare   39b
bladder   vescica   12a
blade (for cutting)   lama   23c
blade (razor)   lametta da barba
25f

blank endorsement   girata in
bianco   26a
blanket   coperta   23b, 35b
blasphemy   blasfemia   11d
bleed   sanguinare   39c
blender   frullatore   23c
bless   benedire   11d
Bless you!   Salute!   16c
blessing   benedizione   11d
blind (for a window)   avvolgibile
23a
blind (sightless)   cieco, accecare
12d
blindness   cecità   12d
blink   battere le palpebre   3f, 12d
blister   vescica   40a
blog   blog   20b
blond, blonde   biondo (-a)   11a
blood   sangue   12a, 39c, 40a
blood group   gruppo sanguigno
12a
blood pressure   pressione del
sangue   12a
blood test   analisi del sangue
40a
blood transfusion   trasfusione del
sangue   40a
blood vessel   vaso sanguigno
12a
bloom   sbocciare   14a
blouse   camicetta, blusa   25k
blow a fuse   fare saltare una
valvola   23d
blue   azzurro   7a
blue-collar worker   operaio (-a)
38d
blueberry   mirtillo   14d, 24g
blueprint   copia cianografica
28b
blues   blues   25j, 28c
blush   arrossire   11a
boa   serpente boa   15c
board   salire a bordo   32a
board of directors   consiglio
d'amministrazione   38d
boarding   imbarco   32a
boarding pass   carta d'imbarco
32a

boastful   vanaglorioso   21a
boat   barca   27b, 36b
body   corpo   11a, 12a
body (of a letter)   contenuto   19c
body-building   culturismo   27b
bodyguard   guardia del corpo   39b
boil   bollire   24a
boiling point   punto di ebollizione, dell'acqua bollente   6c, 13c
boldface   grassetto   19c
Bolivia   Bolivia   30b
Bolivian   boliviano   30e
Bologna   Bologna   30c
bolt   bullone   23d, 25b
bolt down   bullonare   23d
bomb   bomba   44d
bond   obbligazione   26a
bone   osso   12a
boo   fischiare   28e
book   libro   20a, 25n, 37b
bookcase   libreria   23b
bookmark   segnalibro   37f
bookseller   libraio (-a)   38a
bookshelf   scaffale   23b
bookstore   libreria   25n
boot   stivale   25m
border (political)   frontiera   13d, 31
bored   annoiato   21a
boredom   noia   21a
Bosnia   Bosnia   30b
Bosnian   bosniaco   30e
botanical   botanico   14a
botanical gardens   giardino botanico   36a
botany   botanica   14a, 37e
both   ambedue, tutti e due   3b
bothersome, irksome   noioso   11e
bottle   bottiglia   23c, 24k
bottle opener   cavatappi   23c
bottled   imbottigliato   23c
bottom   fondo   3c
boulder   macigno   13b
boundary   confine   3d

bow (archery)   arco   28c
bow   inchino, inchinarsi   3f
bow tie   farfalla   25k
bowl   scodella   23c
bowling   bowling   27b
bowling alley   pista   27b
bowling ball   boccia   27b
bowling pin   birillo   27b
box, tin   scatola   3e, 23b
box office   botteghino   28a
boxer   pugile   27b
boxing   pugilato   27b
boy   ragazzo   11a, 11b
boyfriend   amico, ragazzo   10c
bra   reggiseno   25k
braces   apparecchio per i denti   40b
bracelet   braccialetto   25i
braggart   spaccone (-a)   21a
brain   cervello   12a
brake   freno, frenare   33a, 33c, 34
branch (bank)   filiale di una banca   26a
branch (company)   succursale   38d
branch (tree)   ramo   14a
brand   marca, marchio   20c, 25a
brash, bold   sfacciato   11e
brass   ottone   13c
brass instruments   ottoni   28c
brawny   poderoso   11a
Brazil   Brasile   30b
Brazilian   brasiliano   30e
bread   pane   24c
bread basket   cesta del pane   23c
bread knife   coltello da pane   23c
bread store, bakery   panificio   24m
breadstick   grissino   24c
break   pausa   38d
break a limb   fratturare un arto   40a
break a record   battere un record   27b

break and enter scasso 39b

break off a friendship rompere un'amicizia 10b

breakfast prima colazione 24a, 35a

breakfast included colazione compresa 35a

breast seno, petto 12a, 24a

breast-feed allattare 11c

breath respiro 12b

breathe respirare 12b

breathing respirazione 12b

breeding allevamento 15a

bribe bustarella 39b

bribery corruzione 39b

brick mattone 13c

bricklayer muratore 13c, 38a

bride sposa 11c

bridesmaid damigella 11c

bridge ponte 33a

brief, short breve 4c, 37f

briefcase cartella 25c

briefly in breve 4c, 17b

bright acceso, brillante 7b, 12d

brilliant brillante 11e

bring portare 25a

British britannico 30e

broad chin mento largo 11a

broad forehead fronte spaziosa 11a

broad-minded di ampie vedute 11e

broad-shouldered con le spalle larghe 11a

broadcast trasmissione, trasmettere 20b

broccoli broccoli 14e, 24f

brochure opuscolo 20c, 30a

broiled arrostito 24a

broke (financially) al verde 7a

broken spezzata 2b

broken bone osso rotto 39c

bronchitis bronchite 40a

bronze bronzo 13c

bronze sculpture scultura in bronzo 28b

brooch spilla 25i

brood covata, nidiata 15b

brook ruscello 36b

broom (sweeper) scopa 23b

broth brodo 24b

brother fratello 10a

brother-in-law cognato 10a

brow, forehead fronte 12a

brown marrone 7a

brown eyes occhi castani 11a

brown skin pelle bruna 11a

bruise livido 40a

brush spazzola, pennello 7b, 12f, 25f, 28b

brush against sfiorare 3f

brush oneself spazzolarsi 12f

brusque brusco 11e

bucket secchio 3e

buckle allacciare, fibbia 25g, 25l, 32c

Buddhism buddismo 11d

Buddhist buddista 11d

budget, balance bilancio 26a, 38d

budget prediction bilancio preventivo 38d

buffalo bufalo 15a

build costruire 23f

build (of the body) fisico 11a

building edificio 23e, 36a, 39a

bulb bulbo 14a

Bulgaria Bulgaria 30b

Bulgarian bulgaro 30e

bull toro 15a

bulldog mastino 15a

bump sbattere 39c

bump into imbattersi in 3f

bumper paraurti 33c

burglar alarm allarme antifurto 23a

burial sepultura 11c

burlap tela di sacco 13c

burn bruciatura, bruciare, ustione 39a

burp, belch rutto, ruttare 12b

burrow, den tana 15a

bury seppellire 11c

bus autobus 34

bus driver autista 34
bus station, depot capolinea 34
bus tour viaggio in pullman 30a
business and commerce facoltà di economia e commercio 37a
business card biglietto da visita 19d, 25c, 38c
business consultant consulente commerciale 38a
business letter lettera commerciale 19e
business person persona d'affari 38a
bustle about darsi da fare 3f
busy, occupied signal occupato 18b
but ma, però 8i
butcher macellaio (-a) 38a
butcher shop macelleria 24m
butter burro 24h
buttercup ranuncolo 14b
butterfly farfalla 15d
button bottone 25g, 25l
buy comprare 23f, 25a
buy a travel ticket fare il biglietto 30a
buzz ronzare 15d
by da 8f
by boat, by ship con la nave 30a
by cable via cavo 42a
by chance per caso 8j
by now ormai 8j
by plane in aereo 30a
by the way a proposito 17b, 44e
by train in treno 30a
bypass, highway raccordo stradale 36a
byte byte 42b

C

cabbage cavolo 14e, 24f
cabin cabina 32c
cabinet armadietto 23b
cabinet (political) gabinetto 43a

cabinet head capo di gabinetto 43a
cabinet meeting consiglio di gabinetto 43a
cable cavo 18a
cable television televisione via cavo 20b
cadaver cadavere 11c
cafeteria mensa 24l, 37c
Cairo il Cairo 30c
cake, pie torta 24c
Calabria Calabria 30d
calcium calcio 13c
calculate calcolare 1f
calculation calcolo 1f
calculator calcolatrice 25c, 37b, 38c
calculus calcolo 1g
calendar calendario 5b, 25c
calf (animal) vitello 15a
calf (of the leg) polpaccio 12a
call chiamare 17a
call (a meeting, etc.) convocare 43a
call the fire department chiamare i pompieri 39a
call the police chiamare la polizia 39c
calling (business) card biglietto da visita 16b
calm calmo 11e
Cambodia Cambogia 30b
Cambodian cambogiano 30e
camel cammello 15a
camellia camelia 14b
camera macchina fotografica 25d
cameraman cameraman 20b
Campania Campania 30d
camping campeggio 35a
campus campus 37c
can of hairspray bomboletta spray 25f
Can you tell me ...? Mi sa (sai) dire dove...? 9, 36c
Canada Canada 30b
Canadian canadese 30e
canary canarino 15b

cancel a subscription annullare l'abbonamento 20a
canceled cancellato 32b, 34
cancer cancro 40a
Cancer Cancro 5d
candy caramella 24c
canine canino 40b
cannelloni cannelloni 24b
canoe canoa 27b, 36b
Cantonese cantonese 30e
canvas tela 28b
cap berretto 25k
capacity capienza, capacità 3b
cape capo 13b
capital (money) capitale 26a
capital (of the country) capitale 36a
capital town (of a region) capoluogo 36a
cappuccino cappuccino 24j
Capricorn Capricorno 5d
captain comandante 32c
caption leggenda 20c
captivating accattivante 21a
car macchina 34
car body carrozzeria 33c
car dealer(ship) concessionario 33c
car door portiera 33c
car race corsa automobilistica 27b
car racing automobilismo 27b
car roof tetto 33c
car seat sedile 33c
car window finestrino 33c
car-ferry nave traghetto 34
carafe, decanter caraffa 23c
carat carato 25i
carbon (element) carbonio 13c
carbon (solid), coal carbone 13c
carbonated gassata, frizzante 24j
carburetor carburatore 33c
card, record, file scheda 19d, 38c
cardboard cartone 13c

cardboard box scatola di cartone 3e
cardinal cardinale 1d, 11d
cardiovascular system sistema cardiovascolare 12a
care for volere bene a 11c
career carriera 11f, 38d
carefree spensierato 11e
careful cauto 11e
careless spericolato 11e
Caribbean Caraibi, caraibico 30b, 30e
carnation garofano 14b
carpenter falegname 38a
carpet tappezzeria 33c
carrot carota 14e, 24f
carry out a sentence eseguire una sentenza 41
cart, movable tray carrello 23b
carte blanche carta bianca 7a
cartilage cartilagine 12a
carton paper cartoncino 37b
cartoon cartone animato 28a
cartridge cartuccia 19d, 25c, 38c, 42b
case cassa 3e
cash contanti 25a, 26a
cash a check incassare un assegno 26a
cash register cassa 25a
cashier cassiere (-a) 25a, 26a, 38a
cask barile 3e
casserole casseruola 23c
cast a glance gettare uno sguardo 12d
cast iron ghisa 13c
cat gatto 15a
catalogue catalogo 25n, 28d, 37f
Catanzaro Catanzaro 30c
cataract cateratta 40a
catarrh catarro 40a
catch afferrare 3f
catch (the ball) prendere 27b
catch a chill prendere freddo 40a
catch fire incendiarsi 39a

catcher's mask   maschera   27b

catechism   catechismo   11d

caterpillar   bruco   15d

cathedral   cattedrale   11d, 36a

Catholic   cattolico (-a)   11d

Catholicism   Cattolicesimo   11d

Caucasian   caucasico   30c

cauliflower   cavolfiore   14e, 24f

cautious   cauto   21a

cave   grotta   13b

cavity, tooth decay   carie   40b

CD reader, drive   lettore CD   42b

CD-ROM   CD-ROM   25c, 38c, 42b

ceiling   soffitto   23a

celery   sedano   14e, 24f

cell   cellula   12a

cell phone   cellulare, telefonino   4d, 18a

cellist   violoncellista   28c

cello   violoncello   28c

cellulite   cellulite   40a

Celsius   Celsius   6c

cement truck   betoniera   34

censor   censurare   20a

censorship   censura   20a, 44b

center   centro, centrare   2a, 19c, 42b

center (political)   di centro   43a

Centigrade   centigrado   6c

centimeter   centimetro   3a

century   secolo   4b, 43b

ceremonious   cerimonioso   21a

chaffinch   fringuello   15b

chain   catena   25i

chair   sedia   23b

chair a meeting   presiedere una riunione   38d

chairlift   seggiovia   36b

chalice   calice   11d

chalk   gesso   13c, 37b

chamber music   musica da camera   25j, 28c

chamber (representative)   camera dei deputati   43a

chamomile tea   camomilla   24j

champion   campione   27b

change (money)   resto   25a

change gears   cambiare marcia   33a

change room   spogliatoio   27b

change the oil   cambiare l'olio   33a

change the subject   cambiare soggetto   17a

channel   canale   13b, 20b

chant   canto   28c

chapel   cappella   11d, 36a

chapped hands   mani screpolate   11a

chapter   capitolo   25n, 28d

character   carattere, personaggio   19c, 25n, 28d

charade   sciarada   27a

charge (someone)   incolpare   41

charity   carità   21a

charming, fascinating   affascinante   11e

charter flight   volo charter   30a

chartered accountant   commercialista   38a

chase   inseguire   3f

chat   chiacchierare   17a

cheap   a buon mercato, economico   24n

cheat   imbrogliare   27a

cheater   imbroglione (-a)   27a

cheating   imbroglio, truffa   27a

check (money)   assegno   25a, 26a

check (shape, figure)   quadretto   3d

checkbook   libretto degli assegni   26a

check clearing   compensazione degli assegni   26a

check the oil   controllare l'olio   33a

check-in   accettazione, check-in   32a

check-out vehicle   condizioni del veicolo in uscita   33d

checker piece   pedina   27a

checkered   a scacchi, a quadretti   3d, 25l

checkers dama 27a
cheek guancia 12a
cheekbone zigomo 12a
cheeky, cocky sfacciato 21a
cheer, acclaim acclamare 17a
Cheers! Cin, cin! Salute! 16c, 24k
cheese formaggio 24h
chemical chimico 13c
chemical war guerra chimica 44d
chemistry chimica 13c, 37e
cherry ciliegia 14d, 24g
cherry (tree) ciliegio 14c
chess gioco degli scacchi 27a
chest petto 12a
chest infection infezione polmonare 40a
chest of drawers cassettone 35b
chest protector corazza 27b
chestnut castagna 14d, 24g
chestnut (tree) castagno 14c
chiaroscuro chiaroscuro 28b
chick pulcino 15b
chick peas ceci 14e, 24f
chicken, hen gallina, pollo 15b, 24d
chickenpox varicella 40a
chief executive direttore (-trice) generale 38a
chief of police commissario di polizia 39b
child fanciullo (-a), bambino (-a) 10a
childbirth parto 11c
childhood fanciullezza 11b
children bambini 11b
children's program programma per i bambini 20b
Chile Cile 30b
Chilean cileno 30e
chill, shiver brivido 40a
chimney camino 23a
chin mento 12a
China Cina 30b
Chinese cinese 30e
chip (computer) chip 42b

chip (wood) scheggiatura 33d
chisel cesello, cesellare 23d, 25b, 28b
chlorine cloro 13c
chocolate cioccolato 7b
chocolate candy cioccolatino 24c
choir coro 11d, 28c
choke (of a car) valvola dell'aria 33c
choke strozzarsi 12b
cholesterol colesterolo 12b
chop, cutlet cotoletta 24a
chopping (butcher's) knife coltello da macellaio 23c
chopping board tagliere 23c
chord accordo 28c
Christian cristiano (-a) 11d
Christianity cristianesimo 11d
Christmas Natale 5f, 29a
chrysalis crisalide 15d
chubby grassottello 11a
chum compagno (-a) 10b
church chiesa 11d, 36a
church candle cero 11d
cigar sigaro 25e
cigarette sigaretta 25e
cinema cinema 28a
cinnamon cannella 24i
circle cerchio 2a
circuit circuito 3d
circular, round circolare, rotondo 3d
circulate circolare 3f
circulation circolazione 3f
circumference circonferenza 2a
circus circo 27a, 29b
citizen cittadino (-a) 43a
citizenship cittadinanza 11f, 31, 43a
citrus cedro 24g
city città 36a, 38b
city block isolato 33a
city hall municipio 36a
city map pianta della città 36a
city dweller, citizen cittadino (-a) 36a

civic duty   dovere civico   43a
civil affairs   affari civili   43a
civil right   diritto civile   41, 43a
civil servant   funzionario   43a
civil war   guerra civile   43b
claim   rivendicazione   26b
clam   vongola, mollusco bivalve   15c, 24e
clamp   morsetto   23d, 25b
clap   applaudire   3f
clarinet   clarino, clarinetto   28c
clarinetist   clarinettista   28c
clash   cozzare   12c
class   classe, lezione   30a, 37d, 37f
classical music   musica classica   25j, 28c
Classicism   Classicismo   28b, 43b
classified ad   piccola pubblicità   38d
classroom   aula   37c
clause   proposizione   8a
clay   argilla   13c, 14a
clean   pulire, pulito   11a, 23f, 25g
clean oneself   pulirsi   12f
cleaning cloth   straccio   23b
clear (a check)   compensare   26a
clear   sereno   6a, 12d
clear skin   pelle chiara   11a
clear the table   sparecchiare   23f
clear, delete   annullare   19c, 42b
clearness   chiarezza   12d
clematis   clematide   14b
clergy   clero   11d
clerk   impiegato (-a)   19e, 35a
clerk's window   sportello   19e
click   cliccare   19f, 42b
clientele   clientela   25a, 38d
cliff   scogliera   13b
climate   clima   6a, 13d
climb, go up   salire   3f
climber   alpinista   27b

cling on   appiccicarsi, stringersi   3f
clip   grapetta, clip   19d, 38c
clock   orologio   4d
cloister   chiostro   11d
Close   Chiudi   42c
close an account   chiudere un conto   26a
close friend   amico (-a) intimo (-a)   10b
closed   chiuso   25a, 33b
Closed for holidays   Chiuso per ferie   33b
closed-circuit television   televisione a circuito chiuso   20b
closed-door hearing   udienza a porte chiuse   41
closet   armadio   35b
closing   chiusa   19c
closing (time)   chiusura   25a
cloth   stoffa   13c
clothes   abiti, abbigliamento   25g, 25k
clothes basket   cestino del bucato   25g
clothes closet   guardaroba   23a
clothes dryer   asciugatrice   23b
clothes hanger   attaccapanni   23b, 35b
clothes rack   attaccapanni   23a
clothespin   molletta   25g
clothing store   negozio di abbigliamento   25k
cloud   nuvola   6a
cloudburst   nubifragio   6a
cloudy   nuvoloso   6a
clown   pagliaccio   27a, 29b
clue   indizio   39b
clutch   frizione   33c
coach (sports)   allenatore (-trice)   27b
coach (train)   vagone   34
coalition   coalizione   43a
coast, coastline   costa   13b
coat   cappotto   25k
cobbler, shoe-repairer   calzolaio (-a)   38a
cobra   cobra   15c

cocaine cocaina 44c
cockroach scarafaggio 15d
cocoon bozzolo 15d
cod merluzzo 24e
codfish merluzzo 15c
coed school scuola mista 37a
coffee caffè 24j
coffee pot bricco del caffè 23c
coffin bara 11c
cohabit, live together coabitare, convivere 11c
cohabitation convivenza 11c
coin moneta 27a
coin collecting numismatica 27a
colander colino 23c
cold (sickness) raffreddore 40a
cold freddo 6a
cold cuts affettati 24d
cold water acqua fredda 35b
colitis colite 40a
collapse crollare 3f
collar colletto 25g, 25l
colleague collega 10b
collect call telefonata a carico del destinatario 18b
collecting collezionismo 27a
collection colletta, raccolta 11d, 25n, 28d
collector collezionista 27a
collide sccontrarsi 39c
collision, smash scontro, scontrarsi, investirsi 39c
cologne acqua di Colonia 25f
Colombia Colombia 30b
Colombian colombiano 30e
colon due punti 19c
color colore, colorare 7b
color monitor schermo a colori 25c
color one's hair tingersi i capelli 11a
colored a colori 7b
colorful, vivacious vivace 28d
column (in a newspaper) rubrica 20a
column colonna 3d

columnist, reporter cronista 20a
comb pettine 12f, 25f
comb oneself pettinarsi 11a, 12f
come venire 3f
Come in! Avanti! Prego! 16b
Come off it! Ma va! 21a
Come on! Su! Dai! 21a
come to light venire alla luce 13a
comedy, play commedia 20a, 28d, 28e
comet cometa 13a
comic book rivista a fumetti 20a, 25n
comic, comedian comico (-a) 28e
comics fumetti 28d
comma virgola 19c, 19f
command comando 42b
commandment comandamento 11d
commerce, trade commercio 37e, 38d
commercial spot 20b
commercial channel canale commerciale 20b
commercial school istituto commerciale 37a
commission commissione 43a
commission of inquiry commissione d'inchiesta 43a
committee comitato 43a
communicate comunicare 17a
communication comunicazione 9b, 17a
communication media mezzi (m, pl) di comunicazione 9b
communication sciences scienze della comunicazione 37e
communion comunione 11d
communiqué comunicato stampa 20a
communism comunismo 43a
commuter pendolare 34, 36a
compact compatto 3b
compact car utilitaria 34

compact disc compact disc 20b, 28c

company ditta 38d

company lawyer giurista d'impresa 38a

company policy politica aziendale 38d

compare paragonare 17a

comparison paragone 17a

compartment scompartimento 34

compass bussola, compasso 2b, 13d, 34, 37b

compatible compatibile 42b

compatible software software compatibile 25c, 38c

compensate indennizzare 26b

compete concorrere 27b

competent, skilled competente 11e

competition concorrenza, agonismo 25a, 27b, 38d

competitor concorrente 38d

compiler of a volume curatore (-trice) 28d

complain lamentarsi 17a, 21a, 35a

complaint lamentela 17a, 21a, 35a

complementary complementare 2b

complex complesso 1d

complexion carnagione 12a

complicated complicato 22a

Compliments! Complimenti! 29c

composer compositore (-trice) 25j, 28c

composition componimento, tema, composizione 25j, 28c, 37f

compost miscela fertilizzante 14a

compound composto 13c

compound interest interesse composto 26a

compulsory education istruzione obbligatoria 37a

computer computer 19d, 38c, 42b

computer science informatica 42b

computer scientist informatico (-a) 38a

computer-learning apprendimento tramite computer 37f

concave concavo 2b

conceited pieno di sé 21a

conceive concepire 22b

concept concetto 22a

concert concerto 25j, 29b

concise conciso 28d

conclude concludere 17a

conclusion conclusione 17a

concrete concreto 22a

concrete (cement) cemento 13c

concussion commozione cerebrale 40a

conditional condizionale 8a

condom preservativo 25h, 40a

condominium condominio 23e, 36a

conductor conduttore (-trice) 34

cone cono 2a

confederation confederazione 43a

conference convegno 37f

confess confessarsi 11d

confession confessione 11d

confessional box confessionale 11d

confidence vote fiducia 43a

confidential confidenziale 19e

confirm confermare 17a

confirmation cresima 11d

conflict conflitto 44d

conformist conformista 11e

confusing confusionario 28d

Congolese congolese 30e

congratulate congratulare 17a

congratulations congratulazioni 16c, 17a, 29c

congregation congregazione 11d

conical conico 3d

conjugation coniugazione 8a

conjunction congiunzione 8a

Connect Connetta 42c

connection coincidenza 32a, 34

conscience coscienza 22a

conscientious coscienzioso 11e, 22a

consecutive consecutivo 2b

conservative conservatore (-trice) 43a

conservatory conservatorio 25j, 28c, 37a

consonant consonante 8a

conspiracy, frame-up complotto 39b

constant costante 1f

constipation stitichezza 40a

constitution costituzione 43a

consulate consolato 43a

consult, look up consultare 17a

consultant consulente 38a

consumer consumatore (-trice) 38d

consumer good bene di consumo 38d

consumer protection tutela del consumatore 38d

contact contatto 21a

contact lenses lenti a contatto 12d

contain contenere 3e

container contenitore 3e

contents contenuto 3e

contest, dispute contestare 17a

continent continente 13d, 30a

continental continentale 6a, 13d

contraceptive contraccettivo 25h, 40a

contraceptive pill pillola anticoncezionale 25h, 40a

contract contratto 38d

contradict contraddire 17a

contralto contralto 28c

contrast contrasto 28d

contributor collaboratore (-trice) 20a

Control Controlla 42c

controversial, polemical polemico 28d

controversy controversia 41

convalescence convalescenza 40a

convent convento 11d

conventional weapon arma convenzionale 44d

conversation conversazione 17a

converse conversare 17a

convex convesso 2b

convince convincere 22a, 22b, 41

cook cuoco (-a), cucinare 24a, 38a

cooker, stove cucina 23b

cooking pot pentola 23c

cool fresco 6a

coordinate coordinata 2b

copilot copilota 32c

copper rame 13c

copy copia, copiare 19c, 19d, 42c

copy shop copisteria 25c

coral corallo 25i

cordial cordiale 21a

cordiality cordialità 21a

corduroy fustagno 13c

core subject materia fondamentale 37f

cork sughero 13c

cork cap tappo di sughero 23c

corn granturco, mais 14a, 24c

corn, callus callo 40a

cornea cornea 12d

corner angolo 33a

cornflower fiordaliso 14b

coroner magistrato (investigatore) 39b

corporation società 38d

corpulent corpulento 11a

correct, proper corretto 21a

correspondence corrispondenza 19e

correspondence course corso per corrispondenza 37a

correspondent   corrispondente
19e
corridor   corridoio   23a
corrupt   vizioso, corrotto   11e
Corsica   Corsica   30c
Corsican   corso   30c
cortisone   cortisone   25h, 40a
cosecant   cosecante   2b
cosine   coseno   2b
cosmetic   cosmetico   12f, 25f
cosmetics, perfume shop
profumeria   25f
cosmos   cosmo   13a
cost   costare   24n, 25a
cost price   prezzo di costo   38d
Costa Rica   Costa Rica   30b
Costa Rican   costaricano   30e
costly, expensive   costoso   25a
costume   costume   28e
cotangent   cotangente   2b
cotton   cotone   13c, 25l
cough   tosse, tossire   40a
cough syrup   sciroppo contro la
tosse   25h, 40a
coughing fit   colpo di tosse
40a
council   consiglio   43a
Council of Europe   Consiglio
d'Europa   43a
council of ministers   consiglio dei
ministri   43a
councilor   consigliere   43a
count   contare   1f
counter   banco   25a
counterfeit money   moneta falsa
26a
countersign   controfirmare   19e
countersignature   controfirma
19e
country   paese   13d
country of origin   paese d'origine
43a
country, nation   nazione   30a
countryside   campagna, paesaggio
36b
coupon, voucher   buono   20c
courageous   coraggioso   11e
courier   corriere   19e

courier bus, express   corriera
34
course   corso   37a
course, dish   piatto   24a
court   tribunale   41
court for public funds   corte dei
conti   41
court for serious crimes   corte
d'assise   41
court of appeal   corte d'appello
41
court-appointed lawyer
difensore d'ufficio   39b
courteous   cortese   11e
courthouse   tribunale   36a
courtroom   aula del tribunale
41
courtroom hearing   udienza in
tribunale   41
cousin   cugino, cugina   10a
cove   insenatura   13b
cover charge   coperto   24l
cover, covering   fodera   23b
cover, dust jacket   copertina
20a, 25n
covering, bandage   benda   25h
cow   mucca   15a
cowardly   codardo   11e
cowboy movie   film western   28a
crab   granchio   15c
cracker   cracker   24c
crackle, squeak   scricchiolare
12c
crafts   artigianato   36b
crawl   strisciare carponi   3f
crazy   pazzo, matto   11e
creak   cigolio, cigolare   12c
cream   crema   25h, 25f, 40a
creamery   cremeria   24m
creative   creativo   11e, 22a
creativity   creatività   22a
credit   credito   26a
credit card   carta di credito
25a, 26a
credit institute, trust   istituto di
credito   26a
credit letter   lettera di credito
26b

cyclamen   ciclamino   14b
cycling   ciclismo   27b
cylinder   cilindro   2a
cylindrical   cilindrico   3d
cymbal   piatto   28c
cypress   cipresso   14c
cyst   cisti   40a
Czech   ceco   30e
Czech Republic   Repubblica Ceca   30b

D

dad   papà   10a
daffodil   trombone   14b
dahlia   dalia   14b
daily   quotidianamente   4b
daily newspaper   quotidiano   20a, 25n
dairy product   latticino   24h
dairy shop, milk store   latteria   24m
daisy   margherita   14b
damages   danni   26b
Damn it!   Accidenti!   21a
dance   ballo, danza, ballare   28c
dance music   musica da ballo   25j, 28c
dancer   ballerino (-a)   28c
dandruff   forfora   12b
danger   pericolo   39a
Danish   danese   30e
dare   osare   21a
dark   buio, scuro   6a, 7b, 12d
dark blue   blu   7a
dark mood   umore nero   7a
dark room   camera oscura   25d, 28b
dark skin   pelle nera   11a
dark-haired   bruno   11a
darkness   oscurità   12d
dash   trattino   19c
dashboard   cruscotto   33c
data bank   banca dati   42b
data file   file dati   42b
data processing   elaborazione dati   42b
date (calendar)   data   19c, 38b

date (fruit)   dattero   14d, 24g
date (with someone)   appuntamento   29b
date and place of birth   data e luogo di nascita   38b
date of birth   data di nascita   11f
datum, data   dato, dati   42b
daughter   figlia   10a
daughter-in-law   nuora   10a
dawn, sunrise   alba   4b
day   giorno   4b
day after tomorrow   dopodomani   4b
day before yesterday   l'altro ieri   4b
day of the week   giorno della settimana   4b
daycare   asilo nido   37a
deacon, deaconess   diacono (-essa)   11d
deadly sin   peccato mortale   11d
deaf   sordo   12c
deafness   sordità   12c
deal   affare   26b
deal with   trattare   28d
dean, chair of a faculty   preside di facoltà   37a
dear friend   caro (-a) amico (-a)   10b
Dear John   Caro Giovanni   19b
Dear Madam   Gentile Signora   19a
Dear Madam or Sir   Spettabile (Spett.le) Ditta   19a
Dear Mary   Cara Maria   19b
Dear Sir   Egregio Signore   19a
Dearest John   Carissimo Giovanni   19b
Dearest Mary   Carissima Maria   19b
death   morte   11c
death certificate   certificato di morte   11c
death penalty   pena di morte   44b
debate   dibattito, dibattere   17a, 41

debit, bill, debt debito 26a
decade decennio 4b, 43b
decagon decagono 2a
deceased, late defunto 11c
December dicembre 5b
decency decenza 21a
decent decente 21a
decentralization decentramento 43a
decimal decimale 1d, 1f
decipher decifrare 17a
deck chair sedia a sdraio 36b
declarative dichiarativa 8a
declare dichiarare 17a, 31
decline declino 43b
decor, decoration arredamento 23b
decorum decoro 21a
decrease, diminish diminuzione, diminuire 3b
decree decreto 43a
deduction detrazione 26b
deep profondo 3c
deer cervo 15a
defame, libel diffamare 20a
defeat sconfitta, sconfiggere 27b, 43b
defecate defecare 12b
defend one's thesis discutere la tesi 37f
defend oneself difendersi 41
defense difesa 43b
defense lawyer difensore (difenditrice) 39b
deferent deferente 21a
deferred sentence sentenza di rinvio a giudizio 41
deficit deficit 26a
define definire 17a
definite (article) determinativo 8a
definition definizione 20a
deflation deflazione 26a
degenerate degenerato 21a
degree (university) laurea 37f
degree grado 2b, 6c
dehydrated disidratato 40a
dehydration disidratazione 40a

delete cancellare 19c, 42b
Delete Annulla 42c
delicate delicato 11a, 25g, 25l
delicatessen salumeria 24m
delicious squisito 12e
Delighted! Molto lieto (-a)! 16b
delinquency delinquenza 39b
delivery consegna 25a, 38d
democracy democrazia 43a
democratic party partito democratico 43a
democratic society società democratica 43a
demographic demografico 13d
demonstrate dimostrare 22b
demonstration dimostrazione, manifestazione 38d, 43a
demonstrative dimostrativo 8a
Denmark Danimarca 30b
denomination confessione 11d
dense denso 3b
density densità 3b
dent ammaccatura 33d
dental assistant assistente 40b
dentist dentista 40b
dentist's office gabinetto dentistico 40b
deny negare 17a
deodorant deodorante 25f
department reparto 25a
department store grande magazzino 25a
departmental manager caporeparto 38a
departure partenza 32b, 34
dependency tossicodipendenza 44c
dependent persona a carico 11c
deposit versamento, versare 26a
deposit slip modulo di versamento 26a
deposition, testimony deposizione 41
depraved depravato 21a

depressed   depresso   11e, 21a
depressed area   zona depressa   44b
depression   depressione   21a, 40a
depth   profondità   3c
dermatitis   dermatite   40a
descend   scendere   3f
descent   discesa   3f
describe   descrivere   17a
description   descrizione   17a, 39b
descriptive (adjective)   qualificativo   8a
descriptive geometry   geometria descrittiva   1g
desert   deserto   13b
design   disegno   3d, 37e
desk   banco   37b
desperate   disperato   11e, 21a
desperation   disperazione   21a
despite   malgrado, nonostante   8i
dessert   dessert, dolce   24c
dessert dish   coppa da dessert   23c
dessert fork   forchettina   23c
destroy   distruggere   39a
detain   detenere   41
detective movie   film poliziesco   28a
detention   detenzione   41
detergent   detergente   25g
detest   detestare   21b
detoxify oneself   disintossicarsi   44c
devaluation   svaluta   26a
devalue   svalutare   26a
develop   sviluppare   28d
devil   diavolo   11d
devotion   devozione   11d
devout   devoto   11d, 21a
dew   rugiada   6a
diabetes   diabete   40a
diagnose   diagnosticare   40a
diagnosis   diagnosi   40a
diagonal   diagonale   2b
dial   quadrante   4d, 25i

dial the number   comporre il numero, fare il numero   18b
dialogue   dialogo   17a, 28e
Dialogue Window   Finestra di Dialogo   42c
diameter   diametro   2a
diamond   diamante   11c, 25i
diaphragm   diaframma   12a
diary   diario   25n, 28d
dice   dadi   27a
dictionary   vocabolario, dizionario, lessico   20a, 28d
die   morire   11c
die (singular of dice)   dado   27a
diet   dieta   40a
difference   differenza   1f
differential calculus   calcolo differenziale   1g
difficult   difficile   22a
diffusion, spread   diffusione   3c
dig   vangare, scavare   14a
digestion   digestione   12b
digestive system   sistema digerente   12b
digit   cifra   1d
digital   digitale   18a, 42b
digital camera   macchina fotografica digitale   25d
digital photography   fotografia digitale   25d, 28b
digital watch   orologio digitale   4d
diligent   diligente   11e
dimension   dimensione   3b, 3c
dimple   fossetta (del mento)   11a, 12a
dining room   sala da pranzo   23a
dinner   cena   24a
dinner jacket   smoking   25k
diploma   diploma   11f, 37f
diplomatic   diplomatico   11e
direct   diretto   8a, 21a
direct call   telefonata in teleselezione   18b

direction direzione 3c
director regista 28a, 28e
director, CEO dirigente 38a
dirty sporco 11a, 25g, 25l
disadvantage svantaggio 44b
disagree non essere d'accordo 21a
disagreement malinteso, disaccordo 17a, 21a
disappoint deludere 21a
disappointed deluso 21a
disarmament disarmo 44d
disc disco 12a, 20b
disc jockey disc jockey 20b
disc, puck disco 27b
discipline disciplina 37e
disco discoteca 28c, 29b
discomfort malessere 40a
discount sconto 25a, 26a, 38d
discount rate tasso di sconto 26a
discourse discorso 8a
discuss, argue discutere 17a, 41
discussion, argument discussione 17a
disease malattia, morbo 40a
disgust disgusto, disgustare 21a, 21b
disgusted disgustato 11e, 21b
dish piatto 23c
dish cloth strofinaccio per i piatti 23b
dish towel asciugapiatti 23b
dishwasher lavapiatti, lavastoviglie 23b
dishonest disonesto 11e
dishonorable disonorevole 21a
disinterested disinteressato 11e
disk disco 3d
diskette dischetto 19f, 25c
dislike antipatia, non piacere 21b
dislocated slogato 40a
dislocation slogatura 40a
dispatch dispaccio 20a
display, exhibition mostra 25a

disposal, waste scarico 44a
dissatisfaction insoddisfazione 21a
dissatisfied insoddisfatto 21a
dissertation dissertazione 25n, 28d, 37f
dissolute dissoluto 21a
dissuade dissuadere 22a, 22b
distance distanza 3c, 33a
distortion distorsione 42a
distress phone line telefono amico 18b
district quartiere 36a
ditch fosso, fossato 14a
diuretic diuretico 40a
dive tuffarsi 27b
diver tuffatore (-trice) 27b
divide dividere 1e
divided by diviso (per) 1e
dividend dividendo 38d
diving tuffo 27b
division divisione 1e
divorce divorzio, divorziare 11c
divorced divorziato (-a) 11c, 11f, 38b
dizziness giramento di testa 40a
DNA DNA 39b
docile docile 21a
doctor medico, dottore (-essa) 38a, 39c, 40a
doctor's office gabinetto medico 40a
document cartella, documento 38c, 42b, 43b
document cover copertina 38c
documentary documentario, filmato 28a
dodecahedron dodecaedro 2a
dodge schivare 3f
dog cane 15a
doll bambola 27a
Dolomites Dolomiti 30c
Dominican (national) dominicano 30e
Dominican (relig.) domenicano 11d

Dominican Republic Repubblica Dominicana 30b
Don't be stupid (silly)! Non fare (faccia) lo stupido (-a)! 16c
Don't mention it! Figurati! Si figuri! 16c
Don't talk nonsense! Non dire (dica) schiocchezze! 16c
donkey asino 15a
doodle scarabocchio 28d
door porta 23a
doorbell campanello 23a
door-knob maniglia 23a
doorman, doorwoman portiere (-a) 35a
doormat stuoia d'entrata 23b
dosage posologia 25h, 40a
dot punto 3d, 19f
double doppio, raddoppiare 1b, 3b
double bass contrabbasso 28c
double bass player contrabbassista 28c
double bed letto matrimoniale 35b
double-breasted jacket giacca a doppio petto 25k
double chin doppio mento 11a
double citizenship doppia cittadinanza 11f
double room camera doppia 35a
double salary paga doppia 38d
doubt dubbio, dubitare 22a, 22b
doubtful dubbioso 22a
dove colomba 15b
down giù 3c, 36c
down-payment caparra 30a
downhill skiing sci da discesa 27b
downloading downloading (m, inv), scaricare 42d
downpour pioggia insistente 6a
downtown centro 11f, 36a
downtrodden avvilito 11e
dowry dote 11c
dozen dozzina 1b

draft bozza 19d, 28d, 38c
draft beer birra alla spina 24j
draft, promissory note cambiale 26a
draftsperson geometra 11f, 16b
dragonfly libellula 15d
drama dramma 25n, 28d, 28e
draw, design disegnare 2b, 37f
draw, tie pareggio, pareggiare 27b
drawer cassetto 23b
drawing disegno 28b, 37f
drawing instruments strumenti del disegno 2b
drawing paper carta da disegno 37b
dream sogno, sognare 22a, 22b
dress, clothing, suit vestito, abito 25k
dress, get dressed vestirsi 25l
dresser comò 35b
dresser, sideboard credenza 23b
dressing fascia 25h, 40a
dressing room cabina 25k
dressing-table toilette 23b
dried cod baccalà 24e
drill trapano 23d, 25b, 40b
drink, beverage bere, bevanda 12b, 24n, 24j
drinking can lattina 23c
drinking glass bicchiere 23c, 24k
drive guidare 3f, 33a
driver autista, conducente, guidatore (-trice) 27b, 33a, 38d
driver's license patente (di guida) 33a
drizzle pioggerellina 6a
drizzly piovigginoso 6a
drop goccia 6a, 25h, 40a
drop out abbandonare gli studi 37f
drowsiness sonnolenza 40a
drug addict tossicodipendente 44c

drug addiction tossicodipendenza 40a, 44c

drug pusher spacciatore (-trice) di droga 39b, 44c

drug pushing spaccio di droga 39b

drug traffic traffico degli stupefacenti, di droga 39b, 44c

drug trafficker trafficante di droga 39b

drugs droga, stupefacenti 44c

drum, tambourine tamburo 28c

drummer batterista 28c

dry asciutto, secco 6a

dry cleaner lavanderia a secco 25g

dry oneself asciugarsi 12f

dry skin pelle secca 11a

dubbed doppiato 28a

dubbing doppiaggio 28a

duck anatra (anitra) 15b, 24d

duet duetto 28c

dull cupo, spento 7b

dull life una vita grigia 7a

dumplings gnocchi 24b

dung letame 14a

duplicate duplicare 19c, 38c, 42b

duration durata 4c

during durante 4c

dust pan paletta per la spazzatura 23b

dustbin pattumiera 23b

duster piumino 23b

Dutch olandese 30e

duty tax tassa 31

DVD DVD 20b, 25j

dwell, live in abitare 36a

dwelling abitazione 23a

dynamic dinamico 11e

E

e-mail e-mail, posta elettronica 19f, 38c, 42b

e-mail address indirizzo elettronico, e-mail 19f, 38b

e-ticket biglietto elettronico 32a

each, every ogni 3b

eager desideroso 21a

eagle aquila 15b

ear orecchio 12a

ear (of corn) spiga 14a

ear infection otite 40a

eardrum timpano 12a

early presto, in anticipo 4c, 8j, 32b

earn guadagnare 38d

earphone auricolare 18a

earring orecchino 25i

Earth Terra 5c, 13a

earthquake terremoto 13b

easel cavalletto (da pittore) 28b

east est 3c, 13d, 36c

Easter Pasqua 5f, 29a

eastern orientale 3c, 13d

Easterner, Oriental orientale 30e

easy facile 22a

eat mangiare 12b, 24n

Eat up! Buon appetito! 24k

e-banking e-banking (m, inv) 26a

ebony ebano 13c, 14c

ecclesiastic ecclesiastico 11d

echo echeggiare 12c

eclipse eclissi 13a

economics economia 37e

economy economia 43a

economy class classe turistica 30a

Ecuador Ecuador 30b

Ecuadorian ecuadoriano 30e

edge orlo, margine 3c

edge, bank sponda 13b

Edinburgh Edinburgo 30c

edit redigere, editare 20a

Edit Modifica 42c

editing montaggio, editing 28a, 42b

editor redattore (-trice) 20a, 38a

editor-in-chief caporedattore (-trice) 20a

editorial articolo di fondo 20a

editorial offices redazione 20a

educate, instruct istruire 37a

educated   istruito   37f

education   istruzione   37a, 37f, 38b

education (as process)   educazione   37a

education (level)   titolo di studio   11f, 38b

eel   anguilla   15c, 24e

effective   efficace   21a

efficient   efficiente   21a

egg   uovo   24h

egg-beater   frullino   23c

eggplant   melanzana   14e, 24f

egoism   egoismo   21a

egoist, self-centered   egoista   11e

Egypt   Egitto   30b

Egyptian   egiziano   30e

eight   otto   1a

eighteen   diciotto   1a

eighth   ottavo   1b

eighty   ottanta   1a

El Salvador   El Salvador   30b

elaborate   elaborato   28d

elastic   elastico   13c

Elba   Elba   30c

elbow   gomito   12a

elect   eleggere   43a

elected representative   deputato (-a)   43a

election   elezione   43a

electoral campaign   campagna elettorale   43a

electric car   automobile elettrica   33c

electric outlet   presa (elettrica)   23d, 25b

electric piano   piano elettrico   28c

electric razor   rasoio elettrico   12f, 25f

electric toy train   trenino elettrico   27a

electrical   elettrico   13c

electrician   elettricista   38a

electricity   elettricità   13c, 23d

electrocardiogram   elettrocardiogramma   40a

electron   elettrone   13c

electronic file   archivio elettronico   42b

elegant   elegante   11e, 25l

elegy   elegia   28d

elementary school   scuola elementare   37a

elementary school pupil   scolaro (-a)   37d

elementary teacher   maestro (-a)   37d

elephant   elefante   15a

elevator   ascensore   23e, 35a

eleven   undici   1a

eleventh   undicesimo   1b

eliminate   eliminare   27b, 42c

elimination round   girone eliminatorio   27b

elm   olmo   14c

eloquent   eloquente   11e, 17a

emaciated   emaciato   11a

embassy   ambasciata   43a

embezzlement   appropriazione indebita   39b

emblem   emblema   3d

embrace, hug   abbracciare   3f

embroider   ricamare   27a

embroidery   ricamo   27a

emerald   smeraldo   25i

emergency   pronto soccorso   39c

emergency exit   uscita di sicurezza (emergenza)   23e, 39a

Emergency lane   Corsia d'emergenza   33b

emetic   emetico   40a

emigrant   emigrante   44d

emigration   emigrazione   44d

Emilia   Emilia Romagna   30d

emission   emissione   42a

emphasize   sottolineare   17a, 28d

employee   dipendente   11f, 38d

employer   datore di lavoro   11f, 38d

employment   lavoro   11f, 38d

employment agency   agenzia di collocamento   38d

empty   vuoto   3b

enamel   smalto   13c

enchanting   incantevole   21a

enclose, attach accludere, allegare 19c

enclosed, attached accluso, allegato 19c

enclosed, surrounded circoscritto, racchiuso 3d

enclosure recinto 3d

encourage incoraggiare 21a

encouraged incoraggiato 21a

encyclopedia enciclopedia 20a, 25n, 37b

end, finish fine, finire 3f, 4c

endorse avallare 26a

endorsement girata 26a

enemy nemico (-a) 10b

energetic energico 11a

energy energia 13c, 44a

energy conservation conservazione dell'energia 44a

energy crisis crisi energetica 44a

energy waste spreco d'energia 44a

engagement fidanzamento 11c, 29a

engagement ring anello di fidanzamento 25i

engineer ingegnere 11f, 16b, 38a

engineering ingegneria 37e

engineering faculty facoltà di ingegneria 37a

England Inghilterra 30b

English inglese 30e

enjoy oneself, have fun divertirsi 21a, 29b

enlarge allargare 25l

Enlightenment Illuminismo 43b

enough abbastanza 8j, 3b

Enough! Basta! 21c

ensure assicurare 17a

enter entrare 3f, 36c

entire intero 3b

entrance ingresso 23e, 33b, 35a

entrance exam esame d'ammissione 37f

envelope busta 19d, 25c, 38c

envious invidioso 11e

environment ambiente 13b, 44a

environmentalist ambientalista 44a

epidemic epidemia 40a

epigram epigramma 28d

epileptic fit crisi epilettica 40a

episode episodio 25n, 28d

epoch epoca 43b

equality uguaglianza 1f

equation equazione 1f

equation in one unknown equazione a una incognita 1f

equation in two unknowns equazione a due incognite 1f

equator equatore 13d

equilateral equilatero 2a

equinox equinozio 4c, 5c

era era 43b

erase, delete cancellare 19c, 37f, 42b

eraser gomma 25c, 37b

erotic erotico 21a

error errore 37f

erudite erudito 11e

eruption eruzione 13b

escape evasione 39b

esophagus esofago 12a

espionage spionaggio 44d

essay saggio 25n, 28d

essay-writing saggistica 28d

estate (succession) successione 11c

estate, villa, large home villa 23a

estimable stimabile 21a

Estonia Estonia 30b

Estonian estone 30e

estrogen estrogeno 40a

estuary estuario 13b

etching disegno a matita 28b

ether etere 13c

Ethiopia Etiopia 30b

Ethiopian etiope 30e

Etna Etna 30c

Eucharist Eucarestia 11d
Euclidean geometry geometria euclidea 1g
euro euro 26a, 43a
Europe Europa 30b
European europeo 30e
evaluation, grading valutazione 37f
evangelist evangelista 11d
evasive evasivo 21a
even pari , uguale 1d, 3d
even though anche se 8i
evening sera 4b, 25l
evening attire abito, vestito da sera 25k
evening course corso serale 37a
evening school scuola serale 37a
evergreen sempreverde 14c
every once in a while di tanto in tanto 4c
Everybody out! Tutti fuori! 39a
everyone tutti, ciascuno, ognuno 3b, 8h
everything tutto 8h
everywhere dappertutto 36c
eviction sfratto 23e
evidence prove 41
examination esame 37f
examine visitare 40a
examine the witness interrogare il testimone 41
exchange cambio, cambiare 25a, 26a
exclamation mark punto esclamativo 19c
exclamatory esclamativa 8a
excursion, tour gita 30a
excuse scusa 17a
Excuse me! Scusa! Scusi! Mi scusi! 16c
excuse oneself scusarsi 17a
executive esecutivo 43a
exercise esercizio 37f
exhale espirare 12b
exhibition mostra 28b
exist esistere 22b
existence esistenza 22a

exit uscita 23e, 33b, 35a
exit, go out uscire 36c
Exodus Esodo 11d
expand espandere 3b
expansion espansione 3b
expectant mother futura mamma 11c
expectorant espettorante 25h, 40a
expenses spese , uscite 26b
expensive caro 24n, 25a
explain spiegare 17a, 28d
explanation spiegazione 17a
explode, blast scoppiare 12c
exponent esponente 1f
export esportare 26b
express esprimere 17a
express mail posta celere 19e
express oneself esprimersi 17a
expression espressione 11a, 17a
extension estensione 3b, 3c
extension cord filo di prolungamento 23b
external affairs affari esteri 43a
extinguish, put out spegnere il fuoco 39a
extract the root estrarre la radice 1e
extradition estradizione 41
extraordinary straordinario 11e
extremely angry giallo dalla rabbia 7a
extroverted estroverso 11e
eye occhio 12a
eyewitness testimone oculare 41
eyedrop collirio 25h, 40a
eyeliner matita per gli occhi 25f
eye shadow mascara 25f
eyebrow sopracciglio 12a
eyeglasses occhiali 12d
eyelash ciglio 12a
eyelid palpebra 12a

F

fable favola 25n, 28d
fabric tessuto 25g, 25l
façade facciata 23a
face faccia 12a
Facebook Facebook (m, inv) 19g, 42d
Facebook profile profilo 42d
face powder cipria 25f
face, countenance faccia, viso 11a
facial cream crema per il viso 25f
faction fazione 43b
factor fattore, fattorizzare 1f
factorization fattorizzazione 1f
factory fabbrica 38d
faculty facoltà 37a
fade sbiadire 12d
Fahrenheit Fahrenheit 6c
fail essere bocciato 37f
fail (someone) bocciare 37f
fainting spell svenimento 40a
fairy tale fiaba 25n, 28d
faith fede 11d
faithful fedele 11d, 11e
falcon falcone 15b
fall caduta, cadere 3f
fall asleep addoremntarsi 12b
fall down cadere per terra 3f
fall in love innamorarsi 11c
fall in prices ribasso dei prezzi 26b
fallow, uncultivated incolto 14a
false falso 25i
false teeth, denture dentiera 40b
family famiglia 10a
family doctor medico di famiglia 40a
family friend amico (-a) di famiglia 10b
family relation parentela 10a
family tree albero genealogico 11c
fan ventola, ventilatore 23a, 33c

fanatic fanatico 21a
fandango fandango 28c
Fantastic! Fantastico! 16c
far lontano 3c, 8j, 36c
far-fetched, unusual inconsueto 28d
far-sighted ipermetrope 12d
farm fattoria 15a
farmer contadino (-a) 15a, 38a
farmland terreno agrario 13b, 14a
fascinating affascinante 11a
fashion moda 25k
fashion magazine rivista di moda 20a, 25n
fast (from food) digiuno 11d
fast veloce 3f
fat grasso 11a
father padre 10a
father-in-law suocero 10a
faucet rubinetto 23a, 35b
fault, guilt colpa 41
fax fax 18a, 38c
fear, be afraid paura, avere paura (di) 21a
fearful pauroso, timoroso 11e, 21a
Feast of the Assumption Ferragosto 5f, 29a
feather penna 15b
featherweight peso piuma 27b
feature (film) lungometraggio 28a
February febbraio 5b
federation federazione 43a
fee tariffa 42a
feel bad sentirsi male, stare male 12b
feel like avere voglia di 21a
feel nauseous avere la nausea 40a
feel well sentirsi bene, stare bene 12b
feeling sensibilità 21a
felt feltro 13c
felt hat cappello di feltro 25k
felt pen pennarello 7b

female femmina, femminile 11a, 38b

female dog cagna 15a

feminine femminile 8a, 11a

fence recinto 15a

fencing scherma 27b

fencing suit divisa 27b

fender parafango 33c

fennel finocchio 14e, 24f

fermentation fermentazione 14a

ferry traghetto 34

fertilizer fertilizzante 14a

fetid fetido 12e

fettuccine fettuccine 24b

feudal feudale 43b

fever, temperature febbre 40a

fiancé, fiancée fidanzato, (-a) 10b

fiber fibra 13c, 25g, 25l

fiberglass lana di vetro 13c

fiction, narrative narrativa 20a, 25n

fidelity fedeltà 42a

field campo 13b, 27b

field (of study) campo (di studio) 37f

field of grass prato 13b

field trip gita scolastica 37f

fierce violento, feroce 21a

fifteen quindici 1a

fifth quinto 1b

fifty cinquanta 1a

fifty-one cinquantuno 1a

fifty-three cinquantatré 1a

fifty-two cinquantadue 1a

fig fico 14c, 14d, 24g

fight battersi, picchiarsi, lotta 39b, 44d

figure figura 2a

file (office) archivio, file, scheda 38c, 42b, 42c

file (tool) lima 23d, 25b

file away schedare 38c

file folder cartella, scheda 25c, 38c

file manager file manager 42b

file name titolo del documento 38c, 42b

filet filetto 24a

filing cabinet, box file schedario 38c

filing card, filing folder scheda 25c

Filipino filippino 30e

fill riempire 3b

fill a tooth impiombare un dente 40b

fill out compilare 38c

fill up fare il pieno 33a

filling piombatura 40b

film pellicola 25d

film critic critico del cinema 20a

film, movie film 28a

filter filtro 13c, 33c

fin, flipper pinna 15c

final score risultato finale 27b

finalist finalista 27b

finance finanziare 26b

financier finanziere 26a

Find Trova 42c

fine arts belle arti 28b

fine, traffic ticket multa 33a

Fine, Well! Bene! 16a

finger, toe dito 12a

fingernail unghia 12a

fingerprint impronta digitale 39b

finish school finire la scuola 11f

Finland Finlandia 30b

Finnish finlandese 30e

fir abete 14c

fire incendio, fuoco 13c, 39a

Fire! Al fuoco! 39a, 39b

fire (from work) licenziare 38d

fire extinguisher estintore 39a

fire hose pompa 39a

fire hydrant idrante 39a

fire insurance assicurazione contro l'incendio 26a

fire truck autopompa 39a

firearm arma da fuoco 39b

firefighter vigile del fuoco 39a

fireproof antincendio 39a

firing licenziamento 38d

firm, company azienda 38d
first primo, prima 1b, 8a, 8j
first aid pronto soccorso 25h, 39a, 39c
first class prima classe 30a
first course primo piatto 24a
first name nome 11f
first year primo anno 37a
first-born primogenito 11c
fish pesce, pescare 15c, 24e, 27a
fish shop pescheria 24m
fishing pesca 15c, 27a, 36b
fishing rod canna 15c
fishmonger pescivendolo 38a
fist pugno 12a
fitted carpet moquette 23b
five cinque 1a
five thousand cinquemila 1a
five-star hotel albergo a cinque stelle 35a
fix, repair aggiustare, riparare 25l, 33a
fixed price prezzo fisso 24l, 25a
fixed wage stipendio fisso 38d
fixture, installation impianto 23a
flame fiamma 39a
flamingo fenicottero 15b
flannel flanella 13c, 25g
flash lampeggiare 6a
flash of lightning lampo 6a
flashlight, battery pila 23d, 25b
flat-chested col seno piatto 11a
flat-heeled con tacco piatto 25m
flatter lusingare 21a
flattery lusinga 21a
flatworm verme 15d
flautist flautista 28c
flavor sapore, gusto 12e
flea pulce 15d
flea market mercato delle pulci 25a
flesh carne 12a

fleshy carnoso 11a
flexible flessibile 11e
flier dépliant 20c
flight volo 32b
flight attendant assistente di volo 32c
flight of stairs rampa 23e
fling lanciare 3f
flint selce 13c
flood alluvione 13b
floor pavimento 23a
floor level piano 23e, 35a
floor tile piastrella 23a
Florence Firenze 30c
florist fiorista, fioraio (-a) 38a
flour farina 24c
flow scorrere 13b
flower fiore, fiorire 14a
flower basket canestro di fiori 3e
flower garden, flower bed aiuola 14a
flu, influenza influenza 40a
fluorescent fluorescente 25b
flush tirare lo sciacquone 23f
flute flauto 28c
fly, zipper cerniera 25g, 25l
flying time durata del volo 32c
foam schiuma 13b
focus fuoco, mettere a fuoco 25d
fodder foraggio 14a
fog nebbia 6a
foggy nebbioso 6a
folding chair sedia pieghevole 23b
foliage fogliame 14a
folk music musica folk, musica folcloristica 25j, 28c
follow seguire 3f, 36c
food cibo 24a
food poisoning intossicazione alimentare 40a
food store negozio di alimentari 24m
foot piede 3a, 12a
foot racing corsa podistica 27b
footage metraggio 28a

football (American) football americano 27b
footlights luci di ribalta 28e
footnote nota a piè di pagina 19c
footpath, trail sentiero 36b
footwear calzatura 25m
for per 8f
for example per esempio 44e
for sale in vendita 25a
for three days da tre giorni 4c
forearm avambraccio 12a
forecourt cortile 23a
foreground primo piano 28b
foreign country paese straniero 43a
foreign currency valuta straniera 31
foreigner straniero (-a) 31
forensic science medicina legale 39b
forest foresta, bosco 13b
forger contraffattore (-trice) 39b
forgery contraffazione 39b
forget dimenticare 22a, 22b
forget-me-not miosotide 14b
forgetful smemorato 22a
fork forchetta 23c, 24k
form forma 3d
form (to fill out) modulo 26a, 31
format format, formattare 38c, 42b, 42c
formatted formattato 38c, 42b
Fortunately! Per fortuna! 21c
fortune teller chiromante 29b
forty quaranta 1a
forty-one quarantuno 1a
forty-third quarantatreesimo 1b
forty-three quarantatré 1a
forty-two quarantadue 1a
Forward Avanti 42c
Forward (e-mail) Inoltra 42c
forwarding address recapito 11f
fossil fossile 43b

fossil fuel combustibile 44a
foul weather tempaccio 6a
foundations fondamenta 23a
four quattro 1a
four thousand quattromila 1a
four-sided figure figura a quattro lati 2a
fourteen quattordici 1a
fourth quarto 1b
foyer, lobby atrio 35a
fraction frazione 1d
fractional frazionario 1d
fracture frattura 40a
fragrance fragranza 12e
frail, slender gracile 11a
frame cornice, inquadrare 3d, 28b, 28d
frame (bodily) ossatura 12a
France Francia 30b
franchise appalto 38d
franchiser appaltatore (-trice) 38d
Franciscan francescano 11d
fraternal fraterno 10a
fraud frode 39b
freckles lentiggini 11a, 12a
freckled lentigginoso 11a
free gratis 20c
free sample campione omaggio, esemplare omaggio 20c
free signal libero 18b
freedom on bail libertà su cauzione 41
freehand drawing disegno a mano libera 28b
freeze gelare 6a
freezer congelatore 23b
freezing point punto di congelamento 13c
French francese 30e
French fries patatine fritte 24a
French Riviera Costa Azzurra 30c
frenetic frenetico 21a
frequency frequenza 42a
frequent frequente 4c
fresco painting affresco 28b
fresh fresco 12e

Friday venerdì 5a
fried fritto 24a
friend amico (-a) 10b
friendly socievole 11e
friendship amicizia 10b, 21a
Friuli Friuli 30d
frivolous frivolo 11e
frizzy, fuzzy hair capelli crespi 11a
frog rana 15c
from da 3c, 8f
from my point of view dal mio punto di vista 44e
from now on d'ora in poi 4c
front fronte, facciata 3c
front seat sedile anteriore 33c
frost gelo 6a
frozen gelato, ghiacciato 6a
fruit frutta 14d, 24g
fruit basket canestro di frutta 3e
fruit bowl fruttiera 23c
fruit salad macedonia di frutta 24g
fruit vendor fruttivendolo 38a
fry friggere 24a
frying pan padella 23c
fuel carburante 13c
fugitive evaso (-a) 39b
full pieno 3b
full moon luna piena 13a
fullness ampiezza 3b
fun, enjoyment divertimento 21a
function funzione 1f
funding finanziamento 26a
funeral funerale 11c
funnel imbuto 23b
funny buffo 21a
fur coat pelliccia 25k
furious furioso 21a
furnish one's home ammobiliare la casa 23d
furniture mobili 23b
furrow solco 3d
fuse valvola 23d, 25b
fussy fastidioso 11e
future futuro 4c, 8a

G

gain guadagno 26b
gains, profits entrate 26b
galaxy galassia 13a
gallbladder cistifellea 12a
gallstones calcoli biliari 40a
game gioco 27a
game of chance gioco d'azzardo 27a
game, match partita 27b
garage garage 23a
garbage bin cestino dei rifiuti 23b
garbage truck autoimmondizie 34
garden giardino 14a, 23a
garden seat panchina 14a
gardener giardiniere (-a) 14a
gardening giardinaggio 27a
garlic aglio 14e, 24i
garment indumento 25k
gas benzina, gas 13c, 23d, 33a
gas attendant benzinaio (-a) 33a
gas pedal acceleratore 33c
gas pump pompa della benzina 33c
gas station stazione di servizio 33a
gas tank serbatoio 33c
gate, exit uscita 32b
gauze garza 13c, 39c
gears marcia 33a
gearshift leva del cambio 33c
Gemini Gemelli 5d
gemstone brillante, cristallo 25i
gender (grammatical) genere 8a
general strike sciopero generale 38d
generator dinamo 33c
generosity generosità 21a
generous generoso 11e
Geneva Ginevra 30c
Genoa Genova 30c
genre genere 25n, 28d

gentility, politeness gentilezza 21a

gentle gentile 11e

gentleman signore 11a

geographical geografico 13d

geography geografia 13d, 37e

geometric design disegno geometrico 28b

geometrical geometrico 2b

geometry geometria 1g, 2b, 37e

Georgia Georgia 30b

geranium geranio 14b

German tedesco 30e

German shepherd cane lupo 15a

Germany Germania 30b

gerund gerundio 8a

gesture gesto 3f

get a degree laurearsi 37f

get a diploma diplomarsi 37f

get a doctor chiamare un medico 39c

get a job procurarsi un lavoro 38d

get a suntan abbronzarsi 36b

get better migliorare 40a

get engaged fidanzarsi 11c

get going cominciare 3f

Get lost! Vattene! 21a

get married sposarsi 11c

get out uscire fuori 39a

get out of drugs uscire dalla droga 44a

get up, rise alzarsi 3f, 12b

ghetto ghetto 44b

giant gigante 11a

gift regalo 25a

gill branchia 15c

ginger zenzero 24i

giraffe giraffa 15a

girl ragazza 11b

girlfriend amica, ragazza 10b

give birth partorire 11c

give help dare aiuto 39a

Give my regards to Tanti saluti a, Salutami 19b

give oneself up consegnarsi alla polizia 39b

gladiolus gladiolo 14b

glance sguardo 12d

gland ghiandola 12a

glare at someone fissare qualcuno 12d

glass vetro 13c

glass cabinet vetrina 23b

glimpse occhiata fugace 12d

globe globo, mappamondo 13d

gloomy malinconico 11e

gloss paint, varnish lacca 23d

glove guanto 25k

glove compartment cassetto ripostiglio 33c

glow risplendere 12d

glowworm lucciola 15d

glue colla 19d, 25c, 37b

go andare 3f, 36c

go across attraversare 3f

Go ahead, speak! Di' (Dica) pure! 17b

go around andare in giro 3f

go away andare via, andarsene 3f

go backwards andare indietro 3f

go down scendere 36c

go forward andare avanti, fare marcia avanti 3f, 33a

go on foot andare a piedi 3f

go on strike scioperare 38d

go on the air andare in onda 20b

go on vacation andare in vacanza 29a

go out uscire 3f, 29b

go sightseeing andare in giro 36b

go through a red light passare col rosso 33a

Go to Vai a 42c

go to school andare a scuola 11f

Go to the Devil! Va' al diavolo! 21a

go toward andare verso 3f

go up salire 36c

goal rete, gol 27b

goaltender   portiere   27b
goat   capra   15a
God   Dio, Signore   11d
godchild   figlioccio (-a)   10a
godfather   padrino   10a
godmother   madrina   10a
gold   oro   7a, 13c, 25i
gold ring   anello d'oro   25i
golden   d'oro   11c
goldfish   pesce rosso   15c
golf   golf   27b
Good!   Bene!   16c
good (at heart)   buono   11e
Good afternoon, Hello!   Buon
    pomeriggio! Buona sera!   16a
Good-bye!   Arrivederci!
    ArrivederLa!   16a
good complexion   carnagione
    bella   11a
Good evening, Hello!   Buona
    sera!   16a
good figure, shapely   bella figura
    11a
good, final copy   bella copia
    37f
Good Friday   Venerdì Santo
    11d
Good luck! Best wishes!   Buona
    fortuna! In bocca al lupo! Auguri!
    16a, 16c
good mood   buon umore   21a
Good morning! Good day!   Buon
    giorno!   16a
Good night!   Buona notte!   16a
good time, enjoyment
    divertimento   29b
goose   oca   15b
gorilla   gorilla   15a
Gospel   Vangelo   11d
gossip   pettegolezzo, spettegolare
    17a
govern   governare   43a
government   governo   43a
government bond   buono del
    tesoro   43a
governmental   governativo   43a
grab   afferrare   3f
graceful   grazioso   11e

grade   classe   37a
grade one   prima   37a
grade, mark   voto   37f
graduate   laureato (-a), diplomato
    (-a)   11f
grain   grano   14a, 24c
gram   grammo   3a
grammar   grammatica   8a
grammar book   grammatica
    37b
grammar check   controllo della
    grammatica   42c
granary   granaio   14a
grand piano   piano a coda   28c
grandchild   nipote   10a
grandfather   nonno   10a
grandfather clock   orologio a
    pendolo   4d
grandmother   nonna   10a
granite   granito   13c
grapefruit   pompelmo   14d, 24g
grapes   uva   14d, 24g
graph   grafico   3d, 37f, 42b
graphic interface   interfaccia
    grafica   42b
grass   erba   13b
grasshopper   cavalletta   15d
grate   grattugiare   12c
grateful   grato   21a
grater   grattugia   23c
gravel   ghiaia   13c
gravity   gravità   13a
gray   grigio   7a
gray hair   capelli grigi   11a
graze   pascolare   15a
Great Britain   Gran Bretagna
    30b
great grandchild   pronipote
    10a
great grandfather   bisnonno
    10a
great grandmother   bisnonna
    10a
great-aunt   prozia   10a
great-uncle   prozio   10a
Greece   Grecia   30b
greedy   avaro   11e
Greek   greco   30e

green verde 7a
greenhouse serra 14a
greenhouse effect effetto serra 13c
Greenland Groenlandia 30b
greet salutare 3f, 16a
greeting saluto 16a, 19c
Greetings! Saluti! Salve! 16a, 19a, 19b
grenade granata 44d
grievance lamentela 38d
grilled alla griglia 24a
grind sgretolare 12c
grocer droghiere (-a) 38a
groom sposo 11c
gross national product prodotto nazionale lordo 38d
gross profit guadagno lordo 38d
ground floor pianterreno, platea 23e, 28a, 35a
group work lavoro in gruppo 37f
grow crescere 3b
grow up crescere 11b
growth crescita 3b
grumpy scorbutico 11e
guarantee garantire 17a
guard guardiano (-a) 38a
guard dog cane da guardia 15a
Guatemala Guatemala 30b
Guatemalan guatemalteco 30e
guerrilla warfare guerriglia 44d
guide guida 30a
guidebook guida 25n, 36a
guilt colpevolezza 41
guilty colpevole 41
guitar chitarra 28c
guitarist chitarrista 28c
gulf golfo 13b, 13d
gullible semplice 21a
gully burrone 13b
gums gengive 40b
gun rivoltella 39b
guts ventre 12a
gutter fognatura, grondaia 23a, 36a

gym shoes scarpe da ginnastica 25m
gymnasium palestra 27b, 37c
gymnast ginnasta 27b
gymnastics ginnastica 27b
gynecologist ginecologo (-a) 40a
gynecology ginecologia 40a

H

haggard face viso stravolto 11a
hail grandine, grandinare 6a
Hail Mary Ave Maria 11d
hailstorm tempesta di grandine 6a
hair (bodily) pelo 12a
hair (head) capelli 12a
hair cream brillantina 25f
hairnet retina 25f
hair remover crema depilatoria 25f
hair dye tinta 25f
hairdresser parrucchiere (-a) 12f, 38a
hairdryer asciugacapelli 12f, 25f
hairpin fermaglio 25f
hairspray lacca (per capelli) 25f
hairstyle acconciatura (dei capelli) 11a
hairy peloso 11a
Haitian haitiano 30e
half metà, mezzo 3b
half-brother fratellastro 10a
half-sister sorellastra 10a
hallucination, high allucinazione 44c
hallway corridoio 37c
ham prosciutto 24d
hammer martello 23d, 25b
hamster criceto 15a
hand (of a clock, watch) lancetta 4d, 12a, 25i
hand mano 12a
hand bomb bomba a mano 44d
hand cream crema per le mani 25f

hand luggage bagaglio a mano
31

handbag borsa 3e

handcuffs manette 39b

handful manciata 3b

handkerchief fazzoletto 25k

handle maniglia, manico,
maneggiare '3f, 23a, 33c

handlebar manubrio 34

handrail ringhiera 23a

handshake stretta di mano 16a

hang up riattaccare il telefoono
18b

happen, occur accadere, avvenire
4c

happiness felicità 21a

happy felice, allegro 11e, 21a

Happy Birthday! Buon
compleanno! 11c, 16c, 29c

Happy Easter! Buona Pasqua!
5f, 16c

happy face viso allegro 11a

Happy New Year! Buon anno!
5f, 16c, 29c

hard drive hard drive 19f

hard drug droga pesante 44c

hard-headed cocciuto 21a

hard-working laborioso 11e

hardware ferramenta, hardware
23d, 38c, 42b

hardware store negozio di
ferramenta 25b

hardwood legno duro 13c

hare lepre 15a

harmony armonia 28c

harp arpa 28c

harpist arpista 28c

harpsichord clavicembalo 28c

harvest raccolta, raccogliere
14a

hat cappello 25k

hate odiare 21b

hateful odioso 11e

hatred odio 21b

haughty altezzoso 21a

have avere 40a

have a backache avere mal di
schiena 40a

have a class, a lesson · avere
lezione 37f

Have a good time! Buon
divertimento! 16c

Have a good vacation! Buona
vacanza! 16c, 29c

have a headache avere mal di
testa 40a

Have a nice trip! Buon viaggio!
30a

have a slim waistline avere una
vita snella 11a

have a snack fare uno spuntino
24a

have a sore throat avere mal di
gola 40a

have a sore stomach avere mal di
stomaco 40a

have a temperature avere la
febbre 40a

have a toothache avere mal di
denti 40b

have breakfast fare colazione
24a

have chills avere i brividi 6b

have dinner cenare 24a

Have fun! Buon divertimento!
29c

have lunch pranzare 24a

have patience, be patient avere
pazienza 21a

hawk falco 15b

hay fieno 14a

hazelnut nocciolo 14c

he lui, egli 8g

head testa 12a

head of government capo del
governo 43a

head of state capo dello stato
43a

head of the family capofamiglia
10a

head office sede principale
26a, 38d

heading intestazione 19c

headline titolo 20a

headphones cuffie, auricolari
20b, 32c

headquarters quartiere generale
44d

heal guarire 40a

health salute 12b

health food store negozio
dietetico 24m

healthy sano 12b

hear, feel, sense sentire 12c

hearing (legal) udienza 41

hearing udito 12c

hearing aid apparecchio acustico
40a

heart cuore 12a

heart attack infarto cardiaco
40a

heartbeat battito del cuore 12a

heartburn bruciore di stomaco
40a

heat calore 13c

heater termosifone 23b

heating riscaldamento 23d

heaven, paradise paradiso 11d

heavy pesante 3b, 11a, 25g,
31

heavy-weight peso massimo
27b

hectare ettaro 3a

hectogram ettogrammo, etto
3a

hedge siepe 14a

hedgehog riccio 15a

heel tallone, tacco 12a, 25m

hefty robusto, pesante 11a

height altezza, statura 3a, 11a

hell inferno 11d

Hellenic ellenico 43b

Hello! Pronto! 18b

helmet casco 27b

help aiuto, aiutare 39a

Help! Aiuto! 39a, 39b, 39c

help command comando help,
aiuto 42b

help line il telefono azzurro 7a

hematoma ematoma 40a

hemorrhage, bleeding emorragia
40a

heptagon ettagono 2a

her, to her la, lei, le, a lei 8g

herb erba 24i

here qua, qui 3c, 36c

heredity eredità 11c

hernia ernia 40a

hero, heroine eroe (-ina) 28d,
28e

heroin eroina 44c

herpes erpete 40a

herring aringa 15c, 24e

herself si 8g

hesitant restio 21a

hesitate esitare 17a

hesitation esitazione 17a

hexagon esagono 2a

Hi, Bye! Ciao! 16a

hide-and-seek rimpiattino 27a

high altar altare maggiore 11d

high blood pressure ipertensione
40a

high chair seggiolone 23b

high definition television
televisione ad alta definizione
20b

high forehead fronte alta 11a

high jumping salto in alto 27b

high school, lyceum liceo 37a

high school diploma diploma
(certificato) di maturità 11f, 37f

high school graduate diplomato
(-a) 38b

high school principal preside di
liceo 37d

high season alta stagione 30a,
35a

high, tall alto 3b

high-heeled con tacco alto
25m

highlight sottolineare 28d

highlighter evidenziatore 25c,
37b

highway autostrada 33a, 36b

highway police polizia stradale
33a

hijack dirottare 39b

hijacking dirottamento 39b

hill colle, collina 13b

himself si 8g

Hindu indù 11d

Hinduism Induismo 11d
hinge cardine 23a
hip anca 12a
hippopotamus ippopotamo 15a
hire assumere 38d
hired killer sicario 39b
hiring assunzione 38d
hiss sibilare 15a
historian storico (-a) 43b
history storia 37e, 43b
hit battere, colpire 3f, 27b
hitchhike fare l'autostop 34
hitchhiker autostoppista 34
HIV positive sieropositivo 40a
hive alveare 15d
hoarfrost brina 6a
hobby hobby 27a
hockey hockey 27b
hockey rink campo di ghiaccio 27b
hockey stick bastone 27b
hoe zappa, zappare 14a
hold hands tenersi per mano 3f
hole buco 25g, 25l
holiday giorno festivo 29a
Holland Olanda 30b
Holy Ghost Santo Spirito 11d
Holy Trinity Santa Trinità 11d
holy war guerra santa 44d
home delivery consegna a domicilio 25a
homeless senzatetto 44b
homeopathy omeopatia 40a
homily omelia 11d
homing pigeon piccione 15b
homosexuality omosessualità 44b
Honduran honduregno 30e
Honduras Honduras 30b
honest onesto 11e
honesty onestà 11e
honey miele 24c
honeymoon luna di miele 11c
honorable onorevole 21a
hood cappuccio 25k
hood, bonnet cofano 33c

hoof zoccolo 15a
hook gancio, amo 15c, 23b, 27a
hoop cerchio 27a
hope speranza, sperare 21a
horizontal orizzontale 2b, 3c
hormone ormone 40a
horn (car) clacson 33c
horn (animal) corno 28c
horn player cornista 28c
hornet calabrone (m) 15d
horoscope oroscopo 5d
horror film film dell'orrore 28a
horse cavallo 15a
horse power cilindrata 33c
horse race corsa ippica 27b
horse racing ippica, equitazione 27a, 27b
hose tubo, innaffiare 14a
hospital ospedale 39c
host ostia 11d
hostage ostaggio (-a) 39b, 44d
hostel ostello 35a
hostile party parte avversa 41
hot caldo 6a
hot water acqua calda 35b
hotel albergo 35a
hotel room camera 35a
hound cane da caccia 15a
hour ora 4b
house casa, alloggiare 23a, 23f
house call visita domiciliare 40a
house mortgage mutuo fondiario 26a
house number numero di casa 11f
house painter imbianchino (-a) 38a
housefly mosca 15d
household casa, domicilio, focolare 10a
household soap sapone di Marsiglia 23b
householder proprietario (-a) 23f
how come 9a

How are you? Come sta (stai)? 16a

How come? Come mai? 9a

How do you get to…? Come si fa per andare a…? 36c

How do you say…? Come si dice…? 17b

How lucky! Che fortuna! 16c

how much quanto 3b

How much does it cost? Quanto costa? 25a

How much is it? Quanto è? 25a

How's it going? Come va? 16a

How's the weather? Che tempo fa?, Com'è il tempo? 6b

however tuttavia, comunque 8I, 17b, 44e

howl ululare 15a

hum mormorare 12c

human rights diritti umani 44d

humanity umanità 11e

humble umile 11e

humid, damp umido 6a

humidity umidità 6a

humor umorismo 21a

hunched curvo 11a

hundredth centesimo 1b

Hungarian ungherese 30e

Hungary Ungheria 30b

hunger fame 12b

hunt caccia, cacciare 15a, 27a

hunter cacciatore (-trice) 15a

hunting caccia 27a

hurricane uragano 6a

hurry affrettarsi, sbrigarsi 3f

Hurry! Come quickly! Presto! 39b

hurt fare male a 12b

husband marito 10a, 11c

husky, manly aitante 11a

hut, beach house capanno 23a

hyacinth giacinto 14b

hybrid car automobile ibrida 33c

hydrangea ortensia 14b

hydrogen idrogeno 13c

hyena iena 15a

hygiene igiene 12f

hygienic igienico 12f

hymn inno, cantico 11d, 28c

hypermarket ipermercato 24m

hypertext ipertesto 19f, 42b

hypocrite ipocrita 21a

hypocritical ipocrita 21a

hypotenuse ipotenusa 2b

hypothesis ipotesi 22a

I

I io 8g

I am 55 years old. Ho cinquantacinque anni. 11b

I believe that… credo che… 44e

I can't stand the cold. Non sopporto il freddo. 6b

I can't stand the heat. Non sopporto il caldo. 6b

I can't stand… Non sopporto… 21b

I didn't understand! Non ho capito! 17b

I don't believe it! Non ci credo! 21c

I don't feel like… Non mi va (ho voglia) di… 21c

I don't know if… non so se… 44e

I don't understand. Non capisco. 9a

I doubt that… dubito che… 44e

I think that… penso che… 44e

I want some ne voglio 3b

I was born in 1994. Sono nato (-a) nel 1994. 5e

I wish! Magari! 16c, 21c

I would like to say that … vorrei dire che … 44e

I would like to speak with Posso parlare con 18b

I'll be glad, happy to do it! Lo farò con piacere! 16c

I'm not sure that… non sono sicuro (-a) che… 44e

I'm serious! Dico sul serio! 21c

I'm sorry!   Mi dispiace!   16c, 21c

I'm sorry, wrong number.   Scusi, ho sbagliato numero.   18b

I'm sure that...   sono sicuro (-a) che...   17b, 44e

ice   ghiaccio   6a, 13b

ice cream   gelato   24h, 29b

ice cream parlor   gelateria   24m, 29b

ice skating   pattinaggio su ghiaccio   27b

icon   icona   38c, 42b

icosahedron   icosaedro   2a

idea   idea   22a

idealist   idealista   11e

identification   identificazione   11f

identification card   carta d'identità   31, 35a

identify   identificare   17a

identity   identità   11f

ideology   ideologia   43a

idle   ozioso   21a

if   se   8i

If you don't mind...   Se non ti (Le) dispiace...   16c

ignorance   ignoranza   22a

ignorant   ignorante   11e, 22a

ill-mannered   maleducato   11e

illegal   illegale   41

illiteracy   analfabetismo   25n

illiterate person   analfabeta   25n

illumination   illuminazione   12d

illustrated magazine   rivista illustrata   20a, 25n

image   immagine   25d, 28b, 28d

imaginary   immaginario   1d

imagination, fantasy   immaginazione, fantasia   22a

imaginative   immaginativo   11e

imagine   immaginare   22b

immigrant   immigrante   44d

immigration   immigrazione   44d

immoral   immorale   21a

immune system   sistema immunitario   12a

impatient   impaziente   11e

imperative   imperativo   8a

imperfect   imperfetto   8a

imperialism   imperialismo   43a

impetuous   impetuoso   11e

imply   implicare   17a

import   importare   26b

Impossible!   Impossibile!   21c

impressionable   impressionabile   11e

Impressionism   Impressionismo   28b

imprison   imprigionare, incarcerare   41

imprudent   imprudente   11e

impulsive   impulsivo   11e

in   in   3c, 8f

in a hurry   in fretta   8j

in a little while   fra (tra) poco   8j

in an hour's time   tra un'ora   4c

in conclusion   in conclusione   44e

in fact   infatti   8i

in favor   favorevole   43a

in front of   di fronte, davanti   3c, 36c

in love   innamorato   11c

in my opinion   a mio parere   17b, 44e

in my own opinion   secondo me   17b

in record time   a tempo di record   27b

in slow motion   al rallentatore   28a

in style   di moda   25l

in the afternoon   nel pomeriggio, di pomeriggio   4b

in the city   in città   11f

in the country   in campagna   11f, 36b

in the evening   di sera   4b

in the event that   nel caso che   8i

in the long run a lungo andare 4c

in the long term a lungo termine 4c

in the meanwhile intanto, nel frattempo 4c, 8j

in the middle in mezzo (nel mezzo) 3c

in the morning di mattina 4b

in the mountains in montagna 36b

in the short term a breve scadenza, a breve termine 4c

in the suburbs in periferia 11f

in time in orario 4c

incense incenso 11d

inch pollice 3a

income reddito 26a, 38d

Incoming mail Posta in arrivo 42c

incompetent incompetente 11e

inconsiderate incosciente 11e

incontinence incontinenza 40a

incorruptible incorruttibile 11e

increase aumento, incremento 3b

Incredible! Incredibile! 16c

indecent indecente 21a

indecisive indeciso 11e

indefinite indeterminativo 8a

independent indipendente 11e

index indice 38c, 42b

index finger indice 12a

India India 30b

Indian indiano 30e

indicate indicare 17a

indication indicazione 17a

indicative indicativo 8a

indifference indifferenza 21a

indifferent indifferente 11e, 21a

indigent indigente 11e

indigestion indigestione 40a

indirect (object) di termine, indiretto 8a

individualist individualista 11e

indolent indolente 21a

Indonesia Indonesia 30b

Indonesian indonesiano 30e

industrial industriale 13c

Industrial Revolution rivoluzione industriale 43b

industrialist industriale 38a

industry industria 13c

inept, unfortunate disgraziato 11e

inexpensive a buon mercato, economico 25a

infallible infallibile 11e

infancy infanzia 11b

infantile infantile 11b

infection infezione 40a

inferiority inferiorità 21a

infinitive infinito 8a

inflamed infiammato 40a

inflammation infiammazione 40a

inflation inflazione 26a, 43a

inflation rate tasso d'inflazione 26a

inform informare 17a

informant informatore (-trice) 39b

informatics informatica 37e

information informazione, informazioni 17a, 33b, 42b

information booth sportello informazioni 9b

information counter banco, informazioni 32a

information media mezzi (m, pl) d'informazione 9b

information radio l'onda verde 7a

information theory teoria dell'informazione 9b

infraction infrazione 39b

infrared light luce infrarossa 13a

ingenious ingegnoso 11e, 22a

ingenuity ingegno 22a

ingenuous, naive ingenuo 11e

inhale inspirare 12b

inherit ereditare 11c

inheritor erede 11c

injection, needle iniezione, puntura 25h, 40a
injure, wound ferire 39b
injury, wound ferita, infortunio 39b, 40a
ink inchiostro 25c, 37b, 38c
ink-jet printer stampante a getto d'inchiostro 38c
innocence innocenza 41
innocent innocente 41
inorganic inorganico 13c
input digitare 38c
inputting on the screen videoscrittura 19f, 38c, 42b
insect insetto 15d
insensitive insensibile 11e
Insert Inserisci 42c
inside dentro 3c, 36c
insinuate insinuare 17a
insipid insipido 12e
insistent, unrelenting insistente 11e
insolent insolente 11e
insomnia insonnia 40a
installation installazione 38c, 42b
instant istante 4b
instead invece 8j
institute istituto 37a
instrument strumento 25j, 27a, 28c
insufficient evidence insufficienza di prove 41
insulation isolante 23d, 25b
insulin insulina 25h, 40a
insurable assicurabile 26a
insurance assicurazione 26a, 30a
insurance card carta verde 33a
insurance company società d'assicurazione 26a
insurance policy polizza d'assicurazione 26a
insure assicurare 26a
insured person assicurato (-a) 26a

insurrection insurrezione 43b
integer intero 1d
integral calculus calcolo integrale 1g
integrated circuit circuito integrato 42b
intellectual intellettuale 11e
intelligence intelligenza 22a
intelligent intelligente 11e, 22a
intensive care unit sala di rianimazione 40a
interactive interattivo 19f, 38c, 42b
intercom citofono 18a, 23e, 38c
interest interesse 22a, 26a
interest loan prestito a interesse 26b
interest rate tasso d'interesse 26a
interesting interessante 16c, 22a
interests, hobbies interessi 11f
interface interfaccia 42b
interference interferenza 42a
intermission intervallo 28e
internal affairs affari interni 43a
international call telefonata internazionale 18b
international flight volo internazionale 32b
Internet internet 19f, 20b, 38c
Internet provider provider 19f, 42b
interpret interpretare 17a
interrogate interrogare 17a
interrogative interrogativa 8a
interrupt interrompere 17a
interruption interruzione 17a
intersection incrocio 33a, 36a
interview intervista 20a, 25n
intestine, bowel intestino 12a
intransitive intransitivo 8a
intrepid intrepido 21a
introduce presentare 16b
introduction presentazione 16b

introverted introverso 11e

invest investire 26a

investigation investigazione 39b

investigator investigatore (-trice) 39b

investment investimento 26a

invitation invito, partecipazione 19d, 29b

invite invitare 17a

iodine iodio 13c

Iran Iran 30b

Iranian iraniano 30e

Iraq Iraq 30b

Iraqi iracheno 30e

irascible irascibile 11e

Ireland Irlanda 30b

Irish irlandese 30e

irksome irritante 11e

iron ferro da stiro, stirare 13c, 23f

ironed stirato 25g

ironic ironico 11e, 21a

ironing board tavola da stiro 23b

irony ironia 28d

irrational irrazionale 1d, 11e

irregular irregolare 3d, 8a

irresponsible irresponsabile 11e

irreverent irriverente 11e

irrigation irrigazione 14a

Is Mario in? C'è Mario? 18b

Is Ms. Morelli in? C'è la signora Morelli? 18b

Islam Islam 11d

Islamic Islamico (-a) 11d

island isola 13b

isosceles isoscele 2a

Israel Israele 30b

Israeli israeliano 30e

issue a sentence pronunciare una sentenza 41

It can't be! Non è possibile! 16c

It doesn't matter! Non importa! 16c, 21c

It looks bad on you. Ti sta male. 25l

It looks good on you. Ti sta bene. 25l

it seems that... sembra che..., pare che... 17b, 44e

It was high time! Era ora! 4c

It's 10:00 A.M. Sono le dieci. 4a

It's 10:00 P.M. Sono le ventidue. 4a

It's a bit hot. Fa un po' caldo. 6b

It's a small world Tutto il mondo è paese 13d

It's bad (weather). Fa brutto (tempo). 6b

it's clear that... è chiaro che... 44e

It's cloudy È nuvoloso. 6b

It's cold. Fa freddo. 6b

It's cool. Fa fresco. 6b

It's dark today. Oggi è buio. 6a

It's hot, warm. Fa caldo. 6b

It's humid. È umido. 6b

It's mild. È mite. 6b

It's muggy. È afoso. 6b

It's necessary that... È necessario che... 17b

It's nice (weather). Fa bello. Fa bel tempo. 6b

It's not true! Non è vero! 17b

It's obvious that... È ovvio che... 17b

It's pleasant È piacevole., È bello. 6b

It's raining Piove. 6b

It's raining cats and dogs. Piove a catinelle. Piove a dirotto. 6a

It's snowing Nevica. 6b

It's sunny C'è il sole. 6b

It's thundering. Tuona. 6b

It's true! È vero! 17b

It's very cold. Fa molto freddo. 6b

It's very hot. Fa molto caldo. 6b

It's windy. Tira vento. 6b

Italian italiano 30e

italics corsivo 19c
Italy Italia 30b
itch prudere 12e, 40a
itchiness (itch) prurito 40a
itchy pruriginoso 12e
ivory avorio 7a
Ivory Coast Costa d'Avorio 30c
ivy edera 14b

J

jack cric 33c
jackal sciacallo 15a
jacket giacca 25k
Jamaica Giamaica 30b
Jamaican giamaicano 30e
jamb stipite 23a
janitor bidello (-a) 37d
January gennaio 5b
Japan Giappone 30b
Japanese giapponese 30e
jar, tin barattolo 3e
javelin giavellotto 27b
javelin throwing lancio del giavellotto 27b
jaw mandibola 12a, 40b
jawbone mascella 12a
jazz jazz 25j
jealous geloso 11e
jeer fischiare 17a
jellyfish medusa 15c
jest scherzare 17a
jest, prank scherzo 17a
Jesuit gesuita 11d
Jesus Christ Gesù Cristo 11d
jet lag fuso orario 4c
jewel gioiello 25i
jeweler gioielliere (-a) 38a
jewelry store, jeweler gioielleria, orefice 25i
jingle, clink, jangle jingle, tintinnare 12c, 20c
job mestiere 11f, 38a
jogging jogging 27a
joint articolazione 12a
joke (oral) barzelletta 17a
Jordan Giordania 30b
Jordanian giordano 30e

journalist giornalista 20a, 38a
jovial gioviale 11e
joy gioia 21a
joyous gioioso 11e
Judaism giudaismo 11d
judge giudice, giudicare 22b, 41
judgment, wisdom giudizio 22a
judiciary giudiziario 43a
judo judo 27b
jug brocca 23c
juice succo 24j
juicy succoso 24a
July luglio 5b
jump saltare 3f, 27b
jumper saltatore (-trice) 27b
June giugno 5b
June 23 il ventitré giugno 5e
junior high school scuola media 37a
Jupiter Giove 13a
juridical, legal, authorized giuridico 43a
jurisprudence, law giurisprudenza, legge 37e
juror giurato (-a) 41
jury giuria 41
just, as soon as, barely appena 4c, 8j
justice giustizia 41
justice of the peace giudice di pace 41
justification giustificazione 38c, 42b
juvenile delinquency delinquenza minorile 39b
juvenile delinquent delinquente minorile 39b

K

kangaroo canguro 15a
karate karatè 27b
keep quiet stare zitto 17a
kennel canile 15a
Kenya Kenya 30b
Kenyan keniano 30e

kettle pentolino 23c

key chiave 23f, 28c, 35a

keyboard tastiera 25c, 38c, 42b

keyword parola chiave 42b

kick calciare, dare un calcio, prendere a calci 3f, 27b

kidnap sequestrare 39b

kidnapper sequestratore 39b

kidnapping sequestro 39b

kidney rene 12a

kidney stone calcolo renale 40a

kids' magazine giornalino 20a, 25n

kill uccidere 39b

kill two birds with one stone pigliare due piccioni con una fava 15b

killer assassino, sicario 39b

kilogram chilogrammo, chilo 3a

kilometer chilometro 3a

kindergarten asilo infantile 37a

kindness gentilezza 11e

king re 43a

kingfisher martin pescatore 15b

kiosk, booth chiosco 25a, 36a

kiss bacio, baciare 11c, 21b

kitchen cucina 23a

kitchen scales bilancia 23b

kitchen shelf mensola 23b

kite aquilone 27a

kitten gattino 15a

knapsack zaino 27b

knee ginocchio 12a

kneel inginocchiarsi 3f, 11d

knickers calzoni 25k

knife coltello 23c, 24k, 39b

knit lavorare a maglia 27a

knobby nodoso 12e

knock bussare 3f

knot nodo 13c

knotty nodoso 13c

know sapere, conoscere 22b

know someone conoscere 16b

knowledge conoscenza 22a

knowledgeable ben informato 22a

Koran Corano 11d

Korea Corea 30b

Korean coreano 30e

Kuwait Kuwait 30b

Kuwaiti kuwaitiano 30e

L

label etichetta 25a, 25c, 38c

labor shortage scarsezza di manodopera 38d

labor surplus eccesso di manodopera 38d

labor union sindacato 38d, 43a

laboratory laboratorio 37c

labyrinth, maze labirinto 3d

lace pizzo 13c, 25g, 25l

lack mancare 25a

lack of breath senza fiato 12b

laconic laconico 28d

ladder scala 39a

ladle mestolo 23c

lady signora 11a

ladybug coccinella 15d

lagoon laguna 13b

lake lago 13b, 36b

lamb agnello 15a, 24d

lamp lampada 23b, 35b

land terra, atterrare 13b, 32c

landing (plane) atterraggio 32c

landing (staircase) pianerottolo 23a

landing gear carrello 32c

landscape paesaggio 13b, 28b

lane (traffic) corsia 33a

Lane reserved Corsia preferenziale 33b

languages lingue 37e

languages lyceum liceo linguistico 37a

lanky, long-legged slanciato 11a

Laos Laos 30b

Laotian laoziano 30e

lap, stage tappa 27b

laptop computer computer portatile, laptop 19f, 25c, 37b, 38c

large grosso 11a

large bill banconota di grosso taglio 26a

large garbage can bidone 23b

large loan prestito ingente 26b

lark allodola 15b

laryngitis laringite 40a

lasagna lasagne 24b

lascivious lascivo 21a

laser printer stampante laser 25c, 38c, 42b

last scorso, durare 4c

last a long time durare a lungo 4c

last a short time durare poco 4c

last evening ieri sera 4b

last month il mese scorso 4c

last night ieri notte 4b

last year l'anno scorso 4c

late tardi 4c, 8j

late, delayed in ritardo 32b

Latin America America Latina 30b

latitude latitudine 13d

Latium Lazio 30d

laudable lodevole 21a

laugh ridere 21a

laughter risata 21a

launderette lavanderia automatica 25g

laundry biancheria, lavanderia 23b, 25g

laundry basket cesta del bucato 23b

lava lava 13b

law legge 41

law courts palazzo di giustizia 36a

law faculty facoltà di giurisprudenza 37a

lawn prato (erboso) 14a

lawn bowling bocce 27a, 27b

lawn chair sedia a sdraio 23b

lawn mower falciatrice 14a

laws of the marketplace leggi del mercato 26b

lawsuit querela 41

lawyer avvocato 16b, 38a, 41

laxative purga 25h, 40a

lay person, secular laico 11d

layer, stratum strato 13b

layout stesura 3d

lazy pigro 11e

lead piombo 13c

leaf foglia 14a

leaf through sfogliare 25n

lean scarno 11a

lean against appoggiarsi a 3f

leap balzare 3f

leap year anno bisestile 5b

learn imparare, apprendere 22a, 22b, 37f

learning apprendimento 37f

lease contratto d'affitto 23e

leather pelle, cuoio 13c

leather shoes scarpe di cuoio 25m

leave, depart partire 3f, 34

leave of absence congedo 38d

Lebanese libanese 30e

Lebanon Libano 30b

lecture conferenza 17a

left sinistra 3c, 36c

left turn, exit left svolta a sinistra 33a

left-wing di sinistra 43a

leg gamba 12a

leg (chicken, turkey, etc.) coscia 24a

legal legale 41

legal assistance assistenza legale 39b, 44b

legal consultant consulente legale 38a

legal tender corso 26b

legend leggenda 25n, 28d

legislation legislazione 43a

legislative legislativo 43a

legislature legislatura 43a

leisure svago, tempo libero 29b

lemon limone 7a, 14d, 24g

lemonade limonata 24j

length lunghezza 3a, 3c

lengthen allungare 3c, 25l

lens lente 12d, 25d

Lent Quaresima 11d

lentil lenticchia 14e, 24f

Leo Leone 5d

leopard leopardo 15a

lesbian lesbica 44b

lesion lesione 40a

less meno 3b

lesson, class lezione 37f

Let me introduce you to… Ti (Le) presento… 16b

let off steam sfogarsi 21a

lethargic letargico 21a

letter lettera 18a, 9d

letter carrier postino (-a) 19e

letter opener tagliacarte 19d

letterhead carta intestata 19d, 25c, 38c

lettuce lattuga 14e, 24f

leukemia leucemia 40a

level livello 3b, 3c

Level crossing Passaggio a livello 33b

level of education titolo di studio 37f

level-headed equilibrato 21a

lewd indecente 21a

liability, loan ipoteca, responsabilità 26a, 26b

liar bugiardo 11e

liberal liberale 43a

liberal party partito liberale 43a

Liberia Liberia 30b

Liberian liberiano 30e

libidinous libidinoso 21a

Libra Bilancia 5d

librarian bibliotecario (-a) 37d, 38a

library biblioteca 25n, 36a, 37c

Libya Libia 30b

Libyan libico 30e

license plate targa 33c

lie bugia, dire una bugia 17a

lie down sdraiarsi 3f

life vita 11c

life imprisonment ergastolo 41

life insurance assicurazione sulla vita 26a

life jacket salvagente, giubbotto di salvataggio 32c, 34

lift alzare 3f

lift weights sollevare pesi 27b

light luce 6a, 13a, 35b

light (car) faro 33c

light (weight) leggero 25g, 25l, 31

light (clear) chiaro 7b

light blue, sky blue celeste 7a

light bulb lampadina 23d, 25e

light music musica leggera 25j

light signal segnale luminoso 42a

light, power luce 23d

light-hearted allegro 21a

lighter accendino 25e

lightning (bolt of) lampo, fulmine 6a

Liguria Liguria 30d

likable piacevole 11e

like piacere 21b

liking simpatia 21b

lily giglio 14b

lily of the valley mughetto 14b

lima bean fava 14e, 24f

limb arto 12a

Limited parking Sosta limitata 33b

line riga, linea 2b, 19c

line (fishing) lenza 27a

line (verbal) battuta 28e

line up fare la coda 15b

line, verse verso 25n, 28d

linear algebra algebra lineare 1g

lined a righe 3d

lined paper carta a righe 37b

linen lino 13c, 25g, 25l

lingerie, underclothing biancheria (intima) 25k

linguistics linguistica 37e

lion, lioness leone (-essa) 15a

lip labbro 12a, 40b
lipstick rossetto 25f
liqueur liquore 24j
liquid liquido 13c
Liquid Paper, White-out
 bianchetto 19d, 25c, 38c
liquidate liquidare 26b
liquidation liquidazione 26b
Lisbon Lisbona 30c
listen ascoltare, udire 12c, 17b,
 37f
liter litro 3a
literacy alfabetismo 25n
literal letterale 28d
literature letteratura 25n, 28d,
 37e
Lithuania Lituania 30b
Lithuanian lituano 30e
litigate fare causa 41
litigation, legal case causa 41
litigious litigioso 21a
little, small piccolo 3b
little finger (dito) mignolo 12a
liturgy liturgia 11d
live vivere 11c, 36a
live broadcast trasmissione in
 diretta 20b
live in abitare 23f
live program programma dal vivo
 20b
live somewhere abitare, vivere
 11f
lively animato, spiritoso, vivace
 7b, 11e, 28d
liver fegato 12a, 24d
livestock bestiame 15a
living room salotto, soggiorno
 23a
lizard lucertola 15c
loan prestito 26a
loaner, creditor creditore 26b
lobby ridotto 28a
lobster aragosta 15c, 24e
local agency ente locale 43a
local call telefonata urbana
 18b
local news cronaca cittadina
 20a

locale località 36a
locate localizzare 13d
lock bloccaggio 42b
locket, medal medaglia 25i
locomotive locomotiva 34
lodger, renter, tenant affittuario
 (-a) 23e
lodging, accommodations
 alloggio 35a
loft soffitta 23a
logarithm logaritmo 1f
logarithmic logaritmico 1f
logic logica 22a
logo logo 20c
Lombardy Lombardia 30d
London Londra 30c
long lungo 3b, 25g, 25l, 37f
long jumping salto in lungo
 27b
long-distance call telefonata
 interurbana 18b
long-sighted presbite 12d
long-term a lunga scadenza 4c
longitude longitudine 13d
look (at), watch guardare 12d
look around guardare in giro
 12d
look forward to non vedere l'ora
 di 4c
loose change spiccioli 26a
loose-fitting largo 25g, 25l
loot bottino 39b
loquacious loquace 17a
lose perdere 27a, 27b
lose one's hair perdere i capelli
 11a
lose one's job perdere il lavoro
 38d
lose weight perdere peso 11a
loser perdente 27b
loss perdita 26b, 27b
lost and found ufficio oggetti
 smarriti 32a
lotion lozione 25f
louse pidocchio 15d
love amore, amare 11c, 21b
love affair relazione (amorosa)
 10b

lover   amante   10b
loving   amoroso   11e
low forehead   fronte bassa   11a
low season   bassa stagione   30a, 35a
low-heeled   con tacco basso   25m
lower-case character   carattere minuscolo   19c
Lucania   Basilicata   30d
luggage rack   portabagaglio   33c, 35a
lullaby   ninna nanna   28c
lump sum   somma forfettaria   26b
lunar eclipse   eclissi lunare   13a
lunch   pranzo   24a, 35a
lunch break   pausa mensa   38d
lung   polmone   12a
lusty   lussurioso   21a
Luxembourg   Lussemburgo   30b
Luxembourger   lussemburghese   30e
luxury hotel   albergo di lusso   35a
lymphatic system   sistema linfatico   12a

M
macaroni   maccheroni   24b
Macedonia   Macedonia   30b
Macedonian   macedone   30e
mackerel   sgombro   15c
made-to-measure suit   abito, vestito su misura   25l
Madonna, Virgin Mary   Madonna   11d
Madrid   Madrid   30c
madrigal   madrigale   28c
magazine   rivista   20a, 25n
magic tricks   giochi di prestigio   27a
magician   prestigiatore (-trice)   27a
magistrate   magistrato   41
magnanimity   magnanimità   21a

magnanimous   magnanimo   21a
magnesium   magnesia   13c
magnesium citrate   citrato di magnesio   25h, 40a
Magnificent!   Magnifico!   16c
magnolia   magnolia   14b
magpie   gazza   15b
mahogany   mogano   13c
maid   cameriera   35a
maid-of-honor   damigella d'onore   11c
mail   posta, spedire   19e
mail delivery   distribuzione della posta   19e
mail truck   furgone postale   19e
mail withheld for pick-up   fermo posta   19e
mailbox   cassetta postale, delle lettere   19e, 23a
main   principale   8a
main character   protagonista   28e
main door   portone   23e, 35a
main office   segreteria   37c
main role   ruolo principale   28e
main story   titolo principale   20a
make a call   fare una telefonata   18b
make a connection   collegare   20b
make an appointment   fissare un appuntamento   40a
make bigger   aggrandire   3b
make mistakes   sbagliare   37f
makeup   trucco   12f, 25f, 28e
Malaysia   Malaysia   30b
Malaysian   malaysiano   30e
male   maschio, maschile   11a, 38b
malicious   malizioso   11e
malicious gossip   maldicenza   17a
malign, speak badly of   malignare   17a
malignant   maligno   40a
malleable   malleabile   21a
mallet   mazza   23d, 25b

Malta Malta 30b
Maltese maltese 30e
mammal mammifero 15a
man uomo 11a
management direzione, gestione 38d
management board comitato direttivo 38d
manager direttore (-trice) 26a, 35a, 38d
mandarin orange mandarino 14d, 24g
mandolin mandolino 28c
mandolin player mandolinista 28c
mane criniera 15a
maniacal maniaco 21a
manicure manicure 12f, 25f
manslaughter omicidio preterintenzionale 39b
manual manuale 37b
manure concime 14a
manuscript manoscritto 28d
many molti (-e), tanti (-e) 8h
Many thanks! Grazie mille! 16c
map cartina, geografic, mappa 37b
maple acero 14c
marble marmo, bilia 13c, 27a
marble sculpture scultura in marmo 28b
marbled marmorizzato 3d
march marciare 3f
March marzo 5b
mare cavalla 15a
margin margine 3d, 19c, 42b
marigold calendola 14b
marijuana marijuana 44c
marionette marionetta 27a
marital status stato civile 11c, 11f, 38b
maritime marittimo 13b
mark, correct correggere 37f
marker pennarello 25c, 37b, 38c
market mercato 38d
market price prezzo di mercato 26b

market research ricerche di mercato (di marketing) 38d
marmalade, jam marmellata 24c
marmot marmotta 15a
marriage matrimonio, sposalizio, nozze 11c, 11f
marriage counselor consigliere (-a) matrimoniale 38a
marriage vow promessa di matrimonio 11c
married coniugato (-a), sposato (-a) 11c, 11f, 38b
marry sposare 11c
Mars Marte 13a
martyr martire 11d
martyrdom martirio 11d
Marvelous! Meraviglioso! 16c
mascara mascara 12f, 25f
masculine maschile 8a, 11a
masher pestello 23c
mask maschera 27b
masked ball ballo in maschera 28c
masking tape nastro isolante 23d, 25b
Mass messa 11d
mass massa 3b
mass communications comunicazione (f) di massa 9b
massive massivo 3b
masterpiece capolavoro 28b
match fiammifero 25e
material stoffa 25g, 25l
maternal materno 10a
mathematician matematico (-a) 1f
mathematics matematica 1g, 37e
matrimonial matrimoniale 11c
matter materia 13c
mattress materasso 23b
mature person persona matura 11b
mauve malva 7a
maximum massimo 3b, 6c
maximum temperature temperatura massima 6c

May   maggio   5b
May I help you?   Desideri?
Desidera?   16c
May I introduce you to...?
Posso presentarti (presentarLe)...?
16b
May I speak with...?   Posso
parlare con...?   18b
May I?   È permesso? Posso? Si
può?   16c
mayor   sindaco   43a
me, to me   mi, me, a me   8g
meadow   prato   14a
meal   pasto   24a
mean   significare   17a
mean-minded   meschino   21a
meaning   significato   17a
measles, red measles   morbillo,
roseola   40a
measure, size   misura, misurare   3b
measuring tape   metro   3b
meat   carne   24d
mechanic   meccanico (-a)   33a,
38a
medical checkup   visita di
controllo   40a
medical examination   esame
medico   40a
medical faculty   facoltà di
medicina   37a
medicine   medicina   25h, 37e
medicine chest   armadietto dei
medicinali   23a
medieval   medioevale   43b
mediocre   mediocre   21a, 21b
mediocrity   mediocrità   21a
Mediterranean   mediterraneo
6a, 30c
medium   medio   3b
meet   conoscere   16b
Melanesia   Melanesia   30b
melody   melodia   25j, 28c
melon   melone   14d, 24g
melt   sciogliere   6c
melting point   temperatura del
ghiaccio fondente   6c
membrane   membrana   12a
memoirs   memorie   25n, 28d

memorize   memorizzare   22b
memory   memoria   22a, 38c,
42b
memory capacity   capacità di
memoria   42b
memory stick   chiavetta   19f,
42d
men's clothing store
abbigliamento maschile   25k
men's shoes   scarpe da uomo
25m
men's suit   abito, vestito da uomo
25k
men's watch   orologio da uomo
25i
mend   rammendare   25g
menopause   menopausa   40a
menstruation   mestruazione   40a
mention   menzionare   17a
menu   menù   38c, 24a, 42c
meow   miagolare   15a
merchandise   merce   25a, 38d
merciful   pietoso   21a
merciless   spietato   21a
Mercury   Mercurio   13a
mercury   mercurio   6c, 13c
merge   fondere   38d
Merge   Confluenza   33b
merit, worth   merito   11e
meritorious   meritevole   11e
Merry Christmas!   Buon Natale!
5f, 16c, 29c
message   messaggio   35a, 42a,
42c
metal   metallo   13c
metaphor   metafora   28d
meteor   meteora   13a
meter   metro   3a
meticulous   meticoloso   11e
Mexican   messicano   30e
Mexico   Messico   30b
microphone   microfono   20b
microprocessor   microprocessore
38c, 42b
microscope   microscopio   13c
microwave   microonda   13c
microwave oven   forno a
microonde   23b

middle   mezzo   3c
middle age   mezza età   11b
Middle Ages   Medioevo   43b
Middle East   Medio Oriente   30b
Middle Easterner   mediorientale   30e
middle finger   (dito) medio   12a
middleweight   peso medio   27b
midge   moscerino   15d
midget   nano (-a)   11a
midnight   mezzanotte   4b
midwife   levatrice   38a
migratory bird   uccello migratore   15b
Milan   Milano   30c
mild   mite, tiepido   6a, 24a
mile   miglio   3c
military green   verde militare   7a
military service   servizio militare   11f
milk   latte   24h
milk jug   brocca del latte   23c
millennium   millennio   4b
millimeter   millimetro   3a
millionth   milionesimo   1b
mincer   tritacarne   23c
mind   mente   22a
mineral   minerale   13c
mineral water   acqua minerale   24j
minestrone soup   minestrone   24b
minimum   minimo   3b, 6c
minimum temperature   temperatura minima   6c
minister   ministro   11d
ministry   ministero   43a
Ministry of Education   Ministero della Pubblica Istruzione   37a
minivan   pulmino   34
mink   visone   15a
mint   menta   14e, 24i
minus   meno   1e, 1f, 6c
minute   minuto   4b
mirror   specchio   23a
miscarriage   aborto spontaneo   11c, 40a

mischievous   malizioso, capriccioso   11e, 21a
miss (a bus)   perdere   34
Miss, Ms.   Signorina   11f, 16b
missile   missile   13a, 44d
missionary   missionario (-a)   11d
mist, haze   foschia   6a
mistake   sbaglio   37f
mistletoe   vischio   14b
misunderstanding   fraintendimento   17a
mixed salad   insalata mista   24a
mobile device   dispositivo mobile   19g, 42d
mocking, derisive   beffardo   21a
modal   modale   8a
model   modello   28b
modem   modem   18a, 25c, 38c, 42b
modest   modesto   21a
modest hotel   albergo modesto   35a
moisturizer   crema idratante   25f
molar   molare   40b
Moldavia   Moldavia   30b
Moldavian   moldavo   30e
mole   talpa   15a
Molise   Molise   30d
mollusk, shellfish   mollusco   15c
molotov cocktail   bomba molotov   44d
mom   mamma   10a
moment   momento   4b
Monaco   Monaco   30b
monarchist party   partito monarchico   43a
monarchy   monarchia   43a
monastery   monastero   11d
Monday   lunedì   5a
money   denaro, soldi   26a
Mongolia   Mongolia   30b
Mongolian   mongolo   30e
monk   frate   11d
monkey   scimmia   15a

monologue monologo 28e
monopoly monopolio 38d
Montenegro Montenegro 30b
month mese 4b, 5b
monthly mensile, mensilmente 4b, 5b
monument monumento 36a
moo muggire 15a
mood (emotion) umore 21a
mood (grammar) modo 8a
moody lunatico 21a
moon luna 5c, 6a, 13a
moonbeam raggio della luna, lunare 6a, 13a
mop scopa di stracci 23b
moralistic moralistico 21a
more più, di più 3b
Mormon mormone 11d
morning mattina, mattino 4b
Moroccan marrocchino 30e
Morocco Marocco 30b
morose scontroso 11e
mortar mortaio 23c
mortgage mutuo 26a
Moscow Mosca 30c
mosque moschea 11d
mosquito zanzara 15d
mother madre 10a
mother-in-law suocera 10a
motif motivo 28d
motion mozione 43a
motor motore 32c, 33c
motor scooter motorino, vespa 34
motorcycle motocicletta 34
motorcycling motociclismo 27b
motorway restaurant autogrill 36b
mound pedana di lancio 27b
mount monte 13b
mountain montagna 13b
mountain boots scarponi 36b
mountain chain catena montuosa 13b
mountain climbing alpinismo 27b, 36b
mouse (computer) mouse 19f, 25c, 42b

mouse (rodent) topo 15a
mouth bocca 12a, 40b
Move Sposta 42c
move muovere, muoversi, traslocare 3f, 23f
movement movimento 3f
movie camera cinepresa 28a
movie star stella del cinema 28a
movie theater cinema 28a
movies cinema 29b
moving (residence) trasloco 23f
mow, reap falciare 14a
Mr. Signore 11f, 16b
Mrs., Ms. Signora 11f, 16b
mud, silt fango 13b
muddy fangoso 13b
muffler marmitta 33c
mug boccale 23c
mugginess afa 6a
muggy afoso 6a
mule mulo 15a
mullet triglia 15c
multimedia multimedialità 42b
multinational (company) multinazionale 38d
multiple multiplo 1f
multiplication moltiplicazione 1e
multiplication table tavola pitagorica 1e
multiplied by moltiplicato per 1e
multiply moltiplicare 1e
multiracial society società multirazziale 44d
mumps orecchioni 40a
municipal municipale 43a
mural painting pittura murale 28b
murder assassinio, uccidere 39b
murderer omicida 39b
murmur mormorare 17a
muscle muscolo 12a
muscular muscoloso 11a

museum museo 36a

mushroom fungo 14e, 24f

music musica 25j, 28c, 37e

music stand portamusica 25j, 28c

musical film film musicale 28a

musician musicista 25j, 28c

musicologist musiologo (-a) 28c

Muslim musulmano (-a) 11d

mussel cozza 15c, 24e

mustache baffi 11a, 12a

my mio, mia, miei, mie 8e

My dear John Mio caro Giovanni 19b

My dear Mary Mia cara Maria 19b

My name is … Mi chiamo … 11f, 16b

myself mi 8g

mystery movie film giallo 28a

mystery, detective genre giallo 20a, 25n, 28d

mystic mistico 11d

mysticism misticismo 11d

myth mito 11d, 25n, 28d

mythology mitologia 25n, 28d

N

nail chiodo, inchiodare 23d, 25b

nail file lima per unghie 25f

nail polish smalto 12f, 25f

name nome 11f, 38b

name day onomastico 29a

nanny, housekeeper governante 23f

nape nuca 12a

napkin tovagliolo 23c, 24k

Naples Napoli 30c

narration narrazione 28d

narrative, fiction narrativa 25n, 28d

narrator narratore (-trice) 25n, 28d

narrow stretto 3b, 3c

narrow-minded di vedute ristrette 11e

nasturtium nasturzio 14b

nation nazione 13d

national nazionale 13d, 43a

national press stampa nazionale 20a

national, domestic flight volo nazionale 32b

nationality nazionalità 11f, 31, 38b

natural naturale 13b

natural resources risorse naturali 44a

nature natura 13b

naughty, saucy spinto 21a

nausea nausea 40a

navigate navigare 19f, 38c, 42b

near vicino, presso 3c, 36c, 8j

Near East Vicino Oriente 30b

nearly quasi 3c

neat ordinato 11e

neck collo 12a

necklace collana 25i

needle ago 44c

negative negativo 1d, 25d, 28b

negligent negligente 11e

neigh nitrire 15a

neither…nor non…né…né 8k

neon neon 25b

nephew nipote 10a

Neptune Nettuno 13a

nerve nervo 12a

nerve gas gas nervino 44d

nervous nervoso 11e

nervous system sistema nervoso 12a

nest nido 15b

net (soccer) porta 27b

net profit guadagno netto 38d

nettle ortica 14b

network network, rete 38c, 42a, 42b

neutron neutrone 13c

never non…mai 4c, 8k

New Year Anno Nuovo 5f

New Year's Day Capodanno 5f, 29a

New Year's Eve Vigilia di Capodanno 5f, 29a

New York New York 30c
New Zealand Nuova Zelanda 30b
New Zealander neozelandese 30e
newborn neonato (-a) 11b, 11c
newlyweds novelli sposi 11c
newsflash notizia flash 20b
news item notizia 9b
news item, article, report cronaca 20a
newspaper giornale 20a, 25n
newsroom sala di redazione 20a
newsstand edicola 25a
Nicaragua Nicaragua 30b
Nicaraguan nicaraguense 30e
nickel nichelio 13c
nickname soprannome 11f
niece nipote 10a
Nigeria Nigeria 30b
Nigerian nigeriano 30e
night notte 4b
night work lavoro notturno 38d
night-dress camicia da notte 25k
nightingale usignolo 15b
nine nove 1a
nineteen diciannove 1a
ninety novanta 1a
ninth nono 1b
nipple capezzolo 12a
nitrogen nitrogeno 13c
No! No! 16c
No entrance Vietato l'ingresso 33b
No entry Divieto di accesso 33b
No exit Vietata l'uscita 33b
No left turn Divieto di svolta a sinistra 33b
no more, no longer non...più 8k
no one non...nessuno 3b, 8k
No parking Sosta vietata 33b
No passing Divieto di sorpasso 33b
No right turn Divieto di svolta a destra 33b
No smoking Vietato fumare 33b

No stopping Divieto di fermata 32a, 33b
No thoroughfare Divieto di transito 33b
No U-turn Divieto di inversione a U 33b
No way! Per carità! Macché! 16c, 21a
nod fare un cenno 3f
noise rumore 12c
noisy rumoroso, chiassoso 12c, 21a
non-carbonated liscia 24j
non-confidence vote sfiducia 43a
non-Euclidean geometry geometria non euclidea 1g
non-teaching personnel personale non docente 37d
non-transferrable check assegno barrato 26a
nonconformist anticonformista 11e
noon mezzogiorno 4b
north nord 3c, 13d, 36c
North America America del Nord 30b
North American nordamericano 30e
North Pole Polo Nord 13d
north-east nord-est 3c, 13d
north-west nord-ovest 3c, 13d
northern settentrionale 3c, 13d
Norway Norvegia 30b
Norwegian norvegese 30e
nose naso 12a
nostril narice 12a
nosy ficcanaso 21a
Not bad! Non c'è male! 16a
not even non...neanche (nemmeno, neppure) 8k
not really, not quite non...mica 8k
note (message) appunto, notare 17a, 37f
note (musical) nota 20a, 25j, 28c

notebook, workbook   quaderno 37b

nothing   non…nulla, niente   3b, 8k

nothing to declare   niente da dichiarare   31

notice board   tabella avvisi 25c, 38c

noun   nome   8a

novel   romanzo   20a, 25n, 28d

novelist   romanziere (-a)   25n, 28d

novelistic   romanzesco   25n

November   novembre   5b

now   ora, adesso   4c, 17b

nowadays   oggigiorno   4c, 8j

nowhere   da nessuna parte   3c

nth root   ennesima radice   1e

nucleus   nucleo   13c

nude   nudo   28b

number   numero, numerare   1d, 8a, 38b

numeral   numerale   1d

numerical   numerico   1d

nun, sister   suora   11d

nuptial, wedding ring   anello nuziale   25i

nurse   infermiere (-a)   38a, 40a

nursery   vivaio   14a

nursery school   scuola materna 37a

nutcracker   schiaccianoci   23c

nylon   nailon   25g, 25l

O

oak   quercia   14c

oar   remo   27b, 34

oats   avena   14a, 24c

obedient   ubbidiente   21a

obese   obeso   11a

object   complemento, obiettare 8a, 17a

objective lens   obiettivo   25d

oboe   oboe   28c

oboist   oboista   28c

obsequious   ossequioso   21a

obstetrician   ostetrico (-a)   40a

obstinate   ostinato   11e

obtuse   ottuso   2b, 11e

obtuse-angled   ottusangolo   2a

occasional job   lavoro saltuario 38d

occasionally   di tanto in tanto, ogni tanto   4c

occupant, householder   residente 23f

occupation   occupazione   38a

occupational hazard   rischio del mestiere   38d

ocean   oceano   13b

Oceania   Oceania   30b

octagon   ottagono   2a

octahedron   ottaedro   2a

October   ottobre   5b

October first   il primo ottobre 5e

octopus   polipo   15c

oculist   oculista   38a, 40a

odd   dispari   1d

oddball   bizzarro   21a

ode   ode   25n, 28d

of   di   8f

offend   offendere   17a

offer a job   offrire un lavoro 38d

office   ufficio   38d

office (of an instructor)   studio 37c

office hours   orario d'ufficio 38c, 40b

office supplies   forniture per ufficio   25c, 38c

office worker   impiegato (-a) 38a

official paper   carta protocollo 19d

offspring   discendenza   11c

often   spesso   4c

Oh my!   Mamma mia!   21c

oil   olio   24i, 33c

oil painting   pittura a olio   28b

ointment   pomata   25h, 40a

old   vecchio   11b

old age   vecchiaia, terza età   11b

older   maggiore, più vecchio, più grande   11b

older brother   fratello più grande, fratello maggiore   11b
older person   vecchio (-a)   11b
olfactory   olfattivo   12e
olive   oliva   14d, 24f
olive skin   pelle olivastra   11a
olive tree   ulivo, olivo   14c
Olympic games   giochi Olimpici   27b
omelet   frittata   24h
on   su   3c, 8f
on account of   a causa di   8i
on sale   in saldo   25a
on the air   in onda   20b
on time   in orario   32b, 34
on top   in cima   3c
on vacation   in vacanza   36b
once   una volta   4c
once in a while   ogni tanto   4c
Once upon a time…   C'era una volta…   4c
one   uno   1a
one (in general)   si   8h
one billion   un miliardo   1a
one hundred   cento   1a
one hundred and one   centouno   1a
one hundred and two   centodue   1a
one hundred million   cento milioni   1a
one hundred thousand   centomila   1a
one million   un milione   1a
one thousand   mille   1a
one thousand and one   milleuno   1a
One way   Senso unico   33b
One-800 number   numero verde   18b
one-half   metà, mezzo   1c
one-quarter   un quarto   1c
one-third   un terzo   1c
one-way ticket   biglietto di andata   30a
onion   cipolla   14e, 24f
online   online   38c, 42b
online banking   banca online   26a

online reservation   prenotazione on-line   30a
online shopping   comprare online   25a
only   solo   8j
opal   opale   25i
opaque   opaco   7b
Open   Aperto   25a, 33b
open an account   aprire un conto   26a
open up a mortgage   accendere un mutuo   26a
opening time   apertura   25a
opera   opera   25j, 28c
operate   operare   40a
operating room   sala operatoria   40a
operation   intervento chirurgico   40a
operator   centralino   18a
opinion   opinione   22a
opponent   avversario (-a)   27b
opposite   opposto   2b
optic cable   cavo ottico   20b
optic fiber   fibra ottica   20b
optical reader   videolettore, lettore ottico   42a, 42b
optics   ottica   42a
optimist   ottimista   11e
optional subject   materia opzionale   37f
Options   Opzioni   42c
optometrist   optometrista   40a
oral   orale   17a
oral exam   esame orale   37f
orange (fruit)   arancia   14d, 24g
orange (tree)   arancio   14c
orange (color)   arancione   7a
orangeade   aranciata   24j
orbit   orbita, orbitare   3d, 13a
orchestra   orchestra   25j, 28c
orchestra conductor   direttore (-trice) (d'orchestra)   25j, 28c
orchid   orchidea   14b
order   ordine, ordinare, prendere   11d, 17a, 24n
ordinal   ordinale   1d

ordinate ordinata 2b
oregano origano 24i
organ organo 12a, 28c
organic organico 13c
organist organista 28c
organization chart
  organigramma 38c
origin origine 11f
original originale 11e
ornate adorno 28d
orphan orfano (-a) 11c
orphanage orfanatrofio 11c
orthodontist ortodontista
  40b
orthopedic surgeon chirurgo
  ortopedico 40a
ostrich struzzo 15b
others altri (-e) 8h
otter lontra 15a
Ouch! Ahi! 16c
our nostro (-a), nostri (-e) 8e
Our Father Paternostro 11d
ourselves ci 8g
out fuori 39a
Out of order Fuori servizio 33b
outcome esito 27b
Outgoing mail Posta in uscita
  42c
outlaw fuorilegge 39b
outlet presa 18a
outline, profile profilo, contorno,
  tratteggiare 3d, 28d
outside fuori 3c, 36c
outspoken schietto 17a
oven forno 23b
over sopra, su 8f
overcoat soprabito 25k
overdose overdose 44c
overdue rental morosità 23e
overhead lucido 37b
overhead projector lavagna
  luminosa 37b
overlook guardare su 35b
overpopulation
  sovrappopolazione 44b
overtime work lavoro
  straordinario 38d
owl gufo 15b

ownership papers libretto di
  circolazione 33a
ox bue (buoi, pl) 15a
oxygen ossigeno 13c
oyster ostrica 15c, 24e

P
pacemaker stimolatore cardiaco
  40a
Pacific Pacifico 13b, 30c
pack imballare 25a
package pacco 19e, 25a
package tour viaggio organizzato
  30a
packet plico 19e
packing crate cassa
  d'imballaggio 3e
pad taccuino 19d, 25c, 38c
paddle pagaia 34
pagan pagano (-a) 11d
paganism paganesimo 11d
page pagina 19c
page layout, set-up
  impaginazione 19c, 42b, 42c
pain dolore 40a
painkiller analgesico 25h, 40a
painful doloroso 40a
paint vernice, dipingere,
  imbiancare, pitturare 7b, 23d,
  25b, 28b
paint brush pennello 23d
painter pittore (-trice) 7b, 28b
painting dipinto, quadro, pittura
  7b, 28b
pair paio 3b, 25g
pajamas pigiama 25k
Pakistan Pakistan 30b
Pakistani pachistano 30e
palate palato 12a, 40b
pale pallido 25g
pale cheeks guance pallide 11a
paleontology paleontologia
  43b
Palermo Palermo 30c
Palestinian palestinese 30e
palette tavolozza 28b
palliative palliativo 25h, 40a
palm palma 12a, 14c

pan padella 23c	**partial** parziale 3b
pancreas pancreas 12a	**participle** participio 8a
panda panda 15a	**particle** particella 13c
paneling pannello 23a	**partition, wall** parete 23a
pansy viola del pensiero 14b	**partitive** partitivo 8a
panther pantera 15a	**partner** socio (-a) 38a
pantomime pantomima 28e	**partnership** partnership 38d
pantry dispensa 23a	**partridge** pernice 15b
pants pantaloni 25k	**party** partito 43a
pantyhose, tights collant 25k	**party, feast** festa 29b
papacy papato 11d	**pass** passo, sorpassare, passare 13b, 27b, 33a
paper carta 19d, 25c, 37b, 38c	**pass an exam** superare un esame 37f
paper cup bicchiere di carta 24k	
parable parabola 11d	**pass by** passare davanti 3f
parabola parabola 2a	**pass near** passare vicino 3f
parachuting paracadutismo 27b	**passenger** passeggero (-a) 32c
parade parata 27a, 29b	**passing** approvazione 43a
paragraph capoverso 19c	**Passing lane** Corsia di sorpasso 33b
Paraguay Paraguay 30b	
Paraguayan paraguaiano 30e	**passion** passione 21a
parallel parallela 2b	**passive** passivo 8a
parallelepiped parallelepipedo 2a	**passport** passaporto 31
parallelogram parallelogramma 2a	**passport control** controllo passaporti 31
paralysis paralisi 40a	**password** password 38c, 42c
paramedic paramedico 40a	**past** passato 4c, 8a
parent genitore (-trice) 10a	**past absolute** passato remoto 8a
parenthesis, bracket parentesi 19c	
Paris Parigi 30c	**pasta** pasta 24b
parish parrocchia 11d	**Paste** Incolla 42c
parish priest parroco 11d	**pastel** pastello 28b
parishioner parrocchiano (-a) 11d	**pastille** pasticca 25h, 40a
park parco 36a	**pastry shop** pasticceria 24m
parking parcheggio 33a	**paternal** paterno 10a
parking meter parchimetro 36a	**path** sentiero 14a
parliament parlamento 43a	**pathologist** patologo (-a) 40a
parody parodia 25n, 28d	**patience** pazienza 21a
parrot, budgie pappagallo 15b	**patient** paziente 11e, 40a
parsley prezzemolo 14e, 24i	**patio** terrazza 23a
part parte 3b	**patrol** pattuglia, pattugliare 39b
parted hair capelli con la riga scriminatura 11a	**pattern** modello, modellare 3d
	patterned modellato 3d
	paunch pancia 11a
	pavement, sidewalk marciapiede 36a
	pay paga, pagare 25a, 26a, 38d
	pay bail versare la cauzione 41

pay claim rivendicazione salariale 38d

pay day giorno di paga 38d

pay duty pagare la dogana 31

pay off saldare 26a

pay off a mortgage estinguere un mutuo 26a

payment pagamento 26a

payment on delivery pagamento a pronta cassa 26a

pea pisello 14e, 24f

peace pace 14d, 44d

peach (fruit) pesca 24g

peach (tree) pesco 14c

peacock pavone 15b

peak vetta 13b

peanut (as sold in the USA) nocciolina americana 14d, 24g

peanut (in general) arachide 14d, 24g

pear (fruit) pera 14d, 24g

pear (tree) pero 14c

pearl perla 25i

pearl gray grigio perla 7a

pebble ciottolo 13b

pedal pedale 34

pedestal piedistallo 28b

pedestrian pedone 33a

pedestrian crosswalk passaggio pedonale 33a, 36a

pediatrician pediatra 40a

peel sbucciare 24a

peep, peer sbirciare 12d

pelican pellicano 15b

pelvis pelvi 12a

pen penna 2b, 7b, 19d, 25c

penalty rigore 27b

penance penitenza 11d

pencil, crayon matita 2b, 7b, 25c

pendant pendente 25i

penguin pinguino 15b

penicillin penicillina 25h, 40a

peninsula penisola 13b

pension, retirement pensione 38d

pentagon pentagono 2a

peony peonia 14b

people gente 10b

pepper pepe 14e, 14f, 24i

pepper container pepiera 23c

per hour all'ora 3a

per minute al minuto 3a

per second al secondo 3a

perceive percepire 12b

percent percento 1f

percentage percentuale 1f

percussion instruments strumenti a percussione 28c

perfect perfetto 8a

perfectionist perfezionista 11e

perfidious perfido 21a

performance messa in scena 28e

performer interprete 25j, 28s

perfume profumo 12f, 25f

perimeter perimetro 2b

period (of time) periodo 43b

period (in a sentence) punto 19c

periodical periodico 20a, 25n

peripheral unità periferica 19f, 38c, 42b

periphery, outskirts periferia 3d

perjury falsa testimonianza 39b

permanent memory memoria fissa 38c, 42b

perpendicular perpendicolare 2b

person persona 8a, 10b

personal personale 8a

personal income tax imposta sul reddito delle persone fisiche 26b

personal information dati anagrafici 11f

personal organizer agenda 38c, 42b

personality personalità 11e

personality test test psicologico 38d

perspective, framework ottica 28d

perspire sudare 6b

persuade persuadere 22a, 22b, 41

Peru Perù 30b
Perugia Perugia 30c
Peruvian peruviano 30e
perverted pervertito 21a
pessimist pessimista 11e
pest parassita 14a
pesticide insetticida 14a
pet animale domestico 15a
petal petalo 14a
petroleum petrolio 13c, 44a
petunia petunia 14b
pew banco di chiesa 11d
pharmaceutical farmaco 25h, 40a
pharmacist farmacista 25h, 38a, 40a
pharmacy, drugstore farmacia 25h
pheasant fagiano 15b
phial fiala 25h, 40a
philanthropic filantropico 21a
philanthropy filantropia 21a
Philippines Filippine 30b
philosophy filosofia 37e
phone bill bolletta del telefono 18a
phone book elenco telefonico 18a
phone booth cabina telefonica 18a
phone call telefonata 18b
phone card scheda telefonica 18a
phone keyboard tastiera del telefono 18a
phone number numero di telefono 11f, 18b
phonetics fonetica 8a
phosphate fosfato 13c
photo-sensitive fotosensibile 25d
photocopier fotocopiatrice 19d, 25c, 38c
photocopy fotocopia, fotocopiare 37f
photocopy shop copisteria 19d
photograph foto, fotografia 25d, 28b

photographer fotografo (-a) 25d, 28b
photographic shot ripresa fotografica 25d, 28b
phrase frase 19c
physical fisico 13c
physical education educazione fisica 37f
physical therapist fisioterapista 38a
physics fisica 13c, 37e
pianist pianista 28c
piano pianoforte, piano 28c
pick up one's baggage ritirare il bagaglio 32a
pickpocket scippatore (-trice) 39b
picky, fastidious pignolo 11e
picnic picnic 29a
piece pezzo 3b
piece of furniture mobile 23b
piece work lavoro a cottimo 38d
Piedmont Piemonte 30d
pig maiale 15a
pile mucchio, catasta 3b
pilgrim pellegrino (-a), peregrino (-a) 11d
pilgrimage pellegrinaggio 11d
pill pillola 25h, 40a
pillow cuscino 23b, 35b
pillow case federa 23b
pilot pilota 38a
pimple foruncolo 11a, 12a
pinball machine flipper 27a
pinch pizzicare 3f
pine pino 14c
pineapple ananas 14d, 24g
pink rosa 7a
pipe pipa 25e
pirate program programma pirata 42b
Pisa Pisa 30c
Pisces Pesci (pl) 5d
pistachio pistacchio 14d, 24g
pistol pistola 39b
piston pistone 33c
pitch lanciare 27b

pitch black   nero come la pece 7a

pitcher   lanciatore   27b

pitchfork   forcone   14a

pizza parlor   pizzeria   24l

place   posto, luogo   3c, 19c, 38b

place of birth   luogo di nascita 11f

plain   pianura   13b

plaintiff   querelante   41

plane   pialla   23d, 25b

plane figure   figura piana   2a

planet   pianeta   5c, 13a

planner   agenda   25c

plant   pianta, piantare   14a

plant (manufacturing)   stabilimento   38d

plaque   placca dentaria   40b

plaster   intonaco, ingessatura 13c, 40a

plaster cast   fascia gessata   40a

plasterer   intonacatore (-trice) 38a

plastic   plastica   13c

plastic surgeon   chirurgo estetico 40a

plate   piatto   24k

plate-rack   scolapiatti   23c

platform   programma elettorale 43a

platinum   platino   13c

platter   piatto misto   24a

play (theater)   recita, rappresentazione teatrale   20a, 25n

play (an instrument)   suonare 27a, 28c

play (a game)   giocare   27a

play (action)   gioco, azione   27b

play ball (soccer)   giocare al pallone   27a

play out of tune   stonare   28c

play skipping rope   saltare con la corda   27a

player (sports)   giocatore (-trice) 27b

player (music)   suonatore (-trice) 25j, 28c

playful   giocoso   21a

playing card   carta da gioco   27a

playoffs, championship campionato   27b

playwright   commediografo (-a) 25n

plea   supplica, dichiararsi   41

pleasant, nice   piacevole, simpatico   11e, 21b

pleasant, friendly face   viso simpatico   11a

Please!   Per favore!   16c

pleased, content   contento   11e, 21a

pleated skirt   gonna a pieghe 25k

plebeian   plebeo, plebe   43b

pliers, tongs, tweezers   pinze, tenaglie   23d, 25b

plot   trama   20a, 25n, 28d, 28e

plow   aratro, arare   14a

plug   spina   23d, 25b

plum   prugna, susina   14d, 24g

plumber   idraulico   38a

plumbing   sistema idraulico   23d

plump   pasciuto   11a

pluperfect   trapassato   8a

plural   plurale   8a

plus   più   1e, 1f, 6c

Pluto   Plutone   13a

pneumonia   polmonite   40a

Po river   Po   30c

pocket   tasca   25g

pocket calculator   calcolatrice tascabile   37b

pocket-picking   scippo   39b

poem   poesia   20a, 25n

poet   poeta (-essa)   25n, 28d

poetics   poetica   25n, 28d

poetry   poesia   25n

point   punto   2b, 27b

point out   segnalare   28d

poison gas   gas tossico   44d

Poland   Polonia   30b

polar bear   orso bianco   15a

pole   polo   13d

pole vaulting   salto con l'asta 27b

police polizia 39b, 39c
police headquarters
  commissariato 39b
police officer poliziotto (-a)
  39b
police station questura 36a, 39b
police van furgone della polizia
  39b
police officer carabiniere (-a),
  poliziotto (-a) 33a, 38a
policy (in general) politica
  43a
Polish polacco 30e
politeness, courtesy cortesia
  11e
political science scienze politiche
  37e
politician politicante 43a
polka polca 28c
poll sondaggio 20b, 43a
pollen polline 14a
pollute inquinare 13c
polluted inquinato 44a
pollution inquinamento 13c, 44a
polyester poliestere 25g
polygon poligono 2a
polyhedron poliedro 2a
Polynesia Polinesia 30b
Polynesian polinesiano 30e
pompous pomposo 21a, 28d
pontiff pontefice 11d
poodle barboncino 15a
pool piscina 35a
poor povero 11e
Poor man! Poor woman!
  Poveretto! Poveretta! 21c
pope papa 11d
poplar pioppo 14c
poppy papavero 14b
porcelain porcellana 13c
porch veranda 23a
porcupine porcospino 15a
pore poro 12a
pork maiale 24d
pornographic magazine rivista
  pornografica 20a, 25n
pornographic movie film
  pornografico 28a

pornography pornografia 44b
portable phone telefono portatile
  18a
portable radio radio portatile
  20b
porter assistente ai bagagli 32a
portfolio portafoglio 26a
porthole oblò 34
portion, helping porzione 3b,
  24a
portrait ritratto 28b
Portugal Portogallo 30b
Portuguese portoghese 30e
pose posa 28b
position posizione 3c
positive positivo 1d
possessive possessivo 8a, 11e
post office ufficio postale 19e
postage affrancatura 19e
postal box casella postale 19e
postal card cartolina postale 19e
postal check assegno postale
  19e
postal code codice postale 19e,
  38b
postal money order vaglia
  postale 19e
postal package pacco postale
  19e
postal rate tariffa postale 19e
poster cartellone pubblicitario
  20c
posterior posteriore 4c
pot pentola, casseruola, tegame
  23c
pot-bellied panciuto 11a
potassium potassio 13c
potato patata 14e, 24f
potato masher schiacciapatate
  23c
potato peeler pelapatate 23c
pottery arte della ceramica 27a
pound libbra 3a
pour versare 24a
pouring rain pioggia torrenziale
  6a
poverty povertà 44b
power potenza, potere 1e, 43a

power brake servofreno 33c
power of attorney procura 41
power steering servosterzo 33c
practice esercitarsi 28c
praise lodare, elogiare 17a, 21a
prawn, shrimp scampo, gambero 15c, 24e
pray pregare 11d, 17a
prayer preghiera 11d, 17a
preach predicare 11d, 17a
preacher predicatore (-trice) 11d
preaching, sermon predica 11d
precede precedere 3f
precious prezioso 25i
precipice precipizio 13b
precise preciso 11e
predicate predicato 8a
prefab casa prefabbricata 23a
preface prefazione 25n, 28d
prefer preferire 21b
Preferences Preferiti 42c
pregnancy gravidanza 11c, 40a
pregnant incinta 11c, 40a
prehistoric preistorico 43b
premature birth parto prematuro 11c
premeditated crime delitto premeditato 39b
premiere showing prima visione 28a
preposition preposizione 8a
prepositional contraction preposizione articolata 8a, 8g
prescribe prescrivere 40a
prescription ricetta medica 25h, 40a
present presente 4c, 8a
present perfect passato prossimo 8a
presentable presentabile 21a
presently attualmente 4c
president presidente 43a
president of a university rettore 37d
press stampa 25n

press conference conferenza stampa 20a
press room sala stampa 20a
press agency agenzia di stampa 20a
pressure pressione 13c
pressure cooker, steamer pentola a pressione 23c
presumptuous presuntuoso 11e, 21a
pretentious pretenzioso 11e
pretty carino 11a
price prezzo 24l, 25a, 35a
price list tariffa dei prezzi 25a
price tag etichetta 25a
prickly spinoso, pungente 12e
pride superbia 11d
priest prete 11d
primary school scuola primaria 37a
prime primo 1d
prime minister primo ministro 43a
primrose primula 14b
prince principe 43a
princess principessa 43a
principal preside 37d
print stampare 19f, 38c, 42b, 42c
print (medium) stampa 20a
print run, circulation tiratura 20a
print, mold stampa 28b
printed matter stampe 19e
printer stampante 19d, 25c, 38c, 42b
printing tipografia 20a
prism prisma 2a
prison prigione 41
prisoner detenuto (-a) 39b
private channel canale privato 20b
private detective investigatore privato 39b
private school scuola privata 37a
private television televisione privata 20b

privatize   privatizzare   38d
probation   libertà vigilata   41
probation period   tirocinio   38d
probe   sondare   40a
problem   problema   1f, 22a, 37f
problem to solve   problema da risolvere   1f
proceed   procedere   3f
produce, fruit vendor fruttivendolo   24m
producer   produttore (-trice) 28a, 38d
product   prodotto   1f, 25a, 38d
production   produzione   28a
profession   professione   11f, 38a, 38b
professional   professionista 11f, 38a
professional development aggiornamento degli insegnanti 37f
Professor   Professore (-essa) 11f, 16b
profile   frofilo   19g
profit   profitto, guadagno   38d
profit margin   margine di guadagno   38d
prognosis   prognosi   40a
program   programma   20b, 42b
program instruction   istruzione 42b
program language   linguaggio di programmazione   42b
programmer   programmatore (-trice)   38a, 42b
progressive party   partito progressista   43a
projective geometry   geometria proiettiva   1g
projector   proiettore   20b, 37b
promise   promessa, promettere 17a
promontory   promontorio   13b
promotion   promozione   38d
prompter   suggeritore (-trice) 28e
pronoun   pronome   8a

pronounce   pronunciare   17a
pronunciation   pronuncia   8a, 17a
proof   prova   41
proofs   prove   20a
propeller   elica   34
property   proprietà   23a
propose, suggest   proporre   17a
proposition   proposizione   1f
prose   prosa   25n, 28d
prostitution   prostituzione   44b
protect   proteggere   39a
protest   protesta   43a
Protestant   protestante   11d
Protestantism   protestantesimo 11d
proton   protone   13c
protractor   goniometro   2b, 37b
proud, haughty   orgoglioso 11e
provided that   purché   8i
province   provincia   13d
provincial   provinciale   43a
provision (welfare)   previdenza sociale   44b
provocative   provocante   21a
prudent   prudente   11e
prudish, prim   pudico   11e
prune   prugna, potare   14a, 14d, 24g
psychiatrist   psichiatra   38a, 40a
psychiatry   psichiatria   37e
psychologist   psicologo (-a)   38a
psychology   psicologia   37e
psychosomatic   psicosomatico 40a
psychotherapist   psicoterapista 40a
puberty   pubertà   11b
public channel   canale pubblico 20b
public debt   debito pubblico 26b
public notices   affissioni pubbliche   36a
public phone   telefono pubblico 18a

public prosecutor pubblico accusatore 41
public relations office ufficio pubbliche relazioni 38d
public school scuola pubblica 37a
public television televisione pubblica 20b
public transport trasporto pubblico 34
publish pubblicare 20a, 25n
publisher editore 20a, 25n, 28d
puck disco 27b
pudding budino 24c
pudgy tozzo 11a
Puerto Rican portoricano 30e
Puerto Rico Puerto Rico 30b
pull tirare 3f
pull a tooth estrarre un dente 40b
pulpit pulpito 11d
pulse polso 40a
pump pompa 33c
pumpkin zucca 14e, 24f
punch (paper) perforatrice 19d, 25c, 38c
punch (tool) punzone 25b
punctilious puntiglioso 11e
punctuation punteggiatura 19c
puny smunto 11a
pupil (student) alunno (-a) 37d
pupil (eye) pupilla 12a
puppet theater teatro dei burrattini 27a
puppy cucciolo, cagnolino 15a
purchase acquisto 25a
pure puro 7a, 11e
purgatory purgatorio 11d
purple, violet viola 7a
purse borsa 31
pus pus 40a
push spingere 3f
push button (on a camera) scatto 25d

push drugs spacciare droga 39b
put mettere 3f
put a space interlineare 42b
put down posare 3f
put forward avanzare 17a
put into a mailbox imbucare 19e
put on (clothes) mettersi 25l
put on (shoes) mettersi (le scarpe) 25m
put on makeup truccarsi 12f
put on perfume profumarsi 12f
putrid putrido 12e
puzzle enigma 27a
puzzle section enigmistica 20a, 25n
pyramid piramide 2a
pyramidal piramidale 3d
Pythagorean theorem teorema di Pitagora 2b

Q

quadrilateral quadrilatero 2a
quadrille, square dance quadriglia 28c
qualifications Qualifiche 38b
quality qualità 21a
quantity quantità 3b
quarrelsome litigioso 11e
quart quarto 3a
quarter term quadrimestre 37f
quartet quartetto 28c
quartz watch orologio al quarzo 25i
queen regina 43a
question domanda 37f
question mark punto interrogativo 19c
questioning interrogatorio 39b
queue, lineup fila, coda 25a
quickly velocemente 3f
quiet quieto 11e
Quiet! Silenzio! 16c, 21c
quilt trapunta 23b
quintet quintetto 28c

remember ricordare   22a, 22b
remodeling, renovation rimodernamento   23e
remote control telecomando   20b
Remove Rimuovi   42c
Renaissance Rinascimento   43b
rent affitto, noleggiare, affittare   33d, 23e
rental noleggio   33d
rental place autonoleggio   33d
rented car macchina, auto noleggiata   34
repair riparazione   23e
repeat ripetere   17a, 37f
repetition ripetizione   17a
reply risposta, replicare, rispondere   17a, 19e, 42c
report resoconto, relazione, riferire, riportare   17a
report card pagella   37f
report, news item, feature cronaca   20a
report, reporting servizio   20a
representation (political) rappresentanza   43a
reproach rimproverare   17a
reptile rettile   15c
republic repubblica   43a
republican party partito repubblicano   43a
request richiesta, richiedere   17a
rescue soccorrere   39a
reservation prenotazione   24l, 30a, 32a, 35a
reserve prenotare   35a
reserved riservato   11e, 24l
reservoir cisterna   3e
reside risiedere   11f
residence residenza, domicilio   11f
residential school collegio   37a
resin resina   13c
resistant resistente   13c
resonate risuonare   12c
respectful rispettoso   21a

respiratory system sistema respiratorio   12a
rest, relax riposarsi   12b
restaurant (formal) ristorante   24l
restaurant (informal) trattoria   24l
restless irrequieto   21a
restricted vietato ai minori, minorenni   28a
résumé Curriculum vitae   38b
resuscitate rianimare   40a
retail al dettaglio   25a
retail price prezzo al dettaglio   25a
retire andare in pensione   38d
return tornare, ritornare, restituire   3f, 25a, 29b
return address indirizzo del mittente   19e
return ticket biglietto di andata e ritorno   30a
return vehicle conditions condizioni del veicolo al rientro   33d
Reverend Reverendo   11f, 16b
review recensione, recensire, ripasso, ripassare   20a, 28d, 37f
revolt, riot rivolta   43a
revolution rivoluzione   43a
rheumatism reumatismo   40a
rhinoceros rinoceronte   15a
rhombus rombo   2a
rhubarb rabarbaro   14e, 24f
rhythm ritmo   25j, 28c
rib costola   12a
rice riso   24b
rice with vegetables risotto   24b
rich ricco   11e
riddle indovinello   27a
rifle fucile   39b
right corretto, destra, retto   2b, 3c, 36c, 37f
right away subito   4c, 8j
right prism prisma retto   2a
right to vote diritto al voto   43a

right to work diritto al lavoro 43a

right turn, exit right svolta a destra 33a

right-angled rettangolo 2a

right-wing di destra 43a

Rimini Rimini 30c

ring anello, suonare 3d, 12c, 18b, 25i

ring finger (dito) anulare 12a

ring-binder quaderno ad anelli 19d, 25c

ringed notebook quaderno a anelli 37b

rinse sciacquarsi la bocca 40b

ripe maturo 14a, 24a

rise in prices rialzo dei prezzi 26b

rite rito 11d

rival rivale 27b

river fiume 13b, 36b

river-bed alveo 13b

road, roadway, street strada 36a

road map mappa stradale 33a

road sign segnale stradale 33a

roar ruggire 15a

roast arrosto 24a

rob rapinare 39b

robber, burglar rapinatore (-trice) 39b

robbery, burglary rapina 39b

robin pettirosso 15b

robust, strong robusto 11a

rock roccia 13b

rock music musica rock 25j, 28c

rocking chair sedia a dondolo 23b

Rococo Rococò 28b

rod canna da pesca 27a

rodent roditore 15a

role ruolo 28e

roll of film rullino 25d

roller rullo 23d, 25b

roller skating pattinaggio a rotelle 27b

Roman romano 1d

Roman Empire Impero Romano 43b

romantic romantico 11e

Romanticism Romanticismo 28b, 43b

Rome Roma 30c

roof tetto 23a

room camera, stanza 23a

rooster gallo 15b

root radice 1e, 14a, 40b

rope corda 13c, 27b

rosary rosario 11d

rose rosa 14b

rosemary rosmarino 14e, 24i

rosy cheeks guance rosee 11a

rotten marcio 14a, 24a

rough ruvido 11e, 12e, 25g

rough copy, draft brutta copia 37f

rough skin pelle ruvida 11a

roughness, rudeness rudezza 21a

round box scatola rotonda 3e

round face viso rotondo 11a

round table tavola rotonda 37f

row fila 3d, 28a

rowing, canoeing canottaggio 27b

royalty diritto d'autore 28d

rub strofinare 3f

rubber gomma 13c

rubber band elastico 19d, 25c

rubber gloves guanti di gomma 25h, 40a

ruby rubino 25i

rude rude 11e

rug tappeto 23b

ruin rovina 43b

ruler riga 2b, 19d, 25c, 38c

Rumania Romania 30b

Rumanian rumeno 30e

rumba rumba 28c

rumor diceria, voce 17a

Rumor has it that… Corre voce che… 17a

run correre 3f, 12b, 27b

run away scappare 3f

run into incontrare 16b
runner corridore (-trice) 27b
runway pista 32c
rush hour ora di punta 33a
Russia Russia 30b
Russian russo 30e
rustle frusciare 12c
ruthless spietato 11e

S

sacrament sacramento 11d
sacred sacro 11d
Sacred Scripture Sacra Scrittura 11d
sacrifice sacrificio 11d
sacrilege sacrilegio 11d
sacristan sagrestano 11d
sad triste 11e
safe cassaforte 3e, 26a
safety deposit box cassetta di sicurezza 26a
saffron zafferano 24i
Sagittarius Sagittario 5d
sailing vela 27b
sailor marinaio (-a) 38a
salad insalata 14e, 24a
salad bowl insalatiera 23c
salami sausage salame 24d
sale saldo 25a
sales representative agente commerciale 38a
sales tax IVA 26b
salesman, saleswoman venditore (-trice) 38a
saliva saliva 12a
salmon salmone 15c, 24e
salt sale 13c, 24i
salt container saliera 23c
salt water acqua di mare 13b
salty salato 12e, 24a
salutation saluto epistolare 19c
Salvadoran salvadoregno 30e
sample campione 20c, 25a
San Marino San Marino 30b
sand sabbia 13b
sandal sandalo 25m
sandpaper carta vetrata 23d, 25b

sandwich (bun) panino 24c
sandwich (flat) tramezzino 24c
sap linfa 14c
sapling alberello 14c
sapphire zaffiro 25i
sarcastic sarcastico 11e, 21a
sardine sardina 15c, 24e
Sardinia Sardegna 30d
sardonic sardonico 21a
satellite satellite 13a, 42a
satellite dish antenna parabolica 20b, 42a
satellite television televisione via satellite 20b
satire satira 25n, 28d
satisfaction soddisfazione 21a
satisfied soddisfatto 11e, 21a
Saturday sabato 5a
Saturn Saturno 13a
sauce sugo, salsa 24b
saucepan casseruola 23c
saucer piattino 23c, 24k
Saudi saudita 30e
Saudi Arabia Arabia Saudita 30b
sausage salsiccia 24d
save salvare, risparmiare 26a, 42b, 42c
savings risparmi 26a
savings book libretto di risparmio 26a
saw sega 23d, 25b
saxophone sassofono 28c
saxophonist sassofonista 28c
say, tell dire 17a
scale scala, scaglia, bilancia 13c, 15c, 28c
scalene scaleno 2a
scallop, shell conchiglia 15c
scalp cuoio capelluto 12a
Scandinavia Scandinavia 30b
Scandinavian scandinavo 30e
scanner scanner 19d, 25c
scar cicatrice 40a
scarlet fever scarlattina 40a
scenario, background scenario 28e
scene scena 25n, 28d, 28e

scenery sceneggiatura 28a, 28e
scenic route itinerario panoramico 36b
scented profumato 12e
schedule orario 32b, 34
scheming intrigante 21a
scholarship, grant borsa di studio 37a
scholarship holder borsista 37a
school scuola 37a
school bag cartella 37b
school fee, tuition tassa scolastica 37f
school registration iscrizione a scuola 37f
school yard cortile 37c
school year anno scolastico 5b, 37a
schoolmate compagno (-a) 37d
sciatic nerve nervo sciatico 12b
science scienza 37e
science fiction fantascienza 20a, 25n, 28a
sciences faculty facoltà di scienze 37a
scientific lyceum liceo scientifico 37a
scientist scienziato (-a) 38a
scissors forbici 19d, 25c
score (musical) spartito 25j, 28c
score (game) punteggio, segnare 27b
Scorpio Scorpione 5d
scorpion scorpione 15d
Scotland Scozia 30b
Scottish scozzese 30e
scoundrel scellerato, briccone (-a) 11e, 21a
scrap iron rottame 13c
scratch graffio 33d
scrawny, skin and bones scheletrico 11a
screen schermo 28a, 42b
screw vite, avvitare 23d, 25b
screwdriver cacciavite 23d, 25b

script copione 28e
scrupulous scrupoloso 21a
scuffle baruffa 39b
sculpt scolpire 28b
sculptor, sculptress scultore (-trice) 28b
sculpture scultura 28b
scurvy scorbuto 40a
sea mare 6a, 13b, 36b
sea horse cavalluccio marino 15c
sea lion otaria, leone marino 15a
seabed fondo del mare 13b
seafood frutti di mare 24e
seagull gabbiano 15b
seal foca 15a
search ricerca, perquisizione 19f, 39b, 42b
search warrant mandato di perquisizione 39b
seaside area zona balneare 30a
seaside vacation vacanza al mare 30a
season stagione 5c
seat posto, sellino 32c, 34
seat (political) seggio 43a
seat belt cintura di sicurezza 32c, 33c
secant secante 2b
second secondo 1b, 4b
second course secondo piatto 24c
second job, moonlighting secondo lavoro 38d
Second World War Seconda Guerra Mondiale 43b
second year secondo anno 37a
secondary school scuola secondaria 37a
secretary segretario (-a) 37d, 38a
sect setta 11d
section sezione 3c
security services servizi di sicurezza 43a
sedative sedativo 25h, 40a
seductive seducente 11a, 11e
see vedere 12d

See you later! A più tardi! 16a
See you soon! A presto! 16a
See you Sunday! A domenica! 16a
See you! Ci vediamo! 16a
seed, sow seme, seminare 14a
segment segmento 2b
Select Seleziona 42c
self-confident, sure sicuro 11e
self-examination autopalpazione 40a
self-learner privatista 37d
self-sufficient autosufficiente 11e
self-taught autodidatta 37f
sell vendere 23f, 25a
semester semestre 37f
semicolon punto e virgola 19c
seminar, workshop seminario 37f
senate senato 43a
send spedire 3f, 19e
sender mittente 19e
Senegal Senegal 30b
Senegalese senegalese 30e
senile senile 11b
senior anziano (-a) 11b
sense, feel, smell sentire 12b
sense of smell olfatto 12e
sensible sensato 11e, 22a
sensitive sensibile 11e, 21a
sensitivity sensibilità 21a
sensuous, sensual sensuale 21a
Sent mail Posta inviata 42c
sentence (judgment) sentenza 41
sentence (grammar) frase 8a, 19c
sentimental sentimentale 11e
separated separato (-a) 11f
separation separazione 11c
September settembre 5b
September 15 il quindici settembre 5e
Serbia Serbia 30b
Serbian serbo 30e
serene sereno 11e

serial, series programma a puntate 20b
serious serio 11e
serious accident incidente grave 39c
sermon sermone 11d
serve servire 24n
server server 19f, 42b
service servizio 24l, 35a
servile servizievole 21a
session sessione 43a
set insieme 1f
set a record stabilire un record 27b
set algebra algebra di insiemi 1g
set of drums batteria 28c
set the table apparecchiare 23f
set up a page impaginare 42b
seven sette 1a
seventeen diciassette 1a
seventh settimo 1b
seventy settanta 1a
several parecchio 3b
severe severo 11e
sew cucire 25g, 25l, 27a
sewage acque di scarico 44a
sewage system fognatura 44a
sewing machine macchina per cucire 23b
sex sesso 11a, 38b
sextet sestetto 28c
sexy sexy 21a
shade, nuance sfumatura 28b
shadow, shade ombra 6a
shake agitare 3f
shake hands dare la mano, stringere la mano 3f, 16a
shake one's head scuotere la testa 3f
shaman sciamano 11d
shamanism sciamanismo 11d
shame vergogna 21a
shameful vergognoso 21a
shameless svergognato 21a
shampoo shampoo 12f, 25f, 35b
shark squalo, pescecane 15c

shave farsi la barba 12f

shaving cream crema da barba 25f

shawl mantello 25k

she lei, ella 8g

shed light on gettare luce su 13a

sheep pecora 15a

sheet (of paper) foglio 19d, 25c

sheet metal laminato 13c

sheets (bed) lenzuola 35b

shelf (book) ripiano, palchetto di uno scaffale 23b

shell (sea) conchiglia 15c

shellfish crostacei 24e

shelter rifugio 44b

shepherd pastore (-a) 15a

shift work turno di lavoro 38d

shin stinco 12a

shine brillare 12d

shingle tegola 23a

shingles fuoco di Sant'Antonio 40a

shirt camicia 25k

shoe scarpa 25m

shoe horn calzascarpe 25m

shoe repair (shop) calzolaio 25m

shoe size numero (di scarpa) 25m

shoe store negozio di scarpe 25m

shoelace stringa 25m

shoot, kick tirare 27b

shoot (fire) sparare 39b

shoot a movie girare un film 28a

shooting on location riprese in esterni 28a

shop negozio, fare delle spese 25a

shop for food fare la spesa 24n

shop window vetrina 25a

shopkeeper negoziante 25a

shopping bag sacchetto della spesa 23b

short basso, corto 3b, 11a, 25g, 25l

short (film) cortometraggio 28a

short coffee caffè ristretto 24j

short story novella 25n, 28d

short-sighted miope 12d

short-story writer novellista 28d

short-term a breve scadenza 4c

short-wave onde corte 20b

shorten accorciare 3b, 25l

shorts pantaloncini, pantaloni corti 25k

shot, kick tiro 27b

shot (movie) ripresa (cinematografica) 28a

shoulder spalla 12a

shoulder blade scapola 12a

shout grido, gridare 17a, 39a

shovel, spade pala, vang 14a, 25b

show spettacolo 20b

show-off sfarzoso 11e

shower acquazzone, doccia 6a, 23a, 35b

shred stracciare 19d, 38c

shrewd perspicace 11e

shriek squillare 12c

shrimp gambero 24e

shrine, sanctuary santuario 11d

Shut up! Zitto (-a)! 21c

shutter, blind persiana 23a

shuttle vehicle navetta 32a

shy, timid timido 11e

Siberia Siberia 30b

Siberian siberiano 30e

Sicily Sicilia 30d

sick malato 12b

sick person ammalato (-a) 40a

sickle falce 14a

sickly malaticcio 40a

side lato 2b

side dish contorno 24a

side mirror specchietto 33c

Siena Siena 30c

sight vista 12d

sight test controllo della vista 12d

sign firmare 11f, 19c, 26a

signal light luce di posizione 33c

signatory, signer firmatario (-a) 26a

signature firma 11f, 19c, 26a, 38b

signs of the zodiac segni dello zodiaco 5d

silence silenzio 17a

silent silenzioso 17a

silhouette sagoma 3d

silk seta 13c

silk worm baco da seta 15d

silly sciocco 11e, 21a

silver argento 7a, 11c, 13c, 25i

silver ring anello d'argento 25i

simple semplice 11e, 22a

simple interest interesse semplice 26a

simultaneous simultaneo 4c

simultaneously simultaneamente 4c

sin peccato, peccare 11d

since da, poiché 4c, 8i

since Monday da lunedì 4c

since yesterday da ieri 4c

sincere sincero 21a

sine seno 2b

Singapore Singapore 30b

Singaporean singaporiano 30e

singer cantante 25j, 28c

single celibe, nubile 11f, 38b

single bed camera singola 35a

single-breasted jacket giacca a un petto 25k

singular singolare 8a

sink lavandino 23a

sinner peccatore (-trice) 11d

sinusitis sinusite 40a

siren sirena 39a

sister sorella 10a

sister-in-law cognata 10a

sit down sedersi 3f

sitting (of the house) seduta 43a

six sei 1a

sixteen sedici 1a

sixth sesto 1b

sixty sessanta 1a

size misura 3b

size (of clothes) taglia 25g

skate pattino, pattinare 27b

skateboard skateboard 27a

skater pattinatore (-trice) 27b

skating pattinaggio 27b

skeleton scheletro 12a

sketch schizzo 28b

ski sciare 27b

ski jumping salto 27b

ski resort campo di sci 36b

skier sciatore (-trice) 27b

skiing, ski sci 27b

skin pelle 12a, 24a

skinny magro 11a

skip a class saltare una lezione 37f

skip school, play hooky marinare la scuola 37f

skirt gonna 25k

skit sketch comico 28e

skull cranio 12a

skunk puzzola 15a

sky cielo 6a

Skype Skype (m, inv) 42d

slab, block lastra, piastra 13b, 14a

slant eyes occhi a mandorla 11a

slash sbarra obliqua 19c

Slavic slavo 30e

sleep sonno, dormire 12b

sleeping bag sacco a pelo 36b

sleeping coach vagone letto 34

sleeping pill sonnifero 25h, 40a

sleepless night notte bianca 7a

sleet nevischio 6a

sleeve manica 25g, 25l

slice fetta, affettare 3d, 24a, 24n

slide (photograph) diapositiva 37f, 25d, 28b

slide, slip   scivolare   3f
sliding door   porta scorrevole   23a, 35b
slim, lean   snello   11a
sling   bendaggio   25h, 40a
slipper   pantofola, ciabatta   25m
slippery   scivoloso   6a, 12e
slogan   slogan   20c
slope   pendio   13b
sloppy, disorganized   disorganizzato   11e
slouch   fannullone (-a)   21a
Slovak   slovacco   30e
Slovakia   Slovacchia   30b
Slovenia   Slovenia   30b
Slovenian   sloveno   30e
slow   lento   3f
slow down   rallentare   3f, 33a
slowly   lentamente   3f
small, little   piccolo   3b, 11a, 25g, 25l
small bill   banconota di piccolo taglio   26a
small garden   giardinetto   14a
small package   pacchetto   25a
small villa, cottage home   villino   23a
small writing pad   blocchetto   25d
smell, odor   odore, odorare   12e
smile   sorriso, sorridere   11a, 21a
smoke   fumo, fumare   13c, 39a
smoke bomb   bomba fumogena   44d
smooth   liscio   12e, 25g, 25l
smug   compiaciuto   21a
smuggling   contrabbando   39b
snack   spuntino   24a
snack bar   snack bar   24l
snake   serpente   15c
sneeze   starnuto, starnutire   40a
snobbish   altezzoso   11e
snow   neve, nevicare   6a
snow-capped   coperto di neve   6a
snowball   palla di neve   6a
snowdrop   bucaneve   14b
snowflake   fiocco di neve   6a

snowman   pupazzo di neve   6a
snowstorm   bufera di neve   6a
so that   affinché, perché   8i
So, so!   Così, così!   16a
So?   E allora? E con ciò?   9a
soap   sapone   12f, 25f, 35b
soap bar   saponetta   35b
soap-dish   portasapone   23b
soap-opera magazine   fotoromanzo   20a, 25n
soap powder   sapone in polvere   25g
sober   sobrio   21a
soccer   calcio   27b
soccer ball   pallone   27b
soccer player   calciatore (-trice)   27b
sociable   socievole   21a
social assistance   assistenza, previdenza sociale   44b
social media   i media sociali   19g, 42d
social worker   assistente sociale   38a
socialism   socialismo   43a
socialist party   partito socialista   43a
sociology   sociologia   37e
sock   calzino   25m
sodium   sodio   13c
sodium bicarbonate   bicarbonato di sodio   25h, 40a
sodium citrate   citrato di sodio   25h
sofa, divan   divano   23b
soft   soffice   12e
soft drug   droga leggera   44c
software   software   38c
solar eclipse   eclissi solare   13a
solar energy   energia solare   44a
solar system   sistema solare   13a
soldier   soldato   38a
sole (fish)   sogliola   15c, 24e
sole (of a foot)   pianta del piede   12a
sole (of a shoe)   suola   25m
solid   solido   2a, 13c

solid figure figura solida 2a
solid geometry geometria solida 1g
solo assolo 28c
soloist solista 28c
solstice solstizio 5c
solution soluzione 1f
solve risolvere 1f
solve a problem risolvere un problema 22b, 37f
Somalia Somalia 30b
Somalian somalo 30e
some alcuni, alcune, qualche 3b, 8c, 8h
some of it ne 3b, 8h
someone qualcuno 8h
something qualcosa 8h
somewhere da qualche parte 3c
son figlio 10a
son-in-law genero 10a
song canzone 25j, 28c
sonnet sonetto 25n
soon tra poco 4c
sooner or later prima o poi 4c
soprano soprano 28c
sorrow dolore 21a
soul anima 11d
sound suono 12c
sound signal segnale sonoro 42a
sound technician tecnico del suono 28a
sound track colonna sonora 28a
soup minestra 24b
soup (thick) zuppa 24b
sour amaro 12e, 24a
south sud 3c, 13d, 36c
South Africa Sud Africa 30b
South African sudafricano 30e
South America America del Sud 30b
South American sudamericano 30e
South Pole Polo Sud 13d
south-east sud-est 3c, 13d
south-west sud-ovest 3c, 13d
southern meridionale 3c, 13d

sow scrofa 15a
space spazio 2b, 3c, 13a
space bar barra spaziatrice 19f, 42b
space shuttle navetta spaziale 13a
spacious spazioso 3c
spade vanga 14a
spaghetti spaghetti 24b
Spain Spagna 30b
Spanish spagnolo 30e
spare wheel ruota di scorta 33c
sparkplug candela 33c
sparkle scintillare 12d
sparrow passero 15b
spasm spasimo 40a
speak, talk parlare 17a
speak badly of malignare, parlare male di 17a
speaker cassa acustica, microfono 18a, 20b
special correspondent inviato speciale 20a
special education teacher insegnante di sostegno 37d
specialization course corso di specializzazione 37a
species specie 14a
speech, talk discorso 17a, 43a
speech therapist logopedista 38a
speech therapy logopedia 40a
speed velocità 3a, 33a
Speed limit Limite di velocità 33b
speed up accelerare 33a
speedometer tachimetro 33c
spell check controllo dell'ortografia 42b
spelling ortografia 19c
spend (time) passare, trascorrere 4c
spendthrift spilorcio 21a
sphere sfera 2a, 3d
spherical sferico 3d
spice spezia 24i

spicy   piccante   12e, 28d, 24a

spider   ragno   15d

spiderweb   ragnatela   15d

spinach   spinaci   14e, 24f

spine   spina dorsale   12a

spiral   spirale   3d

spiral notebook   quaderno a spirale   37b

spit   sputo   12a

splash   spruzzare   12c

spleen   milza   12a

splint   stecca   39c

spoke   raggio   34

sponsor   sponsor   20c

sponsoring   sponsorizzazione   20c

spontaneity   spontaneità   21a

spontaneous   spontaneo   21a

spoon   cucchiaio   23c, 24k

sporadic   sporadico   4c

sporadically   sporadicamente   4c

sports car   macchina, auto sportiva   34

sports event   gara   27b

sports fan   tifoso (-a)   27b

sports jacket   giacca sportiva   25k

sports program   programma di sport   20b

sports reporter   cronista sportivo   20a

sporty   sportivo   25g, 25l

spot, stain   macchia   25g, 25l

spotlights   riflettori   28e

spotted   macchiato, chiazzato   3d

spouse   coniuge, consorte   11c

sprain   distorsione, storta   40a

spraying   polverizzazione   14a

spread   diffondere   3c

spread gossip   seminare zizzania   17a

spread out   spargere   3c

spreadsheet   foglio elettronico   38c, 42b

spring   primavera   5c

spring (of a watch)   molla   25i

sprinkler   spruzzatore   14a

spy   spia   44d

spy movie   film di spionaggio   28a

spy-hole   spioncino   23a

square   quadrato   1d, 2a, 3d

square (of a town)   piazza   11f, 36a

square box   scatola quadrata   3e

square centimeter   centimetro quadrato   3a

square kilometer   chilometro quadrato   3a

square meter   metro quadrato   3a

square millimeter   millimetro quadrato   3a

square root   radice quadrata   1e

squared   al quadrato   1e

squared paper   carta a quadretti   37b

squash   squash   27b

squat   rannicchiarsi   3f

squeal   strillare   12c

squid   calamaro   15c, 24e

squint   strabismo   40a

squirrel   scoiattolo   15a

Sri Lanka   Sri Lanka   30b

stab   pugnalare   39b

stadium   stadio   27b

staff, personnel   personale   38a

stage   palcoscenico   28e

stained-glass window   vetrata dipinta, finestra a vetri colorati   23a

stainless steel   acciaio inossidabile   13c

staircase, stairwell   scale   23e

stairs   scale   23a, 35a

stamp   francobollo   19e

stamp collecting   filatelia   27a

stand up, get up   alzarsi   3f

standings   classifica   27b

stanza   strofa   25n

staple   graffa   19d, 25c

stapler   cucitrice   19d, 25c

star   stella   3d, 5c, 6a, 28e

starch   amido   25g

stare   fissare   12d

start the car   mettere in moto   33a

starting wage   stipendio iniziale   38d

state, affirm, maintain   asserire   17a

state   stato   13d

state of war   stato di guerra   44d

statement   affermazione, verbale   17a, 39b

station   stazione ferroviaria   34

stationery store   cartoleria   25c

statistical   statistico   1f

statistics   statistica   1g, 37e

statue   statua   28b

statute   statuto   43a

Stay still!   Sta' (Stia) fermo (-a)!   16c

stay-at-home job   lavoro a domicilio   38d

steadfast   costante   21a

steak   bistecca   24a

steal   rubare   39b

steam iron   ferro da stiro   23b

steel   acciaio   13c

steep   ripido   13b

steering wheel   volante   33c

stem   stelo   14a

step   gradino   23a

step forward   fare un passo avanti   3f

stepdaughter   figliastra   10a

stepfather   patrigno   10a

stepmother   matrigna   10a

stepson   figliastro   10a

sticky   appiccicoso   12e

stiff   rigido   12e

stiff neck   torcicollo   40a

stiffness   rigidezza   40a

still, yet, again   ancora   4c, 8j

sting   pungere   15d

stink   puzzo, puzzare   12e

stinky   puzzolente   12e

stir, mix   girare   24a

stitch   punto   25g, 25l, 40a

stock, share   azione   26a

stock corporation   società per azioni   38d

stock exchange   borsa   36a

stock market   borsa valori   26a

stockbroker   agente di cambio   38a

stockholder   azionista   38d

stocking   calza   25m

stocky   tarchiato   11a

stomach   stomaco   12a

stomachache   mal di stomaco   40a

stone   pietra, sasso, calcolo   13b, 40a

stool   sgabello   23b

stop   fermare, stop   33b, 34

Stop it! That's enough!   Basta!   16c

stopover   scalo   32c

storage room, shed   ripostiglio   14a

storage space   deposito   23a

store   negozio, immagazzinare   24m, 25a, 42b

store chain   catena di negozi   25a

store clerk   commesso (-a)   25a, 38a

store window   vetrina   25a

stork   cicogna   15b

storm   tempesta   6a

story   storia   17a

stove (heating)   stufa   23b

stove (kitchen)   cucina   23b

stove air vent   cappa   23d

stove element   fornello   23b

straight   retta, piatto   2b

straight ahead   diritto (dritto)   36c

straight hair   capelli lisci   11a

straw   paglia   13c, 14a

straw hat   cappello di paglia   25k

strawberry   fragola   14d, 24g

streaked   vergato   3d

streaked hair   capelli striati   11a

street   via, strada   11f, 36a, 38b

street sweeper netturbino (-a) 38a
strength forza 11a
stress stress 40a
stretch stirare 3f
stretcher barella 40a
strict severo 21a
strike sciopero 38d
striker scioperante 38d
string corda, spago 25c, 25l, 28c, 38c
string bean fagiolino 14e, 24f
string instruments strumenti a corda 28c
stripe, streak striscia 3d
striped a strisce, a righe 25g, 25l
stroke (cerebral) ictus cerebrale 40a
stroke (caress) lisciare 3f
stroll passeggiata, , fare una passeggiata 3f, 29b
strong forte 11a, 11e, 40a
strong desire voglia 21a
stubborn testardo 11e
student studente (-essa) 37d
study studio, studiare 22a, 22b, 37f
stuff roba, farcire 13c, 24a
stumble inciampare, incespicare 3f
Stupendous! Stupendo! 16c
stupid stupido 11e
stuttering balbuziente 11e
style stile 19c, 28d, 42b
stylistics stilistica 25n, 28d
subject materia, soggetto 8a, 37e
subjunctive congiuntivo 8a
subordinate subordinata 8a
subscribe abbonarsi 20a
subscription abbonamento 20a, 42a
subscription fee canone d'abbonamento 42a
subsidiary filiale 38d
substance sostanza 13c
substantive sostantivo 8a
subtitle sottotitolo 28a

subtract sottrarre 1e
subtraction sottrazione 1e
suburb sobborgo, periferia 36b
subway metropolitana 34
subway entrance entrata della metropolitana 34
subway station stazione della metropolitana 34
Sudan Sudan 30b
Sudanese sudanese 30e
sue querelare 41
suede shoes scarpe di camoscio 25m
sufficient sufficiente 3b
sugar zucchero 24i
sugar bowl zuccheriera 23c
suggest suggerire 17a
suit vestito, abito 25k
suitcase valigia 31
sulfur zolfo 13c
sulky scontroso 21a
sullen cupo, tetro 11e, 21a
sum somma 1f
sum up sommare 1f
summarize riassumere 17a
summary riassunto 17a
summer estate 5c
summer vacation vacanze estive 30a
summit cima 13b
summons citazione 41
sun sole 5c, 6a, 13a
sun ray raggio solare 13a
sun tan abbronzatura, tintarella 36b
sundial meridiana 14a
sunstroke colpo di sole 40a
sunbathe prendere sole 6a
sunbeam raggio di sole 6a
Sunday domenica 5a
sunflower girasole 14b
sunglasses occhiali da sole 6a
sunlight luce solare 13a
sunny pieno di sole 6a
sunrise alba 4b
sunset, twilight tramonto 4b
supermarket supermercato 24m

superstitious superstizioso 11e
supplement supplemento 3b
supplementary supplementare 2b
supplies viveri 44d
supply cupboard armadietto delle forniture 38c
suppository supposta 25h, 40a
supreme court corte di cassazione 41
sure, certain sicuro 21a
surf cresta dell'onda 13b
surface superficie 3c
surfing surfing 27b
surgeon chirurgo (-a) 38a, 40a
surgery chirurgia 40a
surgical appliance protesi 40a
surname cognome 11f, 38b
surplus eccedente 26a
surprise sorpresa, sorprendere 21a
surprised sorpreso 21a
survey sondaggio 38d
surveying topografia 3d
surveyor geometra 38a
swab tampone 40a
swallow rondine 15b
swamp palude 13b
swan cigno 15b
swarm sciame 15d
swear, avow giurare 17a
swear, curse bestemmiare 17a
sweat sudore, sudare 40a
sweater maglia, maglione 25k
Sweden Svezia 30b
Swedish svedese 30e
sweet dolce 11e, 12e, 24a
swell gonfiare 40a
swelling gonfiore 40a
swim nuotare 27b
swimmer nuotatore (-trice) 27b
swimming nuoto 27b
swimming cap cuffia 25k
swimming pool piscina 27b
swimming suit costume da bagno 25k

swimming trunks pantaloncini da bagno 25k
swings altalena 27a
Swiss svizzero 30e
switch interruttore 23a, 35h
Switzerland Svizzera 30b
swollen gonfio 40a
sword spada, sciabola 27b
swordfish pesce spada 15c
symbol simbolo 1f
symbolic simbolico 28d
symbolism simbolismo 28d
symbols table tavola dei simboli 42b
sympathetic comprensivo 21a
sympathy comprensione 21a
symphony sinfonia 28c, 25j
symposium simposio 37f
symptom sintomo 40a
synagogue sinagoga 11d
synthetic sintetico 13c
syphilis sifilide 40a
Syria Siria 30b
Syrian siriano 30e
syringe siringa 40a, 44c
systems analyst analista di sistemi 38c

T
T-shirt T-shirt 25k
tab tabulatore, tabulare 19f, 42b
table tavolo, tabella 24k, 42c
table lamp lampada da tavolo 23b
table of contents indice delle materie 25n, 28d
tablecloth tovaglia 23c, 24k
tablet compressa 25h, 40a
tableware posate 24k
tack puntina 19d, 25c, 38c
tackle contrastare 27b
tadpole girino 15c
tail coda 15a
tailor sarto (-a) 25a, 38a
take prendere 25a
take a trip fare un viaggio 30a
take attendance fare l'appello 37f

take off (airplane) decollo, decollare 32c

take off (clothes) spogliarsi 25l

take off (shoes) togliersi (le scarpe) 25m

take one's temperature misurare la febbre 40a

take out portare via 24n

take place avere luogo, svolgersi 4c

take-home pay busta paga 38d

takeover bid offerta pubblica d'acquisto 38d

talc, talcum powder talco 25f

tale racconto 25n, 28d

talk, speech discorso 17a

talk show talk show 20b

tall alto 11a

tame addomesticare 15a

tangent tangente 2a, 2b

tango tango 28c

tank carro armato, serbatoio 3e, 44d

tanker autocisterna 34

Tanzania Tanzania 30b

Tanzanian tanzaniano 30e

tap dancing tip tap 28c

tape nastro 13c, 20b

tar catrame, pece 13c

tarantella tarantella 28c

target bersaglio 27b

target practice tiro 29b

tariff tariffa 31

tartar tartaro 40b

task, duty incarico 43a

taste gusto, sapore 12e

tasteless sciocco 12e

tasty gustoso 24a

Taurus Toro 5d

tax tassa 26a

tax evasion frode fiscale 39b

tax on salary imposta sul reddito 38d

tax payment prelievo d'imposta 26b

tax collector esattore (-trice) 26a

taxable income imponibile 26a

taxation office ufficio delle imposte 26b

taxi driver tassista 38a

tea tè 24j

teach insegnare 37f

teacher training school istituto magistrale 37a

teacher, instructor insegnante, docente 37d, 37f, 38a

teaching aids materiale didattico

teacup tazzina 23c

team squadra 27b

teapot teiera 23c

tear squarcio 33d

tear gas gas lacrimogeno 44d

teaspoon cucchiaino 23c, 24k

technical consultant consulente tecnico (-a) 38a

technical school istituto tecnico 37a

technician tecnico (-a) 37d

technology tecnologia 42a

teen magazine rivista per adolescenti 20a, 25n

telecommunications telecomunicazione 18a, 42a

teleconference teleconferenza 38c, 42a

telegram telegramma (telegrammi, pl) 19e

telephone number numero di telefono, numero telefonico 38b

television televisione 20b

television advertising pubblicità televisiva 20c

television broadcasting telediffusione 20b

television camera telecamera 20b

television direction booth cabina di regia 20b

television game show telequiz 20b

television movie telefilm 20b

television network rete televisiva 20b

television news telegiornale
20b
television report telecronaca
20b
television reporter telecronista
20b
television studio studio televisivo
20b
tell (a story), recount raccontare
17a
tell a joke raccontare una
barzelletta 17a
teller cassiere (-a) 26a
teller's window sportello 26a
temperature temperatura 6c
template sagoma 2b
temple tempio 11d
temporarily temporaneamente
4c
temporary temporaneo 4c
temporary work lavoro
temporaneo 38d
ten dieci 1a
tenacious tenace 21a
tenant inquilino (-a) 23e
tender tenero 11e
tenderness tenerezza 21a
tendon tendine 12a
tennis tennis 27b
tennis court campo da tennis
27b
tennis player tennista 27b
tennis racket racchetta 27b
tennis shoes scarpe da tennis
25m
tenor tenore 28c
tense tempo 8a
tent tenda 36b
tenth decimo 1b
terminal terminal 32a, 38c, 42b
termite termite 15d
terrace terrazza, terrazzo 23a
territory territorio 13d
terrorism terrorismo 44d
terrorist terrorista 44d
terse, succinct lapidario 28d
test prova 37f
test tube provetta 13c

test-tube baby figlio in provetta
11c
testify, vouch testimoniare
17a, 41
testimony testimonianza 41
tetanus tetano 40a
tetrahedron tetraedro 2a
text testo 19c, 25n, 28d
text message SMS (m, inv),
messaggino 19g, 42d
textbook libro di testo 25n, 37b
texture, textile tessuto 13c
Thai tailandese 30e
Thailand Tailandia 30b
thank ringraziare 17a
Thank God! Grazie a Dio!
16c
Thank goodness! Meno male!
21c
Thank you! Grazie! 16c
thankfulness gratitudine 21a
thanks to grazie a 8i
that is to say cioè, vale a dire
17b, 44e
that, those quel, quell', quello,
quei, quegli, quella 8d
thaw disgelo, sgelare 6a
the il, l', lo, i, gli, la, le 8b
The line is busy. La linea è
occupata. 18b
The line is free. La linea è libera.
18b
The pleasure is mine! Il piacere è
mio! 16b
The sky is clear. Il cielo è sereno.
6a
The watch is fast. L'orologio va
avanti. 4d
The watch is slow. L'orologio va
indietro. 4d
The weather is foul. Fa un tempo
da cani. 6a
theater teatro 28e, 29b
theatrical agent agente teatrale
38a
their, your (pl, pol) loro 8e
them, to them li, le, gli loro, a
loro 8g

theme tema (temi, pl) 25n, 28d
themselves si 8g
then allora, poi 4c, 8j
theologian teologo (-a) 11d
theology teologia 11d
theorem teorema 1f
therapist terapista 40a
therapy terapia 40a
there là, lì 3c, 8j
There's no doubt that… non c'è dubbio che… 44e
therefore allora, dunque, quindi 8i, 17b, 44e
thermal energy energia termica 44a
thermometer termometro 6c, 13c, 25h, 40a
thermostat termostato 6c, 35b
thesis tesi 37f
they loro 8g
thick spesso, fitto 3b
thickness spessore 3b
thief ladro (-a) 39b
thigh coscia 12a
thin, fine fino 3b
think pensare 22b
third terzo 1b
thirst sete 12b
thirteen tredici 1a
thirteenth tredicesimo 1b
thirty trenta 1a
thirty-one trentuno 1a
thirty-third trentatreesimo 1b
thirty-three trentatré 1a
thirty-two trentadue 1a
this, these questo (-a), questi (-e) 8d
thorn spina 14a
thought pensiero 22a
thousandth millesimo 1b
threat minaccia 17a
threaten minacciare 17a
three tre 1a
three hundred trecento 1a
three million tre milioni 1a
three thousand tremila 1a
three-elevenths tre undicesimi 1c

three-twenty-fifths tre venticinquesimi 1c
thresh trebbiare 14a
thriller thriller 25n, 28a
throat gola 12a
through per, attraverso 3c, 8f
throw tirare, gettare 3f, 27b
thumb pollice 12a
thunder tuono, tuonare 6a
thunderstorm temporale 6a
Thursday giovedì 5a
Tiber River Tevere 30c
tick zecca 15d
ticket biglietto 27b, 30a, 32a, 34
ticket agent bigliettaio (-a) 32a, 34
ticket machine biglietteria automatica 34
ticket office, counter biglietteria 34
tide marea 13b
tie cravatta 25k
tiger tigre 15a
tight stretto 25g, 25l
tight-fitting aderente 25g, 25l
tighten stringere 25l
till vangare 14a
time (hour) ora 4b
time (in general) tempo 4b
time (occurrence) volta 4b
time difference fuso orario 32c
Time flies! Il tempo vola! 4c
Time is money! Il tempo è denaro! 4c
Time is short! Il tempo stringe! 4c
timetable, schedule orario 4c, 25c
tin latta, stagno 13c
tin box scatola di latta 3e
tincture of iodine tintura di iodio 25h, 39c, 40a
tinfoil stagnola 23c
tint tinta, tingere 7b
tip mancia, (to) dare la mancia 24l

tiptoe camminare in punta di piedi 3f
tire gomma, pneumatico 33c, 34
tired stanco 11e
tiredness, fatigue fatica 12b
tissue tessuto 12a
title titolo 11f, 16b, 25n, 28d
to a 3c, 8f
to him lo, lui, gli, a lui 8g
to Sarah's place da Sara 3c
to someone's place da 3c
to speak badly of malignare 17a
to sum up insomma 17b
to the east a est 3c, 36c
to the fourth power alla quarta potenza 1e
to the left a sinsitra 3c, 36c
to the north a nord 3c, 36c
to the nth power all'ennesima potenza 1e
to the right a destra 3c, 36c
to the south a sud 3c, 36c
to the west a ovest 3c, 36c
to this day, till now tutt'oggi 4c
To Whom It May Concern A Chi di Competenza 19a
toad rospo 15c
toast brindisi, brindare 17a, 24n
tobacco tabacco 25e
tobacconist tabaccaio 25e
toboggan, slide slitta 27a
today oggi 4b, 8j
together insieme 8j
toilet toletta, bagno, gabinetto 23a, 32c
toilet (bowl) gabinetto 23a
toilet paper carta igienica 23b, 35b
toiletries articoli da toilette 25f
tolerance tolleranza 21a
tolerant tollerante 21a
toll pedaggio 33b
toll booth casello (stradale) 33a
tomato pomodoro 14e, 24f

tomb tomba 11c
tombstone lapide 11c
tomorrow domani 4b, 8j
tomorrow afternoon domani pomeriggio 4b
tomorrow evening domani sera 4b
tomorrow morning domani mattina 4b
tomorrow night domani notte 4b
ton tonnellata 3b
tone tono 25j, 28c
toner toner 25c
tongue lingua 12a, 40b
tonic tonico 25a, 25h, 40a
tonight stasera, stanotte 4b
tonsillitis tonsillite 40a
tonsils tonsille 12a
Too bad! Peccato! 16c, 21c
too much troppo 3b
tool attrezzo 23d, 25b
toolbox cassetta degli arnesi 3e
tooth dente 40b
tooth extraction estrazione 40b
toothache mal di denti 40b
toothbrush spazzolino da denti 12f
toothless sdentato 11a
toothpaste dentifricio 12f, 40b
toothpick stuzzicadenti 24k
top cima 3c
topaz topazio 25i
topology topologia 1g
tornado tornado 6a
torso, trunk torso 12a
tortuous tortuoso 3d
total totale 3b
totalitarian totalitario 44d
totalitarianism totalitarismo 44d
touch tatto, toccare 3f, 12e
touchy, over-sensitive permaloso 21a
tough duro 11e
toughness durezza 11e
tour giro 30a
tourism turismo 30a

tourist turista 30a

tourist information office ufficio d'informazioni turistiche 36b

tourist place posto di villeggiatura 36b

tournament tournée 27b

tourniquet laccio emostatico 40a

tow the car rimorchiare la macchina 33a

tow truck autosoccorso, autorimorchiatore 34

Tow-away zone Zona rimozione 33b

toward verso 3c

towel asciugamano 12f, 23b, 35b

towel rack portasciugamani 23a

tower torre 36a

towing rimorchio 33a

town (hamlet), village paese 36b

town (market-town) borgo 36b

town (small city) cittadina 36b

town council comune 36b

toxic tossico 44a

toy giocattolo 27a

toy box scatola dei balocchi 3e

toy car macchinina 27a

toy soldier soldatino 27a

trace calcare 28b

track binario, pista 27b, 34

track and field atletica leggera 27b

traditional tradizionale 11e

traffic traffico 33a

traffic accident incidente stradale 39c

traffic jam ingorgo 33a

traffic lights semaforo 33a

traffic policeman vigile (-essa) 33a

tragedy tragedia 20a, 28d

train treno 27b, 34

train station stazione ferroviaria 34

trainer, coach allenatore (-trice) 27b

training formazione, allenamento 27b, 37f

tranquil, calm, serene tranquillo 11e

tranquilizer calmante 25h, 40a

transformer trasformatore 25b

transit transito 32b

transit passenger passeggero (-a) in transito 32b

transitive transitivo 8a

translate tradurre 17a

translation traduzione 17a

transmission trasmissione 42a

transparent trasparente 7b, 25g, 25l

transplant trapianto 40a

transport truck autocarro 34

transportation trasporto 34

trap trappola 15a

trapezium trapezio 2a

Trashed mail Posta eliminata 42c

travel viaggiare 30a

travel agency agenzia di viaggi 30a

travel agent agente di viaggio 30a

traveler's check traveler's check 26a

tray vassoio 23c, 24k, 32c

treasurer tesoriere (-a) 26b, 43a

treasury tesoreria 43a

treatise trattato 25n

tree albero 14a

Trentino Alto-Adige Trentino Alto-Adige 30d

trial processo 41

triangle triangolo 2a

triangular triangolare 3d

tributary affluente 13b

trigonometric trigonometrico 2b

trigonometry trigonometria 1g, 2b, 37e

trimester trimestre 37f

trimmer potatore (delle piante) 14a

trio trio 28c

trip, journey   viaggio   30a
triple   triplo   3b
tripod   treppiede   25d, 28b
trombone   trombone   28c
tropic   tropico   13d
Tropic of Cancer   Tropico del Cancro   13d
Tropic of Capricorn   Tropico del Capricorno   13d
tropical   tropicale   6a, 13d
troublemaker   attaccabrighe   21a
trout   trota   15c, 24e
trowel   cazzuola   14a
truce   tregua   44d
truck   camion   34
trumpet   tromba   28c
trumpeter   trombettista   28c
trunk (container)   baule   3e, 33c
trunk (of a tree)   tronco   14a
trust   fiducia, fidarsi (di)   21a
try on   provarsi, provare   25l
tub   tino, vasca   3e
tuba   tuba   28c
Tuesday   martedì   5a
tulip   tulipano   14b
tumor   tumore   40a
tuna   tonno   15c, 24e
tune   aria, accordare   25j, 28c
Tunisia   Tunisia   30b
Tunisian   tunisino   30e
tunnel   galleria, tunnel   33c
turbulence   turbolenza   32c
Turin   Torino   30c
Turkey   Turchia   30b
turkey   tacchino   15b, 24d
Turkish   turco   30e
turn   svolta, girare   3f, 33a
turn around   girarsi   3f
turn left   girare, voltare a sinistra   3f, 33a
turn off   spegnere   20b, 35b
turn on   accendere   20b, 35b
turn right   girare, voltare a destra   3f, 33a
turquoise   turchino   7a
turtle, tortoise   tartaruga   15c
turtledove   tortora   15b

Tuscany   Toscana   30d
tusk   zanna   15a
tweezers   pinzette   25f
twelfth   dodicesimo   1b
twelve   dodici   1a
twenty   venti   1a
twenty-eight   ventotto   1a
twenty-five   venticinque   1a
twenty-four   ventiquattro   1a
twenty-nine   ventinove   1a
twenty-one   ventuno   1a
twenty-seven   ventisette   1a
twenty-six   ventisei   1a
twenty-third   ventitreesimo   1b
twenty-three   ventitré   1a
twenty-two   ventidue   1a
twig   ramoscello   14b
twin   gemello (-a)   10a
twinkle   luccicare   12d
twist   torcere   3f
twisting, winding   avvolgente   3d
Twitter   Twitter (m, inv)   19g, 42d
two   due   1a
two billion   due miliardi   1a
two copies   doppia copia   19d
two hundred   duecento   1a
two hundred and one   duecentouno   1a
two million   due milioni   1a
two thousand   duemila   1a
two thousand and one   duemilauno   1a
two years ago   due anni fa   4c
two-fifths   due quinti   1c
two-piece suit   costume a due pezzi   25k
two-thirds   due terzi   1c
type in   digitare   38c, 42b
typhoon   tifone   6a
typographical error   errore tipografico   20a
Tyrrenean Sea   Tirreno   30c

U
Uganda   Uganda   30b
Ugandan   ugandese   30e

Ugh! Uffa! 21c
ugly brutto 11a, 25l
ulcer ulcera 40a
ultrasound ecografia 40a
ultraviolet light luce ultravioletta 13a
Umbria Umbria 30d
unacceptable inaccettabile 21b
unbearable insopportabile 21a
Unbelievable! Incredibile! 21c
uncle zio 10a
unconscious inconscio 40a
under sotto 3c
underline sottolineatura 19c, 42b
underpants, underwear mutande 25k
underpass sottopassaggio, passaggio sotterraneo 33b, 36a
undershirt canottiera, maglietta 25k
underskirt sottoveste 25k
understand capire 22b
undress spogliarsi 25l
unemployed disoccupato 38d
unemployment disoccupazione 38d
unemployment benefits cassa integrazione 38d
uneven disuguale 3d
unfaithful infedele 21a
unflustered pacato 21a
unfocussed sfocato 25d
unfortunately purtroppo 8j, 21c
ungrateful ingrato 21a
unhappy scontento 11e
union member sindacalista 38d
union negotiation trattativa sindacale 38d
unit of information unità d'informazione 9b
United Nations Nazioni Unite 44d
United States Stati Uniti 30b
universal suffrage suffragio universale 43a

universe universo 13a
university università 37a
university chair cattedra 37a
university degree laurea 11f
university graduate laureato (-a) 38b
unknown incognita 1f
unless a meno che 44e
unmarried celibe, nubile 11c, 11f
unpleasant spiacevole, 21b
unsatisfied insoddisfatto 11e
unscrew svitare 23d
unscrupulous senza scrupoli 21a
untidy disordinato 11e
until fino a, finché 4c
until now finora 8j
unwind distendersi 27a, 29b
up su 3c
Update Aggiorna 42c
uphold, maintain sostenere 17a
upholsterer tappezziere (-a) 38a
upholstery tappezzeria 23b
uploading uploading (m, inv), caricare online 42d
upper school scuola superiore 37a
upper-case character carattere maiuscolo 19c
upright piano piano verticale 28c
upset, angry adirato 21a
Uranus Urano 13a
urban dweller urbano (-a) 36a
urinary tract apparato urinario 12a
urinate urinare 12b
urine urina 12b
urologist urologo (-a) 40a
Uruguay Uruguay 30b
Uruguayan uruguaiano 30e
us, to us ci, noi, a noi 8g
USB stick chiavetta 19f
user utente 19f, 38c, 42b
User name Nome utente 42c

user-friendly   di facile uso   38c
usher   maschera   28e
usually   di solito   4c
utensil   utensile   23c

V

vacation   vacanza   5f, 29a
vacation in the mountains
  vacanze in montagna   30a
vaccinate   vaccinare   40a
vaccination   vaccino   40a
vacuum cleaner   aspirapolvere
  23b
vagabond   vagabondo   21a
vain   vanitoso   11e
valley   valle   13b
valve   valvola   33c
van   furgone   34
vandal   vandalo (-a)   39b
vandalism   vandalismo   39b
vanilla   vaniglia   24i
vapor   vapore   13c
variable   variabile   1f
varicose vein   vena varicosa   40a
variety program   programma di
  varietà   20b
vase   vaso   23c
vasectomy   vasectomia   40a
veal   vitello   24d
vector   vettore   2b
vegetable garden   orto   14a
vegetables, greens   verdura
  14e, 24f
vegetation   vegetazione   13b
vehicle   veicolo   34
veil   velo   11c
vein   vena   12a
veined, grainy   venato   3d
velvet   velluto   13c
venereal disease   malattia venerea
  40a
Venetia   Veneto   30d
Venezuela   Venezuela   30b
Venezuelan   venezuelano   30e
vengeful   vendicativo   11e
Venice   Venezia   30c
Venus   Venere   13a
verandah   veranda   23a

verb   verbo   8a
verdict   verdetto   41
versatile   versatile   11e
vertex   vertice   2b
vertical   verticale   2b, 3c
Very well!   Molto bene!
  Benissimo!   16a
vest   gilè, panciotto   25k
vestry   sagrestia   11d
Vesuvius   Vesuvio   30c
via satellite   via satellite   20b
vice, bad habit   vizio   11d
victim   vittima   39a
video camera   videocamera,
  cinepresa   25d
video cassette   videocassetta
  20b, 28a
video conference
  videoconferenza   42a
video disc   videodisco   20b,
  25d
video game   videogioco   27a,
  42a
video recorder   videoregistratore
  25j
video telephone   videotelefono
  42a
Vienna   Vienna   30c
Vietnam   Vietnam   30b
Vietnamese   vietnamita   30e
view   veduta   35a
viewer   telespettatore (-trice),
  mirino   20b, 25d
vigorous   vigoroso   11a
vileness, baseness   viltà   21a
village   villaggio   36b
vine   vite   14a
vinegar   aceto   24i
vineyard   vigna   14a
viola   viola   28c
viola player   violista   28c
violate a right   violare un diritto
  43a
violence   violenza   39b
violet   viola   14b
violin   violino   28c
violinist   violinista   28c
viper   vipera   15c

viral infection   infezione virale 40a

virgin wool   lana vergine 13c

Virgo   Vergine   5d

virile   virile   11a

virtual   virtuale   38c, 42b

virtue   virtù   11d

virtuous   virtuoso   11e

virus   virus   38c, 40a

visa   visto   31, 44d

visit   visita, visitare, andare a trovare   29b

visiting hours   ore di visita 40a

visual arts   arti figurative 28b

vitamin   vitamina   25h, 40a

vocabulary   vocabolario, lessico 17a

vocal cord   corda vocale   12a

volatile   mutevole   21a

volcano   vulcano   13b

volleyball   pallavolo   27b

voluble   volubile   11e

volume   volume   3a, 25n, 28d, 42a

vomit   vomito, vomitare, rimettere 40a

voracious   vorace   21a

vote   voto, votare   43a

vow   voto   11d

vowel   vocale   8a

vulgar   volgare   21a

vulgarity   volgarità   21a

vulnerable   vulnerabile   11e

vulture   avvoltoio   15b

W

wage, stipend   stipendio   38d

wage increase   aumento di stipendio   38d

waist   vita   12a

waistline   vita   11a

wait (for)   aspettare   19e, 34

waiter, waitress   cameriere (-a) 24l, 38a

waiting room   sala d'aspetto 32a, 38c, 40a

wake up   svegliarsi   12b

wake-up call   sveglia (telefonica) 35a

Wales   Galles   30b

walk   camminata, camminare 3f, 12b, 27a, 29b

wall   muro   23a

wall painting   quadro   23b

wallpaper   carta da parati   23d, 25b

walnut   noce   14c, 14d, 24g

walrus   tricheco   15a

waltz   valzer   28c

wander   girovagare   3f

war   guerra   44d

warehouse   magazzino   25a, 38d

warm up   riscaldarsi   6b

warn   avvertire   17a

warning   avvertimento   17a

warrant   mandato   39b

wart   verruca   40a

wash   lavare   23f, 25g

washbasin   lavabo   23a

wash dishes   lavare i piatti   23f

wash one's hair   lavarsi i capelli 12f

wash oneself   lavarsi   12f

washable   lavabile   25g

washing machine   lavatrice 23b

Washroom   Toilette, Servizi 33b

wasp   vespa   15d

waste   rifiuto   44a

wastebasket   cestino   19d, 38c

waste disposal   scarico delle immondizie   44a

watch   orologio   4d, 25i

watchmaker   orologiaio   25i

water   acqua   13c

water bottle   bottiglia da acqua 24k

water color   acquerello   28b

water colorist   aquerellista 28b

water fountain   fontana   36a

water glass   bicchiere da acqua 23c

water pollution inquinamento delle acque 44a
water polo pallanuoto 27b
water skiing sci nautico 27b
water tank cisterna dell'acqua 3e
water-heater riscaldatore dell'acqua 23b
waterfall cascate (cascata) 13b
watermelon anguria 14d, 24g
wave onda 13b
wavelength lunghezza d'onda 42a
wavy, undulating ondulato 3d
wavy hair capelli ondulati 11a
wax cera 23b
wax museum museo delle cere 28b
we noi 8g
weak debole 11a, 11e, 40a
weakness debolezza 11a
weapon arma 39b, 44d
wear indossare 25l
weather tempo 6a
weather bulletin bollettino meteorologico 6c
weather conditions condizioni meteorologiche 6c
weather forecast previsioni del tempo 6c
weather report bollettino metereologico 20b
webcast trasmissione web 20b, 42d
website sito web 19f, 38c, 42b, 42d
wedding nozze 11c, 29a
wedding dress abito, vestito da sposa 25k
wedding invitation partecipazione 11c
wedding suit (men) abito, vestito da sposo 25k
wedding ring fede 11c, 25i
Wednesday mercoledì 5a
weed erbaccia 14a
week settimana 4b
weekend fine settimana 5a
weekly settimanalmente 4b
weigh pesare 3b, 25a

weight peso 3a, 11a, 31
weight lifting sollevamento pesi 27b
Well done! Bravo (-a)! 16c
well-built ben fatto 11a
well-disciplined disciplinato 21a
well-done ben cotto 24a
well-mannered educato 11e
Welsh gallese 30e
west ovest 3c, 13d, 36c
western occidentale 3c, 13d, 30e
wet paint vernice fresca 23d
whale balena 15a
What? Che? Cosa? Che cosa? 9a
What a bore! What a drag! Che noia! Che barba! 16c, 21c
What a fool! Che sciocco! 16c
What a jam! Che guaio! 16c
What a mess! Che pasticcio! Che imbroglio! 16c
What a nice surprise! Che bella sorpresa! 16c
What a nuisance! Che seccatura! 16c
What color is it? Di che colore è? 7a
What day is it? Che giorno è? 5a
What does it mean? Che significa? Che vuol dire? 9a
What month is it? Che mese è? 5b
What time is it? Che ora è?, Che ore sono? 4a
What year is it? Che anno è? 5e
What's the date? Che data è? 5e
What's your name? Come ti chiami? Come si chiama? 16b
wheel ruota 33c
wheelchair sedia a rotelle 40a
when quando 4c, 9a
When were you born? Quando è (sei) nato (-a)? 5e

where dove 3c, 9a
which (one) quale 9a
while mentre 4c
whimsical estroso, capriccioso 11e, 21a
whine piagnucolare 17a
whipping cream panna montata 24h
whirlpool gorgo 13b
whiskey whiskey 24j
whisper sussurrare 17a
whistle fischiare 12c
white bianco 7a
white-collar worker impiegato (-a) 38d
Who? Chi? 9a
Who is it? Chi è? 18b
Who knows? Chissà? 17b
Who's speaking? Chi parla? 18b
whole-wheat bread pane integrale 24c
wholesale all'ingrosso 25a
wholesale price prezzo all'ingrosso 25a
whooping cough pertosse 40a
Why? Perché? 9a
wide largo 3b, 3c
widow vedova 11c, 11f
widower vedovo 11c, 11f
width larghezza 3a
wife moglie 10a, 11c
wig, hair piece parrucca 25f
wild boar cinghiale 15a
wild rose rosa canina, rosa selvatica 14b
will testamento 11c
willow, weeping willow salice, salice piangente 14c
wilt appassire 14a
wily, sly furbo 11e
win vincita, vincere 27a, 27b
wind (a watch) caricare 4d, 25i
wind (air) vento 6a
wind gust raffica di vento 6a
wind instruments strumenti a fiato 28c

windbreaker giacca a vento 25k
window finestra, finestrino 32c, 38c, 42c
window frame telaio 23a
window ledge, sill davanzale 23a
windpipe trachea 12a
windshield parabrezza 33c
windstorm bufera 6a
wine vino 24j
wine cellar cantina 23a
wine glass bicchiere da vino 23c, 24k
wine list lista dei vini 24l
wine shop enoteca 24m
wing ala 15b, 32c
wings (of a stage) quinte 28e
winner vincitore (-trice) 27b
winter inverno 5c
winter vacation vacanze invernali 30a
wiper tergicristallo 33c
wire filo 23d, 25b
wireless senza fili 42a
wiring impianto elettrico 23d
wisdom sapienza 22a
wisdom tooth dente del giudizio 40b
wise saggio 11e
wistaria glicine 14b
with con 8f
with a drop of alcohol caffè corretto 24j
with a drop of milk caffè macchiato 24j
With cordial greetings Con i più cordiali saluti 19a
with double bed camera matrimoniale 35a
with espresso coffee caffè espresso 24j
with friends presso amici 11f
with ice, on the rocks col ghiaccio 24j
With kind wishes Un caro saluto 19a

with one's parents   con i genitori
11f
with sauce   al sugo   24a
with two beds   camera a due letti
35a
withdraw   prelevare   26a
withdrawal   prelevamento   26a
within   entro   4c
within two days   entro due giorni
4c
without   senza   8f
witness   testimone   11c, 41
witty, spirited   spiritoso   11e, 17a
wolf   lupo   15a
woman   donna   11a
women's clothing store
abbigliamento femminile   25k
women's magazine   rivista
femminile   20a, 25n
women's shoes   scarpe da donna
25m
women's suit   abito, vestito da
donna, tailleur   25I, 25k
wood   legno   13c
wood box   scatola di legno   3e
wooden spoon   cucchiaio di legno
23c
woodpecker   picchio   15b
woods   bosco   13b
wool   lana   13c
woolen   di lana   25l
word   parola   17a
word processing   word processing
19f, 38c
workday   giorno lavorativo   5a
work (labor)   lavoro, lavorare
11f, 38d
work (of art)   opera   28d
work associate   collega   38d
work contract   contratto di lavoro
38d
work experience   esperienze
lavorative   11f
work in a bank   lavorare in banca
26a
Work in progress   Lavori in corso
33b
work out   fare ginnastica   27b

workstation   stazione di lavoro
38c, 42b
worksite   cantiere   36a
workday   giorno di lavoro   5a
working hours   orario di lavoro
38d
world   mondo   13a
World Cup   Coppa de Mondo
27b
worm   verme   15d
worried   preoccupato   11e, 21a
worsen, deteriorate   aggravarsi
40a
worship   adorazione, venerazione
11d
worthy   meritorio   21a
wound, injury   ferita   39c,
40a
wrap   incartare   25a
wrapping paper   carta da pacchi
25c
wreath   ghirlanda   11c
wrench   chiave inglese   23d,
25b
wrestle   lottare   27b
wrestler   lottatore (-trice)   27b
wrestling   lotta   27b
wrinkles   rughe   11a
wrist   polso   12a
wristwatch   orologio da polso
4d, 25i
write   scrivere   19e, 28d, 37f
writer   scrittore (-trice)   25n,
28d, 38a
writing   scrittura   25n, 28d
writing desk   scrivania   23b,
37b, 38c
writing pad   blocco   25c
written exam   esame scritto
37f
wrong   sbagliato   37f
wrong number   numero sbagliato
18b
wrongfulness   torto   22a
wrought iron   ferro battuto   13c

X
X-rays   raggi X   39c

Y

Yah! Sure! There!   Ecco!   16c
yawn   sbadigliare   17a
year   anno   4b
yearly   annuo, annuale   4b
yell, scream   urlare   17a
yellow   giallo   7a
yellow pages   pagine gialle
  18a
yes   sì   8j
yesterday   ieri   4b
yet   ancora   4c
yield   rendimento, precedenza
  26b, 33b
yogurt   yogurt   24h
you   tu, Lei, voi, ti, te, a te, vi, a
  voi,   8g
You're welcome!   Prego!   16c
young   giovane   11b
young lady   signorina   11a, 11b
young man   giovanotto   11b
young person   giovane   11b
younger   minore, più piccolo
  11b
younger sister   sorella più piccola,
  sorella minore   11b

your   tuo, tua, tuoi, tue, vostro
  (-a), vostri (-e)   8e
yourself   ti, si   8g
youth   gioventù, giovinezza   11b
youthful   giovanile   11a
YouTube   YouTube (m, inv)
  42d
Yuch!   Che schifo!   21a

Z

Zambia   Zambia   30b
Zambian   zambiano   30e
zealous   zelante   11e
zebra   zebra   15a
zero   zero   1a, 6c
zigzag   zigzag   3d
Zionism   sionismo   11d
Zionist   sionista   11d
zipper   cerniera   25g
zodiac   zodiaco   5d
zone   zona   3c, 13d
zoo   zoo   15a
zoological   zoologico   15a
zoology   zoologia   15a, 37e
zoom   zoom   25d
zucchini   zucchine   14e, 24f